The Dictionary of Symbols in Western Art

For centuries, religious and mythological themes, often charged with profound symbolic significance, have played a major role in the subject matter of Western art. Only through an awareness of these themes can we fully comprehend the complexities and subtleties of an artist's interpretation.

The Dictionary of Symbols in Western Art is a highly illustrated A-to-Z reference guide to the understanding and appreciation of Western painting and sculpture. Symbolic meanings can be ascribed not only to figures, objects and historical episodes, but also to posture, color and weather. Concentrating especially on the biblical subjects that have dominated Western art from the early Christian period, and on the mythological subjects that were a potent influence from the Renaissance onward, the book examines common emblems and coded references used by artists.

The detailed entries on saints, heroes, heroines, miracles, martyrdoms, and ravishments are given generous space, and are highly readable and authoritative. Reference is made to specific paintings and artists; for example:

- Pieter Bruegel the Elder painted the *Tower of Babel* as an image of the folly of man. His fantastic structure is not unlike the Colosseum in Rome, but it would have been impossible to build.

- The centaur, a mythological creature with the body and legs of a horse and the torso, arms, and head of a man, may represent the base or animal aspect of humanity, as illustrated in Botticelli's *Pallas and the Centaur*, in which the coarse creature cowers before the wise Minerva.

- In the 1660s, Jan Steen painted *Beware of Luxury* and *The Dissolute Household*, in which playing cards appear as a reminder of the expression, "Cards, women, and drink have ruined many a man."

Continued on back flap

The Dictionary of Symbols in Western Art

Sarah Carr-Gomm

AN INFOBASE HOLDINGS COMPANY

For Solomon Sam Culling Poulos

The Dictionary of Symbols in Western Art

First published in the United States in 1995 by Facts On File, Inc

Facts On File
460 Park Avenue South
New York NY 10016

Conceived, Edited and Designed by
Duncan Baird Publishers
Sixth Floor
Castle House
75-76 Wells Street
London W1P 3RE

Editors: Judy Dean, Alice Peebles, Caroline Bugler
Designer: John Laing
Commissioned artwork: Ron Hayward Studios

Library of Congress Cataloging-in-Publication data
Carr-Gomm, Sarah.
Dicitonary of Symbols in Western Art / by Sarah Carr-Gomm
p. cm
Includes bibliographical references and index.
ISBN 0–8160–3301–3 — ISBN 0–8169–3326–9
1. Art—Dictionaries. 2. Signs and Symbols—Dictionaries.
I. Title
N7740.C29 1995
704.9'46'03—dc20
95–17577
CIP

Typeset in Times NR MT
Colour reproduction by IGS, Bath
Printed in Hong Kong

2 4 6 8 10 9 7 5 3 1

Contents

How To Use This Book

This dictionary has entries on saints, martyrs, mythical, biblical and religious characters and episodes, and major symbols in art, all arranged in A–Z order. Interspersed alphabetically with these entries are highlighted feature panels on the treatment in art of major themes and general topics (Adam and Eve, Landscape, Zodiac and so on).

Cross-references in the margin relate to entries elsewhere that expand upon subjects to which reference is made in the text.

Footnotes in the margin refer to selected documentary sources. (*Met* is used as an abbreviation for Ovid's *Metamorphoses.*)

The illustrations are mostly inspired by works of art dating from the Middle Ages until the 19th century. In all cases the artist has simplified for the sake of clarity.

The Index of Artists (p.233), arranged in alphabetical order of artist, refers to all artists and works of art that are cited in the main dictionary. The Index of Supplementary Words (p.238) covers symbols, and minor characters and episodes that are not themselves subjects of a main entry in the dictionary.

Foreword

The aim of this book is to serve as a useful introduction to the meanings of works of art. Most of the works covered date from the period of the late Middle Ages to modern times when figurative art predominated. It is the figures that often embody the principal message of a painting or sculpture: images and episodes from the lives of the saints, for example, were commissioned because they were considered exemplary and their lives worthy of imitation. Most of the entries in the book are, therefore, about individuals: religious, historical and mythological. Also included are fictitious characters and their authors, themes and topics of art-historical relevance, as well as symbols, emblems, attributes and personifications of abstract qualities.

A symbol may be defined as an object, living or material, that represents a concept. Many objects, however, take on symbolic meaning only within a certain context; the dove, for example, represents the Holy Spirit at Christ's baptism but when accompanied by Venus is associated with love. Thus, the symbolic meaning is not always the same. Moreover, it cannot be assumed that the object is *always* a symbol: it may be included for aesthetic or naturalistic reasons.

A figure that takes on a symbolic role is known as a personification, and is male or female according to the gender of the word. Thus Victory (*Victoria* in Latin) is female not because of any feminine qualities that the notion embodies, but because of grammar. Since the Renaissance, subjects drawn from classical antiquity became increasingly popular, especially figures from mythology. In this book, their Roman titles, rather than Greek, are given because this is standard usage in the Renaissance and Baroque ages. The deities, especially Minerva, Diana, Apollo, Venus and Mercury, were often used as personifications – Minerva, for example, as Wisdom – and were thus useful references for allegory. The stories of gods and goddesses describe a vast range of human emotions and provided artists with a challenge to the imagination and the joy of portraying beautiful people in arcadian settings.

An attribute is an object that identifies a particular individual, such as the wheel of St Catherine or the shaggy tunic of St John the Baptist. Although the keys of St Peter may be seen to symbolize the Kingdom of Heaven, more importantly they are the objects by which the saint himself is recognized. Attributes usually derive from an episode in the life of the figure concerned and, unlike the keys of St Peter, they often have no symbolic meaning. Attributes are not necessarily objects; Tobias, for example, may be seen as the attribute of the Archangel Raphael. There are also collective attributes, which identify a type: the crown of regents, the palm of martyrs or the shell of pilgrims. These are an important part of iconography and are a direct clue to the subject of a painting. This book includes entries for many of the principal symbols, personifications and attributes, but the index should also be used.

It has been fashionable in art history to seek complex levels of meaning and erudite solutions for problematic paintings. Recently, however, scholars have pointed out that this not necessarily a fruitful approach and have shown that when esoteric subjects were painted they often had an inscription to identify the subject or explain the message. However, there were certain conventions understood by the educated. One of these is the tradition known as type and anti-type, whereby many Old Testament figures and narratives were taken as prefigurations of those from the New. In his book *The City of God*, St Augustine explained that "The Old Testament is nothing but the New covered with a veil, and the New is nothing but the Old unveiled." Thus, for example, Isaac was seen as a "type" of Christ, because Abraham, his father, was prepared to sacrifice his son as evidence of his faith. There were also medieval bestiaries, developed from writings known as "Physiologus" (The Naturalist) which professed to describe the nature and habits of creatures, real and mythical, from which moral and religious lessons were drawn. Similarly, numerous flowers were likened to the Virgin or to the Passion of Christ.

Alongside many entries are footnotes on certain literary sources which, for the most part, are readily available today. Herein lies another fascinating question, as there were, and still are, variations of the same story and often numerous editions and translations of the same text. Some were very widely known. *The Golden Legend* of *c.*1260 by Jacobus de Voragine, for example, which tells the lives of the Virgin and the Saints, organized according to the feast days of the liturgical calender, was widely read and was translated into many Western European languages. Until the production of several printed books on iconography in the mid-16th century, there was no authoritative dictionary to explain the meanings of things; moreover, symbols and attributes were not standardized. Even since then, patrons, artists and their advisers have not been consistent in their choice of reference, more than one source might be used and there was always room for invention. The student of iconography must, therefore, be cautious in the quest for meanings.

Although ideas as to the original intention of a work of art can be formed from a knowledge of its subject matter, many other factors must be considered. These include artistic style and technique, social and political history, the original location of the work, and the intention of its patron; such topics are, however, beyond the scope of this book.

With so many questions to answer, the study of art history is never-ending, and the subject is a delight because it involves looking at, and thinking about, the splendid products of the human imagination.

Sarah Carr-Gomm

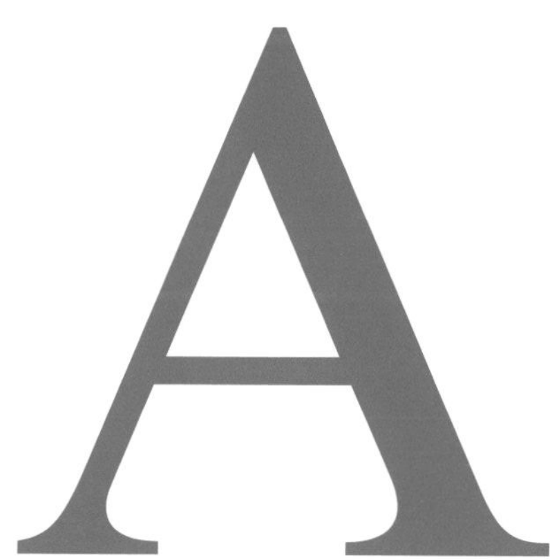

Aaron
In the Old Testament, Aaron was the eloquent elder brother of Moses. While Moses was on Mount Sinai, Aaron fashioned the Golden Calf for idolatry, and in *The Adoration of the Golden Calf* Poussin shows him encouraging his people to worship. Yet God was forgiving and Aaron was chosen to be High Priest of his people. His elaborate vestments are described in detail.[1] The Levite Korah contested Aaron's position, but when Korah was asked to bring his followers and give incense as an offering to God, a rite reserved only for priests, "the earth opened her mouth, and swallowed them up, and their houses and all the men that appertained unto Korah, and all their goods".[2] Aaron was considered the archetypal High Priest, and in *The Punishment of Korah* (Sistine Chapel, Vatican, Rome) Botticelli depicts him in a papal tiara, swinging his censer. The subject, therefore, is a warning to those who would contest Papal authority.

To confirm Aaron's primacy, the leaders of the 12 tribes of Israel were each ordered to bring a rod and place it on the tabernacle. The next day, Aaron's rod was found to have miraculously flowered and yielded almonds. Aaron appears in paintings or cycles of the life of Moses, as either a priest or a patriarchal figure with a long beard. He may be seen carrying a rod or a censer.

Abraham
A great Patriarch of the Old Testament and father of many Hebrew nations, Abraham was told by God to leave his birthplace and set out with Sarah, his wife, and Lot, his nephew.[1] Abraham settled in the land of Canaan, while Lot settled in Sodom and had all his possessions seized. Abraham pursued the raiders, recovered the stolen loot and on his triumphal return to Canaan was blessed and given bread and wine by Melchizedek, king of Salem.

Sarah bore no children and offered her handmaid Hagar to Abraham so that he might have a son; thus Ishmael was conceived. However, Hagar

Aaron: *see* Almond; Moses; Pig
[1] *Exodus 28*
[2] *Numbers 16:32*

Abraham: *see* Lot
[1] *Genesis 12:1–5*
[2] *Genesis 16:12*
[3] *Genesis 22:1–13*

Abstinence: *see* Alexander the Great; Antiochus and Stratonice; Chastity; Scipio

Abundance: *see* Cornucopia

began to despise Sarah. As a result, Hagar was driven into the wilderness. An angel instructed her to return to her mistress, and predicted that Ishmael would be "a wild man; his hand will be against every man, and every man's hand against him;"[2] yet God promised that he would beget 12 princes and rule a great nation.

Eventually, despite their old age, a son, Isaac, was born to Sarah and Abraham. The baby's arrival had been prophesied by three angels to whom Abraham had shown hospitality. Jealous of Isaac, Ishmael and his mother were banished. As they began to die of thirst, an angel led them to water.

To test his faith, God demanded that Abraham sacrifice Isaac and, early in the morning, Abraham saddled his ass with wood for the burnt offering, and took Isaac to the appointed place. Just as Abraham was about to slay his son on an altar, an angel intervened and a ram was substituted for the sacrifice.[3]

Artists have represented many episodes from the life of Abraham. Giambattista Tiepolo, in *The Angel Appearing to Sarah*, shows an aged Sarah before the angel; and Claude Lorrain painted picturesque landscapes with Hagar and the Angel. However, the Sacrifice of Isaac was the most frequently chosen theme, since Abraham was seen as the paragon of unquestioning faith in God, and Isaac as a "type" of Christ: God sacrificed his son as Abraham was prepared to, the wood of the burnt offering representing the Cross. In 1401 this was the subject of the competition to decorate the great portals of the Baptistry in Florence, for which both Ghiberti's and Brunelleschi's panels still exist. Caravaggio's *Sacrifice of Isaac* shows the scene with customary violence, while Ferdinand Olivier, in *Abraham and Isaac*, shows the two on their way to the sacrifice.

Absinthe

This green liqueur flavoured with wormwood was first used medicinally by French troops in the 19th century. It is both addictive and poisonous; Zola describes the bitterness and sorrow it causes in his novel *L'Assommoir* (1877) and Degas painted the eternally depressing image of *The Absinthe Drinker*.

Abstinence

Sexual continence is usually illustrated in art by figures from antiquity famous for their self-restraint. Seleucus, King of the Eastern Empire, gave his young wife to her step-son, who was dying of love for her; Alexander the Great did not take sexual advantage of the defeated family of Darius; the Roman general Scipio refused a young girl betrothed to another. In allegory, an adolescent Cupid (Eros) may be taken from the arms of a naked woman by wise Minerva (Athene), as in Pietro da Cortona's fresco in the Room of Venus (Pitti Palace, Florence).

Abundance

The female figure of Abundance represents the prosperity brought about by peace and justice. Her attribute is a cornucopia, the horn of plenty, which may be full of ripe fruit and jewels. She may be shown near a sheaf of corn or surrounded by children and once-wild animals that have clearly been tamed.

Academy
Named after the garden near Athens where Plato (*c*.427–347BC) taught philosophy, the term was loosely applied to any scholarly circle in the Renaissance. The first Academy of Art was founded in Florence in 1562 by Giorgio Vasari under Duke Cosimo I. An academy was established in Rome in 1593, in France in 1648, and in England in 1768, and by the end of the 18th century there were over 100 in Europe. Zoffany painted *The Academicians of the Royal Academy* in 1770, showing intellectuals discussing the merits of numerous masterpieces.

Academies promoted "history painting", which derived in both style and subject matter from classical antiquity. Monumental, didactic, narrative painting was considered the highest form of art, since it contained universal moral truths and provided inspiration to noble ideals. The rigidity of the French academic system led the Impressionists to find alternative means of exhibiting their works from 1874. Since then respect for academic art has declined.

Achilles
The legendary Greek hero of Homer's *The Iliad*, a work that describes Achilles' part in the Trojan War. Later writers added the story of how his mother, the sea-nymph Thetis, knew that his fate would be to die in this war, and so dipped him in the river Styx to render him invulnerable.[1] However, the heel by which she held him remained dry and he later died from an arrow wound to this one weak spot. Sources differ as to whether Paris or Apollo fired the shot that finally killed him.

Achilles was educated by the centaur, Chiron.[2] Regnault's *The Education of Achilles* shows him learning how to draw a bow. To prevent him from joining the Trojan War, his mother disguised him as a girl and hid him at the court of King Lycomedes. Here he fell in love with Deidamia, the King's daughter, by whom he had a son, Neoptolemus. Achilles' disguise was revealed by Ulysses (in Greek myth, Odysseus), who, laying gifts before the court, noticed his disregard for feminine luxuries and fondness for weapons.[3]

In the 1630s Rubens made *The Achilles Tapestries* of these scenes, together with others from the Trojan War, now hanging at the Boyamns-Van Beuningen Museum, Rotterdam, and in Detroit.

Actaeon
In mythology, Actaeon[1] was the grandson of Cadmus, the founder of Thebes. One day while out hunting he strayed deep into some woods, where lay a pool of clear spring water. Here he spied Diana, goddess of chastity (in Greek myth, Artemis), bathing with her nymphs. In punishment for having seen her naked, Diana turned him into a stag. He fled, amazed by his own speed, but as he paused to look at his new reflection in the water, his hounds caught him and gorged themselves on his flesh. Titian, in *Diana and Actaeon*, shows Actaeon astounded by Diana's beauty; while in his *The Death of Actaeon* the hero, in the process of transformation, flees from the vengeful huntress.

ADAM AND EVE
See panel on following page.

Achilles: *see*
Centaur; Polyxena; Thetis; Trojan War
[1] Statius, *Achilleid I:269* and Hyginus, *Fabulae CVII*
[2] Philostratus the Elder, *II:2*
[3] Hyginus, *Fabulae XCVI*

Actaeon: *see*
Cadmus; Diana; Stag
[1] Ovid, *Met III: 138–252*

Adonis: *see*
Venus
[1] Ovid, *Met X:503–739*

ADAM AND EVE: *see*
Apple; Creation; Fig Leaf; NUDE; True Cross
[1] *Genesis 1:26*
[2] *Genesis 2:7–22*
[3] *Genesis 3*

Adonis: *see*
Cupid; Venus

ADAM AND EVE

In the Old Testament, God created Adam in his own likeness to "have dominion over the fish of the sea, and over the birds of the air, and over the cattle, and over all the earth, and over every creeping thing that creeps upon the earth".[1] Having formed Adam from the dust of the earth, God breathed life into him and he became a living soul; God then placed Adam in the Garden of Eden, and forbade him to eat of the Tree of Knowledge.

Adam named the animals and God created Eve from Adam's rib, to be his companion.[2]

The cunning serpent tempted Eve to know good and evil by eating the forbidden fruit, and she in turn persuaded Adam to taste it. At once their eyes were opened and, ashamed, they took fig leaves to hide their nakedness. In punishment, God commanded the snake to go on its belly and eat dust, and, for their Original Sin, expelled Adam and Eve from the Garden of Eden. Eve was to bear children in sorrow and Adam to toil the thorny ground.[3]

The Creation, Temptation and Fall of Adam and Eve were highly popular themes in medieval and Renaissance art because they represented Original Sin and mankind's need, accordingly, for redemption through Christ.

Adam and Eve with the Tree of Knowledge, after a late 13th-century miniature found in a Hebrew Bible.

These themes were illustrated on their own or as a cycle. The Temptation and the Expulsion from Paradise introduce the fresco cycle by Masolino and Masaccio, *The Life of St Peter* (Brancacci Chapel, Florence). The Fall may also be seen in the background of an Annunciation painting in reference to Christ's mission to redeem mankind; similarly, Adam's skull may appear at the foot of a Crucifixion scene.

Adonis

In mythology, Adonis was the offspring of the incestuous relationship between Myrrha and her father, Cinryas, king of Cyprus. Myrrha begged to be released from her guilt and was turned into the tree that bears her name; Adonis was born from its trunk. He grew into an extremely beautiful youth, and Venus (in Greek myth, Aphrodite), pierced accidentally by Cupid's arrow, fell passionately in love with him. She knew he would die while hunting and

A detail showing Adonis, after Venus and Adonis *by Titian (1553–1554, Prado, Madrid).*

tried to dissuade him from this pursuit. Titian's *Venus and Adonis* shows a naked Venus clinging to the hunter as he sets off to meet his fate. Adonis was killed by a wild boar and, as Venus found him dying, she turned the blood flowing from his wound into an anemone, which became associated with sorrow and death.

Aeneas

The legendary Trojan hero of Virgil's epic poem *The Aeneid*, Aeneas was to become the forefather of the Romans.

The subject was sculpted by Bernini and was popular in Rome because it illustrated the city's Trojan origins as well as noble values of family respect and piety.

The son of Venus (in Greek myth, Aphrodite) and Anchises, he was variously aided and thwarted by the gods, especially the vengeful Juno (Hera), who had sided with the Greeks against the Trojans. The difficulties thrown in his way were often offset by Jupiter's (Zeus') guidance, which Virgil used as proof that the origins of Rome were divinely sanctioned. The story tells of Aeneas' flight from burning Troy, leading his son, Ascanius, and carrying his father, with the sacred relics and images of their household gods.[1]

Aeneas' quest for Italy led him over land and sea, through storms whipped up by Juno and calmed by Neptune (Poseidon), to the island of Delos. Here the king and priest, Anius,[2] showed Aeneas and his father, son and companions the holy site where Apollo was born. The scene is the subject of Claude Lorrain's *Coast View of Delos with Aeneas*. Aeneas and his company later landed at Carthage where Venus told him how Queen Dido founded the city.[3] Fearing an outbreak of war between Aeneas and Carthage, Venus engaged Cupid (Eros) to contrive a love affair between Dido and Aeneas.[4] In *Dido Receiving Aeneas and Cupid Disguised as Ascanius*, Francesco Solimena shows the stately Dido welcoming Aeneas and his son to a banquet in their honour. Cupid, disguised as Ascanius, kisses her hand to make her fall in love with Aeneas.

Turner's *Dido and Aeneas* shows them setting out to hunt with a magnificent re-creation of Carthage in the distance. Their affair began during a storm, and Giovanni Romanelli's *Dido and Aeneas* illustrates them hurrying to shelter in a cave where their love was consummated.[5] Forgetting their duties, they spent the winter together until Jupiter sent Mercury (Hermes) to rebuke Aeneas and remind him of his destiny. A distraught Dido pleaded with Aeneas to remain, but he was resolute. She constructed her own funeral pyre, aided by her sister, Anna, and after watching Aeneas and

Aeneas: *see* Cupid; Juno; Romulus and Remus; Stag; Venus; Virgil; Trojan War

[1] Virgil, *Aeneid II:705–730*
[2] Ovid, *Met XIII: 625–635*
[3] Virgil, *Aeneid I:335–370*
[4] Virgil, *Aeneid I:657–723*
[5] Virgil, *Aeneid IV:160–173*
[6] Virgil, *Aeneid IV:634–705*
[7] Virgil, *Aeneid V*
[8] Virgil, *Aeneid VI*

Aesculapius: *see* Apollo; Caduceus
[1] Ovid, *Met II:628–632*
[2] Ovid, *Met XV: 622–744*

Agatha, Saint: *see* Martyrs
[1] *Golden Legend, St Agatha*

his fleet sail out of Carthage, fell on the sword left by her heartless lover. Juno took pity on her and sent Iris, goddess of the rainbow, to release her spirit. As she flew across the sky, Iris trailed a thousand colours sparkling like dew in the light of the sun.[6] As he headed away, Aeneas looked back to see the city aglow with the flames of Dido's funeral pyre.

Aeneas landed on Sicily where he held games in honour of the first anniversary of his father's death.[7] Having reached the Italian mainland, Aeneas visited the Cumaean Sibyl and requested to see Anchises once more.[8] Accompanied by the Sibyl and bearing a gift of a golden bough for Proserpina (Persephone), queen of the Underworld, Aeneas descended into its shadows. He passed disease, fear, hunger, evil, poverty, sin and war, and saw a multitude, including his kinsmen, who had been denied burial. These souls were destined to roam aimlessly for a hundred years before they could be put to rest. Aeneas was rowed by Charon across the Styx, and, in a myrtle wood, he saw Dido reunited with her former husband. Finally he reached the Land of the Blessed in the Fields of Elysium, where he found his father. Anchises foretold how Aeneas would marry Lavinia, who would bear him a son, Silvius, and how his destiny would be fulfilled through his descendant Romulus, the founder of Rome, and illustrious figures in Roman history, until Virgil's own day.

Aeneas and the Trojans continued their journey to the mouth of the Tiber in Latium and were welcomed by King Latinus, father of Lavinia. However, at Juno's intervention, the Fury Allecto whipped up hatred for the Trojans. Hostilities began when Ascanius shot a stag from the royal herd, tamed by Princess Silvia, a scene depicted by Claude Lorrain in *Landscape with Aeneas Shooting the Stag of Silvia.* Aeneas then reluctantly engaged in a series of wars, and as Boucher shows in *Venus Requesting Arms for Aeneas from Vulcan*, Venus asked Vulcan, the god of fire, to make a set of armour for him. This included a shield embellished with the events that would shape the future of Rome.

Aesculapius

Aesculapius (in Greek myth, Asklepios) was the god of medicine and the son of Apollo. His mother, Coronis, was loved by Apollo but was unfaithful to him. A raven informed the god who, in a jealous rage, shot her with his deadly arrow and learned as she died that she was about to bear his child. Apollo turned his anger on the raven who became black for ever more; and he snatched the child from his mother's womb as she lay on her funeral pyre. Aesculapius was brought up by the wise centaur Chiron, from whom he learned the art of healing.[1] He was introduced to Rome from Greece during a severe plague, arriving disguised as a snake. He resumed his divine appearance on the Tiber Island, and the plague ceased. The caduceus, a serpent twined around a staff, is his attribute.[2]

Agatha, Saint

Legend[1] claims that in the 3rd century AD the noble Agatha was pursued by Quintianus, the lecherous Roman consular official in Sicily, but nothing would persuade her to give in to his demands, as her resolve was with

AGES OF MAN

A detail after The Three Ages of Man, *painted by Titian in 1516 (private collection).*

The span of human life may be divided into several ages, and these ages of man were popular themes in Renaissance art. Sometimes there are four, corresponding to the seasons, and sometimes three. Children may play near a dead tree to represent the cycle of life; youth may be shown as a soldier or pair of lovers; and old age may be a man contemplating a skull. Where there is a fourth figure, it is usually that of the mature man, placed somewhere between youth and age. Usually it is the transience of life that is implied, but Titian's painting of the subject uses the three ages of man as an allegory of prudence. In this work, the faces of three different generations are placed above those of a dog, lion and wolf to suggest that the present should learn from the past in order that it might profit for the future.

AGES OF MAN: *see* Ages of the World; SEASONS

Christ. Infuriated, Quintianus threw her in prison, tortured her cruelly and cut off her breasts. St Peter appeared and restored her, but she was then rolled naked over live coals strewn on the ground, and a tremendous earthquake shook the city of Catania. Agatha died in prison, and a year after her martyrdom Mount Etna erupted; the inhabitants of Catania brought her veil to the volcano, and it miraculously stopped the flow of molten lava and saved the city. Breasts are Agatha's attribute, and in paintings she is often shown carrying them on a plate. Because of their shape, she was adopted as the patron saint of bell founders.

AGES OF MAN

See panel, above.

Ages of the World

In mythology, the four Ages of the World were known as the Ages of Gold, Silver, Copper or Bronze and

Ages of the World: *see* AGES OF MAN; NUDE

[1] Ovid, *Met I: 89–150*

Agnes, Saint: *see* Brothels; Martyrs
[1] *Golden Legend, St Agnes*

Agrippina:
[1] Tacitus, *Annals II:71–72* and *III:1*

Iron.[1] The Golden Age was free of fear and conflict, in a season of everlasting spring; its rivers flowed with milk and nectar, and the animals lived in harmony. Jupiter introduced the four seasons in the Age of Silver, forcing men to seek shelter. In the Age of Bronze men became fiercer and inclined to conflict, but they were still free from wickedness. The Age of Iron introduced treachery, deceit, violence, greed and war. Pietro da Cortona likened the Four Ages of the World to the Ages of Man in frescoes in the Sala della Stufa (Pitti Palace, Florence). Gold represents youth and bounty, and Silver the agrarian life; Bronze reaps the rewards of middle age; Iron brings violence and death.

Agnes, Saint

St Agnes[1] can often be identified in paintings by her attribute, a lamb, which she probably acquired because *agnus*, Latin for lamb, sounds like her name. She is generally represented as a young girl with long hair. Agnes was an early Christian martyr who lived in Rome. The son of a Roman prefect fell in love with her but she scorned his promise of wealth, declaring that she had become a bride of Christ. When she refused to worship the pagan goddess Vesta, the prefect had her stripped and taken nude to a brothel, but miraculously her hair grew and covered her nakedness. An angel appeared in the brothel and provided her with a cloak of heavenly light which converted everyone inside and frightened away those who came to harm her. Her suitor was struck dead by a demon when he tried to ravish her, and her executioners were burned by the flames they intended for her. A knife was finally plunged

A detail of St Agnes with a lamb, after a painting by Andrea del Sarto (Cathedral of St Agnes, Pisa).

into her throat in AD304 and she died aged thirteen.

She appears as an elegant figure holding her lamb, for example in Duccio's *Maestà*. Emerantiana, her half-sister, was stoned to death and sometimes appears with her in paintings, often with a pile of stones in her lap.

Agrippina

The story of the noble Agrippina, granddaughter of Emperor Augustus, is one of fidelity in marriage. She dearly loved her husband, the wise and popular Roman general, Germanicus, named after his successful conquests in Germany. He was poisoned by his political enemies in Syria, and Agrippina, grieving, brought his ashes back to Italy. Her intimate friends, several officers and many who had served under Germanicus went to Brindisi to meet her fleet. As Agrippina disembarked with her two children, clasping the funeral urn, her eyes were riveted to the earth and there was a universal sigh from the crowds of mourners.[1] She may be seen descending from her ship, and the American painter Benjamin West, in his painting *Agrippina Landing at Brundisium with the Ashes of Germanicus*, shows the grieving Agrippina with the ashes of her husband.

Ajax

After the death of Achilles in the Trojan War, the Greek heroes, Ajax and Ulysses (Odysseus), vied for his armour.[1] To resolve the dispute, Minerva (Athene) awarded the armour to Ulysses. In anger, Ajax planned to kill his commanders, but Minerva thwarted the assault by driving Ajax mad so that he slaughtered only a flock of sheep. When his sanity returned, Ajax was so humiliated that he thrust his sword into his side. Hyacinths grew where his blood fell on the earth, although Poussin in *The Kingdom of Flora* curiously shows a carnation.

Alcestis

In mythology, a beautiful princess, Alcestis, believed that the sorceress Medea could rejuvenate her aged father, King Pelias of Iolcus; and so, directly following the witch's instructions, she and her sisters cut up the body or drained the blood of the king (accounts vary). However, the scheme was just a ruse by Medea to bring about the death of Pelias.

Alcestis married King Admetus of Pherae, who had been promised to be spared death if another agreed to die in his place.

When it was time for him to die, Alcestis offered to sacrifice herself on his behalf, to appease the shade of her father.[1] In *The Death of Alcestis*, Pierre Peyton shows her on her deathbed as the epitome of a devoted wife. Hercules, touched by her virtue, fought with death and brought her back to earth.[2]

Alchemy

Alchemy was originally an Arab science with methods inherited from the Egyptians and Babylonians, before its practice was brought to Europe. Based on the Aristotelian idea that there was a "prime matter" for all substances, alchemy is best known for attempting to turn base metals into gold, through the imaginary "philosopher's stone", which was thought to be the Elixir of Life: the secret of immortality. The art was practised in monasteries during the Middle Ages, by alchemists who believed that their experiments would receive divine guidance.

The alchemist is usually seen at his furnace surrounded by flasks, crucibles and other objects of his craft. Vasari and his associates illustrated such a practitioner in *The Alchemist's Laboratory*, Studiolo of Francesco I, *c.*1570.

Alexander the Great

Alexander (356–323BC), king of Macedonia, conquered the Persians, occupied Egypt and founded Alexandria.[1] He was told by the Delphic Sibyl at the Temple of Apollo that he was invincible. His conquests included Gordium, capital of the Phrygians, where there was a chariot fastened with knotted cords. According to tradition, the empire of

Ajax: *see* Minerva; Trojan War; Ulysses
[1] Ovid, *Met XIII:1–398*

Alcestis: *see* Medea
[1] Euripides, *Alcestis*
[2] Apollodorus, *The Library I ix 15*

Alexander the Great: *see* Abstinence; Apelles; Aristotle
[1] Plutarch, *Lives, Alexander*

Almond: *see* Aaron; HALO

[1] *Numbers 17:8*

the world was reserved for the man who could untie this knot. Some accounts report that Alexander could not undo the Gordian knot and so he sliced it with his sword; some maintain that he was able to untie it easily.

Alexander was taught by Aristotle and commanded a cavalry at the age of 18. He is often depicted on his horse, Bucephalus, usually shown as a white charger, which responded only to his gentle control. At the Greek city of Thebes, which he sacked, his captain raped the noblewoman Timoclea and demanded her money. She led him to a well where she claimed she had thrown her valuables and, as he looked over, pushed him in. Pietro della Vecchia's *Timoclea Brought Before Alexander* shows Alexander, in recognition of her resourcefulness and dignity, releasing her and her children.

In 333BC Alexander conquered the Persians in the narrow plain of Issus. In *Battle of Issus*, Albrecht Altdorfer shows his mighty army as a mass of tiny figures. Fighting in the foremost ranks, Alexander wounded and put to flight Darius, the Persian king. Although Alexander's army pillaged the Persian camp, Darius' mother, wife and two daughters were treated with respect and consideration. Veronese in *The Family of Darius Before Alexander* shows Alexander and his friend Haephestion visiting Darius' family after the battle. At first Darius' mother mistook the taller Haephestion for her conqueror, but Alexander put her at ease by saying that Haephestion was another Alexander.

Alexander pursued Darius and found him on the point of death, fatally wounded by his own men. As Darius died he paid homage to his enemy, who covered him with his cloak. Alexander was restrained on all accounts. He believed that it was better to rule through goodwill than force and tried to fuse diverse customs.

He married Roxana, who was, in some accounts, the daughter of Darius and in others the daughter of a chieftain of conquered Asia. This greatly pleased the Persians and Alexander exercised restraint until their union was legalized. Sodoma painted frescoes of scenes of his life, including *The Marriage of Alexander and Roxana* (Villa Farnesina, Rome), which accords with a description by Lucian of a classical painting.[2]

Lysippus was Alexander's official court sculptor and Apelles his court painter – considered the greatest in antiquity. Scenes of Alexander, often helmeted and in armour, may show his magnanimous and honourable behaviour.

Almond

Almonds (in Italian, *mandorle*) may symbolize divine favour. They occur in the biblical story in which God chooses Aaron to be High Priest by way of a miracle: "the rod of Aaron for the house of Levi had sprouted and put forth buds and produced blossoms, and it bore ripe almonds".[1]

As a convenient pictorial shape, heavenly light in the form of an almond may enclose the figure of Christ in various contexts, which include the Last Judgment, the Transfiguration, the Harrowing of Hell, the Ascension, Christ appearing to the Apostles, and Christ in Majesty; a similar aureole may surround the Virgin of the Assumption.

Alpha and Omega (A and Ω)
The first and last letters of the Greek alphabet represent the totality of God. "I am the Alpha and the Omega, the beginning and the ending, says the Lord God, who is and who was and who is to come, the Almighty."[1] They appear with the Chi Rho in early Christian art and in mosaics such as the image of Christ in San Miniato al Monte, Florence.

Amalthea
In mythology, Amalthea was the nymph who fed the infant Jupiter on the milk of a she-goat. In gratitude,

A detail of Amalthea, after Poussin's The Nurture of Jupiter *(c.1636, Dulwich Picture Gallery, London).*

Jupiter broke off one of the goat's horns and gave it to her as the "cornucopia", claiming that it would give her all she desired. He then turned his nurse and the horn into a star.[1] Alternatively, Amalthea is the name of the she-goat.

Amazons
In mythology, the Amazons were a nation of female warriors who lived near the Black Sea. Their name is Greek for "without breast", since they burned off their right breasts in order to draw their bows more easily; but this is not represented in painting. They invaded Athens but were driven back by Theseus.[1] Rubens' *The Battle of the Amazons* shows the violent battle of the sexes in which the women were overcome.

Ambrose, Saint
Ambrose (died AD397) is one of the four Latin Fathers of the Church, with Augustine, Jerome and Gregory the Great. He studied law in Rome and was made prefect of Milan, the administrative centre of the western Empire. Disagreements broke out between the Arians, who did not believe in the divinity of Christ, and the Christians, over the election of a new bishop; and during the dispute a child was supposed to have cried out, "Ambrose shall be bishop." He was duly elected, even though he had not been baptized.

Ambrose was a great orator and resolute theologian; when, in AD390, the Emperor Theodosius I ordered a savage massacre in punishment for the death of the Roman governor, Ambrose instructed him to do public penance, thereby asserting the superiority of the Church over secular rulers. He introduced the Ambrosian chant, the first successful form of hymn, into the church service.

St Ambrose, after a painting by Martin des Vos (mid-15th century).

Alpha and Omega: *see* Chi Rho; God
[1] *Revelation 1:8*

Amalthea: *see* Cornucopia; Jupiter
[1] Ovid, *Fasti V:111–129*

Amazons: *see* Hercules; Theseus
[1] Plutarch, *Lives, Theseus*

Ambrose, Saint: *see* Augustine, St; Bee
[1] *Golden Legend, Saints Gervasius and Protasius*
[2] *Golden Legend, St Ambrose*

Andrew, Saint: *see*
Martyr
[1] *Mark 1:16*
[2] *Golden Legend, St Andrew*

Andrians: *see*
Bacchus
[1] Philostratus the Elder, *Imagines I: 25*

ANGELS: *see*
Gabriel; Michael; Putto; Raphael
[1] Pseudo Dionysius, *Celestial Hierarchy*
[2] *Revelation 12:9*

An early 6th-century mosaic in San Ambrogio, Milan, shows him as a middle-aged man in classical dress. However, he is more frequently seen as a bishop, often one of the four Doctors of the Church, as in the wings of a mid-15th-century triptych by Antonio Vivarini and Giovanni d'Alemagna. He may also be seen with the twin brothers, Saints Gervase and Protase, who according to legend[1] were martyred for their faith and revealed the site of their relics to Ambrose in a vision. In the early 16th century, Ambrogio Bergognone painted scenes from Ambrose's life, beginning with the saint as a baby in his cradle with bees buzzing around the window and over his face, without harming him, and his father predicting his illustrious future.[2] In other paintings he may have a bee hive, symbolizing his future eloquence, and a book with the words, "be nourished by food, but the food of angels not human". This alludes to his name, since ambrosia is the food of the gods; however, it is also the name of the whip with which he drove the Arians out of Italy.

Andrew, Saint (Apostle, Disciple)

Andrew (d. *c.*AD60) was a fisherman on Lake Galilee and the first of the followers of Christ, who summoned him with his brother, Simon, later named Peter.[1] Accounts of his later life are uncertain but, according to legend,[2] he travelled into Russia through Greece and Asia Minor, preaching, performing miracles and converting. He converted a boy who was able to extinguish the flames of a burning house on fire with a few drops of water; he cured a man of lust; he caused lightning to strike dead a woman who had falsely accused her son of attempting to violate her; he expelled from a city demons that appeared to him as dogs; and he brought back to life forty men who had drowned on their way to receive his blessing. Even after his martyrdom he came back as a pilgrim to save a bishop from the Devil disguised as a beautiful woman. Among those whom Andrew converted was the wife of the proconsul who, unable to make the saint worship false gods, had him bound with ropes to the X-shaped cross which became his attribute.

Andrew is usually painted as an old man with long hair and a beard, together with his cross, as in a painting by El Greco. His statue was carved to Bernini's designs in the 17th century for St Peter's, Rome, which possessed the relic of his head. He may also be shown with a fish or fishing net. He is the patron saint of Russia, Greece and Scotland.

Andrians

In mythology Bacchus (in Greek myth, Dionysos) made a river of wine flow on the island of Andros.[1] The inhabitants, known as Andrians, danced and sang and their voices became thick with wine from the river, which "makes men rich, and powerful in the assembly, and helpful to their friends, and beautiful". At the mouth of the river, Tritons blew wine from sea shells, and Bacchus moored his ship in the harbour to lead Laughter and Revel, and reap the river's harvest.

Titian's painting of the scene shows a merry crowd in which some people are becoming amorous in their revelry.

ANGELS

Angels and archangels are said to be divine messengers, the Greek word for angel meaning "bringer of news". Angels appear frequently throughout the Old and New Testaments, and not only bring God's word to mankind but also deliver his protection or punishment. They are often depicted as young men with wings and haloes; young winged boys are called *putti.*

In Christian theology, angels are grouped in three hierarchical orders, each of three types.[1]

In the first hierarchy Seraphim surround the throne of God and are often red in colour; Cherubim know and worship God, and are depicted as gold or blue; and Thrones, wearing judges' robes, support his seat and represent divine justice, which they confer on the second hierarchy.

This second hierarchy consists of Dominions, Virtues and Powers, who govern the stars and the elements, and light up the third hierarchy with the Glory of God. Dominions are depicted with crowns, sceptres or orbs to represent the power of God; Virtues have white lilies or red roses, themselves symbols of the Passion of Christ; and Powers are militant figures, who are seen fighting ubiquitous devils.

The third hierarchy, consisting of Princedoms, Archangels and Angels, maintains contact between Heaven and Earth and executes God's will. Princedoms oversee territories; Archangels are the independent figures Michael, Gabriel, Raphael and Uriel, who together with Angels bring God's messages to mankind.

The Assumption of the Virgin by Botticini, which is part of the Palmieri Altarpiece, shows the three orders of angels, each with its three ranks.

The Rebel Angels were those who fell with Lucifer, who was later renamed Satan, from Heaven.[2] Domenico Beccafumi's *Archangel Michael and the Fall of the Rebel Angels* shows them vanquished by St Michael and metamorphosing into demons as they tumble down to Hell.

A putto *after* The Madonna with the Divine Child *by Andrea Solario (1495, San Pietro, Murano).*

A detail of cherubs, after A Group of Cherubs in the Clouds, *by Giandomenico Tiepolo (*c.*1760).*

Angels, a detail after The Worship of Venus *by Titian (1518–19, Prado Museum, Madrid).*

Angelica:
[1] Ariosto, *Orlando Furioso I:viii–ix*
[2] Ariosto, *Orlando Furioso VIII:xviii–l*
[3] Ariosto, *Orlando Furioso X:xcii–cxiii*
[4] Ariosto, *Orlando Furioso XIX:xix-xxxvi*

Animals: *see*
Ape; BIRDS; Bull; Cat; Dog; Lion; Orpheus; Unicorn
[1] *Genesis 1:24,25*
[2] *Genesis 6:19*

Anna, Saint: *see*
Joachim and Anna
[1] *Golden Legend, The Birth of the Blessed Virgin*

Angelica

Orlando Furioso, an epic poem by Ariosto (1474–1533), published, in 1516 in Ferrara, Italy, recounts the legend of Charlemagne, the Saracen invasion of France, and the conflict between Christians and Muslims.

The poem takes the form of a parody of medieval romances, with combative knights, damsels in distress, monsters and witchcraft. Orlando, or Roland, was driven mad by his love for the beautiful but fickle Angelica. She was promised to either Orlando or his cousin Rinaldo, depending upon which of them slaughtered more Saracens.[1] She fled from her suitors, and had many adventures. In *Angelica and the Hermit* Rubens shows how a lustful hermit put her to sleep with a magic potion, but when he tried to satisfy his desire with the sleeping maiden he found he was too old to perform.[2]

Ingres' *Ruggiero Delivering Angelica* illustrates how Angelica was chained to a rock on the Isle of Tears to feed the orc, a huge sea-monster. She was seen there by Ruggiero, or Roger, a Saracen champion, who flew down on a hippogriff (a mythical creature with the hindquarters of a horse and the wings and head of an eagle) to slay the monster and save her.[3]

By Cupid's will Angelica fell in love with Medoro, a young Moorish soldier who was wounded by a Scottish knight. She healed him with the juice of herbs from the mountains; they were married among herdsmen, and proclaimed their love by carving their intertwined initials on the bark of trees.[4]

ANGELS

See panel on previous page.

Angelus, The

The Angelus is the prayer devoted to and giving thanks for the Annunciation. It is said at morning, noon and sunset, and its name comes from the opening words, *Angelus Domini* ("the Angel of the Lord"). Jean-François Millet's painting of peasants praying in the fields at the sound of the Angelus bell is an image of religious devotion. The picture became widely known through reproductions and was perversely re-interpreted by Salvador Dali.

Animals

In mythology, Orpheus tamed the animals with his music. In the Old Testament God created the animals in the Garden of Eden, Adam named them,[1] and Noah gathered them in pairs for the Ark.[2] These stories represent a time, like the Golden Age, when humans lived in harmony with animals. And yet the Old Testament also tells of animals being sacrificed to God. Mankind has also slaughtered animals on a massive scale in sacrifice to the gods of antiquity, believing that revenge would follow if they did not provide food for the divine world: the Parthenon was said to smell like a slaughterhouse. Overcoming a wild or fabulous beast usually represents strength or good triumphing over evil. Medieval bestiaries outlined the various characteristics of real and imagined animals, and accorded them extensive moral symbolism.

Anna (Anne), Saint

The cult of Anna (1st century AD), mother of the Virgin, first came to the West with Christian refugees fleeing from Muslim conquests, and an early

A detail after Virgin and Child with St Anne and St John the Baptist, *Leonardo da Vinci (1507–8, National Gallery, London).*

image of her *c.*AD650 appears in Santa Maria Antiqua, Rome, where she is shown with the Virgin. By the 14th century she was a popular figure, partly because her motherhood at an advanced age confirmed the doctrine of the Immaculate Conception of the Virgin. She usually appears with her daughter, and their lives are inextricably linked. Legend[1] claims that she was married three times and had three daughters, and she is depicted in the late Middle Ages with her extended family, known as the Holy Kinship, by artists such as the Master of St Veronica. In 1479 the Carmelites in Frankfurt formed a brotherhood of St Anne and commissioned an altarpiece devoted to her, illustrating scenes from her life. She may adopt a matriarchal position but is most frequently portrayed as a maternal figure with her daughter, particularly in Renaissance Florence; the most graceful examples are by da Vinci in his *Virgin and Child with St Anne and St John the Baptist*, and in his *Burlington House Cartoon.*

Ansanus, Saint

A nobleman of Siena, Ansanus (died *c.*AD304), was brought up as a Christian by his nurse, and was openly preaching the faith by the age of 19, in spite of persecutions under Emperor Diocletian. He was whipped, thrown into a pot of boiling oil and finally beheaded. A patron saint of Siena, he appears as a young man with a banner and a cross, primarily in the art of that school. With St Margaret, his image by Lippo Memmi flanks the altarpiece of Simone Martini's *Annunciation*, which was originally intended for his chapel in the Cathedral of Siena, and is now in the Uffizi, Florence.

Anthony, Saint (the Great or Abbot)

According to legend,[1] the 18-year-old Anthony (AD251–356) gave all his worldly goods to the poor in order to live with hermits in the desert near the Nile, where he suffered countless torments by demons. A popular theme in art was the saint tempted by lust: Veronese painted him struggling with the Devil as a sensual female scratches his hand with her extremely long fingernails; Cézanne concentrated on the enticing voluptuous nudes. In a dream Anthony was told of St Paul, thought to be one of the earliest Christian hermits (died AD347), who had taken refuge from persecution in the Theban desert and lived in a cave until a great age. He was led to him by a centaur, satyr and wolf, and on his arrival Paul's daily ration of bread brought by a crow doubled. Dürer shows them together

Anthony, Saint:
[1] *Golden Legend, SS Anthony and Paul the Hermit*

Anthony of Padua, Saint:
[1] *Luke 12:34*

Antiochus and Stratonice: *see* Abstinence
[1] Plutarch, *Lives, Demetrius*

Antiope:
[1] Hyginus, *Fabulae VIII* and Ovid, *Met VI:111*
[2] Philostratus the Elder, *Imagines I:10*

in the forest. When Paul died, Anthony buried him with the help of two lions. St Anthony was sought out for his wisdom and guidance. He advocated self-denial and is thought of as the founder of monasticism. As he was apparently over 100 when he died, he is depicted as a bearded old man with a crutch wearing a hooded robe. Pisanello shows him with a pig, probably symbolizing gluttony, and a bell with which he exorcized demons.

Anthony of Padua, Saint
Anthony (1195–1231) was from Portugal. Having pursued religious studies at Coimbra, he joined the Franciscan friars, teaching and preaching in Morocco, France and Italy with remarkable knowledge and powers of oration. He is the patron saint of Padua, where he died, and many miracles are credited to him. For the high altar of San Antonio, Padua, Donatello cast scenes of *The Miracle of the Ass,* the story of a man who refused to believe in the presence of the Eucharist unless his ass knelt before it, so the animal obliged; and *The Miracle of the Irascible Son*, in which the saint restored a boy's leg, cut off in remorse for having kicked his mother. Another tale tells how, at a miser's funeral, Anthony preached, "For where your treasure is, there will your heart be also."[1] The miser's heart was found in his treasure chest and consequently Anthony became the patron saint of lost property. He is shown as a young man in Franciscan robes; he may be holding a lily, or a flaming heart, or carrying the Christ Child because of a vision he had of the Virgin and Child.

The Miracle of the Wounded Woman, *after a series of frescoes of the miracles of St Anthony by Titian (1511, Scuola del Santo, Padua).*

Antiochus and Stratonice
Son of Seleucus, king of Asia, Antiochus fell desperately in love with his father's young wife, Stratonice, and so resolved to die by refusing nourishment. The court physician, Erasistratus, realized the cause of his illness and informed the king, who immediately annulled his marriage and united Antiochus and Stratonice, making them king and queen of Upper Asia.[1] In *Erasistratus Discovering the Cause of Antiochus' Illness* Jacques-Louis David shows Antiochus lying ill as a dignified Stratonice is brought to him.

Antiope
In mythology, Jupiter disguised himself as a satyr in order to ravish Antiope, daughter of the king of Thebes,[1] as depicted by Ingres in *Antiope and the Satyr*. She bore the twins Amphion and Zethus and fled to avoid her father's anger, but he

killed himself in despair. Antiope was then imprisoned by her uncle and tormented by his wife, Dirce. When she finally managed to escape, her grown-up sons took revenge: they deposed her uncle and tore Dirce apart on the horns of a bull. The twins ruled Thebes and built its walls. Amphion played the harp so beautifully that the stones fell into place on their own.[2] Giambattista Tiepolo painted *Amphion Building the Walls of Thebes with his Song* as part of an allegory of eloquence.

Ape

An ape or monkey may represent the base instincts of man. In Molenaer's *Lady World* a monkey slips his paw into a slipper, as a representation of lust. An ape may also be used to satirize human affectation, folly and vanity. Artists were aware that they "aped" or imitated nature, as Chardin shows in *The Monkey Painter*; while 19th-century caricaturists mocked students as apes imitating their masters. Alternatively, apes or monkeys may appear as part of an exotic menagerie, as in Gentile da Fabriano's *Adoration of the Magi*.

Apelles

Apelles was court painter to Philip and Alexander the Great of Macedonia in the 4th century BC. He was considered the greatest of classical painters, and one story relates how his painting of a horse was so life-like that it made a real horse neigh. He possessed such courtly manners that Alexander frequently visited his studio. Apelles wrote treatises on art but neither these nor any of his paintings have survived. Among the latter were portraits of Alexander, *Aphrodite Rising from the Sea* and *Calumny*. Apelles was allowed to paint Alexander's favourite courtesan, Campaspe, in the nude, but as he painted he fell in love with her; whereupon Alexander did him the honour of presenting her to him.[1] Giambattista Tiepolo painted himself as Apelles and his wife as Campaspe in *Alexander and Campaspe in the Studio of Apelles*.

Apocalypse

Common to both ancient Hebrew and Christian literature, prophetic writing hailed the end of the world and the triumph of good over evil. In the Old Testament Daniel had apocalyptic visions, but in the New Testament the apocalypse is most closely associated with the Revelation ascribed to St John the Evangelist. It was written at a time when Christians were suffering persecution, possibly in the lst century AD, and is difficult to read today as many of the images are no longer clearly understood. The significance of certain numbers, especially seven, is likewise obscure, but some allusions may be to Roman emperors. In the Revelation angels speak, mighty forces clash, and saints are rewarded; God faces huge opposition but is finally triumphant.

Some passages from the Revelation are well known: God as the Alpha and Omega; the apocalyptic beasts surrounding the throne of heaven, resembling a lion, a calf, a man and a flying eagle, which were adopted as the attributes of the Evangelists; and the visions of God, of the Lamb and of the Seven Seals.[1] Each seal opened to reveal a vision. The first four seals disclosed the four horsemen of the

Apelles: *see*
Alexander the Great; Calumny
[1] Pliny the Elder, *Natural History XXXV:85–89*

Apocalypse: *see*
Alpha and Omega; Angels; Evangelists; Michael, St; Satan
[1] *Revelation 6:1–8*

Apollo: *see* Aesculapius; Aurora; Cassandra; Daphne; Diana; Hercules; Hyacinthus; Marsyas; Mercury; Midas; Niobe; Phaeton; Trojan War

[1] Ovid, *Met I:416–451*

[2] Apollodorus, *The Library, II vi 2*

[3] Ovid, *Met XIV:130–153*

apocalypse: a conquerer with bow and crown, on a white horse; War, the destroyer with a sword, on a red horse; Hunger, with a pair of scales, on a black horse; and Death, the pale horseman, with Hell on his heels.

The fifth seal revealed the souls of those slain for preaching the word of God, who were given white robes. The sixth seal brought a great earthquake, when the sun blackened, the moon became blood red, the stars fell, heaven departed and men hid in the mountains from this day of wrath. An angel anointed the "seal of the living God" on the foreheads of his servants, while four angels held back the four winds of the earth. Silence filled heaven when the seventh seal was opened, until an angel threw a censer to earth and caused thunder, lightning and earthquakes. The call of seven trumpets released further revelations, of the wonders of heaven, of the Devil and his angels cast out of Heaven, and of the "whore of Babylon", the scarlet woman, mother of harlots and of the earth's abominations. The last decisive battle was fought at Armageddon before the Day of Judgment

During the Middle Ages scenes from Revelation illustrated manuscripts and stained-glass windows, and featured in frescoes and carvings on Romanesque churches. Dürer made a series of woodcuts, *The Apocalypse*, and El Greco painted *The Opening of the Fifth Seal*. The most popular subject, however, was St Michael vanquishing the rebel angels.

Apollo

In mythology, Apollo was one of the 12 gods of Olympus. The son of Jupiter (in Greek myth, Zeus) and Latona, and the brother of Diana (Artemis) and father of Aesculapius (Asklepios), Apollo was the god of poetry, music (especially that of the lyre) and prophecy. Like his sister he was a hunter, and he acted as the protector of athletes and young men in war. The god of light, he was also known as Phoebus Apollo or Apollo "The Bright". At his birth, on the island of Delos, a blaze of light shone over the island and sacred swans flew around it seven times. He was also the god of healing, because his light nurtured plants.

Apollo and Diana, abandoned by their mother, were nourished on ambrosia and nectar, hence their dazzling appearances. Like the idealized Apollo Belevedere, he was a personification of youth and beauty. His attributes are various: a lyre, a bow and arrow, a golden chariot drawn by four horses or rays of the sun, a laurel wreath or a crown.

Apollo set out to find a suitable place to give truthful oracles to mankind. He found it in the valley of Delphi in the heart of Greece, but the Python, a monster of darkness, guarded its entrance. He slew the creature with a thousand arrows.[1] Turner shows him resting after his triumph in *Apollo and the Python*. Apollo's oracles were communicated through a priestess, Pythia, who sat on a sacred tripod of gold placed over a chasm in the rock. Only Hercules contested Apollo's possession of the oracle, because he did not receive the answer he required. He tried to carry away the sacred tripod, but Apollo came to the priestess' defence and Jupiter settled the quarrel by throwing a thunderbolt between his two sons.[2] The shrine at Delphi was famous: in

Coastal View of Delos Claude Lorrain shows the picturesque landscape where Aeneas came to consult the oracle and was told that his descendants would rule earth's widest bounds.

Among those loved by Apollo was the Cumaean Sibyl, who asked to live as many years as there were grains in a heap of dust. Salvator Rosa's *River Scene with Apollo and the Sibyl* shows her holding the dust in her hand before the god. She scorned his love, and as she had forgotten to ask for eternal youth, the god condemned her to the misery of a protracted old age.[3]

As the god of light, Apollo inherited two distinct characteristics. First, he was the physical light of the sun god, Sol (in Greek myth, Helios), drawing a four-horse chariot across the sky each day, often preceded by the figure of Aurora. The subject lent itself to paintings on Baroque ceilings, such as Guido Reni's *Aurora* (Casino Rospigliosi, Rome) and Giambattista Tiepolo's *Course of the Chariot of the Sun* (Palazzo Clerici, Milan) in which Apollo blazes across the four continents. He is also seen rising or setting, as in the pair of tapestry designs by Boucher, *The Rising and Setting of the Sun*, or with Phaeton, who asked to drive the god's chariot and foolishly flew too near to the ground, scorching some nations.

Secondly, Apollo represented the light of truth and therefore knowledge and reason. He was also guardian of the Muses, by whom he was worshipped on Mount Parnassus.

Artists such as Poussin and Raffael Mengs were influenced by Raphael's painting of Parnassus (Stanza della Segnatura, Vatican, Rome), where Apollo sits surrounded by the Muses and the great poets. Along with Calliope, the muse of epic poetry, Apollo provided inspiration to poets and bestowed on them his sacred crown of laurels, a reference to his unrequited love for Daphne.

Apollo was also associated with the protection of flocks and herds. He clothed himself as a shepherd with a crook, and in this bucolic guise he is often portrayed with satyrs. As god of music, his supremacy was contested by the satyr Marsyas and Pan. Apollo could be cruel, and as the archer-god, he rounded viciously on the Greeks in the Trojan War. His arrows rained down killing ranks of men and his poisoned darts brought disease. He is, however, usually depicted as the god of the civilized arts.

Apollonia, Saint

Apollonia, a deaconess of the church, was martyred in Alexandria during a revolt against the Christians in AD249. According to legend,[1] her persecutors pulled her teeth out, an episode shown in a 15th-century Umbrian School painting, and when they threatened to burn her alive, she walked into the flames of her own volition. She was invoked against toothache and her attribute is a pair of forceps grasping a tooth, as shown by Francisco Zurbarán.

Apostles

After Christ's Resurrection, eleven of the twelve disciples became the Apostles, or messengers of his gospel: Andrew, Bartholomew, James the Great, James the Less, John, Jude, Matthew, Peter, Philip, Simon and Thomas. The twelfth Apostle was Matthias, who replaced Judas Iscariot. The early missionaries Barnabus and Paul may also be included.

Apollonia, Saint: *see* Martyrs
[1] Golden Legend, *St Apollonia*

Apostles: *see* individual names

Apple: *see* ADAM AND EVE; Atalanta; Hercules; Hesperides; Paris; Venus

Arachne: *see* Minerva

[1] Ovid, *Met VI:1–145*

Arcadia: *see* Pan; Satyr

Archimedes:

[1] Plutarch, *Lives: Marcellus*

Apple

The golden apple, or Apple of Discord, is the attribute of Venus. Discord (Eris) was not invited to the wedding of Thetis and Peleus, at which the gods of Olympus were present, and in her anger she threw down a golden apple to be given to the most beautiful woman. Venus (Aphrodite) won the prize, incurring the fury of Juno, which ultimately brought about the Trojan War.

In the garden of Paradise, Eve ate the forbidden fruit from the Tree of Knowledge. Although the fruit is not specified in the Bible, it was taken to be an apple, perhaps because *malus* is Latin for both apple and evil. An apple therefore represents the Original Sin and Fall of Man. It may be the attribute of Eve the temptress.

The inclusion of an apple in a painting may refer to sin. Augustus Egg, for example, in *Past and Present* shows a mother cast out of her comfortable home for committing adultery; the apple in the painting creates a parallel with Eve's expulsion from the Garden of Eden. In contrast, an apple may be held by the Christ Child to signify salvation and redemption from Original Sin.

Arachne

In mythology,[1] Arachne was a young woman famous for her talent at spinning. Her movements were so graceful that the river nymphs would come to watch her at work, and she even gained the praise of her teacher and patron, Minerva (in Greek myth, Athene). Filled with conceit, Arachne foolishly denied that she had ever been taught to spin, and challenged the goddess to a contest. Minerva wove a tapestry showing the 12 gods enthroned. Tintoretto's *Minerva and Arachne* depicts the goddess watching Arachne weave scenes of the gods metamorphosing to consummate their earthly loves; her work was flawless.

Minerva, furious at her rival's success and angered by the choice of subject, tore it to pieces and beat Arachne until the girl attempted to hang herself. Minerva then took pity on her and turned her into a spider, so that Arachne could spin a web eternally.

Arcadia

Arcadia, a mountainous area in the Peloponnese, where Jupiter (in Greek myth, Zeus) was said to have been born, takes its name from Arcas, son of Jupiter and Callisto.

It was associated with an ideal of rustic life. As the home of Pan, nymphs, satyrs, shepherds and shepherdesses, it inspired ancient Greek and Roman pastoral poetry. The theme of *Et in Arcadia Ego* warns that death exists even in an earthly paradise.

In Poussin's painting of the theme, shepherds come across a tomb bearing the inscription *Et in Arcadia Ego* as a reminder of mortality. The alternative interpretation, "I too was once in Arcadia," became a nostalgic lament for youth and an appropriate epitaph.

Archimedes

The Greek Archimedes (287–212BC) was one of the greatest mathematicians of antiquity.[1] He was also an astronomer and physicist, and in mechanics discovered the principle of the lever. He is said to have shouted "*Eureka*" ("I have found it") when he

ARCHITECTURE

The symbolic meaning of architecture in painting depends on both context and contemporary style. In 15th-century Flemish painting the nave of a church may be Romanesque with a Gothic east end, brightly lit through tall narrow windows, to represent the coming of the new Order with the birth of Christ. In Jan van Eyck's *Madonna with Chancellor Rolin* the town in the landscape behind the donor is early Gothic, while a corresponding one behind the Virgin and Child is high Gothic. The capitals of pillars near Christ may be carved with scenes of the Fall of Man to illustrate that he has come to redeem Original Sin. In the Arena Chapel, Padua, Giotto painted the Virtues within Gothic canopies, while the Vices are framed by Romanesque arches. Buildings in ruin are often found in scenes of the Adoration of the Magi and the Nativity, and imply the delapidation of the old Order and the establishment of the new Order with the advent of Christ. Elaborately carved architectural elements in scenes of the Passion of Christ refer to the status of his tormentors, especially Pilate; Christ and his Apostles were themselves poor.

Architecture may have a political as well as a religious meaning. The Florentine Renaissance rejected the Gothic style favoured north of the Alps and, politically affiliated to Rome, re-adopted classical elements of architecture. In Rome, enthusiasm for the antique inspired reconstructions of the past, as shown in Raphael's cartoons of *St Paul at Athens* and *The Blinding of Elymas*. The cartoons also provided settings as affirmation of the noble heritage of Paul and Elymas.

The use of the Orders on columns may be significant: the plain Doric signifies simplicity and restraint; Ionic scrolls suggest learning; and the highly carved Corinthian or Composite Orders signify important figures or settings and are also used for rich decoration. In stage design, classical architecture was used for tragedy; Gothic for comedy. Later inclusions of classically inspired buildings might signify nostalgia for the past or, in the 18th century, might advertise the fact that the learned patron had visited classical sites on the Grand Tour.

realized how to test the purity of metal from observing the volume of bath water displaced by his body. Archimedes died when the Roman general Marcellus captured his city, Syracuse, during the second Punic War (218–201BC).

His inventions had prevented the Roman invasion for two years. Archimedes did not notice that his city had been taken, so engrossed was he in a mathematical problem, and when commanded by a soldier to come before Marcellus he refused until the problem had been solved. The enraged soldier drew his sword and ran him through.

Sebastiano Ricci depicted this scene in *Archimedes and the Hero of Syracuse*.

Arethusa:
[1] Ovid, *Met V:572–641*

Ariadne: *see*
Bacchus; Minotaur; Theseus
[1] Catullus, *Poems LXIV*, Philostratus the Elder, *Imagines I:15*
[2] Ovid, *Heroides X*

Arion: *see*
Apollo
[1] Ovid, *Fasti II:79–129*

A detail showing Ariadne as Bacchus leaps toward her, after Bacchus and Ariadne *by Titian (1522–3, National Gallery, London).*

ARCHITECTURE
See panel on previous page.

Arethusa
In mythology,[1] the nymph Arethusa was cooling herself in clear waters when her beauty attracted the river-god Alpheus. He chased her, still naked, and she could not outrun him. As his shadow stretched before her and his breath stirred her hair, she cried out for help. She is seen in art being rescued by Diana (in Greek myth, Artemis), who hid her in a cloud. However, the persistent Alpheus waited for her to appear. In order that she might remain undiscovered, Arethusa was turned into an underground stream.

Ariadne
Ariadne,[1] daughter of King Minos of Crete, fell in love with Theseus, who dared to encounter the savage Minotaur, risking death for the reward of glory. He slew the monster in the heart of its labyrinth and was able to retrace his steps with Ariadne's help: she had given him a ball of thread to unwind as he entered the maze and then follow back to its source on his return journey. They sailed to the island of Naxos, where Bacchus was worshipped, but Theseus cruelly abandoned Ariadne on the shore. Accounts differ about her first meeting with Bacchus. One describes her asleep when he appeared; another recounts that she was lamenting her fate, incredulous at Theseus' empty vows. Bacchus, afire with love, greeted her with his companions, some brandishing garland-covered points, some waving limbs torn from a bullock, some entwined with serpents, and some playing instruments or beating tambourines.[2] Bacchus turned Ariadne's crown into a circle of stars, which brought her eternal glory, and in some accounts they were wed. In *Bacchus and Ariadne* Titian has the god leaping down from his chariot to claim her, followed by his rowdy throng; while in Sebastiano Ricci's *Bacchus and Ariadne*, Hymen presides over their marriage as Bacchus gently takes Ariadne by the hand.

Arion
An ancient Greek poet, whose story is mainly legendary,[1] Arion played the lyre so beautifully that he would make birds and wild animals halt in their tracks. Diana (in Greek myth, Artemis) compared his playing to that of her brother, Apollo. Sailing from Italy, where he had amassed wealth, his ship was attacked. Arion begged to play a final melody and as soon as it was finished he jumped overboard. He rode ashore on the back of a dolphin which, with the ocean waves, had been charmed by his music. Dürer shows him in *Arion* with his harp on the back of curious-looking fish. (See illustration, page 31.)

Aristotle
A Greek philosopher, scientist and pupil of Plato, Aristotle (384–322BC) founded the Peripatetic School in Athens, named after his habit of walking up and down while teaching. He wrote on Logic, Physics, the Soul, the Heavens, Animals, Metaphysics, Poetics, Rhetoric, Politics and Ethics. He was the great sage of reason and Raphael gave him place of honour alongside Plato in *The School of Athens* (Stanza della Segnatura, Vatican, Rome).

Aristotle taught Alexander the

A detail of Arion, after Dürer's Arion on the Dolphin *(15th–16th century, Kunsthistorisches Museum, Vienna).*

Armour: *see*
Don Quixote; George, St; Liberale, St; Mars; Michael, St; Minerva; *Putto*; Trojan War; Victory; Vulcan

Arrow: *see*
Apollo; Christina, St; Cupid; Diana; Sebastian, St; Teresa, St; Ursula, St
[1] Ovid, *Met I: 469–472*

Great. A medieval legend relates how he expounded that women are the downfall of men. Aristotle tried to persuade Alexander to abandon his favourite courtesan, Campaspe (who in some accounts is called Phyllis). In revenge, Campaspe charmed the old philosopher. To prove his love, she insisted that Aristotle allow her to ride on his back, and Alexander saw how a woman could undo the wisest of men. The subject was often painted on domestic furniture along with related themes, such as Samson and Delilah.

Armour

Armour is used in art to identify warriors. Those warriors most notable in mythology are Mars (in Greek myth, Ares), god of war, his female counterpart, Bellona, and Minerva (Athene), goddess of war and wisdom. Armour and weapons litter the forge of Vulcan (Hephaestus). Personifications of Peace and Victory may be shown over a pile of armour, and the theme of love triumphant may be represented by a *putto* standing on armour and weapons or, with or without Venus, near a sleeping warrior. Fortitude wears armour, as does Europe because of her skill in the art of war.

Several Christian saints wear armour, among them the Archangel Michael, Saint George and Saint Liberale. The Roman soldiers and sometimes Pontius Pilate, tend to be clad in armour in the Passion of Christ.

Because of the nature of epic drama and poetry there have been numerous warrior heroes and anti-heroes from the Trojan War to Don Quixote. In 15th-century Italy a popular topic of debate was the value of a career dedicated to arms or to letters, the ideal being a combination of the two; Federigo da Montefeltro, the Duke of Urbino, was portrayed by Berruguete, dressed in armour, sitting reading a book.

Arrow

In mythology Cupid (in Greek myth, Eros) had two kinds of arrow: one "which kindles love is golden and shining, sharp-tipped; but that which puts it to flight is blunt, its shaft

Artemesia:
[1] Pliny the Elder, *Natural History XXXVI:30–32*

Ass: *see*
Don Quixote, Midas, Silenus
[1] *Isaiah 1:3*
[2] *Numbers 22:21–34*

tipped with lead".[1] He was sent by the gods to play havoc with the lives of their companions and of mortals.

A bow and arrow is also the attribute of Apollo and of Diana (Artemis) the Huntress. At the beginning of Homer's *The Iliad* Apollo's arrows rain down on the Greek camp bringing death and disease. The ancient belief that his arrows brought the plague may have had some influence on the legend of St Sebastian. In Christian iconography arrows killed the martyrs Christina and Ursula, but they failed to kill Sebastian, who recovered from his wounds. He therefore became a popular saint to be invoked against the plague; in Renaissance Italy Sebastian was frequently painted bristling with arrows. An angel pierced the heart of St Teresa of Avila with a divine arrow which gave her both intense pain and spiritual ecstasy.

Artemisia

Artemisia, queen of Caria in Asia Minor, built a large tomb for her husband, Mausolus, in *c*.353BC at Halicarnassus. This first mausoleum was one of the seven wonders of the world.[1] In *Artemisia Building the Mausoleum*, Simon Vouet shows her studying an architect's drawing.

Arthur

The Arthurian legends were collected and edited by many sources, including Sir Thomas Malory (died 1471) in *Le Morte d'Arthur* and Chrétien de Troyes. Arthur, a vaguely historical figure, was mentioned in the 7th century but the first tales appeared with Geoffrey of Monmouth's *Historia Regum Britanniae* of 1136. French, English and Welsh romances extended the story.

Arthur proved his royal blood by removing the invincible sword Excalibur from a stone. Later, however, he lost Excalibur, and it was returned to him by the Lady of the Lake. Arthur gathered the best knights in the land to his Round Table at his court in Camelot. His circle included his nephew Sir Gawain, his magician and counsellor Merlin, his half-sister the enchantress Morgan le Fay, and his wife Guinevere. The quest for the Holy Grail dispersed the knights and proved the valour of Sir Galahad and Sir Percival. Arthur's downfall came as a result of the love between Queen Guinevere and Sir Lancelot. He died from a fatal wound inflicted by his son, Sir Mordred.

The Celtic story of Tristan and Isolde is also connected with Arthur. Sir Tristan, one of the knights of the Round Table, was sent to Ireland to escort his uncle's bride, Princess Isolde, to Cornwall. On board ship the two unwittingly drank a magic potion and fell eternally in love, with tragic consequences.

The Arthurian legends embody the chivalric qualities that appealed to English medieval revivalist painters such as William Morris and Dante Gabriel Rossetti in the latter half of the 19th century.

Ass

At the Nativity the humble ox and ass recognized Christ as the Son of God. Their presence was prophesied by Isaiah: "the ox knoweth his owner, and the ass his master's crib".[1] An ass with a millstone around its neck implies obedience. Asses carry wood for the burnt offering in the story of the Sacrifice of Isaac, and bear the

Astraea: *see* Ages of the World

A detail of Atalanta retrieving the golden apples, after Guido Reni's Atalanta and Hippomenes *(*c.*1620, Galleria di Capodimonte, Naples).*

Virgin on the Flight into Egypt and Christ on the Entry into Jerusalem. Balaam, sent to curse the Israelites, was unable to see that an angel of the Lord barred his way. His ass, however, saw the angel and could not proceed, whereupon Balaam beat it furiously. The beast was given the power of speech, Balaam's eyes were opened and he was converted.[2]

In myths and legends the ass has a somewhat comic role. The drunken Silenus, Bacchus' (in Greek myth, Dionysus') follower, and Sancho Panza, Don Quixote's squire, both ride asses.

The animal is often considered lazy and stupid. *The Golden Ass* or *Metamorphoses* of Apuleius, 2nd century AD, tells the story of young Lucian who is turned into an ass by the maid of a sorceress. He is ill-treated by all until he eats the roses that transform him back into human form. An ass makes a hideous noise and was therefore considered to be tone-deaf. Apollo gave Midas ass's ears in punishment for preferring Pan's music to his own.

Astarte

An ancient Syrian deity, Astarte was identified with Venus (Aphrodite). The painting *Astarte* by Dante Gabriel Rossetti represents the mysterious goddess of love whose realm lay between the sun and the moon.

Astraea

Astraea, associated with Justice, lived happily in the Golden Age but later, in the Bronze and Iron Ages, could not live with the wickedness of men and

Atalanta: *see* Meleager
[1] Ovid, *Met X:560–707*

Atlas: *see* Giants; Hercules
[1] Ovid, *Met IV:621–663*

Attis:
[1] Ovid, *Fasti IV:225–247*

Augustine, Saint: *see* Ambrose, St; Gregory the Great, St; Jerome, St; Monica, St

became the "Starry Maid", the constellation of Virgo.

Atalanta

In myth, the beautiful Atalanta could run faster than the fastest man, and Apollo warned her that her husband would be her downfall.[1] She set a competition for her many suitors: she would marry the man who out-ran her, and those who failed would die. Undeterred by the cruel fate that had befallen others and anxious to win the prize, Hippomenes, great-grandson of the King of the Ocean, took up the challenge. He asked for Venus' (Aphrodite's) help, and she offered him three golden apples to distract Atalanta as she ran. He threw them off-course, but, as Guido Reni shows in *Atalanta and Hippomenes*, Atalanta could not resist running to fetch them. Having won the race, Hippomenes failed to thank Venus and her sympathy then turned to anger. She induced the couple to defile a sacred spot and had them turned into lions. These beasts drew Cybele's.

Atlas

In mythology, Atlas was a Titan punished by Jupiter for his part in the War of the Titans. He was condemned for ever to hold the heavens on his shoulders. His home became identified with the Atlas mountains in North Africa, from the legend that they supported the heavens. It was also said that Atlas gave an unfriendly welcome to Perseus, who therefore turned him into a mountain by showing him the severed head of the gorgon Medusa.[1] Atlas took part in Hercules' quest for the apples of the Hesperides. His name has described books of maps since his image, with the world on his shoulders, appeared in Rumold Mercator's collection of maps, published in 1595.

Attila the Hun

Attila (*c.*AD406–53), king of the Huns, ruled most of the land between the Rhine and the Caspian Sea. When Rome failed to pay tributes he invaded Gaul, but in AD452 abandoned his efforts to capture Rome itself. Raphael's *Repulse of Attila* (Stanza del Eliodoro, Vatican, Rome) shows how Saints Peter and Paul appeared in the sky to halt the invasion on behalf of the Church.

Attis

In mythology,[1] Attis was driven mad by love, so castrated himself and died; violets were thought to have sprung from the blood of his wound.

Augustine, Saint

Saint Augustine of Hippo (AD354–430), with Ambrose, Jerome and Gregory the Great, was one of the four Latin Fathers of the Church. He studied law and taught rhetoric in Rome and Milan and was converted to Christianity by his mother, Monica, and Ambrose, then Bishop of Milan, who baptized him. He became Bishop of Hippo in his native Numidia, now Algeria, where he remained for the rest of his life and formed a loose monastic community, dying of fever aged 76 during a siege by the Vandals. Augustine advocated that Christianity could be served by using the best of classical culture. He was a prolific writer, whose *Confessions* and *The City of God* were highly influential. In the church dedicated to him in San Gimignano, Benozzo Gozzoli frescoed scenes

A detail of Aurora in her chariot, after Aurora, *a fresco by Guercino (1621–23, Casino Ludovisi, Rome).*

Augustus: *see*
Sibyl

Aurora: *see*
Cephalus and Procris; Achilles; Trojan War

[1] Ovid, *Met XIII:576–622*

from his life in Rome, Milan and Hippo, emphasizing his scholarly nature. A predella panel by Botticelli (Uffizi, Florence) illustrates the legend that Augustine was one day walking by the sea and came across a boy endeavouring to pour the ocean into a hole in the sand. When Augustine commented that this was impossible, the child replied, "No more than you for explaining the mysteries on which you are meditating." Augustine often appears as a scholar reading and teaching, as a bishop, or in the black habit of his rule; he may have a flaming heart, sometimes pierced by an arrow.

Augustus

Gaius Julius Caesar Octavianus (Octavian, 63BC–AD14) was the first emperor of Rome, and adopted the title Augustus, meaning venerable, from 27BC. He gave his name to the Augustan Age, one of outstanding literary achievement.

According to legend, prior to the birth of Christ, the Tiburtine Sibyl told Augustus that a Son of God would be born.

Aurora

In mythology, the rosy-fingered, saffron-robed goddess of the dawn (in Greek myth, Eos) set out before Apollo's chariot to herald the coming of the day. Aurora flew or drove a chariot as she rose in the east, and her sons, the fresh morning winds, were felt at her approach. She had several love affairs with mortals, notably Cephalus, and when infatuated she neglected her duty and the sun-god's chariot lay idle. She was struck by the beauty of the youthful Tithonos, carried him off and secured his immortality. They married, but she had forgotten to ask for his eternal youth. Tithonos grew older and older, and eventually she could no longer bear his decrepit figure and locked him away.

Their son, Memnon, was killed in the Trojan Wars: the tears she wept for him became the drops of dew found at dawn.[1] The image of the goddess scattering petals from the sky perfectly suited the decoration of 17th-century ceilings, as in Guercino's *Aurora* (Casino Ludovisi, Rome).

Babel, The Tower of:
[1] *Genesis 11:1–9*

Bacchus: *see*
Andrians; Ariadne; Midas; Satyr; Silenus
[1] Apollodorus, *The Library, III.xiv.7*

Babel, The Tower of

The Bible states that humanity originally shared a common language, but when people tried to build a tower in order to reach the heavens God stopped this presumptuous project by making them speak in many tongues so that they might not understand each other.[1] He then scattered the people abroad, so the tower was left unfinished. Pieter Bruegel the Elder painted *The Tower of Babel* as an image of the folly of man; his fantastic structure is not unlike the Colosseum in Rome.

The Tower of Babel, after an illustration in the Bedford Book of Hours *(c.1424, British Library, London).*

Bacchus

Bacchus, the Roman equivalent of the Greek Dionysos, was the god of wine, who dispelled care and inspired music and poetry. He was the son of Jupiter (Zeus) and Semele, and spent a blissful childhood brought up by Silenus (a rural god, depicted as a fat drunkard but also as having the gift of prophecy), nymphs, satyrs, herdsmen and vine-tenders. As a youth, he set out to teach the art of wine-growing, with fatal consequences: Bacchus fell in love with Erigone, daughter of his host, Icarios, and seduced her; her father, however, was killed by drunken shpeherds,[1] and on hearing the news Erigone hanged herself.

A detail showing Bacchus offering wine, after Caravaggio's Bacchus *(1593–4, Uffizi, Florence).*

When his divine nature was contested, Bacchus always emerged victorious. He was once kidnapped by Lydian pirates but covered their oars and sails with ivy. Wild beasts appeared and when the sailors jumped overboard in madness or fear, they turned into dolphins.

Bacchus is often accompanied by Silenus, satyrs, and the Maenads, or "mad women" – female followers of Bacchus, also known as the Bacchants, who dance around him in a drunken frenzy. The Romans held the festival of the Bacchanalia in the god's honour and, from the Renaissance, this inspired images of revelry and intoxication. Francesco Zuccarelli's *Bacchanal* shows nymphs and satyrs dancing in an idyllic landscape while Silenus reclines on an urn. Other paintings depict the more lecherous aspect of Bacchus, for he was also worshipped as the god of fertility in the form of a goat, hence his association with Pan, Silenus and satyrs. Such ceremonies became wild orgies in which animals were consumed raw.

Bacchus may be seen with his rowdy throng or alone, but either way is himself depicted as a beautiful youth, crowned with grapes and vine leaves or holding a cup or *thyrsus* (staff). He may wear an animal skin and he rides in a chariot drawn by wild animals. Caravaggio's *Bacchus* provocatively offers the spectator a glass of wine.

Barbara, Saint

According to legend,[1] the beautiful Barbara (dates unknown) was locked in a tower by her heathen father to keep her from her many suitors. She managed, however, to admit a Christian priest, disguised as a doctor, and was converted. She had a third window made in her tower to represent the divine light of the Trinity. On discovering her new faith, her father handed her over to the authorities, who ordered him to cut off her head, but he was struck dead by a bolt of lightning before he could behead her, and subsequently it became the custom to invoke Barbara against sudden death. She is depicted as a young, elegant maiden and her attribute is a tower, as seen in Memling's *Donne Triptych*.

Bare Feet

Christ and his disciples are often depicted barefoot, showing their obedience to his command to "carry neither purse, nor scrip, nor shoes".[1] Following his example, some religious orders are barefoot (although most wear sandals), notably the Discalced Carmelites founded in the 16th century by St Teresa. Pilgrims are often depicted barefoot as a sign of humility or poverty.

Barbara, Saint:
[1] *Golden Legend, St Barbara*

Bare Feet:
[1] *Luke 10:4*

St Barbara with her tower, after an engraving by a follower of Mancantonio (Albertina, Vienna).

Barnabas, Saint: *see*
Martyrs; Paul, St
[1] *Acts 15:35*
[2] *Golden Legend, St Barnabus*

Bartholomew, Saint: *see*
Martyrs
[1] *Golden Legend, St Bartholomew*

Bat: *see*
Melancholia

Bathsheba: *see*
David
[1] *II Samuel 11*

Bee and Beehive: *see*
Amalthea; Ambrose, St; Bernard, St; Cupid

Barnabas, Saint (Apostle)
Barnabus (1st century AD) is depicted as less prominent than St Paul, with whom he preached in Antioch.[1] He was a missionary in his native Cyprus, where he is considered Father of the Church and where, as Veronese shows, he apparently cured the sick by laying the Gospel of St Matthew over them. He was said to have been either burned alive or stoned to death.[2]

Bartholomew, Saint (Apostle, Disciple)
Little is known of St Bartholomew (1st century AD). Legend[1] claims that he preached, exorcized demons and

A detail showing the martyrdom of St Bartholomew, after an engraving.

baptized in India, then Armenia. Here he refused to worship pagan gods and was flayed alive. His attribute is the knife with which he was skinned – shown, for example, by Giambattista Tiepolo (San Stae, Venice).

Bathsheba
In the Old Testament the beautiful Bathsheba was bathing when she was seen by David as he walked on his roof. She was the wife of one of his soldiers, Uriah the Hittite, but David desired her and sent messengers to bring her to him. Consequently she conceived a child. David then instructed that Uriah be placed "in the forefront of the hottest battle", so that he was killed.[1] David married Bathsheba, but their child died in punishment for their sin. Their second child was Solomon. Painters usually depict Bathsheba at her bath in various degrees of modesty, but Jacopo Amigoni, in *Bathsheba*, shows her responsive to the message brought to her by David's slave.

Bavo, Saint
Born in the Low Countries, the wealthy Bavo (*c.*AD589–654) led a dissolute life until middle age, when he determined to mend his ways. He gave all his goods to the poor, became a hermit, and lived in a hollow tree. The patron saint of Ghent, he may be shown as a hermit or nobleman, sometimes with a falcon.

Bean King, The
A national custom of Flanders took place on Twelfth Night, when a bean was hidden in a pie and everyone received a slice. The one who found the bean was proclaimed the "bean king" or head of the table for the evening. This theme was painted by Jacob Jordaens in *The Bean King*.

Bee and Beehive
Bees, beehives and honey appear frequently in myth. For example, Jupiter (in Greek myth, Zeus) was raised on milk and honey by a she-goat sometimes known as Amalthea. Cupid (Eros) was stung by a bee while

stealing a honeycomb, only to be told by an unsympathetic Venus (Aphrodite) that he inflicted far greater wounds himself; this scene is amusingly depicted in a painting by Lucas Cranach.

Because of their production of honey, bees and beehives also represent the honeyed words of eloquence. The Athenean and Attic Bee were titles conferred on Plato and Sophocles, and legend claims that Pindar was nurtured on honey. A beehive is the attribute of Saints Ambrose and Bernard of Clairvaux because their words were said to be sweetly persuasive. The bee is the emblem of the Barberini family.

Beggar

Many beggars occur in the lives of Christ and his saints, notably Peter and Laurence, and are blessed or given alms. In the parable of Dives and Lazarus it is the poor man who finds his reward in Heaven. The Blind Leading the Blind may be depicted as beggars. In *King Cophetua and the Beggarmaid* Edward Burne-Jones painted the romantic story of King Cophetua, an imaginary king of Africa who married a beggarmaid.[1]

Belisarius

Belisarius (*c.* AD505–65) was the greatest general under the Byzantine emperor Justinian I. His triumphs were the defeat of the Vandals in Africa and the Goths in Italy. However, he was subsequently accused of treason, imprisoned and later pardoned. A story from the 10th century, illustrating how the mighty fall, also tells how Belisarius had his eyes gouged out and was reduced to begging in the streets of Constantinople. Jacques-Louis David's *Belisarius Recognized by the Soldier* shows Belisarius, as a blind beggar receiving alms from a woman, being recognized by a soldier who had served under him.

Bellerophon

Queen Anteia of Argos fell in love with the Greek hero Bellerophon and begged him to satisfy her passion. When he refused, the Queen told her husband that he had tried to ravish her.[1] The king therefore sent Bellerophon to the court of Lycia with a message requesting that his death be arranged. After a nine-day feast he was charged with the impossible task of destroying the monstrous Chimera which was devastating the country. Bellerophon, mounted on the winged steed Pegasus, slew the beast. His subsequent tasks were to fight the fierce tribe of the Solymi and the Amazons, both of whom he defeated. Impressed, the king of Lycia offered Bellerophon his daughter's hand and gave the hero half his kingdom. Later Bellerophon angered the gods by presuming to ride Pegasus to reach the top of Mount Olympus. As a result, the gods killed two of his three children, and he wandered off in solitude, heart-broken and avoiding all contact with men.

Belshazzar

Belshazzar, son of Nebuchadnezzar and king of Babylon, gave a great feast for a thousand of his lords and their wives and concubines. As they drank wine from golden vessels taken from the Temple of Jerusalem, the fingers of a hand appeared and wrote on the wall of the palace, "MENE, MENE, TEKEL, UPHARSIN".

Beggar: *see* Belisarius; Blind and Blindfold
[1] Percy, *Reliques I.II.6*

Bellerophon: *see* Amazons; Chimera; Pegasus
[1] Homer, *Iliad VI:160–211*

Belshazzar: *see* Daniel
[1] *Daniel 5*

Benedict, Saint: *see* RELIGIOUS ORDERS
[1] *Golden Legend, St Benedict*

Benjamin: *see* Jacob; Joseph
[1] *Genesis 35:18* and *42:4*

This scene was dramatically painted by Rembrandt in *Belshazzar's Feast*. Full of fear, the king offered rich rewards to the man who could understand the words, but all his wise men and astrologers failed. Daniel was summoned, and he warned that the king was not humble in his heart and had taken the vessels from the house of the Lord; he interpreted the writing on the wall as the fall of Belshazzar's kingdom. Belshazzar was slain that night and his kingdom divided.[1]

Benedict, Saint

Benedict[1] (c.AD480–547) was born in Umbria and was sent to Rome to study, but abandoned the dissolute life of the city to become a hermit. In *c.*AD529 he founded his Order, the first in Europe, at Monte Cassino. His reputation spread, and his advice was sought by King Totila the Ostrogoth. He was buried in the same grave as his sister, St Scholastica.

Little more is recorded about his life, but there are numerous legends. Some of these were frescoed in the 14th century by Spinello Aretino at San Miniato, Florence. Benedict's nurse followed him to Rome, where she borrowed a sieve; when it broke into pieces Benedict miraculously restored it. As a hermit, he was fed by a monk who let him know whenever food had been left for him by ringing a bell on the end of a string. He was tempted by the image of a woman, and managed to quell his lust by rolling naked in thorns and brambles. When he asked a community to observe a stricter life, they apparently tried to poison him, whereupon Benedict blessed the poisoned glass, which shattered as if struck by a stone. The blade of a scythe or axe belonging to a man clearing brambles fell into a deep lake; Benedict thrust the shaft into the water and it came out with its blade re-fastened. Maurus and Placidus were young men in his care. When Placidus fell into a fast-flowing river, Benedict enabled Maurus to rescue his friend by walking on the surface of the water, pulling him out by the hair. A malicious priest tried to feed Benedict with a poisoned loaf of bread, but the saint ordered a raven to fly off with it, and a building collapsed on the priest. The Devil tried to hinder the building of Benedict's monastery, said to have been sited on a temple of Apollo, by sitting on the stones and making them too heavy to move and by crushing a young monk; Benedict quickly brought the monk back to life. Benedict threatened two nuns with prompt excommunication if they would not stop gossiping. They died a few days later without having heeded his threat, and were buried in the church. At mass the deacon ordered all to leave who were not in communion, and the two nuns were seen to come out of their tombs and depart.

Benedict exorcized those who were possessed by the Devil and cured those inflicted with diseases. He is usually shown as elderly with a white beard. He may wear the black habit of his original Order or the white of the reformed Order. He may be seen with a raven or crow, or a broken tray.

Benjamin

Benjamin[1] was the youngest of the 12 sons of Jacob, but the only brother to have the same mother as Joseph. Benjamin and Joseph were the sons of

Rachel, while their half-brothers were the sons of Leah and her servants. After Joseph's disappearance at the hands of his half-brothers, Benjamin took Joseph's place as Jacob's favourite son. Unknown to his family, Joseph went to Egypt and eventually became the most important official in the country after intepreting the dreams of the Pharaoh. Years later there was a famine in Canaan and Jacob's sons went into Egypt to buy corn; Benjamin stayed behind as Jacob did not want to lose his favourite a second time. However, at Joseph's request, Benjamin went with the brothers on their next journey to Egypt. Joseph placed his silver cup in Benjamin's sack in order that his brother would be caught as a thief. Joseph declared that the thief of the cup should become his servant, but the other brothers protested, saying that if Benjamin did not return with them to their father, then Jacob would die of sorrow. It was this that led Joseph to reveal his true identity to his brothers.

Bernard of Clairvaux, Saint

Bernard[1] (1090–1153) joined the Abbey of Cîteaux in 1113, from where he expanded and reformed the Cistercian Order. He established a successful house at Clairvaux in Champagne, persuading four of his five noble brothers and 27 friends to join him. He attacked the luxury of the clergy and the abuses of the Roman *curia*. He was a great spiritual leader and his words were heeded by kings of England and France. The devotional quality of his writings earned him the title "Doctor mellifluus", or the "Honey-sweet Teacher". In the late 15th century

A detail of St Bernard at his desk, after The Virgin Appearing to St Bernard, *by Filippino Lippi (*c.*1482–6, Scala, Florence).*

Filippino Lippi and Perugino painted his vision of the Virgin: he appears as a young tonsured monk looking up from his lectern in the white robes of his Order. Ambrogio Bergognone shows him with a dragon chained at his feet representing his supression of heresy (Certosa, Pavia).

Bernardino, Saint

Bernardino (1380–1444), took over the hospital of La Scala, Siena, after most of its staff had died of an outbreak of plague. In 1402 he joined the Franciscans, preached all over Italy, attacking usuary, and tried to establish stricter rules in the Order. He was tried for heresy but acquitted.

Scenes from his life were frescoed *c.*1486 by Pintoricchio in the Bufalini Chapel in Santa Maria in Aracoeli, Rome, but he appears mostly in Sienese painting. Pietro di Giovanni d'Ambrogio's depiction shows him as a skinny, toothless figure in the brown habit of his Order (Pinacoteca,

Bernard of Clairvaux, Saint: *see* RELIGIOUS ORDERS

[1] *Golden Legend, St Bernard*

Bernardino, Saint: *see* IHS

BIRDS: *see*
Dove; Eagle

Blaise, Saint: *see*
Martyrs
[1] *Golden Legend, St Blaise*

Blind and Blindfold: *see*
Belisarius; Elymas, St; Paul, St; Samson; Tobias
[1] *Matthew 15:14*

Siena). He is sometimes depicted with Christ's monogram (IHS), which he used when preaching. Apparently, in order to eliminate gambling, he persuaded the dice-makers of Siena to change their trade and instead to cut ivory discs with the monogram, which he is said to have held up at the end of his preaching.

BIRDS
See panel, right.

Blaise, Saint
Little historical evidence exists concerning St Blaise (thought to have died *c*.AD316). His cult spread during the 8th century, and legend[1] has it that he was Bishop of Cappodocia. It is in this role that he is often depicted, but he led the life of a hermit: birds brought him food and wild animals sought his blessing. He is said to have cured sick animals, and is still invoked to do so. Sano di Pietro depicted a scene in which the saint ordered a wolf to take back a pig that it had stolen from a widow. St Blaise also cured a boy with a fish-bone stuck in his throat, and hence he is also protector against human illnesses, especially sore throats. He apparently refused to worship false gods and was tortured horribly in various ways, notably with iron-carders' combs, which became his attribute; finally, he was beheaded.

Blindness and Blindfolds
A blindfolded figure may personify Ignorance. If the figure is female and holding sword and scales, she might be unpredjudiced Justice; or, with a globe or wheel, unpredictable Fortune. A blindfolded Cupid (in Greek myth, Eros) indicates the

BIRDS
In classical augury the flight of flocks of birds was read as a sign from the gods. For example, crows and ravens were thought unlucky, swallows and storks lucky. Birds may also herald spring. In early Christian art a bird suggested the "winged soul" or the spirit, recalling an idea held by the ancient Egyptians that at death the soul leaves the body as a bird (*ba*).

The Christ Child may hold a bird, often a goldfinch, as a sign of the Resurrection. In Raphael's *Madonna of the Goldfinch*, Christ strokes the bird. The relationship between Christ and the finch is indeed usually one of affection. However, in Michelangelo's *Taddei Tondo* the Infant recoils from the creature, perhaps because the goldfinch was thought to have been a symbol of Christ's Passion.

The bird's association with the Passion may have arisen from a legend that while Christ carried the Cross on the road to Calvary (*Via Dolorosa*), a little bird fluttered onto his head and plucked a thorn from his crown.

In 17th-century Holland, the word for a bird-catcher was a euphemism for copulation, and as a result dead birds may appear in paintings of men and women flirting. A bird that has escaped from a trap might be an allegory of the ephemeral.

However, many artists have painted birds simply as decorative objects of delight or as mere observations; an example is Carel Fabritius' *The Goldfinch*.

blindness of secular love. The subject of Christ healing the blind was taken as an allegory of spiritual blindness before his advent. His parable, "And if the blind lead the blind, both shall fall into the ditch,"[1] was illustrated by Pieter Bruegel the Elder in an anguished painting which warns of the perils of choosing an unfit leader. Tobit (*see* Tobias), Belisarius, Samson and Elymas (*see* Paul, St) all went blind.

Bonaventura, Saint
Bonaventura (AD1221–74) studied, taught and preached in Paris. He acquired his name when he fell ill as a child and his mother took him to St Francis who, upon his recovery, exclaimed "*O buona ventura!*" ("Oh good fortune!"). He joined the Franciscan Order and in 1257 became its head or minister-general; he was considered its greatest friar after St Francis. In 1273 he was made cardinal-bishop of Albano, but maintained a simple way of life. Apparently, when his cardinal's hat was brought to him, he asked for it to be hung on a tree because his hands were dirty from washing dishes; he was so humble that an angel had to bring him the sacraments. He wrote extensively, including a biography of St Francis of Assisi. Zurbarán shows him addressing the assembly at the Council of Lyons in 1274, but he is usually seen reading or writing, dressed as a Franciscan or a bishop; he may have a cardinal's hat.

Book of Hours
A book of hours contains daily prayers for the laity to be said at appointed times, throughout the year. They were often highly decorated; the months may be illustrated with various seasonal farming activities, astrological charts or the pursuits of the aristocracy; the hours may be illustrated with religious scenes related to the prayers. The *Très Riches Heures du Duc de Berry* (Musée Condé, Chantilly), illustrated by the Limbourg brothers, is perhaps the best-known book of hours.

Bread
Bread is the sustainer of life and symbol of Christ's sacrifice. God sent manna to Moses in the wilderness; and Christ said, "I am the bread of life; he that cometh to me shall never hunger."[1] At the miraculous Feeding of the Five Thousand, and in legends of the lives of saints, many people often fed satisfactorily on small amounts of bread. At the Last Supper, Christ broke bread and, with reference to his sacrifice, said, "This is my body which is given for you; this do in remembrance of me."[2] The disciples recognized Christ after the Resurrection when he again broke bread at the Supper at Emmaus. In Christianity, bread is used at the sacrament of the Eucharist, during which it is believed to convert into the body of Christ.

Breasts
Breasts carry associations of Mother Nature and nourishment. Mother Nature is sometimes represented as the goddess Diana of Ephesus, whose many breasts emphasize her fertility. Milk from the Roman goddess Juno's breast (in Greek myth, Hera's), spilt in the heavens while she was nursing Hercules, created the Milky Way.

There are many early paintings of the Virgin giving her breast to the

Bonaventura, Saint: *see* Francis of Assisi, St

Bread: *see* Dominic, St; Moses; Passion of Christ
[1] *John 6:35*
[2] *Luke 22:19*

Breasts: *see* Agatha, St; Cimon and Pero; Diana; Milky Way

Breasts on a platter held by St Agatha, after Zurbarán's St Agatha *(1630–33, Musée Fabre, Montpellier).*

Bruno, Saint: *see* RELIGIOUS ORDERS

Brutus, Lucius Junius: *see* Lucretia
[1] Plutarch, *Lives, Popicola*

Brutus, Marcus: *see* Caesar
[1] Plutarch, *Lives, Marcus Brutus*

Christ Child, just as there are many supposed relics of the Virgin's milk, but this image ceased after the Council of Trent (1545–63) declared its disapproval of unnecessary nudity.

Charity can be personified in art as a woman breastfeeding children, but a young woman suckling an old man probably relates to the theme of Roman Charity illustrated in the story of Cimon and Pero, in which Pero fed her imprisoned father from her breast. The theme was a popular one with Italian and Netherlandish artists during the Renaissance. A bared breast could be a sign of humility, grief or anger, and a platter holding breasts is the attribute of St Agatha.

Bruno, Saint

The noble Bruno (*c.*1033–1101) was the founder of the Order of Carthusian monks. He studied and taught at Rheims but was expelled for accusing its archbishop of selling ecclesiastical privileges. In 1084 he built a church and established a small, isolated community at Chartreuse, near Grenoble, France. In a letter he wrote that only those who have experienced a hermit's life can know the benefit and delight to be had from the quietness and solitude. Summoned to Rome by a former pupil, Pope Urban II; he refused an archbishopric, but was allowed to form another monastery in Calabria. He is usually seen at prayer in the habit of his rule.

A detail of St Bruno bowing before St Hugh, after St Hugh of Grenoble Receiving St Bruno, *by Eustache Le Sueur (1645–48, Louvre, Paris).*

Brutus, Lucius Junius

According to Roman history,[1] Brutus was the nephew of King Tarquinius Superbus, and led an uprising which ousted his uncle. He was one of the first two consuls of the Republic, along with Tarquinius Collatinus. Two of Brutus' sons plotted to kill them and restore the Tarquin monarchy, but their plans were overheard and incriminating letters discovered. Brutus, who was a man of unbending nature, condemned them and watched, unflinching, as they were flogged and beheaded. Jacques-Louis David's *Victors Bringing Brutus the Bodies of his Sons* shows Brutus unmoved as the women weep profusely at the outcome of his patriotic deed.

Brutus, Marcus

Brutus (*c.*85–42BC) was an ardent Republican, whose antagonism to Julius Caesar's ambition induced him to lead the conspiracy to murder Caesar.[1] On March 15 (the Ides) 44BC, Brutus and his collaborators stabbed Caesar to death on the steps of the Theatre of Pompey, now near the Campo dei Fiori, Rome. When Caesar saw that his old friend was one of the assassins, he cried, *Et tu Brute?* ("Even you, Brutus?"). It is thought that Michelangelo carved the bust *Brutus* as a statement of his political beliefs.

Bubbles

A bubble is ephemeral and may refer to the brevity of life, as in Frans van Mieris' *Boy Blowing Bubbles at a Window*, where the boy is watched by an older lady.

The idea has a classical origin in the saying *Homo bulla est* ("mankind is a bubble"). However, Millais' painting *Bubbles* shows his grandson fascinated by a bubble; the work was used to advertise Sunlight soap.

Bull

In Minoan Crete bulls were used in ritualistic games in which athletes leaped over their horns. To the Greeks this animal signified potency and power, not ferocity. Jupiter (Zeus) disguised himself as a bull in order to rape Europa; therefore a bull is one of his attributes.

A bull may also be a representation of the continent of Europe. Hercules captured the Cretan bull as his seventh labour, and fought Achelous in the guise of a bull. The sacrifice of a bull was the principal rite in the cult of Mithras.

Goya and Picasso are among those painters who have been fascinated by the confrontation between toreador and bull.

Bull: *see* Europa; Hercules

Jupiter painting butterflies, which here represent souls: a detail after Dossi's Jupiter, Mercury and Virtue *(*c.*1529, Kunsthistorisches Museum, Vienna).*

Butterfly

Because the winged butterfly emerges as a result of a transformation from caterpillar to pupa to imago, it may symbolize rebirth or resurrection. Images of the Christ Child may show him with a butterfly in his hand or nearby. These delicate creatures may also appear in still lifes as a reminder of transience.

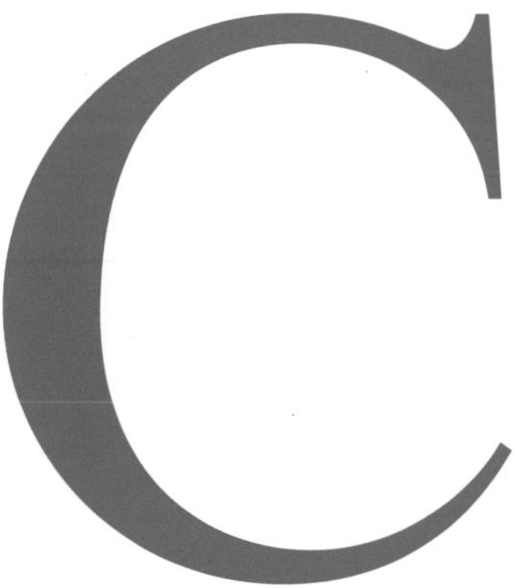

Cadmus: *see*
Actaeon; Minerva; Semele
[1] Ovid *Met III 1–137* and *IV 563–603*

Cadmus

Cadmus,[1] a hero of Thebes, is associated in mythology with violent deaths. He was advised by the oracle of Apollo to find a heifer with a moon-shaped sign marked on her flank: she would lead him to the place where he was to found the city of Thebes. The story tells how he reached the forest where the dragon of Mars dwelled, "with a wonderful golden crest; fire flashed from its eyes, its body was all puffed up with poison, and from its mouth, set with a triple row of teeth, flickered a three-forked tongue." Cadmus was unaware of the danger lurking within and sent some of his men into the forest to fetch water. In *The Followers of Cadmus Devoured by a Dragon* Cornelis van Haarlem shows the dragon with fangs, constricting coils and poisonous breath, in the act of consuming them. To avenge their deaths, Cadmus fought the dragon and killed it after a furious battle.

Minerva (in Greek myth, Athene) then appeared and told Cadmus to plough the earth and sow the dragon's teeth as seeds from which his people would spring. First, spearheads appeared, then plumed helmets, followed by figures weighed down with weapons. One warrior warned Cadmus, "Keep clear of family conflict." The crop of armed heroes began fighting each other until only five remained and agreed to a truce. With these five Sparti (sown men) Cadmus founded Thebes. He married Harmonia, daughter of Mars (Ares) and Venus (Aphrodite), and among his wedding presents from the gods was a beautiful but unlucky necklace made by Vulcan (Hephaestus). The couple had many offspring but the house of Cadmus was ill-fated: his daughter, Semele, was consumed by one of Jupiter's (Zeus') thunderbolts and his grandson, Actaeon, was destroyed by his own hounds. Cadmus and his wife left Thebes, bowed down with old age and sorrow. In reward for killing the dragon of Mars, they were turned into friendly snakes; with their bodies entwined, they disappeared into the shelter of a neighbouring grove.

Caduceus

This wand, entwined with two snakes and sometimes with wings at its tip, is the attribute of Mercury (Hermes) and is carried by messengers as a sign of peace. The belief that snakes have healing powers has ancient origins; in the Old Testament God cured Moses' people with a brazen serpent, usually shown coiled around a stick. The caduceus may also be held by Aesculapius, god of medicine. It is the emblem of the British Royal Army Medical Corps.

Caenis/eus

In mythology Caenis was famous for her beauty and had many suitors, but she refused to marry. Wandering on a lonely shore, she was ravished by Neptune (in Greek myth, Poseidon), who then granted her any request; so that she would never have to endure the injury again, she asked to become a man and was transformed into Caeneus. Later, Caeneus attended the wedding where the centaurs tried to abscond with the Lapith women; he proved his manhood by fighting valiantly. He killed and wounded many centaurs until those remaining hurled rocks and trees upon him; overwhelmed, Caeneus turned into a bird and flew into the clear sky.

Caesar

Caesar was the title adopted by the Roman general Gaius Julius (*c.*102–44BC), and handed on to later rulers of the Roman Empire; from it the modern "kaiser" and "czar" derive. Julius Caesar,[1] was a celebrated Roman general and statesman, conquerer of Gaul (58–50BC), victor in the civil war of 49–46BC, and dictator. In 49BC Caesar crossed the Rubicon, a small river that separated his province from Italy, ruled by Pompey, against whom he launched a civil war. Caesar drove Pompey out of Italy and pursued him to Egypt, but there he learned that Pompey had been murdered. He was said to have been aghast at the sight of his rival's severed head, and wept when given Pompey's seal. A string of victories against foreign powers followed and Caesar's dictatorship was secured. The triumphal march of this, one of the greatest Roman soldiers, was depicted by Mantegna in *Triumph of Caesar*.

Caesar's ambition to remain sole ruler of the empire brought about the Republican plot. On March 15th 44BC he was stabbed to death by Marcus Junius Brutus and his collaborators at the Theatre of Pompey, Rome.

Cain and Abel

These sons of Adam and Eve are described in the Old Testament according to their roles: "Abel was a keeper of sheep, but Cain was a tiller of the ground."[1] Both made offerings to God but Abel's sacrificial lamb was favoured above Cain's crops, and in a jealous rage Cain slew his brother. For his crime God cursed him and sent him to a land east of Eden. The Italian sculptor Lorenzo Ghiberti used episodes from their story for a gilded bronze panel of the doors of the Baptistry in the cathedral of Florence. Titian painted a violent interpretation: *Cain Slaying Abel.*

Callisto

Callisto was an attendant of the goddess Diana (Artemis in Greek myth) and was noticed by Jupiter (Zeus). He came to her disguised as

Caduceus: *see* Aesculapius; Mercury

Caesar: *see* Brutus (Marcus Junius); Cleopatra

[1] Plutarch, *Lives, Caesar, Pompey and Antony*

Cain and Abel:

[1] *Genesis 4:1–16*

Callisto: *see* Diana

[1] Ovid, *Met II 401–530 and Fasti II 153–193*

Mercury, holding the caduceus in his right hand, after a engraving by Hendrik Goltzius (1611).

Calumny: *see* Apelles
[1] Alberti, *On Painting, Book 3*
[2] Lucian, *Slander 4–6*

Cambyses, Judgment of:
[1] Herodotus, *V:25*

Camel: *see* CONTINENTS

Diana to win her confidence, and then he seduced her. While hunting with her nymphs, Diana discovered a cool grove with a stream rippling over its sandy bed and encouraged her companions to bathe. Callisto was reluctant to take off her clothes, and when others undressed her, it became apparent that she was with child. Artists such as Palma Vecchio, in *Diana Discovering Callisto*, show the scene of beautiful nudes surrounding the goddess of chastity as Callisto's condition is revealed. Diana banished her, and Jupiter's wife, the jealous Juno (Hera), changed her into a

A detail of the nymphs uncovering Callisto, after Titian's Diana and Callisto *(1556–9, private collection).*

shaggy she-bear, left to wander, growling, through lonely woods.

When Callisto's son, Arcas, was 15, he was tracking wild creatures when he chanced upon his mother. She tried to approach him but, just as he was about to spear her through the heart, Jupiter swept them up into the heavens, where they became the neighbouring constellations of the Great Bear and the Little Bear.[1]

Calumny

A long-lost painting of *Calumny*, or Slander, by the classical painter Apelles was known of throughout antiquity. It was described by Lucian[1] and often cited by 15th-century artists; Lucien describes the painting as showing a man with very large ears receiving evil counsel from Ignorance and Suspicion, while the beautiful but crafty Calumny holds a lighted torch in one hand and with the other drags her victim by the hair.[2] Her guide is pale and filthy Hatred, and her handmaids are Envy and Fraud. Behind the group stand Penitence, dressed in funeral robes, followed by the young and modest Truth. Several artists of the Renaissance tried to reconstruct this famous picture on the basis of the literary description; the best-known version was by Botticelli.

Cambyses, Judgment of

In the 6th century BC the Persian king Cambyses[1] found that one of his royal judges, Sisamnes, had accepted a bribe. Cambyses had the malefactor executed and flayed, and the seat of judgment covered with strips of his skin to demonstrate the fate of those who were corrupt. He then appointed Sisamnes' son to take his father's place. This severe example of justice was painted by Gerard David in *The Judgment of Cambyses*.

Camel

Camels often appear in Old Testament scenes to give authenticity to the setting. They were also considered royal, and are seen with the Magi following the star. St John the Baptist is often depicted wearing a tunic of camel hair.

Camillus, Marcus Furius

Camillus[1] was a Roman general and statesman of the 4th century BC, from whose story moral lessons were drawn. Francesco Salviati's frescoes depict episodes from his life, exemplifying the modest, just and wise behaviour of a model citizen.

In one famous campaign Camillus laid siege to the Etruscan town of Falerii, during which the beleaguered town's schoolmaster took the children to exercise outside the city walls. Each day he led them further out toward the Romans' camp, until he delivered them right into the enemy's hands, demanding an audience with Camillus. The schoolmaster explained that by this act he had handed over the city. In *Camillus and the Schoolmaster of Falerii* Poussin illustrated the scene in which Camillus, astounded by such treachery, commanded his men to remove the schoolmaster's clothes, tie his hands and let the boys drive him back to the city with rods and scourges. The Falerians acknowledged Camillus' act of justice and surrendered.

However, the general was accused of appropriating Etruscan spoils and, unable to endure the indignity, he went into exile. In 390BC, forgetting his former unjust treatment, he returned to drive the Gauls out of Italy. They had besieged Rome but failed to capture the Capitol because, in the dead of night, the Romans were alerted by the cackling of the sacred geese near the Temple of Juno. The Gallic leader Brennus accepted a ransom of gold in exchange for Rome, but as the gold was being weighed, Brennus attempted to falsify its weight. When accused of this, he threw his sword and belt on to the scales and cried, *Vae victis* ("Woe to the conquered"). Camillus halted the exchange of gold and told Brennus that it was Roman custom to deliver their country with iron, not gold.

Candles and Candlesticks

Candles play an important part in funeral rites, at shrines and in the services and processions of various religions. In Christianity the Eucharist candles represent Christ's presence at Holy Communion; the Paschal candle symbolizes the risen Christ at Easter. On Candlemas Day, February 2nd, all the candles needed for the year are consecrated. The Jewish Menorah, the seven-branched candelabrum in the Temple in Jerusalem, represents Judaism. In Dutch 17th-century still life a candle may suggest the transience of life.

Cards

In the 17th century cards were played frequently in Europe by the upper classes as well as by people in taverns, although moralists considered card-playing a sinful pursuit. In the 1660s Jan Steen painted *Beware of Luxury* and *The Dissolute Household*, and in the foreground of both paintings cards appear as a reminder of the expression, "Cards, women and drink have ruined many a man." In Steen's *Card Players Quarrelling* a fight over a game has broken out between the idle gamblers.

Cupid (in Greek myth, Eros) may be shown holding a blank playing card, referring to the hazards of love, or an

Camillus, Marcus Furius:
[1] Plutarch, *Lives, Camillus*

Candles and Candlesticks: *see*
TIME

Cards: *see*
Cupid; Vices

Carpenter: *see*
Joseph, Husband of the Virgin; Passion of Christ, The

Cassandra: *see*
Ajax; Apollo; Trojan War

Castor and Pollux: *see*
Leda; Meleager; Jason; Jupiter; ZODIAC

[1] Ovid, *Met VIII 372–378*
[2] Ovid, *Fasti V 693–720*

ace of hearts as love triumphant. Generally, however, cards indicate idleness or vice of some kind. The British painter Augustus Leopold Egg used the image of children building a collapsing house of cards as an emblem of a disintegrating home in his moralizing triptych *Past and Present*. Cézanne painted card-players as part of the local life of his native southern France.

Carpenter

Joseph, husband of the Virgin Mary, was a carpenter. The Pre-Raphaelite John Everett Millais' *Christ in the House of his Parents* or *The Carpenter's Shop* shows the young Christ holding up a wound on the palm of his hand; blood drips onto his feet and he is surrounded by many other symbols of his life and Passion.

Cassandra

The Trojan maiden Cassandra, daughter of King Priam, had the powers of prophecy. She was loved by Apollo, but because she refused him, the god ensured that no one believed her predictions, even though they were true. When Troy fell, she was raped by Ajax near an image of Minerva (in Greek myth, Athene), an outrage depicted by Solomon Joseph Solomon in *Ajax Abducting Cassandra*. Cassandra became Agamemnon's concubine and was killed by his wife Clytemnestra.

Cassone

During the Italian Renaissance, a *cassone* was a bride's wedding chest, which usually contained her dowry. Its panels were often painted with scenes from mythology, the Bible or ancient history, suggesting a happy marriage; or with scenes warning men of the captivating power of other women, or warning women of the consequences of disobedience. Some of these panels have now been removed to hang as pictures. In the 16th century richly carved bridal furniture became fashionable and supplanted the *cassone*.

Castor and Pollux

Castor and Pollux (in Greek myth, Polydeuces) were the inseparable twins of Jupiter (Zeus) and Leda. In Latin they were known as the "*Dioscuri*", meaning "sons of Jupiter". A striking pair of warriors, they rode horses whiter than snow. The stories told about them include their rescue of their sister Helen from Theseus, and their part in the Calydonian Boar Hunt[1] and in Jason's quest for the Golden Fleece. Legend claims that worshipping the Dioscuri became a cult in Rome, especially after the epiphany of the two heroes at the battle of Lake Regillus, fought between the young Republic under Aulus Postumius and the forces of Tarquinius Superbus (the last king of Rome) and his Latin allies.

On another occasion, they carried off the daughters of Leucippus to Sparta, a scene made famous by Rubens in *The Rape of the Daughters of Leucippus*. These women were already betrothed to the Dioscuri's cousins, and Castor almost died in the fight caused by the abduction, but Jupiter granted Pollux's prayer that he might share his immortality with his brother; each twin spent alternate days in Hades and Olympus.[2] Jupiter placed the twins in the sky as the constellation Gemini and they were worshipped as gods. "They were

Castor and Pollux, after Rubens' The Rape of the Daughters of Leucippus *(*c.*1618, Kunsthistorisches Museum, Vienna).*

helpful to the storm-tossed bark" and appeared to sailors as the glow of atmospheric electricity on the masts of ships during storms, also known as St Elmo's Fire.

Cat

In paintings, a cat may be shown as a peaceful domestic animal, but a stealthy cat about to pounce suggests that trouble is lurking. In Manet's *Olympia* a black cat, with arched back and bristling tail, announces an intruder into the courtesan's domain. A black cat, or witch's familiar, is also associated with evil.

Catherine of Alexandria, Saint

According to legend,[1] Catherine lived in the 4th century, was beautiful, of noble birth and fully educated in the Liberal Arts. She argued with Emperor Maxentius that he should cease persecuting Christians and worshipping false gods. Overwhelmed by her eloquence and knowledge, and unable to compete, he invited 50 masters of logic and rhetoric to challenge her in Alexandria. Catherine converted them all through her reasoning and faith in Christ. The emperor, beside himself with rage, burned the learned men. Then, unable to persuade this bride of Christ to join him in his palace, he threw her into a dark cell without food for 12 days, but she emerged in full health, having been fed by a dove. The Emperor then constructed a wheel with iron saws and sharp-pointed nails on which Catherine was to be tortured. However, she prayed to God and an angel shattered the wheel, killing 4,000 heathens. Catherine was finally beheaded and her body was taken to Mount Sinai.

Scenes from her life were illustrated by Masolino, and the most popular was the episode of her mystical marriage to Christ. Apparently, Catherine was converted by a hermit who gave her an image of the Virgin and Child. The image prompted a vision in which the Christ Child turned toward her and placed a ring on her finger. Veronese is one of several artists who depicted the betrothal of the richly dressed saint. Catherine's attribute is a wheel.

Catherine of Siena, Saint

Catherine (*c.*1347–1380) resisted her parents' attempts to make her marry, and joined the Dominican Order to tend the poor and sick. She had many mystical experiences: in one, Christ offered her a choice of two crowns, one of gold and one of thorns, and she took the latter; in another, she received the stigmata; and, like Catherine of Alexandria, she had a mystical marriage with Christ. Since 1309 the Papacy had been based at

Catherine of Alexandria, Saint: *see*
Martyr

[1] *Golden Legend, St Catherine of Alexandria*

Catherine of Siena, Saint: *see*
Lily; RELIGIOUS ORDERS

St Catherine, after St Catherine Saved from Torture, *by Guido Romano.*

Cato, Marcus Porcius of Utica: *see*
Caesar, Julius
[1] Plutarch, *Lives, Cato*

Cecilia, Saint: *see*
Lily; Martyrs;
MUSIC/MUSICAL INSTRUMENTS
[1] *Golden Legend, St Cecilia*

Centaur: *see*
Hercules; Theseus;
ZODIAC
[1] Ovid, *Fasti V 379–414*
[2] Ovid, *Met XII 210–535*

Avignon, and she went there to beg Pope Gregory XI to return to Rome. But the elections of 1378 precipitated the great Schism, which lasted for 40 years; ignoring the new French pope in Avignon, Rome elected its own, strongly supported by Catherine; the solution of deposing both in favour of another resulted in the concurrent appointment of three popes. Catherine is now a patron saint of Italy and most highly revered in her native city of Siena, where Domenico Beccafumi painted her receiving the stigmata in a white habit, probably to reflect her purity. In other paintings she wears the black-and-white of her Order and may have a lily or rosary, or show her stigmata.

Cato, Marcus Porcius of Utica

The Roman statesman Cato[1] (95–46BC) was a man of absolute integrity. A supporter of the Republic, he strongly opposed Julius Caesar and, after the death of Pompey, took his own life rather than live under tyranny: he read Plato's dialogue on the soul twice, and then plunged his sword into his breast. Charles Le Brun depicted this scene in *The Death of Cato*.

Cecilia, Saint

Little is known of Cecilia[1] although it is certain that a lady of that name founded a church in Trastevere, Rome. In 5th- or 6th- century legend she is said to have been a Roman noblewoman living in the 2nd or 3rd century, who was raised as a Christian. She revealed that she was a bride of Christ to her pagan husband, Valerian, on their wedding night. Because she persuaded him to join her faith, Cecilia and Valerian were given two crowns of roses and lilies, which never lost their fragrance, by an angel. When she refused to worship pagan gods, Cecilia was put into a boiling bath for a night and a day but remained unharmed. Three blows of the axe failed to cut off her head; and, lingering on the point of death for three days, she gave all her possessions to the poor. Scenes from her life may be seen surrounding her image by the Master of St Cecilia, and Stefano Maderno carved her lifeless body. She is the patron saint of musicians because she sang to God in her heart or because of the music at her wedding. Her attributes are musical instruments, particularly the organ, which she may be playing or holding (as in Raphael's famous image of her) and the lily of purity.

Centaur

This mythological creature had the body and legs of a horse and the torso, arms and head of a man. Centaurs were said to come from ancient Thessaly, probably because the inhabitants were known to be excellent horsemen. Their behaviour was often wild and uncouth – Nessus, for example, tried to carry off the wife of Hercules (in Greek myth, Heracles) – and Piero di Cosimo shows them in *Scenes of Primitive Man*. The centaur may represent the base or animal aspect of humanity, as illustrated in Botticelli's *Pallas and the Centaur*, in which the lowly creature cowers beside wise Minerva (Athene).

The centaur Chiron was, however, civilized. He acquired his form because his father, Saturn (Cronos), hoping to conceal an illicit passion from his wife, transformed himself into a horse and made love to the

A detail of a centaur shown preparing his bow and arrows, after a 15th-century Florentine painting.

nymph, Philyra. Chiron was a wise teacher, especially of music and medicine, and he educated many classical heroes including Achilles, Aesculapius and Jason. He died accidentally: Hercules was being entertained by a centaur and asked for wine but the centaur was reluctant to open it as it had been presented by Bacchus (in Greek myth, Dionysos); other centaurs smelled the feast and a battle ensued in which Hercules accidentally shot one of his poisoned arrows into Chiron's knee.[1] In great pain, Chiron relinquished his immortality and, with bow and arrow, became the constellation Sagittarius.

The renowned Battle of the Lapiths and the Centaurs occurred at the wedding of Pirithous to the lovely Hippodamia.[2] The Lapiths had invited the centaurs, but at the sight of the beautiful bride, the fiercest centaur, Eurytus, dragged her off by her hair and the others carried off whichever girl they could. Theseus attacked them on behalf of Pirithous, and a bloody fray followed in which half the centaurs were slain and the rest driven off. The celebrated Elgin Marbles, originally from the Parthenon, Athens, illustrate the violent struggle.

Centurion

A centurion was a Roman officer in charge of 100 men. Christ healed a centurion's servant, and the centurion Longinus was converted at the Crucifixion.

Cephalus and Procris

In mythology[1] Cephalus, just after his marriage to Procris, was abducted by Aurora against his will. Poussin's *Cephalus and Aurora* shows how he rebuffed her and the goddess swore revenge. She planted suspicion in his mind and changed his appearance. The disguised Cephalus returned home to find Procris distraught at the loss of her husband. He resolved to test his wife's fidelity by offering her a bribe to become his mistress. At the moment she hesitated, he revealed his true identity, but Procris, overwhelmed with shame, fled to the mountains. Here Cephalus found her

A detail after Landscape with Cephalus and Procris Reunited by Diana *by Claude Lorrain (*c.*1750, National Gallery, London).*

Cephalus and Procris: *see* Aurora

[1] Ovid, *Met VII 661–865*

Cerberus: *see* Cerberus; Hades; Hercules; Pluto; Sibyl
[1] Virgil, *Aeneid VI:417–424*

Ceres: *see* Proserpina; Pluto
[1] Ovid, *Met V 342–571*

and begged forgiveness, and for years afterwards they lived in harmony.

Diana (in Greek myth, Artemis) had given Procris a matchless hunting dog and a javelin as presents for her husband. While hunting, Cephalus spoke endearingly to the cool winds which soothed him in the midday heat, but his words were overheard and he was mistakenly thought to be wooing a nymph. The rumour reached Procris, who refused to believe it unless she herself witnessed her husband's disloyalty. The next day Cephalus was calling the winds when he heard a moan and the rustling of leaves. Thinking that a wild animal lurked in the bush, he hurled his javelin, only to spear the hidden Procris. In *Cephalus and Procris* Veronese painted her dying in the arms of her husband; as she begged Cephalus not to let the breeze take her place, he realized his dreadful misunderstanding.

Cerberus

Cerberus was the dog of many heads – commonly three – which guarded the entrance to Hades or the Underworld: "throughout that part of the kingdom gigantic Cerberus sends echoing howls".[1] A Sibyl drugged the beast so that Aeneas could pass through, and Orpheus lulled it to sleep with his music. Cerberus may have a serpent's tail and accompany Pluto (in Greek myth, Hades), king of the Underworld.

Ceres

The Roman Ceres (in Greek myth, Demeter), daughter of Saturn (Cronos) and Ops (Rhea) and sister of Jupiter (Zeus), was goddess of the corn, agriculture, and the regenerative

Cerberus, after a bronze statuette dating from the 16th century.

powers of nature. When her daughter, Proserpina (in Greek myth, Persephone) was abducted by Pluto (Hades) and taken to his kingdom in the Underworld, Ceres sought her tirelessly over land and sea. At last, angered by her vain search, she caused the earth to lie barren, until a nymph told her that her daughter was now the sad consort of Pluto.

In response to Ceres' pleas, Jupiter allowed Proserpina to return to earth on condition that she had eaten no food in the Underworld. She confessed that she had innocently placed seven (although accounts vary as to the number) pomegranate seeds in her mouth, so Jupiter resolved that Proserpina should spend equal parts of the year with her mother and new husband.[1] The seasons were thereby created: her stay in the Underworld became autumn and winter, and her return home to her mother was spring and summer. Ceres, like Abundance, may carry sheaves or ears of corn, fruit or a cornucopia, or hold agricultural implements. She was associated with Cybele, and in his painting *Statue of Ceres* Rubens replicated her as a statue in a niche, with swags of fruit and *putti*.

Chains
The gods were highly amused when Vulcan (Hephaestus) exposed the adultery of his wife Venus (Aphrodite) by catching her in a net of chains as she and Mars (Ares) embraced.

Fetters are often used to denote any figure held captive, in reality or symbolically, and are associated particularly with Saints Leonard and Vincent.

Chariot
In mythological art chariots are seen drawn by various animals: Apollo's chariot may be drawn by white horses; Bacchus' (Dionysos') by panthers, tigers or leopards; Cybele's (Rhea's) by lions; Diana's (Artemis') by stags; Juno's (Hera's) by peacocks; Neptune's (Poseidon's) by sea-horses; Pluto's (Hades') by black horses; and Venus' (Aphrodite's) by doves or swans. Chariots are also ridden in triumph by emperors, generals and personifications of the virtues; they may carry souls to Heaven.

Charity
Faith, Hope and Charity[1] were sanctified by the medieval church as the three cardinal virtues. Charity was the "mother of the virtues" and may be personified as a woman giving alms. In many Renaissance paintings, Charity is depicted as a loving mother with two or more children, perhaps nursing one of them, as in Cranach's *Charity*, or *Charity* by Van Dyck.

St Augustine saw charity as the love of God and the bond between God and mankind. It was also an example for ideal citizens to follow, living their lives according to the seven acts of mercy: "For I was an hungred, and ye gave me meat: I was thirsty, and ye gave me drink: I was a stranger, and ye took me in. Naked, and ye clothed me: I was sick, and ye visited me: I was in prison, and ye came unto me."[2] The seventh act of mercy is to bury the dead. Paintings representing these acts were commissioned into the 17th century, particularly by charitable confraternities.

Charles Borromeo, Saint
Charles Borromeo (1538–84) was made a cardinal by his uncle, Pope Pius IV, at the age of 22. In 1564 he became Archbishop of Milan and he took an active part in the Council of Trent and the reform of the Catholic Church. He started Sunday schools, opened seminaries for training the clergy, and practised and preached that life should be charitable and that the sick and needy should be cared for. He was likened to St Ambrose, the patron saint of Milan, and may be shown with him in paintings. He appears wearing various forms of religious dress and in Baroque art he may be seen having a vision of Christ. Daniele Crespi depicted the saint fasting before a simple altar, weeping as he read, his distinctively large, aquiline nose in evidence.

Charon
In mythology Charon is the ferryman who rowed the dead across the River Styx to Hades, demanding a coin for his services. He was described as "a ragged figure, filthy, repulsive, with

Chains: *see*
Leonard, St; Vincent, St; Vulcan

Chariot: *see*
Apollo; Bacchus; Cybele; Diana; Juno; Neptune; Pluto; Venus

Charity: *see*
Cimon and Pero; VIRTUES

[1] *I Corinthians 12:13*
[2] *Matthew 25: 35–36*

Charles Borromeo, Saint: *see*
Ambrose, St

Charon: *see*
Hades

[1] Virgil, *Aeneid VI 300–305*

Chastity: *see* Abstinence; Anthony, St; Benedict, St; Diana; Francis, St; Joseph; Lily; RELIGIOUS ORDERS; Susannah and the Elders; Tuccia

Chimera: *see* Bellerophon
[1]Homer, *The Iliad, VI 180–185*

Chi Rho: *see* Alpha and Omega; IHS; INRI

white hair, copious and unkempt covering his chin, eyes which are stark points of flame, and a dirty garment knotted and hanging from his shoulders. Charon punts his boat with his pole or trims the sails, and so he ferries every soul on his dusky coracle, for though he is old, he is a god, and a god's old age is tough and green".[1] He can be seen in Christian art, such as Michelangelo's *Last Judgment*.

Chastity

Chastity, poverty and obedience are the vows of the monastic Orders, and personifications of Chastity may have a veil or palm of the virgin martyrs, or stand in triumph on a symbol of lust, such as a pig. Chastity might be paired or locked in combat with the figure of Lust. The goddess of Chastity, Diana (in Greek myth, Artemis) might be juxtaposed with Venus (Aphrodite) and Cupid (Eros) representing sensual love. She may carry a shield on which Cupid's golden arrows break, and the chain for binding love. Chastity may also be represented by virtuous Roman women such as Tuccia, or by biblical characters such as the demure Susannah, or Joseph, who refused Potiphar's wife.

In Christian art St Anthony may be shown controlling erotic dreams through prayer; Saints Benedict and Francis throw themselves into thorny bushes to quell their desires; and female saints who preserved their virginity may hold a lily.

Cherry

The cherry or "Fruit of Paradise" may represent the sweetness of good works and is sometimes held by the Christ Child.

The chimera, taken from a bronze Etruscan figure (6th century BC).

Chimera

This monstrous creature[1] was foisted on mankind by the gods. It had a lion's head, a serpent's tail and the body of a goat, and its breath came out in terrible blasts of burning flame. It was killed by Bellerophon, who was ordered to vanquish it because it was ravaging Lycia.

Chi Rho

This early Christian monogrammatic symbol consists of the first two letters, *chi* and *rho*, from the Greek *Khristos* meaning Christ. It may appear with *alpha* and *omega*, the first and last letters of the Greek alphabet.

Christ, The Life of

The Life of Christ, as told by the four Gospels, provided subjects for innumerable painted narrative series and separate devotional images. Most, but not all, of the episodes are told by all four Gospels, but they are not always told in the same sequence.

Christ is also be present in scenes from the lives of the Virgin, Saint Peter, and the other Apostles.

THE NATIVITY AND ADORATION

The Nativity, or birth of Christ, took place in Bethlehem in Judea. The Virgin Mary "brought forth her

A detail of Christ's nativity, after The Adoration of the Shepherds *by Adriden Tsenbrant (16th century, Bruges).*

firstborn son, and wrapped him in swaddling clothes, and laid him in a manger; because there was no room for them in the inn".[1] The Infant is usually shown in a humble crib with an ox and ass looking on, according to the prophecy of Isaiah. An angel appeared to shepherds that night and told them of the birth of the Saviour. They are seen in the **Adoration of the Shepherds**.

Three Magi (also known as the Wise Men or Kings) came from the East, following a star, and seeking "he that is born King of the Jews."[2] At the **Adoration of the Magi**, they worshipped the Infant and offered him gold, frankincense and myrrh; they were usually depicted as a young, a middle-aged and an elderly man. This scene was highly popular in 15th-century Florence, where the most lucrative trades were textiles and banking. Unlike other scenes from the Life of Christ, the subject allowed the depiction of sumptuous costumes and, as the Church condemned usury, the idea of the gift of gold might both ease a banker's conscience and encourage donations to the Church.

King Herod planned to destroy this newborn "King of the Jews", and an angel urged Joseph to escape. The **Flight into Egypt** shows Joseph leading the Virgin and the Infant out of danger. Meanwhile, Herod ordered all children under the age of two to be slaughtered in the **Massacre of the Innocents**.[3] Giotto painted these two scenes in the Arena Chapel, Padua, using a window to divide them in order to avoid the compositional problem that, in the sequence, if the Holy Family walked from left to right they would appear to be walking into the massacre. In Tintoretto's version, in the Scuola di San Rocco, Venice, the Holy Family walks forward as if to come out of the canvas. After the death of Herod, an angel told Joseph to make the **Return to Israel** with his family; they were directed to Galilee and settled in Nazareth. When Christ was 12 years old the Holy Family went to Jerusalem for the Passover. Christ disappeared and was found engaged in a **Dispute with the Doctors** in the Temple, his understanding astonishing those assembled here.[4]

THE BAPTISM AND CALLING OF THE DISCIPLES

At the age of about 30, Christ was baptized by Saint John. At his **Baptism** the Holy Ghost descended as a dove, and God the Father announced: "This is my beloved Son, in whom I am well pleased."[5] For 40 days and 40 nights, he fasted in the wilderness and suffered the **Temptation**, during which the Devil suggested that he turn stones to bread to ease his hunger. Christ's reply was, "Man shall not live by bread alone but by every word that proceedeth out of the mouth of God."[6]

Christ then went to the Sea of

Christ, The Life of: *see* John the Baptist, St; Joseph, Husband of the Virgin; Martha; Passion of Christ, The; Virgin, The; and individual disciples

[1] *Luke 2:7*
[2] *Matthew 2:2*
[3] *Matthew 2:13–16*
[4] *Luke 2:41–47*
[5] *Matthew 3:13–17*
[6] *Matthew 4:4*
[7] *Matthew 4:18–19*
[8] *Luke 5:4–9*
[9] *Matthew 16:18–19*
[10] *Matthew 5–7*
[11] *Matthew 9:12*
[12] *John 8 1–11*
[13] *Luke 7:36–48*
[14] *Luke 10:38–42*
[15] *Matthew 19:13–14*
[16] *Matthew 13:3–9*
[17] *Luke 10:30–35*
[18] *Matthew 15:14*
[19] *Luke 15:11–32*
[20] *Luke 16:19–31*
[21] *Matthew 25:1–14*
[22] *Matthew 8:1–3*
[23] *Matthew 8:5–13*
[24] *Luke 5:18–20*
[25] *John 5:2–8*
[26] *Matthew 9:27–30*
[27] *Luke 7:11–15*
[28] *Mark 5:22–24*
[29] *John 11:1–44*
[30] *Matthew 15:32–38*
[31] *Matthew 8:28–32*
[32] *John 2:1–10*
[33] *Matthew 8:23–26*
[34] *Matthew 14:14–21*
[35] *Matthew 14:23–31*
[36] *Matthew 17:24–27*
[37] *Matthew 17:1–18*

Galilee, where he preached and began to gather his disciples. The first were the fishermen Simon, called Peter, and his brother Andrew. At the **Calling of Simon and Andrew**, Christ said, "Follow me, and I will make you fishers of men."[7] They had been toiling all night but had caught nothing, yet when Christ asked them to cast their nets once more, they returned with so many fish that their boats began to sink. At this, known as the **Miraculous Draught of Fishes**, Peter realized Christ's identity.[8] Later, in **Christ's Charge to Peter**, he declared, "... upon this rock I will build my church ... And I will give unto thee the keys of the kingdom of heaven."[9] In the **Calling of Matthew** Christ summoned Levi, a tax gatherer as he sat in the customs house; he was subsequently known as Matthew. Christ also called James (known as the Great), his brother John, Bartholomew, James the Less, Jude, Philip, Simon, Thomas and Judas Iscariot.

Compassion and Forgiveness

In the **Sermon on the Mount**,[10] Christ summarized his doctrine, including the eight beatitudes (conditions of blessedness) beginning, "Blessed are the poor in spirit; for theirs is the kingdom of heaven." Later, at the **Supper in the House of Matthew**, Christ was rebuked for eating with sinners, to which he replied, "They that be whole need not a physician, but they that are sick."[11] Christ's attitude to repentant sinners was exemplified in the **Woman Taken in Adultery**. The Pharisees brought her to Christ to gain his approval for stoning her to death; his reply was, "He that is without sin among you, let him first cast a stone at her."[12] Another potent image of penitence and forgiveness was **Mary Magdalene Washing Christ's Feet**. This took place in the house of a Pharisee, who could not understand how Christ could allow Mary, a sinner, to approach him. Christ simply said to her, "Thy sins are forgiven."[13]

Mary Magdalene became one of Christ's most devoted followers, and was sometimes thought to be the sister of Martha, a busy housewife, with whom she is contrasted as a spiritual type. In the episode at the **House of Mary and Martha**, Martha was busy serving guests while Mary sat listening to Jesus, so Martha asked, "Lord dost thou not care that my sister hath left me to serve alone?" Christ replied that, of the two, Mary was concerned with more important matters.[14] Another time, his disciples rebuked those who brought children to him, but Christ said, "Suffer little children, and forbid them not, to come unto me; for of such is the kingdom of heaven."[15] **Christ Blessing Little Children** occurs in northern European painting from the 16th century onwards.

Christ's Teachings

Christ often taught through parables. The parable of **The Sower**[16] told how some seed (his teaching) fell on stony ground but some brought forth fruit. **The Good Samaritan** described an act of charity by a Gentile who stopped to tend a wounded man, who should have been his enemy; he took the man to an inn and paid for his care.[17] In the **Blind Leading the Blind**,[18] Christ warned that the Pharisees were misguided. The **Prodigal Son**[19] emphasized God's forgiveness of repentant sinners; while **Dives and Lazarus**[20] contrasted a rich man's sufferings in hell with a beggar's reward in heaven. **The Wise and Foolish Virgins**[21] warned always to be prepared for Christ's Second Coming. Artists chose the particular moment in a parable that had emotional or artistic appeal. For example, Dürer's engraving of *The Prodigal Son* shows the repentant sinner surrounded by swine, kneeling in humility and wringing his hands as he gazes heavenwards.

THE MIRACLES

Christ healed many sick people as he preached, in scenes such as the following: **Christ Healing a Leper**;[22] **Christ Healing the Centurion's Servant**,[23] an extraordinary expression of faith by a Gentile; **Christ Healing the Paralytic**;[24] **The Pool of Bethesda**,[25] where Christ cured a handicapped man; and **Christ Healing the Blind**.[26] He was admonished by the Pharisees for healing a man with a withered hand on the Sabbath; because he showed them that they were wrong, they began to plot his death.

Christ also brought the dead to life, in the **Raising of the Widow's Son of Nain**[27] and the **Raising of the Daughter of Jairus**.[28] Better known is his restoration of the brother of Martha and Mary in the **Raising of Lazarus**. Lazarus had been in the tomb for four days when Christ ordered the stone to be removed; at this, the young man came forth, bound in his shroud.[29] This was painted by Sebastiano del Piombo in *The Raising of Lazarus*. Christ also exorcised those possessed by the Devil – for example, the **Daughter of the Woman of Canaan**.[30] On another occasion, two men were possessed by devils which he cast out into a herd of swine; in this miracle, known as **The Gadarene Swine**, the whole herd rushed headlong into the sea.[31]

Of the many other miracles in Christ's life, the most popular among painters were: the **Marriage at Cana**,[32] when he commanded six pots to be filled with water which turned into wine; the **Calming of the Waters**,[33] in which he was at sea with his disciples and stilled a great storm; the **Loaves and Fishes**,[34] in which he fed a multitude of 5,000 people with five loaves and two fishes; the **Walking on the Waters**,[35] in which he walked on the sea to reach his disciples who were being tossed about on a ship; the **Tribute Money**,[36] in which Christ told Peter to catch a fish, saying that he would find a coin in its mouth with which to pay the temple tax; and the **Transfiguration**, in which Christ took Peter, James and John up a high mountain, and shone as "white as the light:" the prophets Moses and Elijah appeared, and a voice from Heaven said, "This is my beloved Son, in whom I am well pleased." Meanwhile a man had brought his epileptic son to

A detail after The Transfiguration *by Raphael (1518–20, Vatican, Rome).*

Christina, Saint: *see* Martyrs
[1] *Golden Legend, St Christina*

Christopher, Saint: *see* Martyrs
[1] *Golden Legend, St Christopher*

be cured by the disciples, but they failed; on his return, Christ chided them for having little faith and healed the boy himself. Unusually, Raphael painted the **Transfiguration** with the incident of the epileptic boy happening simultaneously in *Transfiguration* (Vatican Rome).

BEGINNING OF THE PASSION
As Christ neared Jerusalem with his disciples, he prophesied that he would be betrayed and condemned to death.[37] In a sequence of paintings on the Life of Christ, the **Entry into Jerusalem** usually marks the beginning of the **Passion of Christ** (see p.168).

Christina, Saint
There is no historical evidence for the existence of this saint, who is said to have been a Roman noblewoman. Legend[1] tells how she suffered terrible ordeals because of her faith, including being thrown into a lake with a millstone around her neck. With Christ's blessing she survived until her martyrdom, when she was shot by arrows. She is venerated at Bolsena in northern Italy, which claims to have her relics. Her attribute is a millstone depicted hanging from her neck, as seen in Signorelli's *Virgin and Child with Saints*.

Christopher, Saint
Christopher is Greek for "Christ bearer" and, according to legend,[1] the saint was a Canaanite of prodigious size and strength. He desired to serve the mightiest sovereign, and began by worshipping the Canaanite king. The king, however, was afraid of Satan, who therefore became Christopher's next figure of idolatry. However, then

*St Christopher, shown carrying the Christ Child over the river, after a painting by Hans Memling (*c.*1480).*

he realized that Satan was afraid of Christ so he chose to adopt the Christian faith. A hermit told him to go to help those who wished to cross a dangerous river, which he did, using a long pole to steady himself as he carried people across. One day a child begged to be taken over the river, so Christopher lifted him on to his shoulders and strode into the water. Little by little the water became more turbulent and the child became as heavy as lead, so that Christopher was in great distress until he reached the other bank. There the child revealed himself as Christ, who was carrying in his hand the weight of the whole world. He told Christopher to plant his staff, and the next morning it bore leaves and fruit.

Christopher recruited many converts and was cruelly tortured because his faith was steadfast. At one time 400 bowmen shot arrows at him but not a single one touched him; suddenly, one turned back and struck his persecutor, the king of Lycia, in the eye, blinding him. Christopher was beheaded the following day, but he had foretold that his blood would restore the tyrant's sight, and when this came true the king was converted to Christianity. As in the *Moreel Triptych* by Hans Memling, Christopher is usually shown striding through the river, balanced by his staff (which may be a branch or a whole tree which he pulled up with his enormous strength), and bearing the Christ Child on his shoulders. Although he has recently been removed from the Roman calendar as there is no proof of his existence, St Christopher has long been venerated as the patron saint of travellers.

Cimon and Iphigenia

Cimon,[1] meaning "brute", was the son of a nobleman of Cyprus, but was uneducated and uncouth. He was sent by his father to tend a farm where one day he spied the beautiful Iphigenia asleep in a meadow and became rapt in admiration. Cimon resolved to become a gentleman, to learn riding and the arts of music, and within four years he was the most perfect cavalier on the island. Iphigenia was betrothed to another, yet Cimon pursued her and the lovers were finally united. Artists have painted the subject of Cimon finding Iphigenia asleep, as in *Cimon and Iphigenia* by Frederic Leighton. Millais' version, of the same title, emphasizes the contrast between Cimon's crude appearance and Iphigenia's beauty.

Cimon and Pero

This story from antiquity[1] tells of filial duty and illustrates the virtue known as Roman Charity. The aged Cimon was condemned to death by starvation in prison but was saved by his daughter Pero, who visited him regularly and suckled him. The subject was popular with painters including the 17th-century Dutch artist Dirck van Baburen.

Cincinnatus

In the 5th century BC Rome was besieged and a former consul, named Cincinnatus,[1] was unanimously elected to resolve the crisis. He had retreated to a farm, and was busy cultivating a field when the representatives of the state sought him out. For 15 days he led the army, surrounded the enemy's camp and forced them to surrender. He then retired once more to his simple rustic tasks. He offered a fine example of modest citizenship, and appeared in paintings such as Giovanni Romanelli's *Representative of the Senate Offering the Dictatorship to Cincinnatus*, with other examples of virtuous figures from Roman history.

Circe

Returning from Troy, the Greek hero Ulysses (Odysseus) landed on the island of Aaea, home to Circe, daughter of the sun. She was a sorceress, and some of Ulysses' men fell prey to her potions and were turned into swine.[1] But Ulysses, fortified with an antidote from Mercury (Hermes), remained immune

Cimon and Iphigenia:
[1] Boccaccio, *Decameron, 5th Day, 1st Story*

Cimon and Pero: *see* Charity
[1] Valerius Maximus, *Book 5, Chapter IV*

Cincinnatus:
[1] Livy, *The History of Rome III xxvi–xxx*

Circe: *see* Ulysses
[1] Homer, *Odyssey 10*

Circle:
[1] Vitruvius, *On Architecture Book 3 Ch 1.3*

Clare of Assisi, Saint: *see* Francis of Assisi, St; Lily

Claudia: *see* Cybele; Vesta and Vestal Virgins
[1] Ovid, *Fasti IV: 291–344*

Circe charming animals using a tablet carved with spells, after Circe and her Lovers *by Dosso Dossi (*c.*1525, National Gallery, Washington, D.C.).*

to her magic and made her restore his men to human form. Circe persuaded the hero to stay on her island, which they did for more than a year, feasting on meat and mellow wine. The sorceress and her castle appear in depictions of the story of Ulysses. She fascinated British Victorian painters such as J. W. Waterhouse, who in *Circe* showed her enticingly offering Ulysses the poisoned cup with which she turned sailors into swine. In the same painter's *Circe Invidiosa*, she is shown consumed with jealousy at losing Ulysses, and poisoning the sea with her anger.

*St Clare with her lily, after a wooden relief carving by Puccio Campana (*c.*1350, Lower Church of St Francis, Assisi).*

Circle
Without beginning or end, the circle represents God's eternal nature. Concentric circles show the universe as an ordered whole, the planets moving around the earth. During the Renaissance a circle was considered the perfect shape. According to the architect Vitruvius (1st century BC): "If a man lies on his back with hands and feet outspread, and the centre of a circle is placed on his navel, his fingers and toes will be touched by the circumference. Also a square will be found described within the figure, in the same way as the round figure is produced."[1] Leonardo da Vinci's "Vitruvian man" is perhaps the best known example of this human geometry. The Renaissance and later periods admired the few surviving ancient circular temples. They inspired Bramante's Tempietto (San Pietro in Montorio, Rome). They were depicted frequently in paintings with classical themes or settings.

Clare of Assisi, Saint
Clare (*c.*1194–1253) was strongly influenced by St Francis of her native town, Assisi. Rejecting her noble family and offers of marriage, she persuaded him to place her in the care of Benedictine nuns. Later she was joined by her sister and widowed mother, and in 1212 they founded their own community under the instruction of St Francis, which Clare led for 40 years. The nuns followed his dictate of poverty and possessed no property of their own; they were therefore called the "Poor Ladies" or "Poor Clares". Clare's image, with scenes from her life, was painted 30 years after her death in the church of Santa Chiara, Assisi, where she appears in a grey tunic. Her attribute is the lily or a monstrance: legend claims that while besieged by the infidel she placed one or other of these things outside her convent, and the enemy fled.

Claudia
A stone image of the earth goddess Cybele (in Greek myth, Rhea) was carried by boat to Rome from

Pergamum (now in western Turkey), and its weight caused the boat to sink into the Tiber's muddy bed. Claudia, a Vestal Virgin, falsely accused of breaking her vow of chastity, begged Cybele for a chance to prove her innocence. With only the slightest effort she pulled the boat upriver, so vindicating her virtue.[1]

Clement, Saint
Pope Clement I (died *c.*AD101) is thought to have been a Bishop of Rome, but little is known of his life. According to legend,[1] he had believed himself an orphan and received Christian instruction from Saints Barnabas in Rome and Peter in Judea. Peter united him with his family and then went to Rome, where he appointed Clement as his papal successor. While preaching, converting and baptizing, Clement caused a riot among the pagans, and was sent to join prisoners condemned to hard labour in the Crimea; directed by a lamb, he struck the earth, whereupon a stream of water flowed out to quench the prisoners' thirst. He was thrown into the sea with an anchor tied around his neck, but the sea later receded to reveal a small temple containing the martyr's body. Scenes from his life were frescoed from the 6th century in San Clemente, Rome. Giambattista Tiepolo showed the saint as an elderly pope with tiara and triple-armed cross before a vision of the Trinity. Clement's attribute is sometimes an anchor.

Cleopatra
Cleopatra VII[1] (68–30BC) ruled Egypt jointly with her brother until he deposed her in 48BC. However, she was reinstated by Julius Caesar, with whom she had a love affair; she bore his son, Caesarion. Egypt subsequently had to pay tribute to Caesar, a scene painted by Andrea del Sarto in *Egypt's Tribute to Caesar* (Villa Medici, Poggio a Caiano).

After Caesar's death civil war broke out in the Roman Empire, and the triumvir Mark Antony was assigned command of the eastern division. In 41BC he summoned Cleopatra to meet him at Tarsus in Cilicia, and so began their famous relationship. She arrived in a barge with a gilded stern, its purple sails outspread while silver oars beat time to the music of flutes and harps. Under a canopy of cloth of gold she lay dressed as Venus, with boys painted like Cupids fanning her and attendant maids in the guise of sea nymphs and graces.

Giambattista Tiepolo's frescoes *The Meeting of Cleopatra and Antony* and *The Banquet of Cleopatra* (both in the Palazzo Labia, Venice) shows the sumptuous banquet with which Antony welcomed her. She told her host, however, that she could produce a dish far more costly than he had provided, and, removing a pearl from her earring, she dissolved it in vinegar and drank it. The union of Antony and Cleopatra was opposed by Octavian (later Emperor Augustus), who destroyed their fleet at Actium in 31BC. Realizing all was lost, they committed suicide, Antony by the sword and Cleopatra by the bite of an asp concealed in a basket of figs. Her death was the subject of many paintings, such as Guido Reni's *Cleopatra*.

Cloelia
During the wars between the Romans and Etruscans the noble woman

Clement, Saint: *see* CROSS; Martyrs
[1] *Golden Legend, St Clement*

Cleopatra: *see* Caesar; Snake
[1] Plutarch, *Lives: Antony*

Cloelia:
[1] Livy, *The History of Rome II xiii*

Club: *see*
Hercules

Clytie:
[1] Ovid, *Met IV 190–273*

Cock: *see*
Passion of Christ, The;
Peter, St
[1] *John 13:38*

Coins: *see*
Danaë; Judas Iscariot;
Matthew, St
[1] *I Timothy 6:10*

Column: *see*
Passion of Christ, The;
Samson; Solomon

Cloelia was taken hostage by the Etruscan king Porsenna. She escaped with companions and crossed the River Tiber on horseback, but when she reached Rome she was returned to Porsenna by the consuls. He was so impressed by her courage that he released her with the companions of her choice.[1] Jacques Stella shows her on the bank of the Tiber about to transport her companions across.

Club
A club may be a sign of strength and may be held by a personification of fortitude. It is the attribute of Hercules (in Greek myth, Heracles) and also of Theseus, who on his travels slew the robber Periphetes, the owner of a huge brazen club with which he battered passers-by to death. It is also the attribute of Saints James the Less and Jude.

Clytie
In mythology[1] Clytie loved Apollo but he scorned her in favour of her rival, Leucothoe. In a fit of jealousy Clytie made the affair known to her rival's father, who buried his daughter alive. But still Apollo ignored Clytie, who pined away and became a sunflower (or marigold). In her transformed state, held fast by her roots, she turned her head to follow the course of the sun with steadfast adoration. Clytie may be shown with sunflowers; Frederic Leighton painted her stretching out her arms to the rising sun.

Cock
The cock is associated with the dawn of a new day, because it crows at sunrise. It was thought to be vigilant and is, therefore, shown on weathervanes. With St Peter a cock indicates his denial of Christ, who had said to him, "Wilt thou lay down thy life for my sake? Verily, verily, I say unto thee the cock shall not crow, till thou hast denied me thrice."[1]

Cockaigne, Land of
This was a fabled medieval land of idleness and luxury where "the houses were made of barley-sugar cakes, the streets were paved with pastry, and the shops supplied goods for nothing".[1] Peter Bruegel the Elder painted *The Land of Cockaigne*, showing a scene of gluttony and sloth with a scholar, a peasant and a soldier lying in idleness.

Coins
Coins or money often suggest avarice, bribery or corruption: "the love of money is the root of all evil".[1] The Apostle Matthew was originally a tax-collector and may be seen with other figures counting money. Christ paid the Tribute Money to the Pharisee, turned the money-lenders out of the Temple, and was betrayed by Judas Iscariot for 30 pieces of silver.

COLOURS
See panel on following page.

Column
A column may indicate strength and is thus found with a figure of Fortitude and on coats of arms. Both Trajan and Marcus Aurelius erected columns in Rome carved with scenes of their wars. Samson broke the columns supporting a building and thereby killed many of the enemy. Christ was whipped on a column at the Flagellation. The spiral columns originating in the palace of the Old Testament king Solomon are known as Solomonic.

COLOURS: *see*
Mary Magdalene; Religious Dress; RELIGIOUS ORDERS; Virgin, The

COLOURS

Throughout the history of art, colours have been used by artists in a variety of ways, not least as an important part of composition. Although black is associated with mourning and death, colours do not usually carry any specific symbolic meaning.

Certain colours are more costly to produce than others. Ultramarine, for example, was made from expensive lapis lazuli, an imported semi-precious stone, and, therefore, its use would reflect the wealth of the patron or the importance that he attached to the work. Red was also expensive. Purple, being made from two costly pigments, came to be associated with royalty.

The colour of a figure's dress may signify his or her identity. Members of religious Orders, for example, are partly recognized by the colour of their habit, while figures who appear more than once in a sequence of events are more easily detected if they are shown in the same colour. However, in Christian iconography, the colour of dress is by no means consistent.

In Italian art the Virgin usually wears blue, while in Northern art she may wear red. Figures may wear different colours to distinguish the stages of their life: the red of Mary Magdalene's clothing may indicate her earlier life as a sinner, and green her chosen path as a penitent hermit.

From the Renaissance to the 19th century, colour has generally been used naturalistically, except for images that delve into the realms of the imagination: for example, when the infernal regions are visualized. Since the 19th century, artists have exploited the decorative and emotive qualities of colour without necessarily any reference to the natural world.

From *c.*1912 onwards, Kandinsky moved toward abstract art, likening the effect of colours to that of music.

Comb

A woman combing her hair, often with a mirror and other worldly effects, may be an indication of vanity. Degas, however, painted women combing their hair as part of their daily toilet. A wool-carder's comb is the attribute of the martyrs Blaise and Bartholomew, who were both flayed alive. The latter is depicted in Michelangelo's *Last Judgment*, holding both the instrument of his torture and his empty skin containing a self-portrait of the artist.

Commedia dell'Arte

The Commedia dell'Arte was an Italian dramatic tradition, popular from the 16th to the 18th century, which influenced many European playwrights and modern pantomimes, and provided subjects for artists, especially Domenico Tiepolo and Watteau. The principal figures wore half-masks; their gesture, speech and costume identified their characters and became loosely standardized for easy recognition. The repertoire, however, relied upon improvisation, allowing for contemporary social

Compasses, Pair of:
[1] *Proverbs :27*

Concord: *see* Fasces

Constantine: *see* Helena; Sylvester, St

satire; it also included acrobatics, mime and dance. Appealing to all levels of society, the plots concerned ill-fated lovers and mistaken identities. Stock characters included *zanni*, or servants who are either witless or conniving and cause various misunderstandings; a Captain, who vainly boasts of his military success and thinks his queen is in love with him; a variant of the Captain, Scaramouche, who brags of his riches and success as a lover; an aged Doctor who believes he offers words of wisdom but only utters empty rhetoric; Pantalone who wears wide, loose trousers and is an earnest but comic figure; greedy, bad-tempered Puncinello who enjoys harming others, and is the forerunner of Punch in "Punch and Judy"; simple-minded Harlequin who is set curious tasks, tries his best but never fully succeeds; and lastly Columbine, Pantalone's daughter.

Compasses, Pair of

A pair of compasses for drawing circles or measuring distances between points is used by astronomers, geometricians and architects, and thus may be seen as their attributes; it may also be one of the objects asociated with Melancholia. In the creation of the world, God "set a compass on the face of the depth"[1] and imposed order on chaos, as represented in William Blake's *The Ancient of Days*. A pair of compasses in art may therefore represent the rational.

Concord

Like Abundance, Concord – the harmony between people or nations – may be expressed by a cornucopia or a sheaf of corn, since peace is believed to bring fruitfulness. A bundle of fasces, or sticks, that symbolize justice, doves of peace or a branch of wise Minerva's (in Greek myth, Athene's) olive tree may be included in a scene to show that relations are amicable.

Constantine

Constantine the Great (*c.*AD274–337) inherited his father's western forces and defeated the army of the emperor Maxentius just north of Rome at the Milvian Bridge. The River Tiber, swollen with autumn rains, caused the bridge of boats to collapse and swept Maxentius away to his death. Constantine thus became undisputed master of the West in AD312. According to Eusebius,[1] before the battle he had had a vision of a flaming cross and heard a voice saying, "*In hoc signo vinces*" ("You will conquer with this sign"), which led to his conversion to Christianity. Bernini carved him on a rearing horse in front of the flaming cross in *Constantine* (Scala Regia, Vatican,

A detail after Piero della Francesca's Dream of Constantine *(1455, San Francesco, Arezzo), showing the Emperor being guarded while he sleeps.*

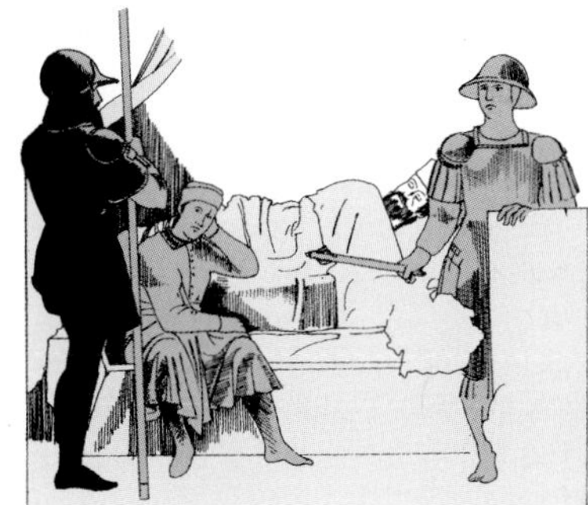

CONTINENTS

Subjects showing the four known continents were popular with Baroque artists such as Giambattista Tiepolo, who painted the sumptuous ceiling fresco *Apollo and the Continents*. Jesuits favoured the subject as it visualized the Order's intention to spread the Catholic faith worldwide.

The Fountain of the Four Rivers (Piazza Navona, Rome), a sculpture by Bernini, shows the continents as personified rivers.[1] Sometimes such personifications recline on urns from which water flows; a veiled head indicates that the river's source was unknown.

Certain indigenous animals associated with each continent may be shown: Africa (the River Nile) may wear coral, be shown with African people or a sphinx, crocodile, snake, lion or elephant; the Americas (the River Plate) may wear a feathered headpiece and be dressed as a hunter, with coins representing rich natural resources; Asia (the River Ganges) is often shown with a camel, a rhinoceros, an elephant, palm trees, jewels or exotic perfumes; Europe (the sea-monster, or the River Danube) could be represented by the bull of Europa or a horse, surrounded by the arts and civilized activities, and bearing a cornucopia and the crown of her supremacy over the others.

A detail showing Asia, after Giambattista Tiepolo's ceiling painting Apollo and the Continents *(1752–53, Würzburg, Germany).*

CONTINENTS: *see* Bull; Europa; Lion; Snake; Sphinx

Rome). Alternatively his conversion may be shown as occurring in a dream, as in Piero della Francesca's fresco *The Dream of Constantine* (San Francesco, Arezzo). Helena, Constantine's mother, a Christian who brought relics of the True Cross to Rome, was thought to have influenced her son. It was also, however, politically expedient to acknowledge Christianity, and in AD313, by the Edict of Milan, tolerance was formally granted. Giulio Romano painted scenes from the emperor's life in the Sala di Constantino frescoes (Vatican, Rome); and they were the subject of a set of tapestries designed by Rubens in 1622.

As the first Christian Emperor, Constantine built huge basilicas in Rome over the graves of the martyrs, the most notable of which was St Peter's. But conservative Romans opposed the new faith and by AD330 Constantine left the West to found Constantinople, now Istanbul, as the

Coral: *see*
CONTINENTS; Medusa; Perseus

Corn: *see*
Abundance; Ceres; Joseph, Son of Jacob; Peace; Sacraments; SEASONS

Cornelia:
[1] Valerius Maximus, *Book 4 Ch V*

new Christian capital in the East. The emperors never again took up residence in Rome. Before Constantine left Rome, he was supposed to have given his territories in the West to the then Pope Sylvester; this act is known as the Donation of Constantine. In the 15th century, however, the document recording this was proved to have been forged during the early Middle Ages in order to assert Papal power over the Holy Roman Emperor.

CONTINENTS
See panel on previous page.

Coral
In mythology, after Perseus had rescued Andromeda from Cetus, the sea-monster (or the River Danube), he laid the Gorgon's head down and immediately the seaweed turned into coral.[1]

Vasari illustrated this on a cabinet door of the Studiolo of Francesco I (Palma Vecchio, Florence) to indicate the precious contents. Coral was thought to be a protection against evil.

Coresus
A priest of Bacchus (in Greek myth, Dionysos), Coresus fell in love with the nymph Callirhoe, who scorned him. He complained to Bacchus, who sent a plague which would only come to an end when Callirhoe was sacrificed to him. In *The High Priest Coresus Sacrifices Himself to Save Callirhoe* Fragonard depicted how Coresus led his beloved to the sacrificial altar but, unable to kill her, stabbed himself instead. The nymph was then filled with remorse, and took her own life.

Corn
Ears or sheaves of corn are the attribute of Ceres (Demeter), and may also appear alongside personifications of Summer, Abundance or Peace.

In the Old Testament Joseph dreamed that a single sheaf of corn in a field stayed upright while others bent toward it, and so prophesied that his brothers would bow down before him. In Christian art ears of corn and vine leaves may represent the sacrament of the Eucharist.

Cornelia
Daughter of the Roman general Scipio Africanus, Cornelia[1] was renowned for her virtue. A lady once showed off her jewelry to Cornelia and asked to see hers in return. Cornelia thereupon produced her two sons and said, "These are the only jewels of which I can boast."

The Cornucopia of Abundance, after a book illustration from the Iconologia *dating from the 18th century.*

Cornucopia

This mythical "horn of plenty" overflows with flowers, fruit and corn. One version of its origin says that the cornucopia was the horn of the she-goat Amalthea, who nursed Jupiter (in Greek myth, Zeus)[1]; while in another version of the cornucopia's origin, Hercules (in Greek myth, Heracles), as one of his 12 labours, fought Achelous as a bull and tore off a horn, but "the naiads filled it with fruits and fragrant flowers, and sanctified it".

This symbol of bounty may be shown with personifications of Abundance, Europe, Peace or the goddess Ceres.

Coronis

In mythology Coronis,[1] the beautiful daughter of King Coroneus, was strolling on the sand when Neptune (in Greek myth, Poseidon) saw her and fell in love. As she did not reciprocate, he resolved to take her by force but she fled and prayed to the gods for help. Minerva took pity on her and turned her into a crow. In *Coronus and Neptune* Giulio Carpioni shows her with wings, flying away from Neptune's grasp.

Cosmas and Damian, Saints

Legend[1] relates how in Syria the Christian twin brothers Cosmas and Damian (thought to have died either *c.*AD287 or *c.*AD303) learned the art of medicine and healed men, women and animals without payment. In one spectacular example of their cures the saints amputated the rotten leg of a man while he slept and replaced it with that of a Moor who had recently died. He woke joyfully to find he had two healthy legs, even though one was

A detail after Cosmas and Damian Heal Justinian the Deacon *by Fra Angelico (1438–40, St Mark's Convent, Florence).*

black and the other white. They refused to make sacrifice to pagan gods and were tortured, bound in chains and thrown into the sea, but an angel pulled them out and sat them before the judge who had condemned them. He thought them magicians and sought to know the secrets of their craft, but two demons appeared and struck him; the saints prayed and the demons disappeared. The twins were thrown into a huge fire, but they remained unharmed while the flames leaped out and burned the heathens. They were then sentenced to be stoned to death, but the stones turned back and wounded the throwers; they were shot at with bow and arrow, but the arrows turned around and shot the archers. They were finally beheaded, and a camel appeared to the Christians telling them to bury the saints in the same tomb.

Cosmas and Damian, the patron saints of physicians and of the Medici family of Florence, feature in Renaissance Florentine painting, where they may be depicted as young martyrs in doctors' robes, perhaps with a phial or other medical instruments. Scenes from their lives were painted in the predella panels of the San Marco altarpiece by Fra Angelico.

Cornucopia: *see* Amalthea; CONTINENTS; Hercules

[1] Ovid, *Fasti V 111–129* and *Met IX 1–97*

Coronis:

[1] Ovid, *Met II 569-587*

Cosmas and Damian, Saints: *see* Martyrs

[1] *Golden Legend, SS Cosmas and Damian*

Crane: *see*
Christ, The Life of; Fish; Peter, St
[1] Pliny the Elder: *Natural HistoriesX:59*

Creation: *see*
ADAM AND EVE
[1] *Genesis 1* and *2:1–3*

Crispin and Crispinian, Saints: *see*
Martyrs

Crocodile: *see*
CONTINENTS; Leviathan; Theodore, St

Crocus:
[1] Ovid, *Met IV: 283–284*

Crow: *see*
Aesculapius; BIRDS

Crane

This bird with long legs and a long neck and bill represented vigilance because it was thought that, while the rest of the flock slept with their heads under their wings, their leader kept watch with his neck stretched out. He signalled a warning by his cry.[1] Cranes appear in Raphael's *Miraculous Draught of Fishes*, on the alert for any fish that might slip out of the net.

Creation

According to the Bible, in the beginning God created the heaven and the earth; on the first day he separated light from dark to make day and night; on the second he divided the waters; on the third he made the land grow plants and trees; on the fourth he made the sun, moon and planets and formed the seasons; on the fifth he brought forth the birds and fish and commanded them to multiply; and on the sixth he created the animals and made man in his own image and gave him control of every living thing that moved upon the earth. On the seventh day he rested and made it a holy day.[1]

Michelangelo chose this story for the central section of the Sistine Chapel ceiling (Vatican, Rome) because it gave him the opportunity for dramatic narrative and potent images. These opening passages from Genesis were illustrated relatively rarely compared to the themes of the Creation of Adam and Eve and the Fall.

Crispin and Crispinian, Saints

The history of these Christian brothers is undocumented, but they were venerated in France by the 6th century. They apparently came from Rome to preach at Soissons where they made and mended shoes and were beaten, boiled in oil and flayed for their faith. In a fresco painting of the late 14th century in the Oratorio di San Stefano by Lentate sul Seveso they are seen as young laymen. They are the patron saints of leather workers and their attribute is a shoe or a shoemaker's model of a foot.

Crocodile

In depictions of the four continents a crocodile may represent Africa or Asia. It is one of the forms of the sea-monster Leviathan, and the attribute of St Theodore.

Crocus

In mythology[1] the beautiful youth Crocus was impatient for the nymph Smilax, and was turned into the crocus flower as punishment.

Crook

A crook usually belongs to shepherds, and therefore may be shown as the attribute of Apollo or of Christ (the Good Shepherd) and his Apostles. A bishop's crook-shaped staff or crozier likewise denotes him as the shepherd of his spiritual flock.

CROSS

See panel on next page.

Crow

In mythology a crow tells her story to the raven before the birth of Aesculapius. She had been a king's daughter and Neptune (in Greek myth, Poseidon) had fallen for her charms. As he intended to take her by force she cried out to the gods for help and Minerva (Athene) transformed her into a crow, after which she

CROSS

A cross has been the emblem of many cults throughout the world. However, since the 5th century in the West it has represented Christ's Crucifixion and, by extension, the Christian faith. Shapes vary: the Latin cross, with a single transverse arm, is the traditional form on which Christ was thought to have been crucified; a double-armed cross is the sign of a bishop; a triple-armed cross is the sign of the Pope; a Greek cross has "arms" of equal length and is thus symmetrical; and St Andrew's is X-shaped like the cross on which he was crucified. The Maltese cross, resembling four arrow-heads meeting, was originally the emblem of the Knights of Malta.

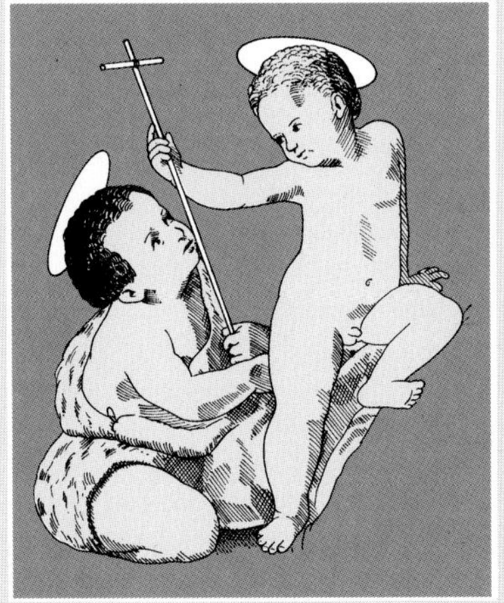

A detail of Christ and John the Baptist with a traditional cross after Madonna Alba *by Raphael (1511, National Gallery, Washington, D.C.).*

St Andrew with his x-shaped cross, after a Renaissance woodcut.

became the goddess's attendant. St Paul the Hermit was fed by a crow.

Crucifix

An image of Christ on the Cross represents the Christian faith. Many saints are seen contemplating a crucifix, especially hermits and penitants, but it may appear in particular with Saints Francis, Jerome, John Gualbert, Nicholas of Tolentino and Scholastica, and between the antlers of a stag before St Eustace.

Crutch

A crutch supports the old or infirm and is the staff of hermits, beggars and pilgrims. It is the attribute of Saints Anthony Abbot and Romuald. Salvador Dalí, who had his own idiosyncratic symbolic vocabulary, often painted limp objects supported by a crutch – for example in *The Enigma of William Tell.*

Cunegunda, Saint

The Holy Roman Emperor Henry II (973–1024) and his wife Cunegunda (died 1033) were dedicated supporters of the Benedictines; Henry founded the see of Bamberg and they are both buried in its cathedral.

As a widow, Cunegunda lived in the monastery she had founded at Kaufungen in Hesse. She is often seen holding a model of Bamberg cathedral or with ploughshares. The latter relate to a legend:[1] Henry suspected her of infidelity with a knight and made her walk barefoot over 15 feet of red-hot ploughshares; she stepped over the glowing mass unharmed, thereby proving her innocence.

Crucifix: *see*
Eustace, St; Francis of Assisi, St; Jerome, St; John Gualbert, St; Nicholas, St; Passion of Christ, The; Scholastica, St; Stag

Crutch: *see*
Anthony, St; Beggar; Romuald, St

Cunegunda, Saint:
[1] *Golden Legend, St Laurence*

Cupid: *see*
Mercury, Psyche; Venus
[1] Ovid, *Met I 468*
[2] Theocritus, *Idyll XIX*

Curius Dentatus, Manius:
[1] Plutarch, *Lives: Marcus Cato*

Curtius, Marcus:
[1] Livy, *The History of Rome VII vi*

Cupid
Cupid (known to the Greeks as Eros) was the Roman god of love, and the son of Venus (Aphrodite); his father may have been Jupiter (Zeus), Vulcan (Hephaestus) or Mars (Ares). He is usually seen as a little winged archer or beautiful young boy who, according to Ovid, had two kinds of arrows, a golden one to kindle love and a lead one, which puts love to flight.[1] He is sometimes shown blindfolded, to imply that love is blind, or may be tying a knot, symbolically bonding a pair of lovers. He often has a mischievous role, perhaps teasing the many lovers of Jupiter, and he may be chastised by Diana (Artemis), Minerva (Athene) or Venus who confiscated his arrows. Cupid was thought to have been taught by Mercury (Hermes). Corregio's *Education of Cupid* shows Cupid engrossed in a book held out by Mercury, which suggests that, having discarded his bow and arrow, he has renounced sensual love in favour of learning.

Cupid was once stung by a bee as he was pilfering honey from a hive. Cranach's *Cupid Complaining to Venus* illustrates him asking Venus how such a tiny creature could cause such pain. Venus replied that he too was a tiny creature yet inflicted far worse wounds.[2]

A detail of Cupid irritated by bees, after Cranach's Cupid Complaining to Venus *(*c.*1540, National Gallery, London).*

Curius Dentatus, Manius
In the 3rd century BC, Curius was three times Roman consul, yet he lived a rustic life in a small cottage. Ambassadors from the enemy Samnites found him there, boiling turnips in the chimney corner, and offered him a bribe of gold.[1] He replied that he had no need of gold and sent them away. He is usually depicted as an example of a virtuous Roman citizen.

Curtius, Marcus
In *c.*360BC a chasm appeared in the Roman forum and an oracle explained that it would close only if Rome sacrificed its most precious possession. The soldier Marcus Curtius[1] understood this to mean that the sacrifice of a young man was required so, fully armed and on horseback, he threw himself into the hole, which immediately closed over his head. Veronese used the subject in his ceiling decoration *Marcus Curtius.*

Cybele
In mythology Cybele was "the Great Mother" and goddess of fertility; she was identified with the Greek earth goddess Rhea (Ops in Roman myth). She turned the huntress Atalanta and her husband Hippomenes into lions which would draw her chariot. She was worshipped as a block of stone that was brought from Pergamum to Rome in 204BC to secure Hannibal's retreat during the Punic Wars: the Sibylline books had advised the Romans that if they wanted victory they must bring the Great Mother to Rome. An oracle had also specified that the stone was to be received by the Roman centurion Cornelius Scipio.

In allegory Cybele represents the Earth, and is commonly shown with an abundance of fruit, as in Rubens' *The Union of Earth and Water*, which invokes peace and prosperity.

Cypress
These trees often grow in cemeteries, so may be associated with the dead,

an allusion made by the Swiss painter Arnold Bocklin in *Island of the Dead*. Van Gogh painted them as indigenous trees of the Mediterranean.

Cyrus the Great
Before his birth it was predicted that Cyrus,[1] founder of the Persian Empire, would overthrow his grandfather Astyages, king of the Medes. In an attempt to defy fate, Astyages ordered his faithful servant, Harpagus, to kill the infant Cyrus. In *Harpagus Bringing Cyrus to the Shepherds*, Sebastiano Ricci illustrated Harpagus, unable to obey the king, giving Cyrus to a cowherd and his wife.

When Astyages by chance recognized his ten-year-old grandson, he punished his servant but was persuaded to let the boy live, despite his dream. When Cyrus reached manhood in Persia, he plotted revenge with Harpagus and together they succeeded in usurping the cruel Astyages, whose army deserted him and surrendered to Cyrus in 550BC.

After inheriting the empire of the Medes, Cyrus had to consolidate his power over Iranian tribes before expanding to the West. He gained control of Asia Minor, captured Babylon, and in 530BC caused heavy losses to the Asian tribe ruled by Queen Tomyris. The queen then marched against Cyrus, slaughtered his army, and searched for his body among the dead. In *Queen Tomyris and the Head of Cyrus* Rubens shows how she placed his head in a bowl of blood saying, "Have your fill of the blood for which you thirsted."

Cythera
This was the name of the Ionian island where Venus (in Greek myth, Aphrodite) came ashore after her birth, and another name for the goddess herself.[1] As a result Cythera was thought of as an earthly paradise where sensual love prevails and young girls find lovers or husbands.

Watteau, in *The Embarkation to Cythera*, seems to represent a departure from the island, giving the painting a melancholic air appropriate to lovers returning to the everyday world.

Cyrus:
[1] Herodotus, *I 108–129* and *214*

Cythera: *see* Venus
[1] Ovid, *Fasti IV 286*

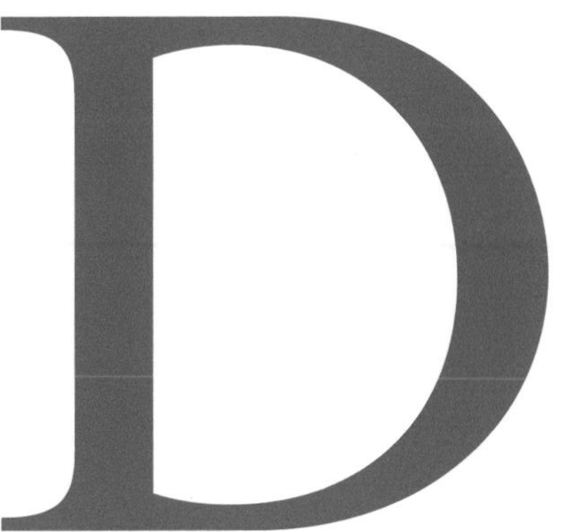

Damocles:
[1] Cicero, *Tusculan Disputations V:xxi*

Danaë: *see* Perseus; Jupiter
[1] Ovid, *Met IV:611*

Danaïds: *see* Danaë; Jupiter
[1] Apollodorus, *II.i.4*
[2] Horace, *3 Ode XI*

Damocles

In the 4th century BC the courtier Damocles praised the wealth of the tyrant King Dionysius of Syracuse, and pronounced the king the happiest of men. However, the king thought this presumptuous, and invited Damocles to experience this so-called happiness for himself. Damocles accepted and was placed on the throne at a banquet and, in order to illustrate the worries of a man in a position of power, directly above Damocles' head hung a sword, held only by a single hair.[1]

A detail showing Danaë, after Titian's Danaë and the Shower of Gold *(1545, Gallerie di Capodimonte, Naples).*

Danaë

In mythology, an oracle predicted that Acrisius, king of Argos, would be usurped by his grandson. He therefore locked his daughter Danaë in a tower, in order that she could not conceive a child. However, Jupiter saw and fell for the maiden and came down to her as a shower of gold.[1] Titian, among others, painted the scene: in *Danaë and the Shower of Gold* he included an ugly nursemaid ignorantly trying to catch the gold, to emphasize Danaë's beauty and higher understanding of her fate. As a result of the coupling, Danaë gave birth to the hero Perseus.

Danaïds

Danaus, a descendent of the supreme god Jupiter, quarelled with his brother Egyptus over their joint rulership of Egypt. He then fled to Argos, where he became king. His fifty daughters, known as the Danaïds, were pursued by the fifty sons of Egyptus. Danaus agreed that they should marry, but on the wedding night he gave each of his daughters a dagger.[1] All but one slew their husbands as they slept. As punishment they were sent to Hades where they were condemned to try to fill holed vessels eternally.[2] Rodin's sculpture of 1885 shows a Danaïd collapsed in despair.

Daniel

In the Old Testament the prophet Daniel interpreted the dreams of Nebuchadnezzar and Belshazzar, the kings of Babylon, for which he was rewarded with land. Daniel's companions, Shadrach, Meshach and Abednego, refused to worship a golden image made by Nebuchadnezzar. They were thrown into a fiery furnace, but an angel protected them and they were unharmed.[1]

A more popular episode in art was that of Daniel being thrown into a lions' den, as a result of his enemies' scheming. When the prophet suffered no harm, the king ordered those who had accused Daniel, and their families, to be thrown to the lions instead.[2] In *Daniel in the Lion's Den* Rubens shows Daniel giving thanks to God for allowing him to survive unscathed.

Another version of the story, in the Apocryphal additions to the *Book of Daniel*, relates how the Babylonians worshipped a dragon which Daniel claimed he could kill without a sword or staff. In order to do this, he fed the dragon pitch, fat and hair, which made it burst. As a result, he was thrown into a den of seven lions for six days, but the lions did not harm him, and he was fed by the prophet Habakkuk. On the seventh day Daniel was released, and those who had imprisoned him were thrown into the den in his place.[3]

Among Daniel's visions was that of a ram which fought with a one-horned goat. The angel Gabriel explained that the two animals represented warring kings and future oppression, and comforted Daniel as he sank to the ground in despair.[4] Rembrandt depicted this episode in *The Vision of Daniel*.

Dante

The Florentine writer and poet Dante Alighieri (1265–1321) was one of the founders of the modern Italian language. *La Vita Nuova* ("The New Life") of 1292 tells of his idealized love for a girl named Beatrice.

When he first saw her she was aged nine, dressed in a delicate crimson dress, tied with a girdle. He saw her again nine years later, walking with two women, dressed in the purest white. She greeted him, "and such was the virtue of her greeting that I seemed to experience the height of bliss."[1] He also saw her again at a wedding feast.

However, Beatrice died prematurely. Inconsolable, Dante continued to contemplate her beauty and goodness, while his friends grew concerned by his grief. In Dante Gabriel Rossetti's *The First Anniversary of the Death of Beatrice*, Dante is seen drawing an angel, oblivious to the presence of others. Rossetti also translated *La Vita Nuova* and painted scenes from it.

Dante is best known, however, for the *Divina Commedia* ("Divine Comedy"), the epic poem concerning mankind's destiny on earth and in the afterlife. The poem falls into three parts: the *Inferno* (Hell) and the *Purgatorio* (Purgatory), in which the poet is led through these regions by Virgil, and the *Paradiso* (Paradise), in

Daniel: *see*
Belshazzar; Gabriel; Habakkuk
[1] *Daniel 3*
[2] *Daniel 6: 12–24*
[3] *Apocrypha, Bel and the Dragon*
[4] *Daniel 8:3–27*

Dante: *see*
Paolo and Francesca; Ugolino; Virgil
[1] Dante, *La Vita Nuova III 1–11*

Daphne's metamorphosis, after Bernini's sculpture, Apollo and Daphne *(1622–25, Borghese Gallery, Rome).*

David, after the sculpture by Bernini (1623, Borghese Gallery, Rome).

which the guide is Beatrice. The poem's journey leads the reader down through the 24 circles of Hell, up the two terraces and seven cornices of Mount Purgatory, and finally to Earthly Paradise, and beyond the planets and the stars to God. The poem contains much political and religious allegory, as well as the personal experiences of its author.

The *Divina Commedia* has provided inspiration for many artists, including Botticelli. Raphael followed a portrait thought to be contemporary in depicting Dante alongside Virgil in *Parnassus*. Dante and Virgil are shown descending into the Underworld together in Delacroix's *The Barque of Dante.*

Daphne

Daphne,[1] a nymph who was born from a river, was pierced by Cupid's lead arrow which puts love to flight; the god Apollo, however, was struck by the golden arrow of new love. As Daphne fled, trying to evade the amorous advances of Apollo, her hair and garments streamed in the wind, enhancing her beauty, and Apollo pursued her until she grew weary. In fear, she called out for help, and as she did so her soft breasts became enclosed in thin bark, her hair turned into leaves, her arms into branches, and her feet became rooted in the ground. Daphne had been transformed into a laurel tree, yet still Apollo loved her. He fashioned a crown from her branches and entwined other branches and leaves around his quivers and lyre.

The subject was popular in Renaissance and Baroque art. Bernini's sculpture *Apollo and Daphne* is a fine example.

Daphnis and Chloe

The son of Mercury and a nymph, Daphnis was a cowherd among the woods and sweet springs of Sicily. A gifted musician, he pleased the goddess Diana (in Greek myth, Artemis) with his shepherd's pipe, which he had been taught to play by Pan; he is also credited with inventing the bucolic or pastoral poem. In one pastoral romance,[1] the nymph Chloe fell in love with Daphnis, and after several adventures they married. In *Daphnis and Chloe* Paris Bordone shows the young couple with Cupid (Eros), who plays his usual wilful part in the story.

David

The Old Testament prophet David has many guises. He may be seen as a personification of physical prowess and courage, or the conqueror of evil. He played the harp and, as the "royal musician" to King Saul, he was depicted on the frontispieces of medieval psalters (he was thought to have composed the Psalms). Seen as a prefiguration of Christ, he was Christ's ancestor through the Tree of Jesse.

The beautiful youngest son of Jesse, David was a shepherd boy chosen by the prophet Samuel to succeed Saul as king of the Israelites. Saul led the Israelite army into battle against the Philistines, whose champion was Goliath, an eight-foot giant clad in heavy armour. Goliath offered a challenge of single combat to the best of the Israelite warriors, and David volunteered for the contest. Refusing the armour that Saul offered him, he picked five smooth stones from a brook for his sling. David killed Goliath with the first stone, which sunk deep into Goliath's forehead; he then stood upon the fallen body, took Goliath's sword, and cut off the giant's head.[1] The Philistines fled.

The victorious youth featured in both Renaissance and Baroque sculpture. The statues by Donatello, Michelangelo and Bernini show different interpretations of David the Giant Slayer. In *The Triumph of David* Poussin shows the Israelites celebrating David's triumphal entry into Jerusalem with Goliath's head.

David's success incurred the envy and wrath of Saul, and the youg hero fled for his life. In *The Cave of Adullam* Claude Lorrain shows the cave in which David hid from Saul with three Israelites who broke through the Philistines' ranks to fetch water for him. However, he would not drink, saying, "is this not the blood of the men that went in jeopardy of their lives?"[2]

David was 30 years old when Saul died and he became king of Judah. Seven and a half years of war ensued, after which David became established as ruler of the 12 tribes of Israel with Jerusalem as his capital. He triumphantly brought the Ark of the Covenant to the city, which was filled with much shouting and the noise of trumpets. David "danced before the Lord with all his might",[3] watched from a window by his wife, Michal.

David had seventeen sons, one of whom, Amnon, raped his half-sister Tamar, and yet the king would not punish him. Another son, Absalom, brooded for two years about his brother's crime, before inviting Amnon to a feast. Here, in order to avenge his sister, Absalom murdered Amnon. Mattia Preti depicted this incident in *The Feast of Absalom*. Absalom fled the city and David mourned the loss of his two sons. After many years they were reconciled, but Absalom led a revolt against his father. During the battle Absalom rode his mule beneath an oak tree and his hair became entangled in the branches. As he hung there helplessly, David's general stabbed him through the heart.[4]

David sent men to greet the wealthy landowner Nabal, in order to acquire food from him. However, the men were rebuffed and David determined revenge. When Nabal's beautiful wife,[5] Abigail, learned of Nabal's rejection of David's men, she determined to make amends and secretly went to meet the Israelites. She threw herself at David's feet and pacified him with quantities of food and drink. On discovering Abigail's indiscretion, Nabal died and David took Abigail as his second wife.

Death

Death is usually represented by a skeleton, sometimes wearing a hooded cloak, and carrying a sword, scythe, sickle or hour-glass. *The Triumph of Death* has been frequently painted: the frescoes by Francesco Traini (Campo Santo, Pisa), painted

A detail of Death, after The Triumph of Death *by Johann Huis (16th century).*

Daphne: *see*
Apollo; Laurel
[1] Ovid, *Met I 452–567*

Daphnis and Chloe:
[1] Longus, *Daphnis and Chloe*

David: *see*
Bathsheba; Saul; Tree of Jesse
[1] *I Samuel 17:20–51*
[2] *II Samuel 23:13–17*
[3] *II Samuel 6:14*
[4] *II Samuel 18:9–15*
[5] *I Samuel 25*

Decius Mus:
[1] Livy, *The History of Rome, X:xxviii*

Democritus:
[1] Juvenal, *Satires X:34*

Denys, Saint: *see* Martyrs

Descent into Hell: *see* Passion of Christ
[1] *The Apocryphal Gospels, Gospel of Nicodemus II, Descent of Christ into the Underworld*

after a series of devastating plagues, depict three richly dressed noblemen reeling back, horrified by three open coffins containing corpses in various stages of decomposition.

Death might be included in a painting as a reminder that no one is spared, regardless of age or status; and a skeleton may appear on or near a tomb as a *memento mori*. The painting may have a Latin inscription to the effect, "I was once that which you are and what I am you also will be." Edvard Munch's *Death and the Maiden* shows the fatal embrace of death as the destroyer of beauty.

Deceit

Deceit or Fraud, in Bronzino's *Allegory of Love*, is depicted as having the face of a beautiful young girl, the body of a reptile and the feet of a lion. With one hand she offers a honeycomb, and in the other she holds the sting of her reptilian tail. Deceit may also be represented by a mask – for example, an old woman wearing the face of a young girl.

Decius Mus

The celebrated Roman consul Decius Mus devoted himself to the service of the state.[1] Rubens made designs for seven tapestries, now housed in the Gallery of the Princes of Liechtenstein in Vaduz, with scenes from the consul's life, including the episode when, in 338BC, he threw himself into the thickest part of the battle against the Latins to spur on his army.

Democritus and Heraclitus

The Greek Democritus (460–370BC) wrote on philosophy, mathematics and music. Having travelled extensively he retired to study in solitude. In *Democritus in Meditation*, Salvator Rosa depicts him among human and animal skeletons, meditating on the futility of life. Nicknamed the "laughing philosopher", he derided the vanities and follies of mankind,[1] and was contrasted with the haughty and melancholic philosopher Heraclitus (active *c.*500BC). Raphael, in his *School of Athens* fresco (Stanza della Segnature, Vaticana), gave the latter the likeness of Michelangelo.

Denys, Saint

Denys, Denis or Dionysius of Paris is the patron saint of France and sometimes associated with the biblical Dionysius the Areopagite. A 9th-century legend tells that he was a missionary, sent to Paris by Pope Clement I. He was said to have been beheaded *c.*AD258 on Montmartre (Martyrs' Hill) and to have carried his own severed head to his burial place, 2½ miles (4 km) from Paris. The abbey of St Denys, which became the burial place of the kings of France, was later built on the site. Henri Bellechose shows Denys as a young bishop receiving his last communion from Christ, and his decapitation. In altarpieces the saint may stand holding his severed head.

Descent into Hell

According to an Apocryphal gospel,[1] after the Entombment Christ went down to Hell or Limbo, a region where souls since Adam had been consigned until his coming. The episode was also known as the Harrowing of Hell. A great voice commanded that the gates be opened so that "the King of Glory shall come in". The dead were released from their chains and the dark places were lit up. Christ sent Satan to Hades but raised Adam, and bade the others to follow him to Paradise. In paintings of the episode Christ is usually depicted in white, holding the banner of the Resurrection at the entrance to a cave, where Adam and numerous bearded patriarchs wait. The Devil may be a small black figure recoiling at Christ's majesty or crushed by the gates on which Christ stands.

Deucalion and Pyrrha

In mythology,[1] the god of the sea, Neptune, angered by mankind's transgressions, struck the earth with his trident and the rivers poured over the plains, flooding the land and leaving only high Mount Parnassus exposed. However, Deucalion and his wife Pyrrha had built an ark, in which they floated for nine days, until Neptune recalled the waters. Once the flood had subsided, they were advised by an oracle to throw behind them the bones of their mother, which they understood to mean "Mother Earth". They duly descended from the ark and, with veiled heads, threw stones behind them. These stones took human form and became a hardy race which repopulated the earth.

Diana

The daughter of Jupiter (in Greek myth, Zeus) and Latona, and twin sister of Apollo, Diana (Artemis) was one of the 12 deities of Mount Olympus, and was extremely beautiful. She was the goddess of chastity and hunting, and may therefore be depicted as athletic, dressed in a short tunic, carrying a bow and arrow, and accompanied by hounds or stags. She was identified with the moon goddess Selene, and a crescent moon is her attribute. She is often surrounded by attendant nymphs, and perhaps a bear, because one of her nymphs, Callisto, was turned into a bear by the supreme goddess Juno (Hera). As Chastity, Diana may be paired with Venus (Aphrodite) or Cupid (Eros), who represent sensual love. She may also carry a shield to protect herself from Cupid's arrows.

The many breasts of Diana of Ephesus emphasize her fertility.

Dice

Dice or a single die may represent fate (as in the saying "the die is cast"). As part of a game of chance, dice may be the attribute of Fortune. At the Crucifixion soldiers gambled for Christ's cloak: "They said therefore among themselves, Let us not rend it, but cast lots for it, whose it shall be".[1]

Diogenes of Sinope

The Greek Diogenes (*c.*412–323BC) was a Cynic philosopher and ascetic. In *Diogenes in the Market Place* Jacob Jordaens illustrates the story of the philosopher's search for an honest man at the market: Diogenes is shown in daylight, carrying a lantern, which represents his search for truth. He rejected all luxuries to the extent of making his home in a large earthenware tub, and cast off all worldly goods except his cloak and a drinking bowl. As Poussin shows in his painting *Landscape with Diogenes*, when he saw a young man drinking from the river with his hands, Diogenes even abandoned his bowl. When Alexander the Great visited his home and asked if there was anything the philosopher required, Diogenes

Deucalion and Pyrrha:
[1] Ovid, *Met I: 313–415*

Diana: *see*
Actaeon; Apollo; Callisto; Endymion; Niobe; Orion

Dice:
[1] *John 19:24*

Diogenes:
[1] Plutarch, *Lives, Alexander*

Dionysius the Areopagite: *see*
Denys, St; Paul, St
[1] *Acts 17:19–32*

Discord: *see*
Feast of the Gods; Paris
[1] Hyginus, *Fabulae*

Doctors: *see*
Ambrose, St; Augustine, St; Gregory the Great, St; Jerome, St; Luke, St

Dog: *see*
Dominic, St; Roch, St

defiantly replied, "Yes, I would have you stand from between me and the sun," meaning that he required nothing other than that which was natural and non-material.[1]

Dionysius the Areopagite

Dionysius heard St Paul preaching at Athens[1] before a council of judges known as the Areopagus which met at Mars Hill (the hill itself was also called the Areopagus). Raphael shows how Dionysius was converted by the saint in *St Paul Preaching at Athens*. Tradition has connected him with St Denys, patron saint of France, and erroneously credited him with mystical writings.

Discord

In mythology, Eris was the goddess of Discord. She was not invited to the Feast of the Gods to celebrate the wedding of Thetis and Peleus, and so she angrily threw a golden apple among the guests, dedicated "To the Fairest".[1] This resulted in the Judgment of Paris, which ultimately led to the Trojan War. In *The Goddess of Discord* Turner painted Eris choosing the apple in the garden of the Hesperides.

Doctor

The four early fathers of the Western Church, known as the Doctors of the Church, are Saints Ambrose, Augustine, Gregory the Great and Jerome, whose writings were treated as special theological authority.

Doctors of Philosophy may be recognized by their gowns, loose-fitting caps, or lecturer's wands; they may carry a book or mark off the points of an argument on their fingers. Theologians may be absorbed in writing.

In the Low Countries, doctors of medicine were sometimes made objects of ridicule; for example, Bosch's *Cure for Folly* shows a man having his skull trepanned (drilled) to release malign spirits. Jan Steen's *The Doctor's Visit*, a popular theme in 17th-century Dutch painting, shows a doctor attending a young woman who appears to be either love-sick or pregnant. In such scenes, there may be a piece of ribbon evident, since a diagnosis was made from the smell that resulted when a ribbon burned; or the doctor may be seen testing the woman's pulse, which was supposed to quicken in the presence of her lover.

The quack doctor was also painted to illustrate a moral. In *The Quack* Gerard Dou shows a pedlar of potions on a stand, beneath which a woman wipes a baby's bottom. The painting's meaning was explained in contemporary emblem books by the motto, "The body, what else is it but stench and shit?"; thus, in Dou's painting the quack's potions may help physical ailments but they will not help the soul.

Important medical research has also been painted, as in Rembrandt's *Anatomy Lesson of Dr Tulp*: public dissections could be attended by anyone for a fee and were by this time considered a respectable professional practice.

Dog

As there are many breeds of dog, so are there diverse qualities ascribed to them. Creatures of fidelity and loyalty, dogs are depicted on medieval tombs lying at the feet of their masters, and in portraits they represent similar qualities. The faithfulness of the dog was sentimentalized by the Victorians. Landseer, for example, in *The Old Shepherd's Chief Mourner* shows a sheepdog resting his head on his master's coffin. Dogs may also have the role of guardian: in myth the three-headed Cerberus stood at the entrance to the Underworld.

Dogs of good pedigree or hunting dogs may be included in portraits of the aristocracy and land-owning classes. Hunting dogs also accompany figures in the chase in scenes of classical mythology.

Dogs may even be used to express carnal desire: *Brothel Scene* by Frans van Mieris the Elder shows a lady pouring a man a glass of wine while a canine pair copulate in the background. They may also signify greed, as in the fable of the dog which, holding a cake in its jaws, looked down into water and lost the cake in an attempt to catch its reflection.

A dog is the attribute of St Roch, and black-and-white dogs in Dominican scenes are, in a pun on the Order's name, depicted as *Domini Canes* or "Hounds of the Lord"; they may be chasing wolves, which represent heretics.

Dominic, Saint

The founder of the Dominican Order, the Spaniard Dominic (1170–1221), became a canon at the age of about 26. In 1206 he was chosen to accompany his bishop, Diego, to Languedoc in order to convert the heretical Albigensians; the mission was, however, unsuccessful. In 1215 Dominic was in Toulouse, where he began to form an Order of preachers bound by vows of poverty. The Order was given Papal approval in 1216 and friaries were founded in Italy, principally in Bologna, and then throughout Europe.

St Dominic appears in numerous altarpieces in chapels devoted to his Order. He wears the black and white robe of the Dominicans and he may hold the rosary – as he was said to have instigated its use as symbol of dedication – or a lily of purity. The presence of a black-and-white dog, reflecting the colours of his habit, is a pun on his name and on his position as the inquisitor of heretics: the *Domini Canis* or "Hound of the Lord". Such dogs appear in the foreground of Andrea da Firenze's fresco (Spanish Chapel of Santa Maria Novella, Florence), in which they appear to have been sent out by the saint to catch wolves in the same way that the Dominicans set out to convert non-believers. St Dominic also appears in altarpieces in the company of other illustrious brothers or founders of monastic Orders, particularly St Francis.

The scenes illustrated from Dominic's life are mostly derived from legend.[1] Before he was born his mother dreamed that she carried a dog with a lit torch in its mouth, which set fire to the earth; and at Dominic's baptism, a brilliant star, which may be used in art as his attribute, appeared on his forehead to shed its light over the world.

A heretic tried to burn Dominic's writings but they jumped out of the fire intact. The Pope withheld his confirmation of the Dominican Order until one night when he dreamed that the Lateran basilica was about to fall into ruins and Dominic ran and held up the tottering building.

Dominic, Saint: *see* Dog; Religious Dress; RELIGIOUS ORDERS

[1] *Golden Legend, St Dominic*

Dorothea, Saint: *see* Martyrs
[1] *Golden Legend, St Dorothea*

Dove: *see* God; Noah; Trinity
[1] *Genesis 8:8–11*

Another legend tells how Saints Peter and Paul appeared to Dominic in a vision, handed him a staff and book and commanded him to go out to preach. He also had a vision of Christ with three spears, which Christ had decided to unleash upon the world to destroy the vices of pride, lust and avarice; however, the Virgin begged for mercy and presented St Francis and St Dominic as Christ's allies on the earth.

Dominic exorcized those possessed by demons, and restored the life of the nephew of the Cardinal of Fossa, who had been thrown from his horse. Once, at supper with his friars, there was little bread but, miraculously, two young men silently brought loaves to the friars and then suddenly disappeared again.

The saint converted heretics or burned those who would not accept the faith.

Don Quixote

Miguel de Cervantes' *Don Quixote*, published in two parts in 1605 and 1615, is a satire on the notion of chivalry. Cervantes' hero, a simple-minded, gaunt knight errant who rides an aged horse, Rosinante, believes that his destiny is to set the world to rights.

Accordingly, he embarks on a series of adventures, each the bizarre product of his deluded imagination, fighting various inanimate and unharmful objects. He is accompanied by his rotund peasant "squire", Sancho Panza, astride a donkey.

To 19th-century French artists, however, Don Quixote was not a figure of ridicule, but a tragic hero in pursuit of idealistic dreams.

A detail of a dove, after a mosaic showing Noah's ark in St Mark's Basilica, Venice (built 1071).

Dorothea, Saint

Legend[1] claims that Dorothea (died *c.*AD303) was persecuted with other Christians in Cappodocia. Two women, who had abandoned Christianity, were sent to make her renounce her faith, but instead she reconverted them, for which she was beheaded. On the way to her martyrdom a man asked her to send flowers and fruit from heaven. Miraculously, a child appeared with a basket of fruit and roses.

Dorothea may appear before the Virgin and Child in a garden, with the basket of flowers, her attribute – as in an early 15th-century painting from the School of Gentile da Fabriano in the Ducal Palace of Urbino.

Dove

In mythological paintings doves may surround female deities, especially Venus (in Greek myth, Aphrodite), as a representation of love. They are also associated with funerary cults, as a dove was believed to carry souls to the afterlife.

In the Old Testament Noah sent out a dove to see if the waters had abated after the Flood, and it returned with an olive branch in its beak, signifying a new peace between God and man.[1]

In Christianity, the dove symbolizes the Holy Ghost, which descended to the Virgin at the Annunciation, and to Christ at the Baptism, and therefore forms part of the Trinity.

Dragon

Compared with other mythical beasts, such as Cerberus or the Chimera, this monster has a less specific make-up, which gave greater freedom for artistic imagination. However, most dragons are depicted as gigantic, scaly, winged reptiles with huge jaws, barbed tails, eagle's legs, and massive claws.

In epic narratives, a dragon is often the last obstacle to be overcome before the quest is successful. Famous dragon-slayers in mythology include Cadmus, Jason and Perseus.

In Christian iconography, the dragon may stand for the Devil. In the war in heaven, St Michael and his angels fought the Devil: "And the great dragon was cast out, that old serpent, called the Devil."[1] The Devil also appeared to St Margaret of Antioch in the form of a dragon, which thus became her attribute.

The story of St George and the Dragon was particularly popular in 15th-century Italian art where the monster may represent the Devil, or alternatively the infidel, vanquished by the Christian knight.

The dragon does not always symbolize evil; it is also used, for example, in heraldry, and is a national emblem of Wales.

Dragon: *see*
Angelica; Cadmus; George, St; Jason; Margaret, St; Michael, St; Perseus

[1] *Revelation 12:9*

Eagle: *see*
Ganymede; John the Evangelist, St; Jupiter; Prometheus

Echo: *see*
Narcissus
[1] Ovid, *Met III: 359–369*

Egg: *see*
Castor and Pollux; Helen of Troy; Jupiter; Leda

Eagle

The eagle, with its strength, speed and soaring flight, is appropriately the attribute of the supreme Roman god Jupiter (in the Greek, Zeus), and also a symbol of the planet Jupiter. The god sent an eagle to peck out Prometheus' liver, and he also transformed himself into an eagle to carry the beautiful Ganymede to Mount Olympus to be his cup-bearer. This powerful raptor followed Aeneas from Troy to Italy, ultimately resulting in its adoption as the Roman insignia. The bird was later used to represent the Holy Roman Empire, America and other dynasties and nations. Its enemy was the snake, which it may hold in its claws to represent its superior power.

The eagle is found carved on medieval Christian fonts, from a belief that in old age it would fly to the sun and then descend to earth and, diving into spring water, rejuvenate itself, just as man is regenerated through baptism. The ascending and descending eagle was also likened to Christ's Resurrection and Ascension.

The eagle is also the attribute of St John the Evangelist, whose gospel is regarded as the most mystical of the four; consequently, lecterns are often carved in the form of the eagle with outstretched wings. It is also one of the four beasts of the Apocalypse.

Echo

In mythology, Juno, queen of the gods (in Greek myth, Hera), punished the nymph Echo for detaining her with endless chatter, when she could have caught her husband Jupiter (Zeus) being unfaithful.[1] Echo's punishment was that she could only repeat the last words of whatever was said to her. The nymph fell in love with Narcissus but, unable to make conversation, she wasted away until only her voice remained. She is often seen in paintings of Narcissus, wistfully gazing at her love.

Egg

In many cultures the egg is regarded as a symbol of renewal. Leda's two sets of twins, Castor and Clytem-nestra, and Helen and Pollux, were born from eggs because Jupiter had fathered them in the shape of a swan.

In 16th-century Netherlandish art an egg with two legs and a knife sticking out of the top is thought to represent a type of demon.

Elements

The four elements – air, earth, fire and water – may be illustrated by figures involved in appropriate activities or by relevant objects; alternatively they may be represented by the gods of antiquity. **Air** may be the peacock of Juno (in Greek myth, Hera), or birds flying, or Boreas, god of the North wind, and Zephyr, god of the West wind. **Earth** may be represented by the goddess Ceres or Ops, who may have a globe or a cornucopia; other representations include Cybele with her lion, and the bountiful Golden Age. **Fire** may be Vulcan (Hephaestus) at his forge, or the sun. **Water** may be pouring from an upturned urn; or may be represented by a seascape, or by a river scene with reeds and fish, or by a river-god, or by Neptune (Poseidon), or by the Birth of Venus from the sea.

Elephant

The second Punic War brought Hannibal over the Alps in 218BC with troops and elephants. Elephants were used to pull chariots in Roman triumphal marches. The animals appear in Old Testament scenes to evoke the East. An elephant may symbolize Africa, or Temperance because it was believed that elephants ate modest quantities of food.

Eligius, Saint

Eligius, or Eloi (*c.*AD588–660), was trained at a mint in Limoges and became a talented engraver. He founded a monastery at Solignac and a convent in Paris. In AD641 he became Bishop of Noyon and Tournai. He is the patron saint of metalworkers. His attributes are an anvil, or the tongs with which he is said to have held the Devil by the nose when the fiend visited his workshop disguised as a young woman. Nanni di Banco's sculpture of *c.*1411 in the niche belonging to smiths on the exterior of Orsanmichele, Florence, shows Eligius as a bishop. The relief below depicts the legend of how he sawed off, shod and miraculously restored to its body, the legs of a difficult horse.

Elijah

The Old Testament prophet Elijah spoke against Ahab, king of Israel, whose wife Jezebel had introduced the heathen cult of Baal. During a drought God sent Elijah east to live by a brook where ravens fed him. When the brook dried up he met a widow of the city of Zarephath whom he found gathering sticks. She gave him food, and, in gratitude, Elijah cured her child of his sickness.[1] After three years of drought and famine, Elijah assembled 450 priests of Baal on Mount Carmel and built two sacrificial altars with King Ahab's blessing, for an offering of bullocks. Both Elijah and the priests of Baal built fires, which were to be ignited by their respective gods. The priests' fire refused to catch alight, but Elijah's ignited immediately. The priests were put to death, thus appeasing the god of Israel, and the rains returned.[2] Fearing Jezebel's revenge, Elijah fled into the desert and prayed for his own death. He slept under a juniper tree

Elements: *see* Ceres; Cybele; Juno; Neptune; Ops; Vulcan; Winds

Elephant: *see* CONTINENTS; Fabricius; Hannibal

Elijah: *see* Jezebel

[1] *I Kings 17:6–22*
[2] *I Kings 18:19–41*
[3] *I Kings 18 :5–8*
[4] *II Kings 2:11*

Elisha: *see* Elijah
[1] *II Kings 4:1–34*
[2] *II Kings 5:1–14*

Elizabeth of Hungary, Saint:
[1] *Golden Legend, St Elizabeth*

Endymion: *see* Diana
[1] Apollodorus, *The Library I vii 5*

Envy:
[1] Ovid, *Met II:760–796*

and was fed by an angel.[3]

On Mount Horeb Elijah encountered the voice of God, who told him to seek out his successor as a prophet. Elijah did so, finding Elisha ploughing a field. They travelled together until one day there appeared a chariot and horses of fire, and Elijah went up to heaven in a whirlwind.[4] As he ascended, Elijah's mantle fell from him, and Elisha took it up. Elijah also appeared with Moses at Christ's Transfiguration.

Elijah appears in art as a bearded old man. Rubens shows him in his fiery chariot in *The Chariot of Elijah*. The prophet being fed in the desert by ravens or by the angel was also a favourite subject, as in Giovanni Lanfranco's *The Prophet Elijah Awakened in the Desert by an Angel*. Elijah was a popular subject for the Carmelite Order, who claim him as their founder.

Elisha

After Elijah's ascent to heaven, Elisha became his spiritual successor and it was his responsibility to anoint Hazel and Jehu, the kings of Syria and Israel, who would later kill Ahab and the followers of Baal.

Elisha once miraculously filled a woman's empty vessels with oil; and a Shunammite woman, who gave Elisha a bed and food, was rewarded with a son, although her husband was old. Later, this child died, but was subsequently resuscitated by Elisha.[1] Naaman, a captain of Syria, suffered from leprosy and Elisha advised him to dip himself into the River Jordan seven times; Naaman did this and was cured.[2] Lambert Jacobsz depicted this scene in *The Prophet Elisha and Naaman*.

Elizabeth of Hungary, Saint

Daughter of the king of Hungary, Elizabeth (1207–31) was happily married to Ludwig IV of Thuringia and had three children. In 1227 Ludwig joined the crusades and died suddenly. According to legend,[1] Elizabeth devoted herself to the seven works of mercy and, when her husband died, became a Franciscan to live in the depths of poverty and dedicate her life to the sick and needy. She was a particularly popular subject with northern European artists. She may be dressed either as a princess with a crown or as a Franciscan. She may have roses in her lap, from the tale that she was caught stealing food from her brother-in-law's castle to give to the poor; when questioned about her actions, she replied that she was merely collecting roses and, miraculously, the food in her basket became these flowers.

Endymion

Endymion, son of Jupiter (in Greek myth, Zeus) and a nymph, was supremely beautiful, and the goddess Diana (Aphrodite) fell in love with him. His father granted him a wish, and he chose eternal sleep, remaining immortal and ageless.[1] The goddess may be depicted gazing at him as she visited him by night. Girodet, in *The Sleep of Endymion*, shows the idealized youth asleep by daylight, watched over by Cupid (Eros).

Envy

According to Ovid,[1] Envy lived in a filthy house in a deep, sunless valley. She fed on snake's flesh and was sickly pale, with a wasted body, horrible squint and rotten teeth; her poisonous breasts were greenish-blue and her

Gattamelata (the "honeyed cat") after Donatello's equestrian monument of the leader (1443–48, Piazza del Santo, Padua).

tongue dripped with venom. She carried a staff circled with thorny briars. In his engraving of the *The Battle of the Sea Gods* Mantegna depicts her as a scrawny old woman with drooping breasts holding the sign *Invidia* ("Envy").

Equestrian Monument

A portrait of a man on a horse expresses power, conquest and authority. There were countless equestrian monuments in ancient Rome, but most have been smashed or melted down. However, the monument of Marcus Aurelius (2nd century BC), now in the Capitoline Museum, Rome, survived because it was erroneously thought to be a statue of Constantine, the first Christian emperor. In the late Middle Ages the equestrian portrait was used for funerary monuments of military leaders, a tradition that continued with Paolo Uccello's *trompe l'œil* fresco of Sir John Hawkwood in the Duomo, Florence. Donatello revived the classical tradition of a free-standing statue in a public area with his portrait of the *condottiere*, or mercenary leader, nicknamed Gattamelata (the "honeyed cat") in Padua. Both he and his follower Verrocchio were drawn to the problem of how to cast a large mass supported only by the horses' slender legs.

Since the Renaissance, numerous European monarchs and illustrious figures in authority have had themselves portrayed on horseback in stone, bronze and paint.

A horse striding forward suggests that the rider is in control, while a rearing horse suggests a man of a more passionate nature.

Erasmus, Saint

Legend claims that Erasmus, Elmo or Ermo (died *c.* AD303) was a bishop in Syria. Poussin depicts his gruesome martyrdom, showing him lying naked on a stone slab, his vestments beside him, as brutal pagans put him to death by winding his intestines around a windlass (Vatican, Rome). The windlass became his attribute; and, because similar machines are used on board ship, Erasmus became the patron saint of sailors. The electrical charges that appear during storms, known as "St Elmo's Fire", were seen as a sign of his protection.

Erichthonius

Erichthonius was born when Vulcan (in Greek myth, Hephaestus) spilled his seed trying to ravish Minerva (Athene), impregnating Mother Earth instead. Minerva took the baby and shut him in a chest, which she put into the care of the three unmarried daughters of Cecrops, a king who was part human and part snake.[1] Minerva had told the daughters not to open

Erasmus, Saint: *see* Martyrs

Erichthonius: *see* Vulcan

[1] Ovid, *Met II:553–561*

Esther:
[1] *Esther 1:5–19*
[2] *Esther 2:2–10*
[3] *Esther 5:1–2*
[4] *Esther 7:1–10*

Europa: *see* CONTINENTS; Jupiter; ZODIAC
[1] Ovid, *Met II:833–875*
[2] Fasti *V:603–621*

the chest, but curiosity overcame them. Rubens shows them untying the knots of the casket in *The Daughters of Cecrops Discovering Erichthonius*. Inside, they found the child with snakes coiled around him, or as other sources say, with legs that had turned into snakes. The sisters went mad with horror and hurled themselves off a cliff. Erichthonius is sometimes associated with Erechtheus, a mythical king of Athens.

Ermine

The name by which the stoat is known in winter. It has immaculate white fur, worn by those of rank and wealth. In Leonardo da Vinci's *Portrait of a Lady with an Ermine*, the sitter is widely assumed to be Cecelia Gallerani: she holds an ermine, known in Greek as *gallée*, and some say that this is a pun on her name.

After A Lady with an Ermine *by Leonardo da Vinci (1485–90, Czartorysky Museum, Cracow).*

Esther

Like Judith, Esther was a Jewish heroine of the Old Testament who saved the Israelites from persecution. Ahasuerus, king of Persia, had dismissed his queen, who, despite being summoned, had refused to appear at a feast in his palace (said to have had coloured hangings, marble pillars and beds of gold and silver).[1] Ahasuerus then desired a new wife, and chose Esther from all the fair young virgins in his kingdom. Esther had been brought up by Mordecai, her cousin, who told her to keep the secret of their Jewish faith.[2] Mordecai discovered that the king's favourite attendant, Haman, had contrived his permission to kill all the Jews in the land. On hearing this, Mordecai tore up his clothes, put on sackcloth and sat outside the king's gate until he could warn Esther of the fate awaiting the Jews.

Death was the penalty for anyone entering the inner court for an unsolicited audience with the king. Esther, however, dressed in her royal garments, dared to do so and the king lowered his golden sceptre over her as a sign of acceptance.[3] She invited the king and Haman to a banquet and made an impassioned speech on behalf of the Jews. As a result of Esther's plea Haman was hanged, Mordecai received high office and wealth, and the enemies of the Jews were put to death.[4]

Esther may be portrayed as a richly dressed queen, and as an example of virtuous womanhood interceding for her people.

The story provided Veronese with much scope for sumptuous costumes and settings in *Scenes from the Story of Esther*. Théodore Chassériau, in *The Toilet of Esther*, shows Esther preparing herself for the meeting with the king.

Euclid

A Greek mathematician of *c.*300BC, Euclid wrote on geometry and the theory of numbers. His image, therefore, may represent geometry, as in Raphael's *School of Athens* (Stanza della Segnatura, Vatican, Rome).

Europa

Europa,[1] daughter of the king of Tyre, used to play with her companions on the sands where cattle were taken down to the shore. Jupiter (in Greek myth, Zeus) fell in love with her, and so, disguised as a bull with placid eyes, a snow-white hide and horns shining like jewels, he joined the herd lowing in the grass. In his painting of 1580 in the Doge's Palace, Venice, Veronese shows how Europa admired the handsome bull, and tentatively held out flowers so that he would kiss her hands. The disguised Jupiter frolicked and played until Europa lost her fear and hung garlands on his horns and finally ventured to mount him. With Europa on his back, Jupiter sped away across the ocean to Crete.

Paintings may show the startled Europa looking back at the sands behind her, while she grasps Jupiter's horn, her garments fluttering in the breeze. Having landed on Crete,

A detail showing Europa, after The Rape of Europa *by de Vos (late 16th century, Museo de Bellas Artes, Bilbao).*

Jupiter made love to Europa, and later she gave birth to sons, one of whom was Minos, king of Crete. Another version of the myth states that one of her children was the continent that bears her name, and she herself was turned into a bull, which became the constellation and zodiac sign of Taurus.[2]

Eustace, Saint

According to legend,[1] Eustace (said to have died AD118) was a pagan Roman general in Emperor Trajan's army. While he was out hunting a herd of deer, a stag of great size and beauty gave chase and, when it came to a halt, Eustace saw a crucifix between its antlers, shining brighter than the sun. The stag is said to have approached Eustace, commanding him to convert to Christianity. A similar story is told of St Hubert, with whom Eustace is sometimes confused. Pisanello shows Eustace dressed as a young nobleman, stopped in his tracks before the stag while hunting in the depths of a forest.

Now followers of Christ, Eustace and his family were converted and

A detail showing Saint Eustace, after The Vision of Saint Eustace *by Pisanello (c.1450, National Gallery, London).*

baptized by the Bishop of Rome. Then followed a series of misfortunes during which they were separated: his wife was taken by pirates, and his sons by a wolf and lion. Miraculously, however, the family was later reunited.

The new Emperor, Hadrian, observed that Eustace and his family would not worship idols, and so threw them into a pit of wild animals. The family tamed the animals, so Hadrian finally had Eustace and his family roasted inside a huge brass bull.

Eustace, Saint: *see* Hubert, St

[1] *Golden Legend, St Eustace*

Evangelists: *see*
Apocalypse; Doctors; Ezekiel; John the Evangelist, St; Luke, St; Mark, St; Matthew
[1] *Ezekiel 1:10, Revelation 4:7*
[2] *Golden Legend, St Luke*

Eyes: *see*
Lucy, St; Trinity
[1] *Psalms 34:15*

Ezekiel: *see*
Evangelists
[1] *Ezekiel 1:10*
[2] *Ezekiel 37:1–10*

The Evangelists, after a detail from Ezekiel's Vision *by Raphael (*c.*1518, Pitti Palace, Florence).*

Evangelists

The four Gospel writers: Matthew, Mark, Luke and John. Each has a winged creature as his symbol: a man or angel, a lion, a bull and an eagle.[1] The medieval explanation for these attributes lies in aspects of the Gospels. Matthew has the winged man or angel because he gives an account of Christ's ancestry; the image may also relate to Christ's incarnation. Mark has the noble lion because his Gospel emphasizes the majesty of Christ, or because he begins his account in the wilderness with the roar of John the Baptist's teaching. Luke has the sacrificial bull because he stresses Christ's sacrifice, or because his Gospel opens with offerings in the temple. John has the soaring eagle because his Gospel is generally regarded as the most mystical; the bird may also represent the grace of the Holy Spirit.[2]

As well as being subjects in their own right, the Evangelists may be depicted holding their Gospels or writing them, or they may have scrolls. Like the Doctors of the Church, they conveniently fill ecclesiastical architectural spaces or the frames or wings of paintings when four figures are required.

Eyes

There are several references to the eyes of God in the Old and New Testaments, "For the eyes of the Lord are over the righteous, and his ears are open to their prayers,"[1] as the omnipresent, all-seeing divinity. The Trinity may be shown as an eye within a triangle. A pair of eyes, often on a platter, is the attribute of St Lucy.

Ezekiel

The prophet Ezekiel had a vision of the throne of God surrounded by a winged lion, a winged man, a bull and an eagle.[1] These four beasts were to become the symbols of the Evangelists. In *Ezekiel's Vision* Raphael shows Ezekiel hovering above them. Another of his visions was of a valley of dry bones, which God covered in flesh; the bones came together and life was breathed into them so that they stood like a great army. This was regarded as a foretelling of the Resurrection of the Dead at the Last Judgment.[2]

Fabricius, Luscinus Gaius

In 280BC the honest Roman Fabricius was sent as ambassador to Pyrrhus, king of Epirus, with whom Rome was at war. Fabricius refused bribes of gold offered to him by the king's soldiers. Thus, Epirus, wishing to unnerve Fabricius, ordered that a huge elephant, an animal that Fabricius would never have seen before, be placed behind a hanging in the room where they talked. In *Pyrrhus and Fabricius* Ferdinand Bol shows the moment at which, with the hanging drawn aside, the elephant raised its trunk and trumpeted hideously. Unmoved, Fabricius said to Pyrrhus, "Neither your money yesterday, nor this beast today, makes any impression upon me."[1]

Fame

In classical antiquity the female figure of Fame bore away on her wings the illustrious dead. By the Renaissance her image had acquired a trumpet with which to herald the famous. Bernardo Strozzi's *Fame* uses a winged young girl as the personification; she holds a gilded trumpet and a plain wooden recorder to represent the good and bad aspects of her proclamations.

Fasces

A bundle of wooden rods around an axe, fastened together with a strap, fasces symbolized authority or power. In ancient Rome they were carried by lictors (attendants) before superior magistrates. They repre-sented the punishments of whipping and beheading, and are therefore associated with Justice. Other figures of authority were allowed to carry fasces; they were awarded different quantities according to rank (a consul, for example, had 12 fasces).

Fates

In mythology, the Fates (in Latin, *Parcae*) were three sisters who controlled human destiny. The length of a single human life was represented by a thread, which they spun together. Clotho held the distaff from which Lachesis pulled the thread, which Atropos, unmoved by the prayers of

Cicero holding a bundle of fasces, after a fresco (late 15th century, Palazzo Vecchio, Florence).

Fabricius, Luscinus Gaius:
[1] Plutarch, *Lives, Pyrrhus*

Fasces: *see* Concord

Faunus and Fauns: *see* Pan; Satyr

Feast of the Gods: *see* Cupid; Discord; Juno; Minerva; Venus; Paris; Trojan War

Felicity, Saint: *see* Martyrs

Fertility: *see* Priapus; Rabbit

A faun, after Piero di Cosimo's A Faun Mourning Over a Nymph *(*c.*1462, National Gallery, London).*

mortals, snipped. They are usually depicted as old and ugly but Rubens, in *The Destiny of Marie d'Medici*, shows them as three elegant youths, presided over by Jupiter (in Greek myth, Zeus) and Juno (Hera), spinning the thread of the yet unborn Marie d'Medici, queen of France.

Faunus and Fauns

Faunus was the ancient Roman chief of the satyrs, worshipped by farmers and shepherds, and identified with the Greek god Pan. Fauns were rural gods with a human form and, like satyrs, had the legs, tails and ears of a goat. They were associated with lust.

Feasts of the Gods

Two wedding feasts attended by the gods are popular subjects in painting: the feast of Cupid (in Greek myth, Eros) and Psyche, and that of Thetis and Peleus.

At the latter the gods sat on their 12 thrones, the Fates and Muses sang, Ganymede poured nectar, and fifty Nereids danced on the sands. The centaurs were also present. However, Eris, goddess of Discord, who stirs up war by spreading rumour, had not been invited. As Juno (Hera), Minerva (Athene) and Venus (Aphrodite) chatted happily together, Eris threw down a golden apple at their feet dedicated "To the Fairest". The Judgment of Paris concluded that the fairest was Venus, a decision that ultimately led to the Trojan War.

The subject of the Feast of the Gods was also painted without reference to these weddings as a great outdoor banquet set in the shade of trees.

Felicity, Saint

According to legend the Roman widow Felicity (died AD165) and her seven sons refused to worship pagan idols. Felicity watched her children being put to death one by one before she was either beheaded or plunged in a vat of boiling oil. In *Saint Felicity* Neri di Bicci shows her as a matronly nun in a dark habit surrounded by her children, with the predella panel representing their martyrdom.

Fertility

In mythology, Priapus was born with enormous genitals and was the god of fertility. Fertility may be represented as a female figure accompanied by a hen with eggs and hatching chicks or with rabbits and hares at her feet.

Fête Champêtre

Fête champêtre or *fête galante* scenes, showing the wealthy pursuing romantic pleasures outdoors, were popular in early 18th-century France. They were painted most notably by Watteau. Fashionably dressed couples are seen amusing themselves by dancing, making music or talking in an idealized pastoral landscape. There is often an air of gentle *ennui* and melancholy pervading the scene.

Fidelity

The secular counterpart of Faith, the personification of Fidelity may have a dog at her feet, and hold a key that signifies her absolute trustworthiness.

Fig Leaf

When Adam and Eve were expelled from the garden of Eden, "they knew that they were naked; and they sewed fig leaves together and made themselves aprons".[1]

Fig leaves were also used to cover the genitalia of statues. Numerous classical works of male nudes in later centuries had the genitalia amputated so that fig leaves could fit more conveniently over the groin; many of these leaves have since been removed. The huge fig leaf that covered the genitalia of the replica of Michelangelo's *David* for the benefit of Queen Victoria and other royal ladies of Britain can be seen behind the statue in the cast room of the Victoria and Albert Museum, London.

Fina, Saint

Fina (238–1253), from San Gimignano, Italy, lay paralysed on a bed of bare boards in her room, plagued by rats in order to increase her torment, so that she might bring herself closer to Christ. Ghirlandaio shows how Pope Gregory the Great came to Fina in a dream and foretold her death (Collegiata, San Gimignano). As her body was carried to her funeral, her hand miraculously seized a crippled boy and healed him. She interceded after her death in order to extinguish a fire, rescue a man falling off a roof and save a ship in distress. She may hold a model of her native city (recognizable by its many tall towers) as her attribute.

Fish

A fish was an early symbol of Christianity because the Greek for fish, *Ichthus*, contains the initial letters of *Jesus CHristos, THeou Uios, Soter* (Jesus Christ, Son of God, Saviour). The variety of fish caught in the Miraculous Draught of Fishes represented the numerous types of people who would adopt the Christian faith. A large fish may be a substitute for Jonah's whale; it also appears as the attribute of Tobias.

Flag

Emperor Constantine had a vision of the Cross before defeating Maxentius in AD312. Henceforth, he used it in his flag, designed as a red cross on a white background. This flag has come to represent Christian triumph. It may be carried by Christ in depictions of the Descent into Hell or at the Resurrection; or by St John the Baptist; or by the Lamb of God. It is also the attribute of St Ursula and the militant saints George and Liberale.

Flora

The Roman goddess of flowers, Flora[1] was originally the Greek maiden Chloris, who was pursued and

Fig Leaf:
ADAM AND EVE; NUDE
[1] *Genesis 3:7*

Fish: *see*
Jonah; Tobias

Flag: *see*
Ansanus, St; Constantine St; George, St; John the Baptist, St; Liberale, St; Ursula, St

Flora: *see*
Adonis; Ajax; Clytie; Flowers; Graces; Hyacinthus; Narcissus
[1] Ovid, *Fasti V:183–228*
[2] Ovid, *Met IV:283*

FLOWERS: *see* Adonis; Ajax; Clytie; Hyacinthus; Iris; Lily; Narcissus; Passion Flower; Rose

FLOWERS

Flowers are the attribute of the goddess Flora. Various flowers sprang from those who died of unrequited love: anemones from Adonis, violets from Attis, sunflowers from Clytie; narcissi from Narcissus; hyacinths from Hyacinthus.

Flowers may indicate Paradise or Eden, and are also used to illustrate the earth's seasons.

In the Middle Ages, many flowers took on a Christian significance: red flowers represented the blood of Christ's Passion; and white, especially the lily, iris and rose without thorns, the Virgin's purity. Cyclamen, jasmine, lily-of-the-valley and violets were also connected with the Virgin, and may be scattered across the ground in depictions of her walled garden. Flowers also had a numerical significance: five petals symbolized the wounds of Christ, and triple leaves the Trinity. The columbine may symbolize the Holy Ghost (Latin *columbus*, which means "dove").

Flowers, after the still life A Vase of Flowers *by Ambrosius Bosschaert the Elder (*c.*1620, Hague, Mauristhuis).*

In still life painting, flowers may represent the impermanence of life as a *memento mori*, but flower painters of the 17th and 18th centuries depict them more often as botanical jewels. Artists may show rare or unknown varieties from the New World or, by including flowers from different seasons, illustrate what it was impossible to achieve in real life, as in *A Vase of Flowers* by Ambrosius Bosschaert.

raped by Zephyr, who then made her his bride. Botticelli's *Primavera* shows the metamorphosis of Chloris, who, once caught in the embrace of Zephyr, began to sprout flowers, and was transformed into Flora. Flora enjoyed perpetual spring in a garden of countless flowers and fruit, where the Graces twined garlands for their hair, and Flora scattered seeds to bring colour to the monochrome earth. In Poussin's *Garden* or *Kingdom of Flora*, she is seen with youths who were turned into flowers: Ajax, Hyacinthus, Narcissus, Crocus[2] and Adonis.

Fools and Folly

From the Middle Ages to the 17th century jesters were the licensed fools of royalty and aristocracy. Giotto's

Folly is a fat youth with a feathered crown, tattered tunic and club. In Bronzino's *Allegory of Love*, Folly is a young boy about to throw petals over Venus; he has bells around his ankles and is grinning, unaware of a thorn piercing his foot.

Fortuna
The classical goddess Fortuna was depicted with a cornucopia, representing the favours she so unevenly meted out. She may appear blindfolded with a wheel or a globe which spins in reference to her inconstancy. She may also stand on gaming dice or have billowing "sails" of drapery, which refer to the variable winds of chance.

Fountain
A fountain may symbolize the waters of eternal life, as in Van Eyck's *Adoration of the Lamb*; it may also represent purification, as in the legend of the unicorn. A popular myth in the 15th century was the Fountain of Youth, which was painted by an anonymous artist (Castello, Mantua): it was thought that when aged people drank from it they were immediately rejuvenated. Bernini's flamboyantly sculpted *Fountain of the Four Rivers* in Rome represents the continents. Ornamental fountains, surmounted by naked Cupids, flow in arcadian Gardens of Love.

Four Crowned Martyrs or Saints
Roman legend claims that there were four skilled sculptors who refused to fashion an idol for the Emperor Diocletian or to make sacrifices to pagan gods. They were encased alive in lead coffins and thrown into the sea.[1] A church is dedicated to these *Quattro Santi Coronati*, as they were called in Italian, on the Caelian Hill, Rome, where 16th-century frescoes show them being forced into their coffins. They were the patron saints of stonemasons; their sculpted images by Nanni di Banco were placed in the niche of the masons' guild on the exterior of Orsanmichele, Florence.

Francis of Assisi, Saint
Francis[1] (*c.*1181–1226) was the son of a wealthy merchant. He led an extravagant life but, aged about 20, after several illnesses and a military expedition, he became pious, solitary, and devoted to God. In 1210, Pope Innocent III sent him and 11 followers to preach under the name of the Friars Minor; their headquarters was established near his native Assisi. Many followed his example, particularly St Clare, and took the vows of chastity, poverty and obedience. Francis tried three times to preach to the Muslims. He set out on a pilgrimage to the Holy Land but was shipwrecked in 1212. Two years later sickness forced him to abandon a journey to the moors in Spain. In Egypt in 1219, he succeeded in preaching to the Sultan. In 1224, while praying in the Apennines, he received the "stigmata", the marks of the five wounds of Christ, which never left him.

St Francis is seen as a tonsured middle-aged man, wearing the brown habit of his Order, and a rope girdle with three knots representing the three vows. He may be depicted barefoot holding the lily of purity or showing his stigmata. In Spanish Counter-Reformation art he is often be shown at prayer. Zurbarán represents him kneeling in

Fountain: *see*
ELEMENTS; Unicorn

Four Crowned Martyrs, Saints: *see*
Martyrs
[1] *Golden Legend, The Four Crowned Martyrs*

Francis of Assisi, Saint: *see*
RELIGIOUS ORDERS
[1] *Golden Legend, St Francis*

St Francis, after St Francis Preaching to the Birds *by Giotto (Church of San Francesco, Assisi, 1287–99).*

meditation, holding a skull.

Several panel paintings and cycles showing episodes from the life of St Francis are displayed in monasteries of his Order. Panels by Sassetta (*Scenes from the Life of St Francis of Assisi*) were originally painted for the alterpiece of the church of San Francesco in San Sepolcro. The most famous fresco cycle is that painted by Giotto and his assistants at San Francesco, Assisi.

Even as a youth Francis was worthy of veneration; a man from Assissi spread his cloak before him. He was dedicated to his "Lady Poverty" and gave alms whenever he could. At his conversion he gave his cloak to a poor soldier. The following night he dreamed of a fine palace containing weapons with crosses; he thought that this was a sign of a military career but later understood it to be a vision of the Order he would found.

At prayer in the church of San Damiano he heard the voice of Christ saying, "Francis, repair my falling house"; and he did so, paying for the work from his father's coffers. His father disinherited him and took him to the Bishop of Arezzo. Francis immediately threw off his clothes to symbolize his renunciation of all wordly goods, and the bishop covered him with his own cloak.

To maintain his chastity Francis would throw himself into a thorny bush or roll about in the snow when tempted by the flesh. Initially Pope Innocent III had reservations about confirming Francis' Order because he thought the rules too severe, but after a dream that the Lateran Basilica was collapsing and that Francis held it up, he confirmed Francis' brotherhood.

Francis was renowned for preaching to the birds. When swallows were chattering he ordered them to be silent and they obeyed; he called all animals his brothers and sisters.

Other episodes painted from St Francis' life include his dream of beautiful thrones in heaven: a voice told him that riches were reserved for him there. He is said to have gone to Arezzo, where he saw demons enjoying civil strife, and ordered his companions to exorcize them. In Syria, Francis proved his faith by walking through fire, which left him unharmed. It was here also that he answered a cry for water by conjuring up a stream.

In order to illustrate the Nativity, he placed a doll in a humble straw manger and thus began the tradition of the Christmas crib.

He was invited to dine with a devout knight and, foreseeing the host's imminent death, suggested that he make his confession. The knight obeyed and promptly died. Francis then became a vehicle for the voice of the Holy Spirit and was even asked to

FURIES
Born from the goddess Gaea or from the blood of the castrated Uranus, the Furies administered revenge, especially on behalf of families. Alternatively, they were the daughters of the Roman god of the Underworld, Pluto. Their heads were covered with serpents and they breathed vengeance and pestilence. They are the usual attendants of Mars, the Roman god of war. Their names were sometimes said to have been Alecto ("relentless"), Megaira ("resentful") and Tisiphomne ("avenger of murder"). The Furies are seen dragging Mars away from Peace in Rubens' *Allegory of Peace and War*.

The Furies, after a painting formerly attributed to Bronzino (17th century, private collection).

FURIES: *see* Mars

speak before Pope Honorius III.

On Francis' death a friar saw the soul of the saint rise to heaven on a white cloud, and a doubting knight was converted by touching the saint's stigmata. Once dead, Francis was succesfully invoked in order to heal a wounded man, to restore a woman to life to make her confession, and to free a penitent heretic.

Francis Xavier, Saint
Francis (1506–52) became a follower of St Ignatius Loyola while studying at the University of Paris, and was one of the first of seven Jesuits who dedicated themselves to God in 1534. In 1541 he went as a missionary to Portuguese India for seven years. Then he went on to Japan for two years, and then to China, where he was taken ill and died. The patron saint of missionaries, Francis Xavier is seen in Jesuit habit tending the sick, or he is shown dying in ecstasy, as in Baciccia's altarpiece in Sant' Andrea al Quirinale, Rome.

Fruit
A cornucopia, represented as a horn or an ornamental bowl, offers an abundant supply of fruit and illustrates nature's bounty. It is often depicted with Ceres (in Greek myth, Demeter), the goddess of agriculture, and with personifications of Abundance, Peace or Summer. Fruit may be included in still-life painting to illustrate the transience of life: Caravaggio's *Bacchus* includes a still-life detail of over-ripe fruit. Exotic or out-of-season fruit might suggest wealth. However, sometimes fruit is chosen as a subject purely to demonstrate the artist's skill.

FURIES
See panel, above.

Francis Xavier, Saint: *see* Ignatius Loyola, St

Fruit: *see* Apple; Pomegranate; Proserpina

Gabriel, Archangel: *see* ANGELS; Daniel; Virgin
[1] *Daniel 8:16*
[2] *Luke 1:28*

Galatea: *see* Polyphemus
[1] Ovid, *Met XIII:738–897*

Gabriel, Archangel
Gabriel was one of God's principal winged messengers and, in particular, brought news of birth. In the Old Testament he explains the visions of Daniel;[1] in the New Testament he is identified with the angel who announced the birth of John the Baptist to Zacharias, and of Christ to the Virgin Mary. His words to Mary were, "Hail, thou that art highly favoured, the Lord is with thee; blessed art thou among women."[2] The Latin equivalent, "*Ave gratia plena Dominus tecum*" or "*Ave Maria*", may be written on paintings of the Annunciation – for example, Simone Martini's. Gabriel often offers the Virgin the lily of purity, which, therefore, may be considered his attribute.

A detail of Gabriel, after Buoninsegna's The Annunciation *(1311, National Gallery, London).*

Galatea
In mythology,[1] the sea-nymph Galatea was in love with the handsome Acis, but she was herself pursued by the giant Cyclops, Polyphemus, a savage monster who raised sheep on an island generally thought to be Sicily. Polyphemus climbed a hill overlooking the sea, and here he played his pipe of a hundred reeds and sang a pastoral love song to Galatea. Later, however,

the Cyclops saw her lying in Acis' arms; so he chased the youth, hurling a huge lump of the mountainside at him, whereupon Acis was turned into a river. Raphael's *The Triumph of Galatea* shows her fleeing on a cockle-shell chariot fitted with paddles and drawn by dolphins; Cupids fly in the air and Tritons and Nereids play in the waves. The scene would have beautifully reflected the view outside the loggia where it was painted, since it originally overlooked the Tiber.

Ganymede

The supreme god Jupiter (in Greek myth, Zeus) fell in love with the shepherd boy Ganymede,[1] and transformed himself into an eagle in order to sweep down and snatch him up into the air. Jupiter then flew with Ganymede to Mount Olympus, where the boy became his cup-bearer. In his painting of the event Rembrandt humorously depicted the young boy as a squealing and incontinent baby.

Garden

In Genesis the Garden of Eden is described as an earthly paradise, from which God expelled Adam and Eve for eating the forbidden fruit of the Tree of Knowledge. The Virgin may be depicted in a flowery garden, which is often walled – the *Hortus Conclusus* – in reference to the Immaculate Conception of Christ. The Rhinish Master (15th century) shows this in *Paradise Garden*.

The medieval garden was confined within the precincts of castles and monasteries. In art it may be shown as a Garden of Love, embodying the pleasures and conventions of a courtier's life. Medieval gardens also appear in illustrations of the early 14th-century poem *Le Roman de la Rose*, in which the young poet is led to a Palace of Pleasure to meet Love, only to be obstructed by Danger, Fear and Slander.

In England, gardens laid out for royalty and the aristocracy were subject to fashion but also reflected social and political change. Until the 1750s geometrical designs, created with avenues, terraces and hedges, were to an extent a reflection of a hierarchical and authoritarian society. In the later 18th century, however, this regularity gave way to the open, gentle curves of Lancelot "Capability" Brown, who designed parks modelled on the classical landscapes of Claude Lorrain, and on literary descriptions of classical gardens, with statues, fountains, grottoes and walks. With the onset of the Romantic movement in 19th-century literature and painting it became fashionable to imitate wild, remote landscapes, which were often the settings for contemporary Gothic novels.

Geminianus, Saint

The bishop of Modena, Geminianus (4th century) was a friend of St Ambrose and was renowned as a healer. Legend has it that he went to Constantinople to exorcize a demon from the Emperor's daughter, and so he may be shown with a demon at his feet. Attila the Hun had a vision of the saint, as a result of which he halted his attack on Modena. Geminianus was also said to have saved Modena from floods. He is depicted by Sebastiano Mainardi as a bishop holding a model of San Gimignano, the many-towered town which adopted his name (Sant' Agostino, San Gimignano).

Ganymede: *see* Eagle; Jupiter

[1] Ovid, *Met X:155–161*

Garden: *see* Pomona and Vertumnus; Virgin, The

Geneviève, Saint: *see* Attila the Hun

George, Saint: *see* Dragon; Martyrs
[1] *Golden Legend, St George*

Geneviève, Saint
The devotion to God shown by Geneviève (*c.*AD420–500) was noticed when she was only eight years old and tending a flock of sheep. She was said to have performed several miracles during her childhood. Her prayers apparently repelled the advance on Paris of Attila the Hun. She arranged for food for the starving during the Frankish siege of Paris, and the enemy leader listened to her pleas for clemency for the captives. In 1129 an epidemic of ergot poisoning suddenly abated when her relics were carried in a procession. She is the patroness of Paris and may be shown holding the keys of the city. The Pantheon in Paris was once dedicated to her. Her story was illustrated on its walls by Puvis de Chavannes.

Genre
The term *genre* was used in the 18th century by the art critic Denis Diderot, with reference to artists who specialized in a specific type of painting. *Genre* is especially used to describe the paintings of everyday life popular in 17th-century Holland; they may illustrate a proverb or an aspect of folklore, which may have both a literal and a symbolic significance, imparting a moral message.

George, Saint
George (late 3rd or early 4th century AD) is said to have been martyred in Palestine, but no historical evidence of his life exists. Carpaccio's cycle in the Scuola di San Giorgio, Venice, depicts the legend[1] of George as a soldier who travelled to Libya where a dragon was terrifying the populace. The people of Libya appeased the monster's fury by offering it every day a youth or maiden selected by lot. Eventually the king's only daughter was picked, but George, mounted on his horse, armed himself with the sign of the Cross and gave the beast a grievous wound, forcing it to the ground. The maiden's girdle was then tied around the dragon's neck, and it followed her, like a dog on a leash, back to the city. The king and all the people were baptized into Christianity, and George slew the dragon.

George, often on a white horse, is usually shown slaying the winged beast, as in Paolo Uccello's *Saint George and the Dragon*. The theme

A detail showing St George, after St George and the Dragon *by Gustave Moreau (1826–98, National Gallery, London).*

was taken to represent the triumph of Christianity over evil. Like Christ of the Resurrection, George may hold a white banner with a red cross.

Later episodes from his life are less frequently painted. He is said to have fallen into the hands of persecutors and to have survived torture. He was subjected to the rack and fire, had salt rubbed into his wounds, was poisoned, and survived a wheel fitted with sharp knives, and a cauldron of molten lead. He is said to have prayed to God to destroy the pagan temple, whereupon the building immediately caught fire. Then he was dragged through the streets and finally he was beheaded.

George's cult was brought to Europe by the crusaders, and *c.*1348 his image was adopted by Edward III of England as the patron of the Order of the Garter. He is the protector of England.

Giants

In mythology, the giant Titans were the offspring of Uranus and Gaea. There are usually said to have been 12 of them, six males and six females, all of enormous size and strength.

According to Ovid,[1] they sought to overthrow the gods of Mount Olympus. They piled two other mountains on top of each other to reach the summit, prompting Jupiter (in Greek myth, Zeus) to hurl his thunderbolts at them to halt their attack.

The subject was popular in Baroque times: Giulio Romano's *trompe l'œil* frescoes in the Palazzo del Tè, Mantua, were an example to later artists of the dramatic possibilities offered by the episode.

In the Old Testament David slew the giant Goliath in single combat during the war between the Israelites and Philistines, an act that ultimately led to his succession as king of Israel.

St Christopher, the patron saint of travellers, is often represented as a giant, carrying the Christ Child in his arms or on his shoulders.

Gideon

In the Old Testament Gideon was one of the judges of Israel. He was threshing wheat when an angel told him that he would save his people from the Midianites.

However, he needed repeated proofs of God's support, to confirm his own and his followers' faith, so he laid a fleece on the ground and asked God that the morning dew should fall only on the fleece and not on the ground. In the morning he wrung a bowlful of water from the fleece yet the ground had remained dry. The next night he asked for the reverse to happen, and indeed the following morning the fleece was dry while the ground was covered in dew.[1]

Gideon did not wish to conquer with superior numbers so, with God's guidance, he carefully selected 300 men from his troops – numbering more than 30,000 in all – by leading them to water: those who drank like dogs – an unwise action when the enemy is nearby – were dismissed; those who drank from water cupped in their hands were enlisted. Gideon and his troops attacked at night, blowing on trumpets, crying, "The sword of the Lord, and of Gideon." and the Midianites fled[2]

In *The Battle of Gideon Against the Midianites* Poussin painted a night scene in which the trumpeters are seen causing chaos; and in *The Sword of the Lord of Gideon* Stanley Spencer showed tents collapsing to reveal the startled Midianites.

Giles, Saint

Little is known of Giles, who may have been a hermit near Arles, in the south of France, some time before the 9th century AD. He was highly

Giants: *see* Christopher, St; David
[1] Ovid, *Met 1:151–162*

Gideon:
[1] *Judges 6:36–40*
[2] *Judges 7:5–21*

Glaucus and Scylla:
[1] Ovid, *Met XIII:898–968* and *XIV:1–74*

Globe: *see* Fortune; God

popular in the late Middle Ages, and over 150 churches in England were dedicated to him.

The Master of St Giles (*c*.1500) shows the episode when a deer, which had been wounded by hunters, came to Giles for protection. When the hunters eventually tracked down the deer, they found that the arrow had transferred itself from the animal to the saint. The deer is the attribute of St Giles, who may also be shown with an arrow in his arm.

Glaucus and Scylla

In mythology,[1] the nymph Scylla was bathing in the cool water of a secluded cove when Glaucus appeared before her. Once a fisherman, Glaucus had been transformed into a sea-god when he had eaten a herb that rendered fish immortal: he is depicted with a rusty green beard, sweeping hair, huge shoulders, dark blue arms, and a writhing fish-tail for legs. He fell in love with Scylla, pursued her and appealed to her with his story. Scylla rejected him, so Glaucus turned to the sorceress Circe for help to win his love. However, Circe fell in love with him; when he rejected her, she turned Scylla into a sea-monster. In *Glaucus and Scylla*, Salvator Rosa shows Scylla shrinking from Glaucus as he rises from the waters.

*A detail showing Glaucus and Scylla, after a painting by Salvator Rosa (*c.*1650, National Gallery, Brussels).*

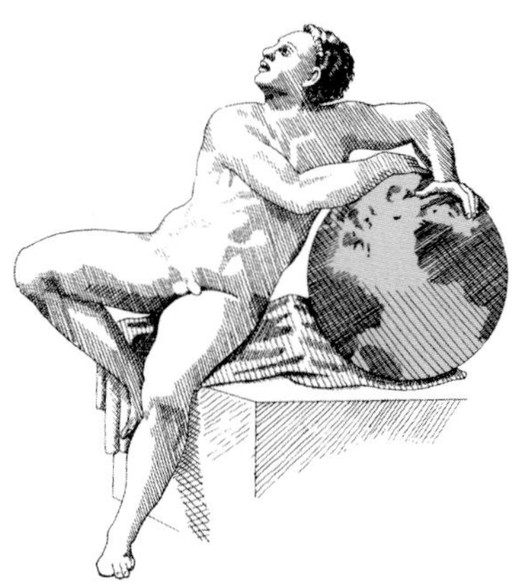

A detail showing a man leaning on a globe, after Der Traum *(National Gallery, Vienna), an engraving after a work by Michelangelo .*

Globe

A globe or sphere may be held in the hand of a deity or monarch to signify dominion. Surmounted by a cross it represents Christ's rule; alternatively, God may stand on a globe as the great architect of the world. A globe may be held by personifications of the Virtues, indicating their universal significance, but Fortune may also stand on a globe as a symbol of her inconstancy.

In Hans Holbein's *The Ambassadors* the inclusion of a globe with other learned objects may signify education. In the 17th century, a period of discovery and expansion, globes and maps reveal an interest in new territories; they may also refer to the

GODS AND GODDESSES OF CLASSICAL MYTHOLOGY

Set out below are the most important Roman gods and goddesses and their Greek equivalents. The summit of Mount Olympus in Greece was thought to be their home, set in a cloudless sea of limpid air, illuminated by white radiance. Episodes from the lives of the gods and the myths about them provided artists with a variety of subjects. As personifications of human qualities, gods and goddesses play an important role in allegory.

Roman deity	Greek deity	Associations
Apollo	Apollo	Light; the arts; healing
Bacchus	Dionysos	Wine; ecstasy
Ceres	Demeter	Agriculture
Cupid	Eros	Love
Diana	Artemis	Hunting; chastity; the moon
Juno	Hera	Queen of heaven; marriage
Jupiter	Zeus	Supreme deity; ruler of the skies
Mars	Ares	War
Mercury	Hermes	Communication
Minerva	Athene	Wisdom
Neptune	Poseidon	Ruler of the seas
Pluto/Dis Pater	Hades	Ruler of the Underworld
Saturn	Cronus	Agriculture; time
Venus	Aphrodite	Love and beauty
Vesta	Hestia	Home and hearth
Vulcan	Hephaestus	Forge and fire

GODS AND GODDESSES OF CLASSICAL MYTHOLOGY: *see* Giants; and individual names

absence of someone on a journey abroad. In Dutch painting a globe or map combined with other references to sensual delights often alluded to earthly desires, as in Willem Buytewech's *Merry Company*.

Goat

The goat carries both mythological and religious significance. The animal was sacred to the Roman supreme god Jupiter (in Greek myth, Zeus), because a she-goat had suckled him. Goats may also be associated with Bacchus or Pan and his lusty satyrs. The goat is the Zodiac sign of Capricorn.

Among the Israelites a goat was sacrificed to the Lord, and the scapegoat took the sins of the world into the wilderness.[1] Holman Hunt painted a forlorn image of *The Scapegoat*.

In the Gospel of St Matthew goats are likened to the unbelievers: when all nations come before Christ, "he shall separate them one from another, as a shepherd divideth his sheep from the goats."[2]

Goat: *see* Amalthea; Zodiac
[1] *Leviticus 16:10*
[2] *Matthew 25:32*

God

In the New Testament Christ told his disciples to "teach all nations, baptizing them in the name of the

God: *see* Alpha and Omega; Hand; Trinity
[1] *Matthew 28:19*

Graces, Three: *see* Venus

Grammar: *see* LIBERAL ARTS

[1] Plutarch, *Moralia, The Education of Children 9*

A detail after an illustration in the French Bible Historiale *of 1411 showing God in the act of creation.*

Father, and of the Son, and of the Holy Ghost",[1] from which the doctrine of the Holy Trinity derives.

In late medieval imagery God may be shown as part of the Trinity: either as the Father, creating the world; or in the shape of Christ; or, as the Holy Ghost, in an Annunciation, represented by shafts of light or by a dove.

In the Renaissance God came to be depicted as a static, paternal figure with long white hair and a beard, as in Masaccio's *Trinity*. Michelangelo's representation of God creating the world (Sistine Chapel, Rome) has affinities with depictions of Jupiter (in Greek myth, Zeus).

The attributes of God may be a triangular halo representing the Trinity, a globe in order to represent his capacity as the creator of the world, or an *alpha* and *omega* to signify his position as the beginning and the end of all things.

GODS AND GODDESSES OF CLASSICAL MYTHOLOGY

See panel on previous page.

A detail showing the Three Graces, after Botticelli's Primavera *(c.1478, Uffizi, Florence).*

Graces, Three

In mythology the Three Graces were personifications of beauty and charm, and attended a greater goddess, usually Venus (Aphrodite), the goddess of love, whose attributes they adopted. Their names are said to have been Aglaia, Euphrosyne and Thalia. The depiction of three beautiful women, inspired by classical prototypes, was popular with both painters and sculptors: famous examples are the painting by Rubens and the sculpture by Canova.

Grammar

One of the Liberal Arts, Grammar was described as the "learned and articulate voice, spoken in a correct manner", and was traditionally depicted as a sage, or a teacher with a whip for discipline. In the 17th century

A detail after The Allegorical Figure of Grammar *by Laurent de la Hyre (1650, National Gallery, London).*

a new image emerged, showing Grammar as a woman watering plants: "Just as plants are nourished by moderate application of water in succession, in the same fashion, the mind is made to grow by properly adapted tasks."[1] This idea was taken up by Laurent de la Hyre in his *Allegorical Figure of Grammar.*

Granida and Daifilo

The first pastoral play written in Dutch, *Granida*, by Pieter Hooft, was performed in 1605 and inspired several artists during the 17th century. Granida, daughter of the king of Persia, lost her way while hunting and came across the shepherd Daifilo, who fell in love with her at first sight. He followed her back to court and became the page of Tisiphernes, a prince who asked for Granida's hand in marriage. Granida had several suitors and decided that the one who defeated all his rivals in a series of duels should become her husband. Daifilo fought in Tisiphernes' place and was the victor. Granida and Daifilo eloped but they were caught and taken prisoner. Tisiphernes, moved by their love, intervened and eventually Granida and Daifilo married. Gerrit van Honthorst, in *Granida and Daifilo* (1625), was perhaps the first to paint these lovers.

Gregory the Great, Saint

Gregory (*c.* AD540–604) was one of four Latin Doctors of the Church, the others being Saints Ambrose, Augustine and Jerome. Gregory, known as "the Great", was elected Pope in AD590. He was a remarkable administrator and a prolific writer, and spent large amounts of money on those suffering through war, illness and hunger, sending missionaries throughout Europe. Missions were sent especially to England because Gregory saw some Anglo-Saxon slaves in a Roman market; when he was told their nationality, he replied, "*Non Angli, sed Angeli*" ("Not Angles, but Angels").[2]

In AD590 a virulent plague swept through Rome. As Gregory led a procession past Hadrian's mausoleum, he had a vision of the Archangel Michael on the top of the tomb. Michael indicated that the plague would soon be over. A chapel was built on the spot and the structure was renamed the Castel Sant'Angelo.

Gregory is thought to have been concerned with liturgical music and to have established what is known as the Gregorian chant.

He is usually shown as an elderly pope, often with the three other Doctors of the Church. He may have a dove, which whispers in his ear, inspiring his writings. Some Flemish and German paintings of the Renaissance show him kneeling at an altar, relating to the legend that when Gregory prayed for a sign to convert a disbeliever in his congregation, Christ

Gregory the Great, Saint: *see* Ambrose, St; Augustine, St; Doctors; Jerome, St; Michael, St; Trajan

[1] *Golden Legend, St Gregory*

Guarini:
[1] Guarini, *The Faithful Shepherd Act 2*
[2] Guarini, *The Faithful Shepherd Act 4*

Guilds of Florence, The: *see* individual names of saints

Gyges and King Candaules:
[1] Herodotus, *I:8–12*

on the cross appeared above the altar, with the instruments of his Passion.

Grotesque
The term, derived from the Italian *grotta* (meaning "cave"), originated at the end of the 15th century, when lavishly decorated chambers were discovered in the Golden House of Nero (1st century AD). This style of decoration interweaves humans, animals, flowers and foliage, classical urns and motifs. It was especially popular in the 16th century.

Guarini, Giovanni (Il Pastor Fido)
The play *Il Pastor Fido* (The Faithful Shepherd) of 1590 by Giovanni Guarini, which combines tragedy and comedy, provided artists with pastoral scenes populated by beautiful nymphs. Mirtillo, disguised as a woman, joins the game of kissing the nymph Amarillis and at his turn falls in love with her. Amarillis awards him the crown of victory, but he places it on her head, saying that it was her kisses that had made his so sweet.[1] The scene was illustrated by van Dyck in *Amaryllis and Mirtillo*.

The play includes a satyr who grabs the nymph Corisca by the hair, accusing her of deceiving him, but she eludes him by wearing a wig. Meanwhile, the nymph Dorinda is in love with the rich, gallant and beautiful Silvio, who enjoys only the hunt and is unaffected by love. Dorinda, disguised as a shepherd to be near her love, falls asleep under a bush; Silvio unwittingly shoots her with an arrow.[2]

Guilds of Florence, The
In the early Renaissance the guilds of mercantile Florence were leading patrons of the building and decoration of many of the city's principal monuments. For example, they commissioned statues of their patron saints to fill the niches of Orsanmichele, the guilds' church. These included St George, patron saint of the Armourers' Guild; the Four Crowned Martyrs, the Stonemasons' and Woodworkers'; St Philip, the Shoemakers'; St Peter, the Butchers'; St Luke, the Lawyers'; St Joseph, the Furriers'; St Mark, the Linen-workers'; St Eligius, the Smiths'; St Matthew, the Bankers'; St John the Evangelist, the Silk Guild; and St Stephen, the Wool Guild. They also commissioned a statue of St John the Baptist, who was the patron saint of the Cloth merchants' Guild, as well as of the city itself.

Gyges and King Candaules
In the most popularly painted tale of Gyges and Candaules, Gyges was the favourite bodyguard of Candaules, king of Lydia. Candaules thought that his wife was the most beautiful woman in the world.

To prove her beauty, he asked Gyges watch her undressing. Gyges was unwilling because "with the stripping off of her tunic, a woman is stripped of the honour due to her". The king, however, insisted. Jacob Jordaens' *King Candaules of Lydia Showing his Wife to Gyges* shows the naked queen about to climb into bed, while the two men peep around the curtain. The story tells how she noticed Gyges slipping away and in outrage made him choose either to die or to kill the king. Gyges chose the latter, thereby making himself master of the king's wife and territory.[1]

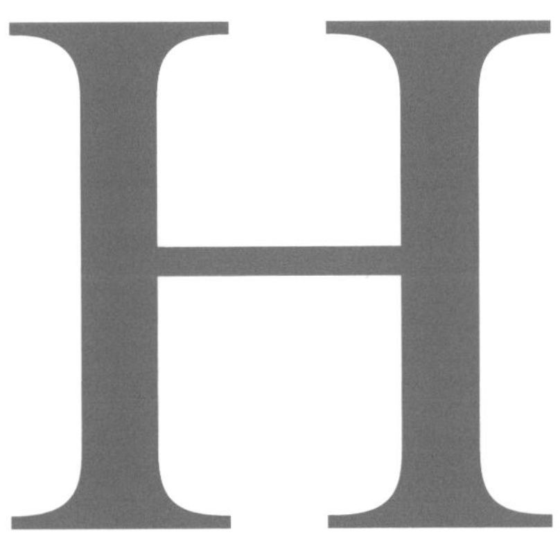

Habakkuk

In the Old Testament book of Habakkuk the prophet prays to God for revenge on the oppressors of his people. Donatello's sculpture *Habakkuk* shows the prophet's harrowed features, while Bernini's of the same name depicts the story of him taking pottage to Daniel in the lions' den. Habakkuk was transported from Judea by an angel who "carried him by the hair of his head and ... set him in Babylon over the den".[1] Habakkuk delivered his food to Daniel and was then returned to Judea by the angel.

Hades

In mythology Hades was originally the Greek god who ruled the Underworld, his Roman equivalent being Pluto or Dis. Later, Hades became the name of the Underworld itself: a gloomy underground region where departed souls went. Its entrance was guarded by the three-headed watchdog Cerberus.

Hades was reached through natural chasms and was situated on the further shore of one of the five rivers of Hades, the Styx (hate), across which the souls of the dead were ferried by Charon. The other rivers of Hades were the Acheron (woe), Cocytus (wailing), Lethe (forgetfulness), and Phlegethon (fire). Minos was the judge of dead souls, directing them to their final abode, which for most was the dreary Plain of Asphodel. Virtuous souls were rewarded with the paradisal Fields of Elysium. However, gloomy Tartarus, where unbearable torments were only temporarily eased by Orpheus' music, was the destiny for those who had outraged the gods. It is this last area that equates with the Christian perception of hell, and was painted in Pieter Bruegel the Younger's *Rape of Persephone*.

HALO

See panel on following page.

Hand

References to the hand of God are numerous in the Old Testament. A hand in painting often represents God the Father, because of an implicit

Habakkuk: *see* Daniel

[1] *Apocrypha, Bel and the Dragon*

Hades: *see* Cerberus; Ixion; Pluto; Passion of Christ; Proserpina; Sisyphus; Tantalus; Tityos

Hand: *see* Christ, The Life of; Pantocrator; Passion of Christ

[1] *Exodus 33:20*

HALO

In Christian art a halo or nimbus is the light shining around the head of the divine.

Haloes appeared in art from the 5th century AD, but were little used after the Baroque. They are commonly depicted as circular, but those of Christ or God the Father may be triangular to represent the Trinity; Christ might also have a cross behind his head for a halo. An aureole or mandorla – a larger area of light, sometimes surrounding the whole figure – is reserved for God the Father, Christ and the Virgin.

Above: *A detail after* The Virgin and Child with Angels *by a follower of Fra Angelico (National Gallery, London).*

Top right: *An eastern Orthodox halo, after* Christ's Blessing *(School of Nonantola, 9th century).*
Bottom right: *The mandorla, after* Christ Enthroned *(12th-century Romanesque Gospel).*

HALO: *see* Almond; Saints

Hannibal: *see* Elephants

prohibition on depicting his head: "Thou canst not see my face; for no man shall see me and live."[1] God's hand may be seen releasing the dove at the Annunciation to the Virgin.

A hand paying Judas the 30 pieces of silver or holding a bag of coins denotes the Betrayal of Christ. A hand also became an Instrument of the Passion owing to the scene in which Christ's face was slapped during his mockery; this incident is shown in a fresco by Fra Angelico in San Marco, Florence. Traditionally, the right hand was considered powerful, the left weak.

Hannibal

A great Carthaginian leader, Hannibal (247–182BC) marched an army reported to consist of 90,000 infantry, 12,000 cavalry and a number of elephants across the Alps in 218BC during the second Punic War against Rome. In *Snow Storm: Hannibal and his Army Crossing the Alps* Turner shows how the mighty army, which astounded the Romans, also had to battle with the forces of nature.

Harpy

In mythology a harpy was a monster with a woman's face and breasts and the body, claws and wings of a bird. Harpies defiled everything they touched and were thought to be the grasping, greedy administrators of the gods, or the beasts that snatched the soul away at death. Mantegna's *Allegory of the Fall of Ignorant*

A harpy, after an engraving in Aldrovanoi's Ornithologia, *Volume I Lib. X (1599).*

Humanity shows them supporting a globe on which the fat figure of Ignorance sits holding a rudder, flanked by blindfolded Ingratitude and scrawny Avarice.

Elsewhere harpies appear as decorative motifs on furniture: the harpy table-leg in Cesare da Sesto's *Salome* contributes to the sinister atmosphere of the subject.

Harvest

Harvesting may be part of a scene representing August or Summer, and may represent nature's abundance. However, Jean-François Millet's *The Gleaners* subverts the usual mood: the peasants are so poor that they have to collect the remains left by the harvesters.

Hate

Hate is the pale, filthy guide of Calumny, who is the personification of slander. Mantegna depicted Hate, Fraud, Malice, Jealousy and Suspicion in *Minerva Expelling the Vices from the Garden of Virtue*. In this painting, Hate is a monkey-like hermaphrodite with only one breast. Four bags containing the seeds of evil hang from the creature's shoulders.

Heart

A heart most commonly symbolizes divine love and understanding because "the Lord seeth not as man seeth; for man looketh on the outward appearance, but the Lord looketh on the heart".[1] A flaming heart, sometimes pierced by an arrow, may be held by saints noted for especially fervent religious devotion, such as St Augustine. The attribute of St Ignatius Loyola is the "sacred heart", which is crowned with thorns.

Heaven

In European paintings Heaven, where God abides with the angels and saints, is often represented as a vast blue arch with stars or clouds, or a heavenly garden. It may also be indicated by gates through which divine light shines. In Nardo and Andrea Orcagna's *Paradise* Heaven is a populous throng of saints and angels.

Hecate

The goddess Hecate was associated with black magic and the Underworld. At night she was thought to hold burning torches at crossroads, accompanied by ghosts and hell-hounds. Later, she was depicted as having three bodies, which stood back-to-back looking in different directions.[1] She appears in Shakespeare's *Macbeth* with the three witches and was illustrated by William Blake in his engravings of the play.

Helen of Troy

Outstandingly beautiful, Helen was believed to be the daughter of the god

Harvest: *see*
SEASONS; TIME

Hate: *see*
Calumny

Heart: *see*
Augustine, St; Ignatius Loyola, St
[1] *I Samuel 16:7*

Heaven: *see*
God

Hecate:
[1] Ovid, *Fasti I:141–144*

Helen of Troy: *see*
Feast of the Gods; Leda; Paris; Trojan War
[1] Ovid, *Met XII:1–10*

Helena, Saint: *see* Constantine; True Cross
[1] *Golden Legend, The Birth of Our Lord Jesus Christ, St Silvester, The Epiphany of the Lord*

Heliodorus:
[1] *Apocrypha, II Maccabees 3*

Hell: *see* Hades; Last Judgment
[1] *Matthew 13:41,42*
[2] *Matthew 25:41*

Jupiter (in Greek myth, Zeus) and Leda, whom he ravished in the form of a swan. The wife of the Greek leader Menelaus, Helen was given as a prize to the Trojan prince Paris for judging Venus (Aphrodite) more beautiful than Minerva (Athene) or Juno (Hera). Helen and Paris eloped to Troy, but were pursued by ships bearing Greek warriors, aiming to reclaim Menelaus' wife. This series of events began the Trojan War.[1] *The Abduction of Helen*, by a follower of Fra Angelico, was part of the embellishment for a piece of domestic furniture. Jacques-Louis David portrays Helen blinded by infatuation in *The Love of Paris and Helen*.

Helena (Helen), Saint

The empress Helena (*c.*AD255–330) was the mother of Constantine, the first Christian emperor. Toward the end of her life she made a pilgrimage to the Holy Land, where she donated large amounts of money to the poor and founded churches on holy sites. According to legend,[1] Helena brought to Rome the hay from the manger in which the Christ Child had lain. She also brought to Constantinople the bodies of the Magi, which were later taken to Milan and then Cologne. She is said to have discovered the wood of the True Cross on which Christ was crucified, and may be shown in scenes of the wood's discovery. In a painting by Cornelis Engelbrechtsz she appears beside Constantine, holding a cross and wearing imperial dress.

A detail showing St Helena, after St Helena and the Miracle of the True Cross *attributed to Simon Marmion, (late 15th century, Louvre, Paris).*

Heliodorous

In the Apocrypha[1] Heliodorus, treasurer to the Syrian king, was sent to Jerusalem to sequester from the Temple of Solomon funds that had been collected for widows and orphans. Raphael's *Expulsion of Heliodorus from the Temple* (Vatican Stanze, Rome) shows how, once Heliodorus had taken the money, the priests prayed, and God sent a horse and rider, with two companions, who charged, driving the thief to the ground. This was seen as an example of divine intervention for the Church.

Hell

In the New Testament Christ speaks of the unquenchable fire reserved for unbelievers, proclaiming that he "will send his angels, and they will gather ... all the evil doers, and throw them into a furnace of fire and there shall be wailing and gnashing of teeth".[1] At the Last Judgment he will condemn those who have not lived according to the seven acts of mercy, saying, "Depart from me, ye cursed, into everlasting fire, prepared for the devil and his angels."[2]

In depictions of the Last Judgment hell is always to the bottom right of the composition – that is, on Christ's left – so that the good can rise on his strong right side. The entrance to hell may be depicted as the jaws of the gaping monster Leviathan. The infernal realm may be filled with flames and monsters or composed of successive circles of the damned, as described in Dante's *Inferno*, illustrated closely by Botticelli. Alternatively, groups of the damned are organized and tortured according to which of the seven deadly sins they have committed. In Michelangelo's *Last Judgment* (Sistine Chapel, Vatican, Rome) Charon, ferryman of the Underworld, and Minos, judge of the dead, are borrowed from Hades, the ancient Greek predecessor of hell.

Hercules

Hercules (in Greek myth, Heracles) had superhuman strength and is depicted as a huge, muscular figure with a club, wearing the skin of the Nemean Lion. The classical statue known as the *Farnese Hercules*, discovered in 1540, provided the prototype for numerous images of the hero. He may be a personification of strength, courage and endurance, and his story was also treated as an allegory of good vanquishing evil.

Hercules was the son of the supreme god Jupiter (in Greek myth, Zeus) and the mortal Alcmena. When Hercules was eight months old, Juno (Hera), Jupiter's wife, outraged by her husband's infidelity, sent two huge snakes to kill the baby in his cradle, but he strangled them with his bare hands. As an adult, having been driven mad by Juno,[1] he threw his own children into a fire. In punishment he had to serve Eurystheus, king of the Tiryns, for 12 years. The king set Hercules following 12 dangerous tasks, which he completed successfully, aided by the goddess Minerva (Athene):[2]

1. THE NEMEAN LION Hercules tracked down this invincible beast, choked it to death, skinned it, and donned its pelt, which made him invulnerable. He is often depicted forcing the lion's jaws open.

2. THE LERNEAN HYDRA The monstrous Hydra had nine heads, one of which was immortal. The monster and Hercules are often shown locked in combat. With the help of a companion, Iolaus, Hercules decapitated the Hydra and cauterized the stumps to prevent the heads from growing again. Once the monster was dead, Hercules dipped his arrows in its blood to give them poisoned tips.

3. THE ARCADIAN STAG This animal, known as the Ceryneian Hind in Greek myth, was sacred to the goddess Diana (Artemis), and had golden horns. Hercules' task was to bring it back alive to Mycenae. Finally, after hunting it for a whole year, he wounded the stag and returned with it.

4. THE ERYMANTHIAN BOAR This had been ravaging the area around Mount Erymanthus. Hercules drove it into deep snow and trapped it in his net.

5. THE AUGEAN STABLES In a single day Hercules had to clear the enormous pile of dung produced over 30 years by the 3,000 cattle of Augeas, king of Elis. He succeeded by diverting two rivers to flow through the cattle-yard.

6. THE STYMPHALIAN BIRDS Lake Stymphalus, deep in Arcadia, was the roosting-place of countless murderous birds. By sounding a pair of

Hercules: *see* Amazons; Cerberus; Cornucopia; Jason; Milky Way

[1] Philostratus the Elder, *Imagines II:23*

[2] Apollodorus, *The Library II.iv.8–12* and *II.v.1–12*

[3] Hyginus, *Fabulae XXX*

[4] Apollodorus, *The Library II.v.9*

[5] Virgil, *Aeneid VIII:193–272* and Ovid, *Fasti I: 543–587*

[6] Apollodorus, *The Library II v 11*

[7] Ovid, *Fasti II 303–359*

[8] Xenophon, *Memorabilia II.i.22–34*

[9] Ovid, *Met IX:1–97*

[10] Ovid, *Met IX:98–229*, Hyginus, *XXIII–XXVI* and Philostratus the Younger, *Imagines 16*

[11] Ovid, *Met IX:229–273*

Hercules, after Zubarán's Hercules Seared by the Poisoned Robe *(1634, Prado, Madrid).*

golden castanets given to him by Minerva, Hercules frightened the birds and shot them as they soared.

7. THE CRETAN BULL Hercules went to Crete to capture this savage, fire-breathing creature, which he brought back to Eurystheus.

8. THE HORSES OF DIOMEDES The war-like king Diomedes of Thrace possessed man-eating mares. Hercules slew the king and fed his body to the mares, which then became tame.

9. THE GIRDLE OF HIPPOLYTA Hercules and his companions set out to win this belt from the warrior Hippolyta, queen of the Amazons. A pitched battle ensued in which Hercules killed Hippolyta and secured her belt.

10. THE OXEN OF GERYON Geryon, a three-bodied monster, kept red oxen guarded by a two-headed hound and a giant herdsman. Hercules sailed to his island in the west, on the way setting up the Pillars of Hercules, usually thought to be the rocks either side of the Straits of Gibraltar. He killed the dog, herdsman and Geryon, and brought the oxen back to Greece.

11. THE APPLES OF THE HESPERIDES These had been given by the earth-goddess Gaea to Juno. They were tended by the Hesperides, "daughters of evening", and guarded by a hundred-headed dragon in the Atlas mountains. Hercules slew the dragon and returned to Eurystheus with the apples; in alternative myths, he persuaded the giant Atlas, who held the heavens on his shoulders, to fetch them while Hercules took his place.

12. CERBERUS Pluto granted that Hercules could take his three-headed guard dog, Cerberus, from the Underworld, if he could master it without weapons. In the struggle poisonous aconites grew where foam fell from Cerberus' mouths. Hercules presented the dog to Eurystheus before returning it to the Underworld.

Stories from the Labours of Hercules were selected to make an oblique reference to the power of the patron. For example, Vasari painted *Labours of Hercules* for Duke Cosimo I; and Guido Reni painted the same subject for Ferdinando Gonzaga, duke of Mantua. The depiction of Hercules resting from his labours was also popular. Other adventures of Hercules often depicted are:

HERCULES AND EURYTION According to the Latin author Hyginus (1st century AD), Hercules attacked and slew the centaur Eurytion, whom he found raping a girl.[3]

HERCULES AND HESIONE Laomedon, king of Troy, was ordered to assuage the gods' displeasure by sacrificing his daughter Hesione to a sea-monster. Hercules killed the monster and rescued Hesione.[4]

HERCULES AND CACUS The monster Cacus terrorized the country around the Aventine Hill, near the site of Rome, and tried to steal some of Geryon's cattle from Hercules. But the hero cornered the monster and strangled him. Hercules thereby made the founding of Rome possible.[5]

HERCULES AND ANTAEUS On the quest for the apples of the Hesperides Hercules wrestled with the giant Antaeus, whose strength came from the earth. Hercules lifted him off the ground long enough to strangle him.[6]

HERCULES AND OMPHALE Hercules murdered his friend Iphitus in a fit of madness. In punishment, Mercury (Hermes) sold him to Omphale, the widowed queen of Lydia. Taking Hercules as her lover, they exchanged clothes. In such array they feasted and fell asleep side by side. Pan, smitten with love for the queen, crept into Hercules' bed, thinking the hero to be his love, and was ejected forthwith.[7]

HERCULES AT THE CROSSROADS When passing from boyhood to youth, Hercules had to choose between a life of virtue or of vice. Two women of great stature appeared: Virtue was fair to look upon; Vice was plump, soft and seductive. Each wanted him to follow her, but he chose Virtue.[8]

HERCULES AND ACHELOUS The river-god Achelous fought Hercules for the hand of the princess Deianeira. In the contest Achelous turned himself at first into a snake, then into a bull. Hercules flung himself around the bull's neck and, forcing its head to the ground, broke off one of its horns, which some accounts say became the cornucopia.[9]

HERCULES AND NESSUS The centaur Nessus attempted to abduct Hercules' wife, Deianeira, for which Hercules shot him with a poisoned arrow. Dying, the centaur gave Deianeira his shirt, soaked in his poisoned blood, pretending that it was a love charm. Later, to win back Hercules' affection from Princess Iole, Deianeira sent a messenger, Lichas, to throw the shirt around Hercules and the poison drove him mad. He seized Lichas and flung him into the sea. As Lichas flew through the air, fear drained away the messenger's blood and he turned to stone.[10]

THE APOTHEOSIS OF HERCULES Racked with pain from the poisoned shirt, the wounded warrior built his pyre and lay down on it, the skin of the Nemean Lion beneath him, his head resting on his club. Jupiter, proud of his son's exploits, made Hercules immortal and bore him away to Mount Olympus in his four-horse chariot; there he was reconciled with Juno and married her daughter, Juventas.[11]

Herm

In classical antiquity a herm was a square or rectangular pillar, which usually tapered outwards in elevation, surmounted by a bearded head or

Hermaphroditus and Salmacis:
[1] Ovid, *Met IV:274–388*

Hero and Leander:
[1] Ovid, *Heroids XVIII, XIX*

Herse: *see* Apollo
[1] Ovid, *Met II:708–832*

Hippolytus: *see* Theseus
[1] Ovid, *Met XV:479–546*, Philostratus the Elder, *II:4* and Euripides, *Hippolytus*

armless bust, originally thought to depict the Greek god Hermes. Herms were set up on the street corners of Athens and outside the city as milestones. In bacchanalian scenes, by artists such as Rubens and Poussin, they may have a phallus.

Hermaphroditus and Salmacis

Hermaphroditus[1] was called after his parents' Greek names, Hermes and Aphrodite, who in Roman myth are referred to as Mercury and Venus. Hermaphroditus travelled far afield and came across a crystal pool where Salmacis dwelled – the only nymph unknown to Diana (Artemis in Greek myth), the goddess of chastity. When Salmacis caught sight of Hermaphroditus she longed to possess him and offered herself to him, but he rejected her. Bartholomeus Spranger, in *Salmacis and Hermaphroditus*, painted a voluptuous Salmacis watching Hermaphroditus undress as he prepared to bathe in her pool. Once Hermaphroditus was in the water, Salmacis entwined herself passionately around him. She prayed never to be separated from him, and their bodies fused to become one, joining both male and female as a hermaphrodite.

Hermes Trismegistus

Hermes, or Mercurius, Trismegistus ("thrice greatest") was the name given to the author of a group of writings on mysticism and alchemy. They probably belong to the 3rd century AD, but in the Renaissance were believed to be by a contemporary of Moses, and so contained wisdom close to God. An image of the author as a sage was inlaid on the floor of the nave in Siena Cathedral.

Hero and Leander

In mythology the beautiful Hero, priestess of Venus (Aphrodite), fell in love with the handsome Leander.[1] At night he swam across the Hellespont (the strait linking the Aegean sea with the sea of Marmara) to reach her, guided by a lighted torch at the top of Hero's tower. One stormy night the light blew out and Leander drowned. In despair, Hero threw herself from the top of her tower into the sea below. In *Hero and Leander* Domenico Fetti shows nymphs carrying Leander's body to the shore as Hero is dashed on to the rocks.

Herse

In mythology[1] the maiden Herse was returning home with her sisters from a festival of Minerva (in Greek myth, Athene), still carrying the sacred symbols in flower-wreathed baskets on their heads, when Mercury (Hermes) saw her and was astounded by her beauty. He flew down to earth but her sister Aglauros, who had envy planted deep in her heart, blocked the threshold of Herse's room. Mercury turned Aglauros into a blackened statue. In *Mercury, Herse and Aglauros* Louis Lagrenée shows the lovers on a bed while Aglauros peers around the curtain.

Hippolytus

Hippolytus[1] was desired by his stepmother, Phaedra, who tried to persuade him to dishonour the bed of his father, Theseus. When he continually refused she pretended that he lusted after her, and so his father banished him.

In *The Death of Hippolytus* Rubens shows how, as he fled, a sea-monster sent by Neptune (in Greek myth,

Poseidon) terrified his horses. His chariot struck a tree, throwing him out; and, with his limbs entangled in the reins, he was dragged to his death.

History
History was often personified as a female figure with books, tablets or scrolls. Anton Mengs, in *An Allegory of History*, shows her crowned with laurel in the company of Fame, Time and double-headed Janus.

Holy Family
During the Renaissance paintings of the Holy Family – Mary, Joseph and

A detail of the Holy Family, after The Madonna of the Basket *by Correggio (*c.*1524, National Gallery, London).*

the Infant Jesus – grew out of maternal images of the Virgin and Child. Michelangelo's *Doni Tondo* is a notable example of this development. The subject emphasizes the human aspect of the Incarnation, as the Holy Family are seen doing domestic tasks. For example, in Correggio's *Madonna of the Basket* the Virgin has her sewing beside her, while Joseph, a carpenter, is busily at work.

The Holy Family is also often seen in a landscape, as in the Rest on the Flight into Egypt, which tended to be a popular theme.

Homer
The Greek epic poet Homer is the accepted author of *The Iliad* and *The Odyssey* and probably lived some time before the 7th century BC. In *Parnassus* Raphael depicted him with Dante and Virgil as a dignified old man wearing a laurel wreath. Homer was blind, so is frequently shown dictating his works to a scribe.

Horatii and Curiatii
Two families, the Roman Horatii and the Latin Curiatii of Alba,[1] each had three sons matched in years and strength. To conclude the war between the Romans and Latins, their kings suggested that these young men should fight. Both sets of brothers took an oath that the losing side would peacefully submit to the other. In *The Oath of the Horatii* Jacques-Louis David shows the brothers making this vow before their father.

In the combat, the first advantage fell to the Curiatii who, though wounded, killed two Horatii. The remaining Roman knew that he could not take on three men at once so he ran a distance, followed by the three Curatii, each at a different speed. Fighting the Curiatii one by one, he emerged the victor.

Horatius Cocles
The heroism of the Roman soldier Horatius Cocles[1] saved his city from capture by Lars Porsena and his Etruscan army. With two comrades Horatius held the enemy back at a wooden bridge across the Tiber,

Holy Family: *see*
Joseph, Husband of the Virgin; Virgin, The

Homer: *see*
Trojan War; Ulysses

Horatii and Curiatti:
[1] Livy, *The History of Rome I xxiv–xxv*

Horatius Cocles:
[1] Plutarch, *Lives, Poplicola*

Hubert, Saint: *see* Eustace, St

Hunter/Hunting: *see* Adonis; Diana; Eustace, St; Hubert, St; Unicorn

Hyacinthus: *see* Apollo
[1] Ovid, *Met X:162–219* and Philostratus the Elder, *Imagines I:24*
[2] Lucian, *Diologue of the Gods 16*

Hylas: *see* Jason and the Argonauts
[1] Apollonius of Rhodes, *The Argonautica I:1207–1240*

giving the Romans time to destroy it. Severely wounded, he then dived into the river and swam to the other side. He was rewarded for his courage with as much land as he could plough in a day. A fine example of an ancient Roman hero, his image appropriately adorns public places – for example, Pietro Perugino's *Horatius Cocles* (Collegio del Cambio, Perugia).

Hubert, Saint

In legend, the wealthy Hubert (died AD727) was hunting on Good Friday; he came upon a hart with a crucifix between its antlers, and Christ commanded him to change his life. He became a hermit and later Bishop of Maastricht. The patron saint of hunters, he appears in north European painting from the 15th century. *The Conversion of St Hubert* by the Master of the Life of the Virgin shows him kneeling before the stag.

Hunter/Hunting

Hunting, the sport of rulers and the aristocracy, offered the opportunity to display wealth and power, as well as dynamic configurations of people and animals in a wooded setting.

In mythology, Diana (Artemis), goddess of hunting, was surprised while bathing by the hunter Actaeon, and turned him into a stag. Also, Adonis was killed while hunting.

In Christian art the unicorn was hunted as a "type" of Christ. Saints Eustace and Hubert were hunters.

Hyacinthus

Apollo loved the Spartan youth Hyacinthus[1] beyond all other mortals. They were competing at throwing the discus when Apollo's struck Hyacinthus, killing him. In an alternative version,[2] jealous Zephyr, the wind, who loved Hyacinthus, blew the discus at his head. Apollo transformed the youth's blood into the purple hyacinth, which returns to life every year. In Poussin's *Kingdom of Flora* Hyacinthus stares at the flower that bears his name.

Hymen with his torch, after Rubens' Minerva Protects Pax from Mars *(1629–30, National Gallery, London).*

Hylas and the Nymphs

Hylas,[1] who accompanied Hercules on his adventures with Jason, was looking for water when he found a spring where Naiads danced. One nymph was captivated by Hylas' beauty; as the youth filled his pitcher, she encircled his neck and pulled him underwater. In *Hylas and the Nymphs* J.W. Waterhouse shows him being drawn into their watery domain.

Hymen

Hymen, the god of marriage, was either the son of Bacchus and Venus, or of Apollo and a Muse. He is usually depicted as a boy crowned with flowers, holding a burning torch. He appears in marriage scenes.

Icarus and Daedalus

In mythology[1] Daedalus was a skilled Athenian craftsman, who killed his nephew, Perdix, when the boy showed greater craftmanship. Daedalus fled to Crete, where he proved useful to King Minos, for whom he made a Labyrinth to contain the monstrous Minotaur. Daedalus was later imprisoned in the Labyrinth for providing the thread with which Theseus found his way out of the maze after killing the Minotaur.[2] To enable himself and his son Icarus to escape, Daedalus made them each a pair of wings. He warned Icarus not to fly too near to the sun, but the boy ignored his father's wishes. As he soared higher and higher, the sun melted the wax on his wings and Icarus plunged to his death in the waters below. The story may be read as a warning against ambition. Icarus is usually seen tumbling out of the sky. In *Landscape with the Fall of Icarus* Pieter Breugel shows a shepherd and a ploughman on a cliff, oblivious to the tiny figure falling to his death in the sea.

Ignatius Loyola, Saint

Ignatius Loyola (*c*.1491–1556) was the founder of the Jesuit Order. Of noble Spanish birth, he became a soldier. During his convalescence after the siege of Pamplona he decided to dedicate himself to God. From 1524 to 1534 he studied at the University of Paris, where he inspired faith in seven students, including St Francis Xavier, who intended to become missionaries to the Moslems. The Society of the Jesuits was approved in 1540 by Pope Paul III with *Ad majorem Dei gloriam* ("To the greater glory of God") as its motto. Membership grew to thousands, and missionaries were sent to Europe and further afield to educate non-believers and halt the spread of Protestantism. Loyola's *Spiritual Exercises*, a book of meditations on the purity of the soul, enlightenment and union with God, was highly influential.

The Sacred Heart crowned with thorns, the flaming heart, and the monogram IHS, are the Jesuit emblems with which Ignatius is depicted. He wears the black habit of

Saint Ignatius, after a depiction by H. Wierix (early 17th century, Bibliothèque Nationale, Paris).

Icarus and Daedalus: *see* Minotaur; Theseus

[1] Ovid, *Met VIII:183–235*

[2] Apollodorus, *Epitome I: 5–14*

Ignatius Loyola, Saint: *see* Francis Xavier, St; IHS

IMPRESA: *see* Bull; Dragon; Eagle; Fleur de Lys; Lily; Planets; Tree

IMPRESA

A personal heraldic device is known in Italian as an *impresa*. The term is derived from *intraprendere* ("to undertake"), as the device was often accompanied by a motto or proverb of intention. By the end of the 16th century *imprese* were very fashionable and became highly inventive and complicated in design. They were developed from family emblems and decorated palaces throughout Italy. Some emblems were shared: the Gonzaga Dukes of Mantua, the Este Dukes of Ferrara and the Holy Roman Emperor adopted the eagle of Imperial Rome; the fleur-de-lys was common to the kings of France as well as mercantile Florence. The cross-keys and triple-crowned papal tiara were, however, unique to the Papacy. Below are emblems of families who were significant patrons of the arts:

Family	Place of Origin	Emblem
Barbarini	Florence	Bees
Borgia	Spain	Bull
Chigi	Siena	Pyramids of mounds
Farnese	Rome	Fleur-de-lys
Medici	Florence	Balls
Pamphili	Rome	Fleur-de-lys/Dove and olive branch
Piccolomini	Siena	Crescent moon
della Rovere	Savona	Oak tree/Acorns
Rucellai	Florence	Billowing sail
Sforza	Milan	The Visconti Dragon, with eagles, fleur-de-lys and other heraldry
Strozzi	Florence	Crescent moon
Visconti	Milan	Dragon or serpent spouting humans

IHS: *see* Bernardino, St; Christ, The Life of; Constantine, St; Ignatius Loyola, St; INRI; Passion of Christ, The; RELIGIOUS ORDERS

the Order and a biretta. He may be shown as a missionary, taking his vows, studying or performing miracles.

IHS

The monogram sometimes seen on the Cross at the Crucifixion, IHS was an abbreviation of the original Greek word for Jesus.

Constantine, the first Christian emperor of Rome, had a vision of the Cross before battle, after which IHS was identified with "*In hoc signo [vinces]*" (meaning "With this sign [you will conquer]"). In 1424 St Bernardino of Siena interpreted the initials as signifying *Jesus Hominum Salvator* (Christ the Saviour of Man), and the monogram thus became the saint's attribute.

It is also the emblem of the Jesuit Order, and is gloriously celebrated in Baciccia's *Adoration of the Name of Jesus*.

IMPRESA

See panel, above.

INRI

The first letters of *Iesu Nazarenus Rex Iudaeorum*, or Jesus of Nazareth, King of the Jews,[1] which appears at the top of the Cross in many paintings of the Crucifixion.

Intemperance

In 17th-century Dutch art Intemperance may be illustrated by a figure who has fallen asleep after too much smoking and drinking, in contrast with Temperance, who dilutes her wine with water. Jan Steen's *Effects of Intemperance* shows the folly of such disorderly behaviour:

A detail showing Intemperance offering drink to a parrot, after Effects of Intemperance *by Jan Steen (1663–5, National Gallery, London).*

a young boy steals from the drinker's purse; a maid gives drink to a parrot (that foolish imitator of humans); children feed a cat on food meant for adults; a foolish boy casts roses before a swine. As a reminder of the fate of those who lack self-discipline, the birch of punishment is placed in a basket above Intemperance.

Io

In mythology,[1] the supreme god Jupiter (in Greek myth, Zeus) caught sight of Io, daughter of Inachus, king of Argos, and robbed her of her virginity. To hide his adulterous deed from his jealous wife, Juno (Hera), he had spread dark clouds over himself and the land. However, on seeing the black clouds, Juno suspected what had happened, but Jupiter sensed his wife's appearance at the scene and turned Io into a sleek heifer to prevent her from learning the truth. Juno admired the lovely creature and requested that she be guarded by the hundred-eyed monster, Argus. So that he would not be found out, Jupiter agreed. However, Argus let Io stray near her family, where she conveyed the sad news of her changed shape by writing in the dust with her hoof. They mourned together until Argus moved her on. When Jupiter could no longer bear Io's suffering, Mercury (Hermes) lulled the vigilant Argus to sleep and cut off his head. Juno set his hundred eyes in the peacock's tail and forgave her husband. Io resumed her human form and bore Jupiter a son.

Isolated incidents from the story were depicted in art, such as Juno discovering Jupiter with Io in the form of a heifer, Mercury sending Argus to sleep, and Io being embraced by a black cloud, as in Correggio's *Io*.

Iphigenia

At the outset of the Trojan War Iphigenia,[1] daughter of the Greek leader Agamemnon, was offered as a sacrifice to the gods at Aulis, to induce them to bring wind to his becalmed fleet. Agamemnon brought his daughter to the altar, surrounded by weeping priests, under the pretence that she was to be married to the hero Achilles, as shown in Bertholet Flémalle's *The Sacrifice of Iphigenia*.

INRI: *see*
IHS; Passion of Christ, The

Io: *see*
Bull; Juno; Jupiter; Peacock
[1] Ovid, *Met I:568–746*

Iphigenia: *see*
Trojan War
[1] Ovid, *Met XII:24–38* and Euripides, *Iphigenia in Tauris*

Io embraced by the black cloud, after Correggio's Io *(1531, Kunsthistorisches Museum, Vienna).*

Iris: *see*
Lily
[1] Virgil, *Aeneid IV 693–705*

Isaiah: *see*
Man of Sorrows; Tree of Jesse
[1] *Isaiah 7:14–16*
[2] *Isaiah 11:1*

Ivy: *see*
Bacchus

Ixion: *see*
Hades
[1] Hyginus, *Fabulae LXII*
[2] Ovid, *Met IV:461*

Just as she was about to be killed, the goddess Diana mercifully cast a veil of cloud over the eyes of the assembled company, and substituted a stag in Iphigenia's place.

Iris

In mythology Iris was the goddess of the rainbow, on which she descended to give messages to mortals from the gods, especially from Jupiter (in Greek myth, Zeus) and Juno (Hera), king and queen of the gods. In Homer's *The Iliad* she takes Mercury's (Hermes') place as Jupiter's principal messenger, and in Ovid and Virgil[1] she is the messenger of Juno. In art she is also seen in the realm of the dream god, Hypnos.

Like the lily, the iris flower symbolizes purity and accompanies the Virgin.

Isaiah

One of the great prophets of the Old Testament, Isaiah foretold the coming of Christ: "Behold, a virgin shall conceive and bear a son ... and the child shall know to refuse evil and shall choose the good."[1] He also prophesied that "there shall come forth a rod out of the stem of Jesse, and a branch shall grow out of his roots".[2] The Tree of Jesse, the father of David, names the ancestors of Christ.

Isaiah is depicted in a similar way to other prophets as an old man with a long beard, holding a book or scroll which is sometimes inscribed with his name.

Ivy

Ivy is the attribute of Bacchus (in Greek myth, Dionysos). He may have a crown of ivy, or the plant may cover his thyrsus, or wand; it may also decorate his companions. As an evergreen, ivy may also symbolize immortality. Arthur Hughes' *The Long Engagement* shows an unfortunate curate and his fiancée condemned to a lengthy betrothal: next to them is a tree carved with intitials that have been covered by the slow-growing climber.

Ixion

In mythology Ixion, king of Thessaly, promised gifts to his father-in-law Eioneus; but when Eioneus came to collect them, Ixion dropped him into a pit of burning coals. Jupiter (in Greek myth, Zeus) forgave him the crime, but the ungrateful Ixion then tried to seduce Juno (Hera).[1] Jupiter fashioned a cloud to look like the goddess, which Ixion then embraced. In punishment he was sent to Tartarus in the Underworld, where he was tied to a wheel perpetually turned by a strong wind.[2] Ixion is shown courting Juno in paintings by van Couenbergh and Rubens.

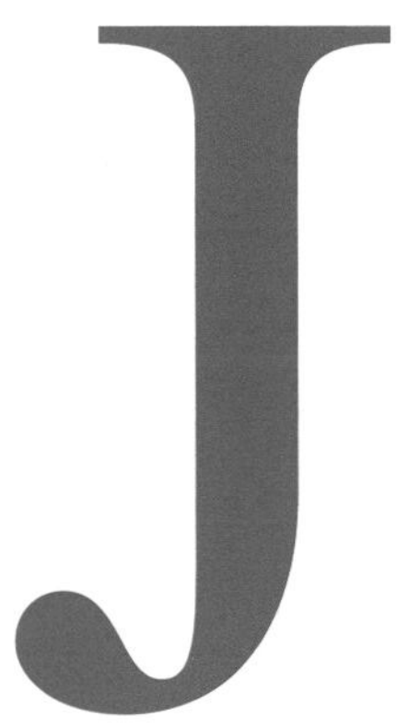

Jacob

In the Old Testament,[1] Jacob was one of the twin sons of Isaac and Rebecca, and was born clinging to the heel of his brother Esau. This was a sign from God that they would head two tribes, and that Jacob, the younger twin, would be stronger than Esau, who would serve him.

Jacob became a herdsman and his mother's favourite, Esau a hunter and his father's favourite. One day, faint with hunger, Esau sold his birthright to his brother for food. When they were older, Rebecca contrived that Jacob should receive his father's blessing in Esau's place: she disguised Jacob as his brother so that the old and nearly blind Isaac would mistake the younger for the elder when giving his (irrevocable) blessing. When Esau discovered this, he swore to kill his twin. These episodes may illustrate part of a series of Old Testament patriarchs.

Rebecca sent Jacob away to escape his brother's wrath, and to marry one of the daughters of his uncle, Laban, so that he would not have to marry a local Canaanite. On his way, "he took stones of that place, and put them for his pillows, and lay down in that place to sleep. And he dreamed, and behold a ladder set up on the earth, and the top of it reached to heaven; and behold there were angels of God ascending and descending on it." During the dream God told Jacob that he and his descendants would prosper.[2] A ladder may therefore appear in art as Jacob's identifying attribute. Tintoretto, however, in *Jacob's Dream*, chose to portray it as a vast flight of stairs.

On his travels Jacob met Rachel, one of Laban's daughters, as she was bringing her father's flocks to water. Jacob rolled back the stone that covered the well. Rachel was very beautiful, and Jacob offered to work for Laban for seven years to win her hand. Laban agreed, but when the time came for their wedding, he put his elder daughter Leah in Rachel's place, because the younger sister could not marry before the elder. Jacob still loved Rachel, however, and he offered to work for seven more

Jacob: *see* Joseph, Son of Jacob

[1] *Genesis 25:20–34*
[2] *Genesis 28:11–14*
[3] *Genesis 29:1–28*
[4] *Genesis 31:3–35*
[5] *Genesis 32:24-30*
[6] *Genesis 32:6–32; 33:1–4*
[7] *Genesis 48*

James the Great, Saint: *see* Christ, Life of; Martyrs; Pasion of Christ; Pilgrims
[1] *Golden Legend, St James the Great*

years so that he might marry her, too; Laban agreed that it would be better to give his daughter to Jacob than to another man.[3] Jacob had many children by both of his wives, and by their handmaids, and after 20 years he resolved to return to Canaan with them all.

They left secretly, Rachel taking her father's household idols. Laban pursued, eventually overtaking them, but Rachel kept the idols hidden by sitting on them.[4] In *Rachel Hiding the Idols from her Father, Laban*, Giambattista Tiepolo shows her feigning innocence while her father questions her as to their whereabouts.

The night before they reached Canaan, Jacob, alone by a brook, wrestled with an angel until daybreak. Unable to throw him, the angel refused to tell his name, but said that Jacob would henceforth be named Israel. Jacob then understood that he had been wrestling with God.[5] The theme was taken as an allegory of good versus evil. Gauguin abandoned his preference for naturalistic subjects and painted *Jacob's Struggle with the Angel.*

As they approached Canaan, Jacob heard that Esau was coming to meet him with 400 men, so he sent his brother part of his herd in appeasement. When they met, the brothers embraced and wept.[6]

In his old age, Jacob blessed the children of Joseph, his favourite son, a tranquil scene depicted by Rembrandt in *The Blessing of Jacob.*[7] He prophesied that in the future his own 12 sons would be the founders of the 12 Tribes of Israel. With Jacob, the sons were portrayed in a series by Zurbarán entitled *Jacob and his 12 Sons.*

A detail after St James the Great Conquering the Moors *by Giambattista Tiepolo (1749, Szempveszeti Museum, Budapest).*

James the Great, Saint (Apostle, Disciple)

The sons of Zebedee, James (died AD44) and his brother John were fishermen who, with Peter, were the favourite disciples of Christ. They witnessed his Transfiguration and the Agony in the Garden of Gethsemane, and they are usually shown in paintings of these scenes. According to legend, King Herod Agrippa ordered the martyrdom of James: he was decapitated by the sword.[1]

In the 7th century a legend arose claiming that James went to Spain and was a successful evangelist. This tradition is a relatively late one, but contributed to the growth of his Spanish cult; he became the patron saint of Spain. In the Middle Ages his shrine at Compostela was one of the major places of pilgrimage, where many miracles were said to have taken place; pilgrims wore his emblem, a cockle shell. St James is often shown as a pilgrim himself with a cockle shell on his hat or on his cloak.

James is believed to have appeared at the Battle of Clavijo in AD844 to help the Spaniards win their first victory against the Moorish invaders, and many artists have shown him as a warrior on horseback.

James the Less (Apostle, Disciple)

James (died *c.*AD62), called the Less in order to avoid confusion with James the Great, was referred to as "the Lord's brother" in the New Testament, and in art he may, therefore, resemble Christ. He was probably the first Bishop of Jerusalem, where the contemporary historian Josephus records that he was stoned to death. However, later legend says that he was instructed to preach about Christ from the roof of the Temple and that for this he was thrown from the roof, stoned and clubbed to death.[1] One man snatched up a fuller's bat with which cloth was beaten, aimed a heavy blow at James' head, and split his skull. James may be shown as a bishop. His attribute is a club, or a flat fuller's bat.

Janus

In ancient Rome, the god Janus was guardian of the threshold and god of beginnings.[1] His image was set up by the principal door of a house. He had two faces so that he could look ahead and behind, and is therefore sometimes represented as a herm (a double-faced head or bust). He gave his name to January, which saw the old year out and ushered in the new, and he was associated with wisdom because he knew the past and could foresee the future.

Jason and the Argonauts

In mythology, Jason was the son of Aeson, king of Iolcus in Thessaly.[1] When the throne was usurped by Pelias, Aeson's brother, Jason was sent away to be cared for and educated by the centaur Chiron. On reaching maturity, Jason undertook to fetch the Golden Fleece in return for his rightful monarchy. This precious fleece hung in a grove in Colchis on the Black Sea, guarded by a dragon. Jason sailed there in the *Argo* with his crew, the Argonauts, passing through the dangerous straits of the Symplegades with the help of the goddess Minerva (in Greek myth, Athene).

King Aeëtes of Colchis agreed to surrender the fleece if Jason could perform certain difficult tasks. The king's daughter Medea, pierced by Cupid's (Eros') arrow, fell in love with Jason and aided him with her magic. Jason successfully completed the tasks, and found the Golden Fleece hanging on a huge oak tree, guarded by the dragon. Medea's sweet voice charmed the dragon, and she sprinkled a potion in its eyes so that Jason could remove his prize safely. These stories appealed to Gustave Moreau, who painted *Medea Enamoured by Jason*, and *The Return of the Argonauts*.

Jephthah

One of the Old Testament judges, Jephthah led the Israelites against the

James the Less (Apostle Disciple): *see*
Martyrs
[1] *Golden Legend, St James the Less*

Janus: *see*
Herm
[1] Ovid, *Fasti I:89–145*

Jason and the Argonauts: *see*
Hercules; Hylas; Medea; Sirens
[1] Apollonius of Rhodes, *Argonautica*

Jephthah:
[1] *Judges 11:30–40*

Jeroboam: *see*
Ambrose, St; Augustine, St; Gregory the Great, St
[1] *I Kings 12:27–33; 13:1–6*

Jerome, Saint: *see*
Ambrose, St; Augustine, St, Gregory the Great, St
[1] *Golden Legend, St Jerome*

Jezebel: *see*
Elijah
[1] *I Kings 21:1–23*
[2] *II Kings 9:30–37*

Ammonites.[1] Before the battle he vowed to God that if he was victorious he would sacrifice the first creature he met on his return home. Victory was secured, but the first person he saw coming out of his door, "with timbrels and with dances", was his only child, a daughter. He tore his clothes in anguish but kept his vow. In *The Sacrifice of Jephthah*, Charles Lebrun showed him standing, knife in hand, about to kill her.

Jeremiah
The Old Testament prophet Jeremiah preached against the sins of the people and foresaw that great suffering was needed for salvation. In *Jeremiah Foreseeing the Destruction of Jerusulem* Rembrandt depicted him as an old man lamenting the city's destruction by the Babylonians. The book of Lamentations in the Old Testament, which deals with the captivity of Jerusalem, was wrongly attributed to Jeremiah.

Jeroboam
In the Old Testament, Jeroboam was the king of a divided Israel whose territories did not include Jerusalem. He set up false altars in Bethel and Dan. One one occasion, as he was burning incense, an angel appeared and admonished him, causing his hand to wither. Jeroboam prayed to God and his hand was restored.[1] Jean-Honoré Fragonard's *Jeroboam Sacrificing to Idols* shows him worshipping a calf.

Jerome, Saint
Jerome (*c*.AD342–420) was one of the four Latin Doctors of the Church, with Saints Ambrose, Augustine and Gregory the Great. He studied in Rome, after which he became a hermit in Syria, where he learned Hebrew. Between AD382 and AD385 he was secretary to the Pope in Rome, who encouraged him to revise the Latin version of the New Testament. In AD386 he settled in Bethlehem, accompanied by one of his followers, the Roman matron Paula. Jerome devoted himself to a scholarly and ascetic life. By *c*.AD404 he had translated almost all of the Old and New Testaments into Latin from Hebrew and Greek. Jerome's versions later became known as the "Vulgate".

Popular in the 15th century was the image of Jerome as an old hermit in the wilderness praying in front of a crucifix or beating his breast with a stone, wearing a cardinal's hat, with a lion nearby, as shown by Cosimo Tura. One day, when Jerome was in Bethlehem with his followers, a lion limped into the monastery. The monks fled but Jerome plucked a thorn from its paw, its wounds healed and thereafter it became his constant companion.[1]

He may also be depicted as a scholar surrounded by books in his study, a room usually furnished as it would have been in the artist's time; Antonello da Messina's depiction is an example. Or he may be dressed as a cardinal – although the office did not exist in his time – holding the Bible, or a model of a church to represent his status as a Doctor of the Church.

Between 1502 and 1507 Carpaccio painted scenes from Jerome's life in the Scuola di San Giorgio, Venice.

Jezebel
In the Old Testament, Jezebel was the wife of Ahab, king of Israel, and has come to be known as the archetypal

A detail after St Jerome Reading in a Landscape *by a follower of Giovanni Bellini (*c.*1480, National Gallery, London).*

wicked woman. Ahab coveted a vineyard owned by Naboth, whom Jezebel contrived to have stoned to death for blasphemy. When Jezebel and Ahab went to take possession of the vineyard, they encountered Elijah, whom God had sent to meet them. Eljah said to them: "In the place where dogs licked the blood of Naboth shall dogs lick thy blood, even thine ... and the dogs shall eat Jezebel."[1] The scene was depicted by Frederic, Lord Leighton, in *Jezebel and Ahab*.

After Ahab's death Jezebel "painted her face and tied her hair" to seduce Jehu, Ahab's general; but Jehu ordered three eunuchs to throw her out of her window. When she hit the ground she was trampled on by horses and eaten by dogs.[2]

Joachim and Anna

According to legend,[1] Joachim and Anna, the parents of the Virgin, were married for 20 years without off-spring. Joachim went to the altar to make an offering but a priest ordered him away, declaring that it was not proper for a man who did not increase the people of God to approach the altar. Joachim was ashamed to go home and face his kinsmen, and went to live among the shepherds. One day an angel appeared to him and told him that Anna would give birth to Mary, conceived not in carnal desire but as a sign of divine generosity. The angel then revealed the same to Anna, establishing the doctrine of the Immaculate Conception. The couple were told to meet at the Golden Gate of Jerusalem, where they embraced tenderly. Giotto recorded these stories in a series of frescoes (Arena Chapel, Padua), including a sacrifice that Joachim made to God after the angel's Annunciation.

Job

In the Old Testament, Job was a blameless and upright man who prospered in the land of Uz. Without his knowledge, he became the subject of an argument between God and the Devil as to the strength of his faith. To test that faith, his herds, children, servants and house were destroyed, and he was afflicted with boils, which caused him great suffering, but despite everything he refused to renounce God. He finally recovered his property and his health, but he never discovered that he had been the subject of a wager. In 1828 an English edition of the Book of Job was published with 18 illustrations by William Blake.

John the Baptist, Saint

Luke[1] gives an account of the life of John the Baptist (died *c.*AD30), the last Old Testament prophet to preach the coming of Christ.

An elderly priest, Zacharias, and his wife, Elizabeth, who lived in the days of King Herod, had no children. But as Zacharias was burning incense in the Temple of the Lord, an angel appeared and announced that he would have a son, named John, who would be great in the eyes of the Lord. Zacharias doubted the angel's words and in punishment was struck dumb. When their child was born, Zacharias was asked what the baby should be called; he wrote "John", and immediately his speech was restored. At the Annunciation to the Virgin, an angel told Mary about the miraculous conception of John, and Mary went to stay with Elizabeth, her

Joachim and Anna: *see* St Anna; Virgin

[1] *Golden Legend, The Birth of the Blessed Virgin Mary*

John the Baptist, Saint: *see* Christ, The Life of; Salome

[1] *Luke 1:5–64*
[2] *Matthew 3*
[3] *Matthew 14:1–12*
[4] *John 1:29*

John Chrysostom: *see* Doctor

A detail after The Baptist in the Wilderness *by Geertgen Tot (*c.*1490–5, National Gallery, Berlin).*

cousin. Their meeting is known as the Visitation.

When he grew up, John preached in the wilderness that the kingdom of heaven was at hand. "And John was clothed with camel's hair, and with a girdle of a skin about his loins." For food he ate wild honey and locusts. He baptized many people, proclaiming: "He that cometh after me is mightier than I." When Christ came to be baptized, "the heavens were opened unto him [John] and he saw the Spirit of God descending like a dove. And lo a voice from heaven, saying, This is my beloved Son, in whom I am well pleased."[2]

John preached that it was unlawful for the governor, Herod, to have married his brother's wife, Herodias, and for preaching this John was imprisoned; but Herod was afraid to put John to death because of the repercussions from John's large following. On his birthday, Herod promised his step-daughter Salome anything she wanted if she would dance for him. Having danced, she was instructed by her mother to ask for the head of the Baptist. John was decapitated, and his head brought to Herod on a charger. Then his disciples buried his body.[3]

Images of the Baptism of Christ, and of Salome with the head of John the Baptist, were frequently painted. Scenes from John's life were also illustrated, and are found appropriately in baptistries, notably in Florence, the city of which he is patron saint. He also appears as a small child in paintings of the Virgin and Child, and of the Holy Family, because he foretold the advent of Christ.

John is usually shown in altarpieces as a wild and unkempt figure, who wears a shaggy tunic and holds a long, thin cross. He may also carry a lamb, in reference to his words, "Behold the Lamb of God, which taketh away the sin of the world," the *Ecce Agnus Dei*, which he said as he saw Christ coming to him for baptism.[4]

John Chrysostom, Saint

John Chrysostom (*c.*AD347–407), whose name means "Mouth of Gold", was born at Antioch and in AD398 was elected Archbishop of Constantinople. One story tells how he had a child by a princess, for which he was required to pay penance by crawling on all fours like an animal; this scene was engraved by Dürer.

Renowned for his eloquence, the saint is counted as one of the four Greek Doctors of the Eastern Church, along with the Saints Athanasius, Basil and Gregory of Nazianzus. He may also appear with the Doctors of the Western Church – for example, sculpted under Bernini's *Chair of St Peter* (St Peter's, Rome).

John the Evangelist, Saint

John (died late 1st century AD) was one of Christ's favourite disciples and also the youngest. He appears as a young man in numerous scenes of the New Testament. Brother of James the Great, John was a fisherman, and they were both mending their nets when Christ bade them follow him.[1] Along with Peter, the brothers were chosen to be present at the Transfiguration and at the Agony in the Garden. John has been identified as the unnamed "disciple whom Jesus loved", who wept on his shoulder at the Last Supper, and to whom Christ entrusted the care of his mother after his death.[2] In the Acts of the Apostles, John is described preaching with Peter. They were imprisoned together, and eventually John was exiled to the island of Patmos. He is said to have spent his last years at Ephesus, where he died. Poussin painted him as an old man writing, for he is traditionally held to be the author of the Fourth Gospel and the book of Revelation.

According to legend,[3] John was returning to Ephesus at the same time as the body of his dear friend Drusiana was being carried out for burial. John ordered her bier to be set down and her body unbound; then he said, "Drusiana, may my Lord Jesus Christ raise you to life! Arise, go to your house and prepare food for me!" As Filippino Lippi depicted, Drusiana rose as if from sleep and did as he ordered (Strozzi Chapel, Santa Maria Novella, Florence).

At another time, a priest of the temple of the goddess Diana wanted proof of John's faith. Two criminals were ordered to drink poison and immediately fell dead, but when John took the cup, he made the sign of the cross, drank the potion and suffered no harm. Similarly, when John went to Rome, he was thrown into a vat of boiling oil, yet emerged unscathed.

At the age of 98 he was called to Heaven, so he dug his own grave, lay in it and ascended in a brilliant light.

John's attribute is an eagle, a representation of divine inspiration, which is found in John's Gospel. Also, he often holds a chalice full of snakes, alluding to the poison that he drank. The Ghent altarpiece by Jan van Eyck shows him with this attribute (Cathedral of St Bavo, Ghent).

John Gualbert, Saint

John Gualbert (in Italian, Giovanni Gualberto) of Florence (AD c.985–1073) was said to have had his brother's murderer at his mercy but pardoned him. John later had a vision of Christ on the Cross bowing his head toward him. He founded the Order of the Vallombrosans in Tuscany, the con-duct of which was drawn from the rule of St Benedict. In Tuscan paintings he is seen wearing the Vallombrosans' light grey habit, sometimes with a crucifix.

Jonah

According to the Old Testament, God ordered the prophet Jonah to visit the corrupt city of Nineveh and warn of its impending destruction; but Jonah feared the reaction of the city's people and took a boat in a different direction. God sent a mighty tempest as a result of Jonah's disobedience, and although the sailors rowed hard, they could not bring the vessel to land. So they took up Jonah and cast him into the sea, whereupon the storm ceased. "Now the Lord had prepared a great fish to swallow up Jonah. And Jonah

John the Evangelist, St: *see* Apocalypse; Christ, The Life of; Evangelists; James the Great; Martyrs; Passion of Christ; Peter, St; Virgin

[1] *Mark 1:19–20*

[2] *John 19:25–27*

[3] *Golden Legend, St John the Evangelist*

John Gualbert, Saint: *see* RELIGIOUS ORDERS

Jonah:

[1] *Jonah 1* and *2*

[2] *Matthew 12:40*

A detail of St John with his chalice of snakes from Saints Matthew, Catherine of Alexandria and John the Evangelist *by Stephan Lochner (c.1445, National Gallery, London).*

was in the belly of the fish three days and three nights." Jonah repented and the fish disgorged him unharmed.[1]

The story of Jonah and the whale was taken as a prefiguration of Christ and the Resurrection, because when the Pharisees demanded a sign from Christ, he said that, like Jonah, "so shall the Son of man be three days and three nights in the heart of the earth", as Jonah had been in the whale.[2] Michelangelo's massive image of Jonah and his whale appears above the altar in the Sistine Chapel in the Vatican, Rome.

Joseph, Son of Jacob

Joseph, Son of Jacob: *see* Benjamin; Chastity; Jacob

[1] *Genesis 37*
[2] *Genesis 39:1–20*
[3] *Genesis 40*
[4] *Genesis 41:1–44*
[5] *Genesis 42–45*

Of Jacob's 12 sons, Joseph was his favourite and the one to whom he gave a coat of many colours.[1] With the exception of Benjamin (the only brother to have the same mother as Joseph), the other sons envied Joseph their father's favouritism. Joseph had a dream that his sheaf of corn stood upright while his brothers' bowed down, and that the sun, moon and 11 stars paid homage to his star. The dream further fuelled the brother's jealousy, and one day, when they were tending their sheep, they stripped Joseph of his coat, threw him in an empty well, and then sold him as a slave for 20 pieces of silver to merchants journeying into Egypt. The coat of many colours was taken back to their father covered in goat's blood, so Jacob would believe that Joseph had been devoured by a wild animal.

In Egypt Joseph was sold to Potiphar, an officer of the Pharaoh, who made him overseer of his house. Potiphar's covetous wife "cast her eyes upon Joseph and she said, 'Lie with me.'" When he refused she accused him of trying to molest her. Potiphar threw Joseph into prison.[2] When the Pharaoh's baker and butler were later imprisoned with him, he interpreted their dreams.[3]

Having been released back into Pharaoh's household, the butler recommended Joseph as an interpreter of the Pharaoh's own strange dreams. The Pharaoh had dreamed that seven fat cattle were devoured by seven lean ones, and that seven fat sheaves of corn were eaten by seven thin ones. Joseph understood these dreams to mean that seven years of plenty would be followed by seven years of famine; and he advised that reserves should be set aside to provide food during the famine. Joseph was rewarded for his prophecy with the Pharaoh's ring, fine linen and a golden chain. He was also made governor of Egypt.[4]

When the famine came, Jacob sent his sons, except for Benjamin (whom he now favoured), to buy corn in Egypt. The brothers bowed down before Joseph, in respect for the Pharaoh's governor, without recognizing him. In return for corn, Joseph demanded that Benjamin be brought to Egypt, keeping another brother, Simeon, as hostage. The brothers were reluctant, fearing for their father's health if another of his sons should come to any harm, but evntually they agreed.

On their return to Egypt with Benjamin, Joseph tormented his brothers still further. He placed the silver cup that he used for drinking and divining in Benjamin's sack, and then declared that there had been a theft. Joseph's steward found the cup, accused Benjamin of being the culprit, and brought the brothers before Joseph. At last Joseph revealed his identity. He was reconciled with his brothers and invited them and Jacob to live with him in Egypt.[5]

The stories of the initially ill-treated Joseph, his rise to Egypt's highest office, his wisdom, and his conciliatory magnanimity, were highly popular, especially in late medieval and Renaissance art. They were used in fresco cycles, furniture and tapestry design, and easel paintings. Individual scenes were also depicted, as in the 17th-century Orazio Gentileschi's *Joseph and Potiphar's Wife*.

Joseph, Husband of the Virgin

All that is known of Joseph appears in the Gospels. He was descended from the house of David,[1] worked as a carpenter and became betrothed to the Virgin Mary, who had already conceived the child "of the Holy Ghost". An angel appeared to Joseph to dispel his fears about marrying Mary, and then again after Jesus' birth to tell him to flee into Egypt with the Virgin and Christ Child in order to avoid Herod's slaughter of all first-born baby boys (the Massacre of the Innocents). When Herod died, the angel appeared to Joseph once more to tell him to return to Nazareth with his family.[2]

Joseph presumably died before Christ's Crucifixion, because on the Cross Jesus entrusted Mary to the care of one of his Apostles, probably St John the Evangelist. Joseph appears in fresco cycles of the Life of the Virgin and Christ, and in individual scenes of the Flight into Egypt and the Holy Family. He is usually depicted as a modest, benevolent old man concerned only for his family's welfare. The idea that Joseph was an elderly man may have come from an Apocryphal Gospel which claims that he had been married previously, had six children and died aged 111 years.[3] His attribute is often the flowering rod, which is said to have miraculously blossomed in the Temple, to show that he was chosen above all other suitors to be the Virgin's husband; or it may be the Virgin's lily of purity.

Joseph of Arimathea

The wealthy Joseph of Arimathea was a follower of Christ and appears in the Gospels as the man who asked Pilate's permission to remove Christ's body after the Crucifixion. Joseph wrapped Christ in clean linen and laid the body in his own tomb, which had been "hewn out in the rock". He rolled a stone over the entrance and then departed.[1]

Joseph is often seen with Nicodemus at the Deposition, lowering Christ from the Cross; he also appears in depictions of the Entombment, such as that by Rogier van der Weyden.

Joshua

In the Old Testament,[1] Joshua succeeded Moses as leader of the Israelites, bringing them into the Promised Land. Having conquered kingdoms and cities, he shared them among the 12 tribes of Israel and the Levites.

After Moses' death Joshua led his people to the River Jordan and ordered his priests to lead the Ark of the Covenant across. As their feet touched the water, it separated, letting the people through. In memory of this miracle, Joshua asked 12 men to take 12 stones from where the priests had stood on the water and set them up on the far bank.[2] On this side lay

Joseph, Husband of the Virgin: *see* Holy Family; Virgin
[1] *Matthew 1:1–16*
[2] *Matthew 2:13–23*
[3] *The Apocryphal History of Joseph the Carpenter*

Joseph of Arimathea: *see* Lamentation
[1] *Matthew 27:57–60*

Joshua:
[1] *Deuteronomy 31:14*
[2] *Joshua 3* and *4*
[3] *Joshua 6:1–20*
[4] *Joshua 10:12–28*

Judas Iscariot: *see* Passion of Christ
[1] *Matthew 26:25*
[2] *Matthew 26:47–48*
[3] *Matthew 27:3–5*

Jude, Saint: *see* Martyrs
[1] *John 14:22*
[2] *Golden Legend, SS Simon and Jude*

Judith and Holofernes: *see* Jeremiah
[1] *Apocrypha, Judith 10:3–5*
[2] *Apocrypha, Judith 13*

Judas shown wrapped in his yellow cloak, kissing Christ, after a fresco by Giotto (1303–6, Arena Chapel, Padua).

the well-defended city of Jericho in the land of Canaan which, at God's command, Joshua and the Israelites besieged for six days. Every day seven priests marched around the city with seven trumpets before the Ark of the Covenant, but on the seventh day they went around seven times, then blew the trumpets. At that, the Israelites gave a great shout, and the walls of the city collapsed.[3] These scenes were recorded in Ghiberti's *Joshua* door panel for the Baptistry in Florence.

John Martin's huge and dramatic *Joshua Commanding the Sun to Stand Still Over Gibeon* shows how God allowed the Israelites time to avenge themselves on their enemy, the Amorites, of whom a great number were slaughtered.[4]

Judas Iscariot (Disciple)

Judas appears in numerous cycles of the Passion as the Apostle who betrayed Christ for 30 pieces of silver. He sits isolated in scenes of the Last Supper. When Christ announced that he would be betrayed, Judas asked, "Is it I?", to which Christ replied, "Thou hast said."[1] While Christ prayed in the Garden of Gethsemane, and Peter, James and John failed to keep watch, Judas brought in Pilate's soldiers, and singled out his master with a kiss.[2] After Christ had been condemned, Judas repented, returned the 30 pieces of silver to the priests, and hanged himself in shame.[3]

Caravaggio's *The Taking of Christ* was one of many treatments of this episode. Judas, usually unattractive, may wear a yellow cloak and may, as in Giotto's *The Stirring of Judas*, have a demon goading him. His attributes may be a money bag, or the rope with which he hanged himself.

Jude, Saint

Jude (1st century AD), also identified as Thaddeus and the author of the last Epistle of the New Testament, was brother of James the Less and one of Christ's disciples. He was also known as "the other Judas, not Iscariot".[1] According to legend,[2] he went with his other brother, Simon, to preach in Persia, where they performed many baptisms and several miracles. Jude was martyred with a club, halberd or lance, which he might hold as his attribute. For an unknown reason, Jude is the patron saint of lost causes and all people in despair.

Judith and Holofernes

Judith, a beautiful widow, was the Apocryphal Old Testament heroine who, as saviour of the Israelites, was seen as the female counterpart of David, the shepherd boy who became king of Israel. Holofernes, chief captain of the Assyrians, was ordered to go west with a huge army, and kill anyone who did not yield to his king's command. He reached Judea and prepared to make war with the people of Israel. Hearing of their plight, Judith bathed and adorned herself in her finest clothes and jewels and, accompanied by her maid and carrying wine and food, she entered the enemy's camp.[1] She pretended that she had come to betray her people to the captain. Seduced by her beauty, Holofernes gave a feast in her honour and, left alone with her, drank too much wine. Judith took hold of his hair, smote his head from his body, and triumphantly bore it back to her people.[2] Terrified, the Assyrians fled.

Judith is usually depicted holding the severed head of Holofernes, sometimes seductively. She may bear a sword, and her maid may hold the sack in which they placed the head.

Judith was popular in the Renaissance and Baroque periods: Christofono Allori and Artemisia Gentileschi both painted famous interpretations.

Julian the Hospitaller, Saint

In legend[1] the wealthy noble Julian (dates unknown) was one day hunting a stag, which turned round and foretold that Julian would kill his parents. To avoid tragedy, Julian fled. He served a prince and married a widow, whose dowry was a castle. Meanwhile his parents, searching for their son, arrived at the castle; Julian was not at home but his wife gave them the matrimonial bed to sleep in. When Julian returned, thinking his wife had taken a lover, he unwittingly murdered his parents.

To pay for his crime, Julian and his wife established a hospice for the poor and ailing near a broad river, across which he ferried travellers. One night he found a leper perishing from cold asking to be carried across the river. Julian took the stranger to his house and put him to bed. The man revealed himself to be an angel and told him that he had served his penance. Castagno frescoed Julian as a humble young man (SS Annunziata, Florence), while Christofono Allori depicted his hospitality. His attribute may be a stag. He is the patron saint of ferrymen, travellers and innkeepers.

Juno

Daughter of Saturn and Ops, Juno (in Greek myth, Hera) was the sister and consort of Jupiter (Zeus). Queen of Olympus, she was also goddess of marriage and childbirth, and the mother of Vulcan (Hephaestus), Juventas (Hebe) and Mars (Ares). She was majestically beautiful, but in the Judgment of Paris she lost the prize for beauty to Venus and, in the ensuing Trojan War, sided with the Greeks against Jupiter's wishes.

In order to distract her husband from his support of the Trojans, Juno obtained the girdle of Venus, which made her irresistible and tricked him into falling asleep in her arms.

There are many legends about Juno's jealousy of her husband's mortal loves, and she is often depicted spying on him. Enraged by his behaviour, she tended to take revenge on the innocent girls, notably Callisto, Io and Semele. In *Juno Discovering Jupiter and Io* Pieter Lastman illustrated the confirmation of her suspicions of Jupiter's infidelity.

Juno's attribute is a peacock: a pair of these birds drew her chariot. It was she who gave the peacock the eyes on its marvellous tail: after Argus, the one-hundred-eyed monster guarding Io, had been slain by Mercury (Hermes), Juno took his eyes and transferred them to the bird's feathers.[1] Antonio Balestra illustrated this in *Juno Placing the One Hundred Eyes of Argus in the Peacock's Tail.*

A temple of Juno Moneta (giver of counsel) was situated on the Roman Capitol. A mint was founded there, and her epithet gave rise to the English word "money". As patroness of commerce, Juno might appear in paintings about financial gain, as in Nicholas Maes' *The Account Keeper*.

Jupiter

Son of Saturn and Ops, Jupiter (in Greek myth, Zeus) overthrew his father to become supreme head of the gods. His image is majestic: he has an

Julian the Hospitaller, Saint:
[1] *Golden Legend, St Julian*

Juno: *see*
Callisto; Io; Jupiter; Paris; Semele
[1] Ovid, *Met I:568–746*

Jupiter: *see*
Antiope; Callisto; Ceres; Danaë; Europa; Io; Juno; Latona; Leda
[1] Homer, *Iliad XV:184–204*

After Judith with the Head of Holofernes *by Lucas Cranach the Elder (c.1530).*

Justina of Antioch, Saint: *see* Martyrs
[1] *Golden Legend, St Justina*

Justina of Padua, Saint: *see* Justina of Antioch, St; Martyrs

athletic form and a long, curly beard and hair. He may be enthroned or hold a sceptre. An eagle, his attribute, may be nearby. As the "aegis bearer" he often bears a shield and wears armour. When he was a baby his mother hid him from his father in a cave on Mount Ida in Crete, where he was nurtured by the nymph Amalthea on goat's milk and honey (some say Amalthea is the name of the she-goat itself). The universe was divided among Jupiter and his brothers by drawing lots: Neptune obtained the sea, Pluto the Underworld, and Jupiter heaven.[1] He was also the law-

A detail after Jupiter and Semele *by Rubens (late 16th century).*

giver, and could foresee the future and change the destiny of mankind. He was known as the "Thunderer" and would hurl thunderbolts when displeased, but he was benevolent to those who were loyal and virtuous. Philemon and Baucis were two such worthy people; they were the only humans to show Jupiter hospitality when he was choosing whom to save before he caused the great flood .

Jupiter was the husband of Juno (Hera) and often provoked her fury by his infidelities. Among his lovers were the goddesses Ceres (Demeter), who bore him Proserpina (Persephone); Latona who bore him the twins Diana (Artemis) and Apollo; and Maia (the daughter of Atlas) who bore him Mercury. He also pursued the mortals Danaë, Io, Europa, Callisto, Antiope and Leda, in disguised form.

Justina of Antioch, Saint

In legend the sorcerer Cyprian, who lived in Antioch (3rd century AD), wanted to seduce the Christian virgin Justina (dates unknown).[1] He invoked the Devil to win her over, but three times was unsuccessful: Justina made the sign of the cross and the Devil fled. Realizing that Christ was greater than the Devil, Cyprian was converted and baptized. Justina and Cyprian were martyred at Nicomedia and may be shown together in art. A unicorn, symbol of chastity, is Justina's attribute.

Justina of Padua, Saint

Justina (dates unknown) was greatly revered in Padua, where a church was dedicated to her in the 6th century. A medieval legend claimed that she was baptized by a follower of St Peter and was martyred by the sword under Nero. She appears in Paduan and Venetian painting; like Justina of Antioch, she may be shown with a unicorn because she retained her virginity under duress, even when the Devil tried to tempt her.

Juventas

Goddess of perpetual youth, Juventas (in Greek myth, Hebe) was the daughter of Jupiter (Zeus) and Juno (Hera), and handmaiden of the gods. Adolph Diez shows the beautiful young girl as the cup-bearer of Jupiter in *Juventas with Jupiter in the Guise of an Eagle.*

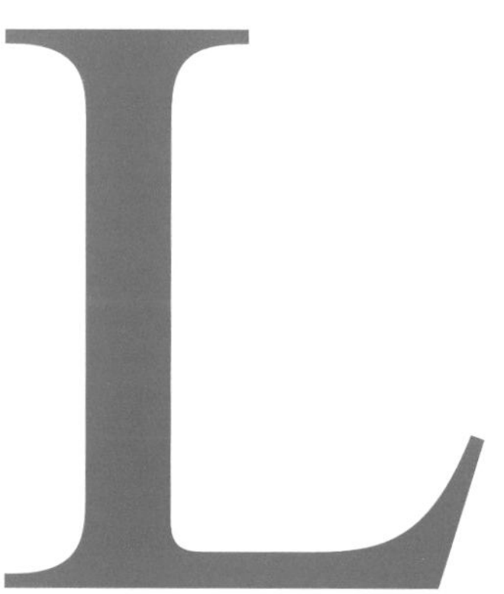

Lamb

In the Old Testament, a lamb (*agnus* in Latin) or ram was frequently sacrificed to God. For example, to protect themselves during plague, the Israelites were instructed to kill a lamb "without blemish" and sprinkle their doorposts with its blood, an act which immunized their first-born children.[1] Because a lamb was substituted for Isaac in the Sacrifice of Abraham, the Sacrificial Lamb or Lamb of God was taken as a type of Christ who shed his blood for the salvation of mankind. The attribute of John the Baptist may be a lamb, with reference to his calling Christ the "Lamb of God", destroyer of sin.[2]

A lamb was used in early Christian and medieval art to represent both the Passion of Christ and Christ of the Resurrection. In depictions of the former theme its blood may flow into a chalice; in the latter it may hold a triumphant banner with a red cross on a white background. In the Book of Revelation a lamb stood on Mount Sion; in this case the lamb may be taken to represent the Church. Jan van Eyck's *Adoration of the Lamb* from the Ghent Polyptych shows the lamb on an altar surrounded by angels holding the Instruments of Christ's Passion, while people gather from all corners of the world; this illustrates another passage from Revelation.[3]

As well as representing the sacrificial figure of Christ, a lamb may also symbolize one of Christ's flock of followers, under the protection of the Good Shepherd.[4] This is illustrated in the early Christian mosaics of the Mausoleum of Galla Placida, Ravenna. Christ sent his disciples out to preach to the Jews, whom he described as the "lost sheep of the house of Israel".[5] After the Resurrection, Christ twice instructed St Peter to "feed my sheep".[6]

A lamb is also the attribute of St Agnes.

Lamentation

Although the Lamentation does not appear in the Gospels, in art this scene of mourners around the body of Christ follows the Deposition and

Lamb: *see*
Abraham; Agnes, St; Christ, The Life of; Isaac; John the Baptist, St; Passion of Christ, The

[1] *Exodus 12:3–7*
[2] *John 1:29*
[3] *Revelation 14:1–4*
[4] *John 10:11*
[5] *Matthew 10:6*
[6] *John 21:16*

Lamentation: *see*
John the Evangelist, St; Joseph of Arimathea; Mary Magdelene; Nicodemus; Passion of Christ, The; Virgin, The

Lamp, Lantern, Light: *see* Lucy, St

[1] *II Samuel 22:29*
[2] *John 9:5*

precedes the Entombment. Christ is usually laid on the ground at the foot of the Cross and the Marys weep near the body. The Virgin Mary may be fainting, while Mary Magdalene may clasp the feet of Christ in a gesture reminiscent of her washing them at the Last Supper. Joseph of Arimathea, Nicodemus and John the Evangelist may also be present. The Pietà ("pity"), a much-depicted version of the Lamentation, usually represents the Virgin alone supporting the dead Christ on her lap. In northern Europe, pictorial emphasis was placed on the harrowing qualities of the subject. However, Michelangelo's early *Pietà* conveys a gentle pathos, harmoniously placing Christ (as a fully grown man) in the lap of his mother; in other Pietàs Christ may be on the ground to avoid compositional difficulties.

Lamp, Lantern, Light

In the Old Testament a lamp signifies divine light: "for thou art my lamp, O Lord; and the Lord will lighten my darkness".[1]

It also symbolizes divine wisdom. Christ's words, "As long as I am in the world, I am the light of the world,"[2] were the inspiration for William Holman Hunt's painting, *The Light of the World*. Caravaggio often included a source of light external to the composition to suggest the divine illuminating the chosen.

In landscape paintings, such as Albert Cuyp's *Milkmaid and Cattle Near Dordrecht*, a scene bathed in a golden glow evokes a rural idyll where mankind is in harmony with nature.

LANDSCAPE

See panel, right.

LANDSCAPE

Until the late 16th century landscape painting did not exist as a subject in Western art, but was simply a backdrop for outdoor scenes. During the Renaissance, however, landscape details became increasingly naturalistic, and since then the interpretation of nature, whether as a subject in its own right or as an enhancement of a theme, has reflected various aims.

Seasons usually convey mood: winter may communicate bleakness and decay; spring and summer the optimism of renewal and vigour; autumn the benefits of plenty. Time of day and treatment of light are also evocative: dawn may suggest hope, while evening light casts ominous shadows.

Landscape may indicate mankind's relationship with nature: the pastoral image recalls a mythical Golden Age when humans and nature existed in harmony; cultivated fields and a clement sky may suggest mankind in control of its environment; while stormy scenes may show the superior forces of nature.

Landscapes may be purely topographical or else be picturesque views with arcadian or heroic connotations. Rural scenes may reveal an intimacy with nature or consciously ignore the impact of the Industrial Revolution.

The Impressionists chose to paint tamed and populated scenes. However, Van Gogh, Cézanne and Gauguin presented a wilder nature more akin to their particular temperaments.

Laocoön, after an antique marble sculpture, artist unknown (Belvedere Courtyard, Vatican Museum, Rome).

Laocoön

The Trojan priest Laocoön[1] warned his people that the huge wooden horse fashioned by their enemy, the Greeks, was treacherous, as he suspected that it contained the men who would bring about the downfall of their city. The Trojans, however, were tricked by a Greek captive into believing that it was a gift to Minerva (Athene in Greek myth).

As Laocoön was sacrificing a bull to Neptune (Poseidon) on the shore, two giant sea-snakes with monstrous coils swam up to him; first they twined themselves around his two little sons before encircling the priest himself. Laocöon strove frantically to wrench the knots apart, but the snake's grip tightened and all were crushed to death. The famous expressive marble group of the 2nd century AD, now in the Vatican Museum, Rome, was rediscovered in 1506; since the late 15th century it has been greatly admired and copied.

Laocoön: *see* Trojan War
[1] Virgil, *Aeneid II*

Last Judgment

The Nicene Creed was the first official statement of Christian belief, made in AD325 at the Council of Nicea. It established the doctrine of the Second Coming of Christ, when the living and the dead would be judged – the "Last Judgment".

The Gospels prophesied that all nations would come before Christ, and "He shall separate them one from another, as a shepherd divideth his sheep [the faithful] from the goats [non-believers]. And he shall set the sheep on his right hand, but the goats on the left."[1] In late medieval and Renaissance churches the Last Judgment was traditionally depicted on or near the wall of the west entrance of churches as a reminder to departing congregations. Christ presides as judge, seated on a throne with the Apostles flanking him as a jury. Near him may be the Virgin as intercessor, St Peter with the keys to Heaven, and angels bearing the Instruments of the Passion. Above Christ appear ranks of angels, martyrs or saints and, below him, St Michael holds the scales in which souls are weighed. Angels sound their trumpets to call up the dead. At the bottom of the composition graves open to release souls and the blessed soar up in a clockwise direction toward Christ's right. On his left the damned are sent to Hell. Here, among flames, Satan may devour and excrete sinners, while those suffering specific tortures may be grouped according to

Last Judgment: *see* Hades
[1] *Matthew 25:32–33*

Latona: *see*
Apollo; Diana; Jupiter
[1] Ovid, *Met VI: 313–381*

Laurel: *see*
Daphne

Laurence, Saint: *see*
Martyrs; Stephen, St
[1] *Golden Legend, St Laurence*

their punishment.

Michelangelo's *Last Judgment* in the Sistine Chapel, Rome, is unusual in being placed behind the altar. This may have been to warn those who questioned the supremacy of the Pope after the Reformation. Christ is no longer passive but seems to storm out of the fresco with a condemning gesture, while saints wait anxiously for his blessing and, in the lower half, the elected throw off their shrouds. The damned sink in despair to be met by Minos, the judge of Hades, whose coiled tail indicates which circle of hell awaits them, and Charon, ready to ferry them to the kingdom of Satan.

Latona

A Titaness, Latona (in Greek myth, Leto) was loved by the supreme god Jupiter (Zeus).[1] She fled from the anger of Jupiter's wife, Juno (Hera), and gave birth to her twins, Apollo and Diana (Artemis), on the Mediterranean island of Delos. Johann Koenig, in *Latona Changing the Lycian Peasants into Frogs*, illustrates how a thirsty Latona stopped to drink from a lake where peasants gathering reeds harried and insulted her. As punishment for their malicious behaviour she turned them into frogs, which even under water continued to bicker.

Laurel

Laurel, or the bay of the laurel family, was sacred to the god Apollo because divine powers turned his mortal love Daphne into a laurel tree. This was to save her from Apollo's embrace, after Cupid (in Greek myth, Eros) had struck him with the arrow of love; Daphne herself had been struck with the arrow that puts love to flight. She is usually shown in painting fleeing from the god's advances as her arms metamorphose into branches.

A crown or wreath of laurels was worn by those worthy of honour, especially poets; hence "poet laureate". Paintings of victorious generals of ancient Rome also show them crowned with laurel.

Laurence (Lorenzo), Saint

It is known that Laurence was a deacon, that he was martyred in Rome in AD258, and that he was buried outside the city, where a church dedicated to him now stands. Legend[1] claims that he was entrusted by Pope Sixtus II with the church's treasure, which he then distributed among the poor. When Laurence was ordered by the prefect of Rome to bring the treasure, he gathered together all the poor and sick and said to them, "See here the eternal treasure, which never diminishes but increases." Laurence was martyred by being laid on an iron grid above roasting coals. Heated iron pitchforks were pressed on his body, whereupon he cried, "You have me well done on one side, now turn me over and eat!"

The martyrdom is shown in Bronzino's painting of 1569. Scenes from his life were also painted by Fra Angelico in the Chapel of Nicholas V in the Vatican. Laurence was one of the patron saints of Florence and of the Medicis; he appears in many paintings commissioned by the family.

Laurence is usually seen dressed as a deacon with a censer, or he may be shown holding a plate of coins in reference to the alms he distributed. His most common attribute, however, is the gridiron of his martyrdom.

A detail showing Leda and Jupiter (as a swan), after Melzi's Leda and the Swan *(c.1550, Uffizi, Florence).*

Leda

In mythology[1] Leda was the wife of Tyndareus, king of Sparta. Jupiter (in Greek myth, Zeus), the supreme god, fell in love with her and appeared to her in the form of a swan. Leda subsequently laid two eggs; from one hatched Clytemnestra and Castor, and from the other Helen of Troy and Pollux. Accounts vary as to the paternity of these children as Leda is said to have slept with her husband on the same night as with Jupiter; most often the latter pair are said to have been the offspring of the god. Michelangelo's cartoon and lost painting of 1530 showing Leda erotically embracing the swan provided the basis for several paintings. Correggio's picture of *c.*1534 similarly emphasizes the sexual nature of the encounter. Leonardo da Vinci's slightly earlier treatment of the theme, which is now lost but exists in copies by other artists, shows Leda standing with the swan, while her infants play on the ground, hatched from eggs.

Leonard, Saint

Little is known of Leonard.[1] He was apparently a hermit, but founded a monastery near Limoges in France in the 6th century. He was held in such esteem that the king of France released any prisoners visited by the saint. His prayers were answered for the queen's well-being and the safe delivery of her child, and he performed many miracles, including freeing some prisoners bound in chains. He is usually dressed as a monk. Fetters are his attribute, as he is the patron saint of prisoners.

Leonidas

At Thermopylae in 480BC Leonidas, king of Sparta, withstood the massive army of his enemy Xerxes of Persia for two days. The following day Leonidas and his 300 men were attacked from the rear and only one man survived.[1] In *Leonidas at Thermopylae* Jacques-Louis David shows Leonidas and his men before battle, depicted as idealized nudes.

Leviathan

This enormous sea-monster usually takes the form of a crocodile, whale or sea-serpent. It is described in the Old Testament as a huge scaly monster that breathes fire and "out of his nostrils goeth smoke, as out of a seething pot, or cauldron".[1] With open jaws it may represent Satan and the descent into hell, as in El Greco's *Allegory of the Holy League*.

LIBERAL ARTS

See panel on following page.

Liberale, Saint

Liberale, an early Christian (dates unknown), was venerated at Treviso

Leda: *see*
Castor and Pollux; Helen of Troy; Jupiter
[1] Apollodorus, *The Library III.x.7*

Leonard, Saint:
[1] *Golden Legend, St Leonard*

Leonidas:
[1] Herodotus, *VII: 203–238*

Leviathan: *see*
Hell
[1] *Job 41*

Liberale, Saint: *see*
George, St

LIBERAL ARTS

During the Middle Ages and Renaissance the seven Liberal Arts were the subjects of secular education. They comprised the *trivium*: grammar, rhetoric and logic (dialectic); and the *quadrivium*: arithmetic, geometry, astronomy and music. The Sages of antiquity might accompany personifications of the Liberal Arts or represent their subjects: Priscian or Donatus, grammar; Cicero, rhetoric; Aristotle, logic; Pythagoras, arithmetic; Euclid, geometry; Ptolemy, astronomy; and the biblical character Tubal-Cain,[1] music. These are shown in Andrea da Firenze's frescoes in Santa Maria Novella, Florence.

Female personifications of the subjects may each have a book and inscriptions to identify them: an example is the throned figures in Pinturicchio's Room of the Liberal Arts in the Vatican, Rome. **Grammar**, the foundation of all subjects, may have writing instruments, a fountain from which scholars drink, fruit that she offers to a child, or a rod for chastisement, or she may point to the slim door of knowledge. **Rhetoric**, a subject learned in adolescence, may have a scroll, a sword and the globe of her universal domain. **Logic** may be shown with a scorpion or snake, perhaps signifying the penetrating nature of the subject. **Arithmetic** is often seen holding her fingers up, to calculate with them, or holding an abacus or tables covered with figures. **Geometry** may be seen with a set square, pair of compasses, measuring rod or other instruments of the science. **Astronomy** may point to the sky and have an astrolabe or a globe marked with the constellations. **Music** may be shown playing instruments and singing.

Rhetoric

Logic

Arithmetic

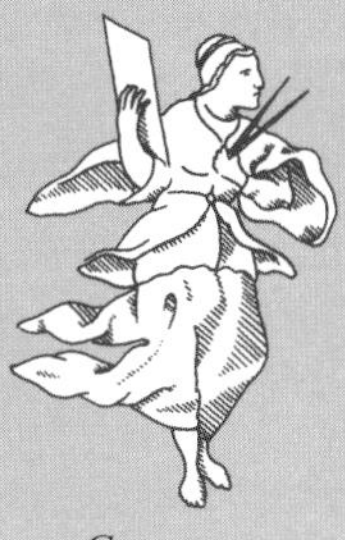

Geometry

Astronomy

Music

LIBERAL ARTS: *see*
Grammar; MUSIC/MUSICAL INSTRUMENTS

[1] *Genesis 4:22*

Lily: *see*
Dominic, St; Gabriel, Archangel; Joachim and Anna; Joseph, Husband of the Virgin; Virgin, The

and the surrounding Veneto, where he is said to have made many converts.

He is usually depicted as a knight in armour with a spear and banner, as in Giorgione's altarpiece in San Liberale, Castelfranco. In this and other paintings he may be confused with St George, who is also often depicted as a knight.

Lily

The lily is the particular attribute of the Virgin and symbolizes her purity. The flower is often depicted at the Annunciation, either held out by Gabriel or standing in a vase near the Virgin. It is also the attribute of those associated with the Virgin, especially Gabriel, Joachim and Joseph, the virgin saints and St Dominic. The fleur de lys (heraldic lily or iris flower with three petals bound at the base) was the French royal coat of arms from the 12th century.

Lion

The lion has an ancient role as the king of beasts, representing strength, courage and fortitude. It has, therefore, been included in many royal and aristocratic emblems. It is, however, a ferocious beast, and so to overcome a lion may be seen as proof of superhuman strength, as shown in the stories of Samson and David in the Old Testament and the Roman hero Hercules (in Greek myth, Heracles). A lion lying peacefully with other animals suggests a Paradise or Golden Age without conflict; Daniel in the lions' den represents God's redemption of his people.

Vigilance is another of the lion's perceived qualities, as stated in the Old Testament: "the lion which is the mightiest among beasts and does not turn back before any."[1] It may therefore be the guardian of doorways or may support church pulpits as a pillar of vigilance.

In mythology lions draw the chariot of Cybele, the personification of Mother Earth. In Christian iconography a lion is an attribute of St Jerome. A winged lion symbolizes St Mark, patron saint of Venice; the city also adopted this as a religious and political emblem.

Longinus, Saint

Longinus (1st century AD) was the name attached in the Middle Ages to the Roman centurion who pierced Christ's side at the Crucifixion and was immediately converted, saying, "Truly this was the Son of God."[1] His attribute is, therefore, the spear. The weapon is one of the relics of St Peter's, Rome, where Bernini's sculpture shows Longinus, arms outstretched, at the moment of his conversion.

Loretto

Loretto, on the Adriatic coast of Italy, was a major place of pilgrimage because, according to legend, the house of the Virgin Mary's birth was miraculously transported there from the Holy Land in 1291. Caravaggio's *Madonna of the Pilgrims* was commissioned to imitate a statue known as the Madonna of Loretto. Giambattista Tiepolo's *Holy House of Loretto* shows the house with the Virgin on its roof being carried through the air by angels.

Lot

In the Old Testament Lot, accompanied by his uncle, Abraham, went into Canaan and then selfishly stated his own claim to the well-watered plain of Jordan. This brought him into contact with the wicked inhabitants of Sodom and Gomorrah.[1] Lot played host to two angels but the people of Sodom threatened to violate his guests. Urged by the angels to "escape for thy life; look not behind thee", Lot and his family fled, but, as God destroyed Sodom and Gomorrah, his wife looked back and was turned into a pillar of salt. To preserve the seed of their father, Lot's daughters made him drunk and slept with him, giving birth to the ancestors of the Moabites and Ammonites.[2] In *Lot and his Daughters* Bonifazio de' Pitati, like many other artists, shows Lot in his drunkenness with his daughters,

Lion: *see*
Cybele; Daniel; David; Evangelists; Hercules; Jerome, St; Mark, St; Samson and Delilah
[1] *Proverbs 30:30*

Longinus, Saint:
[1] *Matthew 27:54*

Lot: *see*
Abraham
[1] *Genesis 13:10–13*
[2] *Genesis 19*

A detail of St Dominic holding the lily of purity, after Virgin and Child with Saints John and Dominic *by Filippino Lippi (1406–69, National Gallery, London).*

Louis IX, Saint: *see* Fleur-de-Lys
[1] *John of Joinville, Life of Louis IX*

Louis of Toulouse: *see* Fleur-de-Lys; Louis IX, St

Lucretia: *see* Brutus; Lucius Janius
[1] Ovid, *Fasti II:721–853* and *Livy, The History of Rome I 1.vii–1.ix*

Lot between his daughters. The detail is after Lot and his Daughters Leaving Sodom *by Guido Reni (*c.*1615, National Gallery, London).*

while Sodom and Gomorrah burn in the background.

Louis IX, Saint

Louis (1214–70), king of France, was profoundly religious and a just and merciful monarch.[1] In 1248 he led a crusade and returned with what were believed to be Christ's Crown of Thorns and a piece of the True Cross, which, along with a sword and the fleurs-de-lys, may be held as his attributes. He died of the plague on his second crusade. He is a national saint of France, and may be dressed as a king with a crown or clad in armour as a knight. In place of a sceptre he may hold a staff surmounted by a hand, as shown in a painting by El Greco.

Louis of Toulouse, Saint

Descended from Louis IX of France, Louis (1274–97) was offered the throne of Naples, but renounced it in favour of his brother, Robert of Anjou, and entered the Franciscan Order. He became Bishop of Toulouse and devoted his life to Christian works, dying at the age of 24. Simone Martini's *St Louis Altar* shows the young saint enthroned, dressed in his bishop's vestments and holding a crozier. Angels appear above, supporting the crown he refused, as he in turn crowns Robert, who kneels beside him. Surrounding the image are French fleurs-de-lys.

Lucretia

The classical story of Lucretia[1] is one of conjugal fidelity and virtue. In Lorenzo Lotto's *A Lady with a Drawing of Lucretia*, the figure, probably herself a 16th-century woman called Lucretia, directs us to a drawing of the legendary Lucretia as such an example. Lucretia, the beautiful wife of Tarquinius Collatinus, served in the army of Sextus, son of the dictator Tarquinius Superbus. One night, Sextus raped her. Lucretia confessed her disgrace to her husband before plunging a knife into her heart. This incident was instrumental in persuading the Romans to overthrow Tarquin. Depictions of Lucretia commonly show either her rape, as in Titian's violent *Tarquin and Lucretia*, or her suicide.

A detail after A Lady with a Drawing of Lucretia *by Lorenzo Lotto (*c.*1530, National Gallery, London).*

Lucy, Saint

Lucy (died *c.* AD304) was martyred in Sicily. Legend[1] claims that she persuaded her mother to pray at the shrine of St Agatha, where she was healed of her usually incurable disease. In gratitude Lucy gave all her goods to the poor but, angered by her faith, her suitor handed her over to the Roman Consul. When she was condemned to a brothel to be violated, she was made miraculously immovable, even by oxen. She survived being drenched in urine and oil and set alight, only to be killed by a sword thrust into her throat. Her name, implying light, explains why her attribute is a lamp.

In another legend, one of her suitors ceaselessly praised her eyes, so she tore them out and sent them to him. Consequently, she may be shown with a pair of eyes on a dish. Giambattista Tiepolo shows her taking her last communion (Santi Apostoli, Venice).

Luke, Saint

Author of one of the Gospels, Luke was a physician and probably travelled with St Paul to Italy. Although in medieval tradition it was thought that he was martyred, he probably died naturally of old age in Greece. Legend claims that he was a painter, who produced several portraits of the Virgin. 15th- and 16-century Flemish paintings by artists such as Rogier van der Weyden show him in this role. St Luke is the patron saint of painters as well as doctors and pharmacists, the latter two professions possibly sharing a guild. As an evangelist Luke may be depicted writing his Gospel. His attribute is the winged bull.

Luxury

Luxury may be closely associated with Lust, one of the Vices. Dutch 17th-century paintings, which appear to be on the theme of "merry company", with richly dressed figures sitting at a dinner table covered with sumptuous objects, may contain warnings of the vanity of earthly possessions and of wastefulness. The etching *Death Surprising a Young Couple* by Jan van de Velde has the inscription: "We often sit in luxury, while Death is closer than we know".

Lucy, Saint: *see*
Agatha, St; Eyes; Lamp, Lantern, Light; Martyrs
[1] *Golden Legend, St Lucy*

Luke, Saint: *see*
Bull; Doctor; Evangelists; Paul, St

Luxury: *see*
VICES

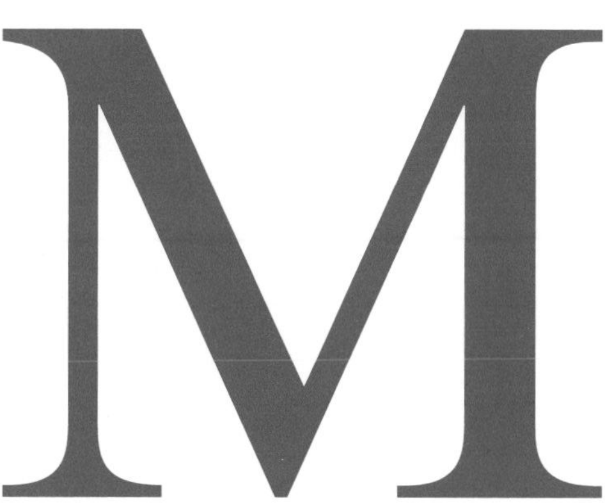

Maccabees:
[1] *Apocrypha, II Maccabees 7*

Man of Sorrows: *see* Passion of Christ, The
[1] *Isaiah 53:3*

Manlius Torquatus:
[1] Livy, *The History of Rome VIII vii*

Maccabees
In the Old Testament Apocrypha the Maccabees are said to have rebelled against the Syrian high priests and kings dominating Palestine.[1] Under a cruel regime, seven brothers and their mother were brought before the king and ordered to eat the forbidden flesh of the pig. When they refused they were dismembered one by one. In art they may be seen in a cauldron, their mutilated limbs in view.

Man of Sorrows
It was prophesied that the Messiah would be "despised and rejected of men; a man of sorrows, and acquainted with grief".[1] The image is not part of the narrative of the Passion of Christ, although in paintings it may include symbols from before and after the Crucifixion. For example, Christ may be standing in the sepulchre, crowned with thorns, displaying his wounds.

Manlius Torquatus
During the war against the Latins in 340BC, the Roman consuls, of whom Manlius Torquatus was one, forbade single combat with the enemy.[1] His son disobeyed the ruling and, although he defeated his opponent, Manlius ordered his execution. Ferdinand Bol illustrated this example of severe justice in *Manlius Torquatus Beheading His Son*, for the Council Chamber of the Admiralty in Amsterdam.

Marat
The Swiss-born Jean-Paul Marat (1743–93), a man of extreme republican views, was a member of the Jacobin club during the French Revolution, and made his name as a friend of the people. This brought him into conflict with the counter-revolutionary Girondins. One of their sympathizers, Charlotte Corday, travelled to Paris from Normandy and stabbed him to death in his bath, believing that she was thereby delivering her country from the threat of Jacobinism. Jacques-Louis David's *Death of Marat* confirmed the painter's sympathies with the Revolution.

Marcus Sextus

With his painting *The Return of Marcus Sextus* Pierre-Narcisse Guérin invented a figure from Roman history who returns from exile to find his wife dead. The artist no doubt intended to allude to the return of émigrés to France after the 1789 Revolution.

Margaret of Antioch, Saint

There is no historical evidence to prove that Margaret existed, yet her cult was popular in the later Middle Ages. Legend states that the Christian maiden was harassed by the prefect of Antioch; after refusing to become his concubine, she was tortured and thrown into prison.[1] Here, the Devil appeared to her in the form of a hideous dragon and swallowed her up, but the power of the cross she was wearing split the dragon in two, leaving her unharmed. She was subsequently beheaded, but not before she had prayed that, just as she had been safely delivered from the dragon's belly, so healthy children would be born to all women who invoked her aid when faced with a difficult labour. She consequently became the patron saint of childbirth. A dragon is her attribute, and she may be depicted trampling it underfoot. She is often shown as an attendant saint in paintings of the Virgin, frequently in the company of Catherine of Alexandria.

Margaret of Cortona, Saint

The daughter of a peasant family in Tuscany, Margaret (*c.*1247–97) became the mistress of a nobleman near Montepulciano. The man was assassinated, whereupon his dog found Margaret and led her to his murdered body. She repented her ways and joined the Franciscans. Baroque artists such as Lanfranco painted her ecstatic vision of Christ. Her attribute is her lover's dog.

Mark, Saint

One of the four Evangelists, Mark (died *c.*AD74) travelled to Rome, where he is thought to have written his Gospel aided by St Peter. He then travelled to Cyprus and Alexandria, where he is said to have become the first bishop, and to have been battered and stoned to death. He is depicted as a middle-aged, dark-haired, bearded man, often shown writing his Gospel,

St Mark with his gospel, after a painting by Andrea Mantegna (1448–9, Stadelsches Kunstinstitut, Frankfurt).

and his attribute is the winged lion.

According to legend, Mark was once caught in a storm off the Adriatic coast and was blown onto the islands of the Venetian Lagoon; an angel appeared to him and announced that he stood on the spot where a city would rise in his honour.

Margaret of Antioch, Saint: *see*
Catherine of Alexandria, St; Dragon, St; Martyrs
[1] *Golden Legend, St Margaret of Antioch*

Mark, Saint: *see*
Evangelists
[1] *Golden Legend, St Mark*

Mars: *see*
Furies; Putto; Venus; Vulcan
[1] Homer, *Iliad V:814–909*
[2] Lucretius, *De Rerum Natura I:32–40*
[3] Homer, *Odyssey VIII:265–346* and Ovid, *Met IV:167–189*

Some 400 years later, settlers began to drive in the foundations of Venice. In AD829 two Venetian merchants induced priests to let them secretly remove St Mark's relics from Alexandria; they managed to conceal them from officials under a consignment of salted pork and transported them to Venice. A basilica was built, dedicated to the saint initially as the Chapel of the Doge's palace, Venice, and his relics were enclosed within a column of marble. With the passing of time their exact location was forgotten, which caused much distress; but one day, during a fast, stones bounced out of the column and revealed the holy casket of the saint's relics. St Mark is, therefore, particularly venerated in Venice, where scenes of his life were painted by Tintoretto and others, and the winged lion was adopted as an emblem of the city.

The Venetians popularized stories regarding the saint's miraculous intervention on behalf of those who invoked his help.[1] In one, a servant made a pilgrimage to the body of St Mark without his master's permission. Tintoretto, in his depiction of the tale, shows how, when the man returned, his master wanted his eyes put out, his feet cut off, his legs broken and his teeth smashed. He was thrown to the ground but, because he had prayed to St Mark, the sharp pointed sticks used to inflict his punishment broke into pieces and the iron tools melted or became blunt. Both master and servant repented.

St Mark is also said to have saved several victims shipwrecked during a storm. Some Venetian merchants had taken passage in a Saracen ship, and seeing that the ship was in imminent danger they climbed into the skiff towed by the vessel and cut the rope, whereupon a great wave sank the ship. One of the Saracens, struggling in the waves, invoked the saint and vowed that he would be baptized if rescued: he was instantly plucked out of the sea and deposited in the skiff. In another tale Saints Mark, Nicholas and George appeared to a fisherman at the height of a storm and told him to row out to sea. They came across demons threatening to destroy Venice and exorcized them, and St Mark gave the fisherman his ring; as Paris Bordone shows, the saint commanded him to tell their story to the Doge and present the ring as evidence.

Mars

In mythology Mars (in Greek myth, Ares), the god of war, son of Jupiter (Zeus) and Juno (Hera), is depicted as a militant figure armed with a helmet and shield and a spear, sword or lance. He may be accompanied by the Furies or by his sisters, Strife and Bellona (the latter being his female counterpart). In the Trojan War, Minerva (Athene), goddess of wisdom, considered Mars a pestilent, double-dealing villain and easily conquered him.[1] He appears in allegories illustrating the triumph of love or wisdom over war. Mars may also be used to emphasize, by contrast, the superior aim of peace, in his negative role of war trampling on civilized pursuits.

His most famous affair was with Venus (Aphrodite), goddess of love, a relationship shown in numerous paintings. Whenever Mars rested in her company he took off his armour and the world was at peace. Painters followed the classical description of the couple together: "Mars potent in arms, rules the savage works of war, yet often casts himself back into your lap, vanquished by the ever-living wound of love."[2] The theme may also be treated humorously, with *putti* disrespectfully playing with Mars' discarded armour. Another episode in the story concerns Venus' husband Vulcan (Hephaestus); informed of his wife's infidelity, he forged an invisible net that caught Venus and Mars in an embrace. This caused much amusement to all except the humiliated lovers and Vulcan.[3]

Marsyas

In mythology the satyr Marsyas became accomplished at playing Minerva's (Athene's) flute, which she had cursed because playing it distorted her face.[1] According to Apollodorus,[2] a competition ensued between Marsyas and Apollo, the god of music, in which they were to play their instruments upside down. However, while Apollo was able to play his lyre in this position, Marsyas could not sound his pipe. His brutal punishment was to be flayed alive for presuming to be able to play as well as Apollo. Satyrs, nymphs and fauns mourned for him and the earth grew wet with their tears until a river was formed.

Renaissance artists were inspired by Roman copies of a Hellenistic image of Marsyas, dating from the 3rd century BC. This shows him bound hand and foot, hanging upside down from a tree before his punishment. However, Titian's *The Flaying of Marsyas* gruesomely depicts the satyr in the throes of being flayed.

Martha

Martha, sister of Mary and Lazarus, represents the good housewife. The Gospels describe how she hospitably received Christ into her house and busied herself serving him while Mary listened to his words. She reproached him for not encouraging Mary to help her, but Christ replied that Mary had chosen the faithful path.[1] Martha is usually shown at work, perhaps with a ladle or pot or wearing a bunch of household keys. Velázquez's *Kitchen Scene with Christ in the House of Martha and Mary* suggests she is somewhat disgruntled with her lot. According to legend,[2] Martha, Mary and Lazarus were set adrift on rafts without food but landed safely on the coast of France near Marseilles. At that time a ferocious dragon was terrorizing the neighbouring community of Tarascon, but Martha subdued it with holy water and a cross.

A detail showing Martha, after the painting Kitchen Scene with Christ in the House of Martha and Mary *by Diego Velázquez (*c.*1618, National Gallery, London).*

Martin of Tours, Saint

Martin (*c.*AD315–97) was a young officer in the Roman army who was born in Hungary. While billeted in France, he converted to Christianity.

Marsyas: *see* Apollo
[1] Ovid, *Fasti VI:693–711*
[2] Apollodorus, *I.iv.2*

Martha:
[1] *Luke 10:38–42*
[2] *Golden Legend, St Martha*

Martin of Tours, Saint:
[1] *Golden Legend, St Martin*

MARTYRS: *see* Saints

He became a recluse, then founded the first monastery in Gaul, and was made Bishop of Tours *c.* AD370. He made many converts and had a reputation as a miracle worker. A figure of great importance in France, Martin was one of the first to be venerated as a saint, although he was not a martyr.

Legend[1] relates that one bitter night Martin came upon a naked beggar and divided his own cloak in two with his sword in order to cover the man; Christ then appeared to him, which led to his baptism. Martin asked for discharge from the army, saying, "I am a soldier of Christ and I am forbidden to fight." He was accused of cow-ardice, but offered to stand in the line of battle armed only with a cross. The following day the barbarian army surrendered. Martin hid when the people of Tours sought to elect him their bishop, as he wished to continue the solitary life, but a cackling goose gave away his hiding place. On one occasion Martin gave. his clothes away to a poor man while on his way to Mass and instructed the archdeacon to fetch him a new tunic. The archdeacon meanly brought one that was far too small, but while Martin was conducting the service angels presented him with gold armlets set with jewels so that his bare arms were decently covered.

The cult of St Martin was widespread. Scenes from his life by Simone Martini (*c.* 1317) decorate the chapel dedicated to him in San Francesco, Assisi. He is particularly venerated in France.

He is depicted as a bishop with the French fleur-de-lys on his cope, or occasionally with a goose, or as a soldier on horseback in the act of dividing his cloak for the beggar.

MARTYRS

The early Christian martyrs, who were persecuted by the Romans until the reign of Constantine, formed the subjects of altarpieces intended for churches and chapels dedicated to them or commissioned by patrons of the same name. Accounts of many of their lives are given in the *Golden Legend* (*c.* 1260) by Jacobus de Voragine; many were converted at an early age, refused to worship pagan idols and were tortured but refused to renounce their faith. Their attributes are often the instruments with which they were tortured or killed, but common to all is the martyrs' palm. Following the Council of Trent (1545–63) images showing their torments were favoured in order to encourage piety.

A particularly gruesome series of frescoes was commissioned by Pope Gregory for the church of San Stefano Rotondo in Rome. The martyrs are also shown in divine rapture, experiencing visions of the Virgin and Child or of Christ, or receiving their last communion from Christ.

Under King Shapur II (AD310–379) the Persians made war against the Roman Empire, which by then had adopted Christianity. In *10,000 Martyrs on Mount Ararat* Carpaccio shows the crucifixion of Armenian Christians by the Persians; Dürer, in *The Martyrdom of the 10,000 Christians under King Sapor*, shows them being executed in a variety of ways.

MARTYRS
See panel, left.

Mary of Egypt, Saint
According to legend,[1] Mary (5th century) was an Alexandrian prostitute who joined a pilgrimage to Jerusalem to find more trade. She was converted to Christianity after being pushed back by an invisible force when she tried to enter a church; looking up, she saw an image of the Virgin. She prayed to the image, and was then able to enter unimpeded. A voice subsequently told her to cross the Jordan; she did so, and thereafter lived as a penitent in the wilderness, sustained by three loaves of bread which miraculously lasted throughout her life. As her clothes wore out, her hair grew to cover her nakedness. When a priest took the sacred Host to the river bank, Mary was able to walk over the water to meet him. On his return the following year, he found her dead; he was unable to dig her grave single-handed but a lion came to his aid. Mary may be represented dressed as a penitent hermit in rags or covered with long hair, and thus may be confused with Mary Magdalene unless the loaves of bread and the lion are shown nearby.

Mary Magdalene
Mary Magdalene (1st century AD) was believed to be a reformed prostitute and is identified as the woman who "was a sinner" at the house of the Pharisee, who washed Christ's feet with her tears, wiped them with her hair and anointed them. Christ then forgave her sins.[1] She was present at the Crucifixion and found Christ's tomb empty after the Resurrection. Initially she

Mary Magdalene with her jar of ointment, after The Magdalene Reading *by Rogier van der Weyden (c.1435, National Gallery, London).*

mistook him for a gardener but then recognized him, and Christ bade her, "Touch me not, for I am not yet ascended to my Father; but go to my brethren and say to them, I ascend unto my Father."[2] This *Noli me tangere* theme was painted both as part of the narrative sequence and as an episode by itself – for example, by Titian.

According to legend,[3] Mary was the sister of Martha and Lazarus, with whom she was set adrift at sea, landing in Marseilles. She made many converts and performed miracles, then retired into the wilderness where she ate nothing but was nourished by angels. A hermit witnessed how angels descended and lifted her up seven times a day, and at the appointed hour of her death a choir of angels brought her to church to be blessed.

In scenes from the Life and Passion of Christ, Mary is often painted with long blond hair, wearing red. Masaccio shows her distraught at the Crucifixion. Her most common

Mary of Egypt, Saint: *see* Mary Magdalene
[1] *Golden Legend, St Mary of Egypt*

Mary Magdalene: *see* Martha; Passion of Christ, The
[1] *Luke 7:36–48*
[2] *John 20:17*
[3] *Golden Legend, St Mary Magdalene*

Mask: *see* Commedia dell'Arte; MUSES

Maurice, Saint: *see* Martyrs
[1] *Golden Legend, St Maurice and his companions*

Medea: *see* Jason; Alcestis
[1] Apollonius of Rhodes, *The Argonautica IV*
[2] Ovid, *Met VII:1–403* & Euripides, *Medea*

Matthew after Saints Matthew, Catherine of Alexandria and John the Evangelist *by Stephan Lochner (*c.*1445, National Gallery, London).*

attribute is her jar of ointment; Rogier van der Weyden shows her carrying this in his mid-15th-century *Braque Triptych*. Mary is also depicted as a penitent both young and old; Donatello carved her as a haggard elderly figure, her long hair covering her naked body. She may also be seen contemplating a skull, a crucifix or an open book, or in divine rapture.

Mask
In the plays of ancient Greece, actors wore the masks of comedy and tragedy, which are also the attributes of the comic and tragic muses Melpomene and Thalia. The characters of the Commedia dell'Arte also wore masks. A mask implies concealment and may thus be an attribute of Deceit.

Matthew, Saint
The attribute of the Apostle Matthew, or Levi, is a winged angel or winged man. Matthew was a tax gatherer for the Roman government. One day, as he sat in the customs house, Christ called him, "and saith unto him, Follow me. And he arose, and followed him." There is no authenticated account of the rest of his life, but legend relates that he preached in Ethiopia, where the king lusted after a Christian virgin. Matthew reprimanded him for desiring to violate a bride of Christ, and for this he was martyred by the sword or axe. Like the other Evangelists, Matthew may be shown writing his Gospel, usually guided by an angel. He may have the coins or purse of his former trade; in Florence he was the patron saint of money changers or bankers. Caravaggio depicted his Calling and Martyrdom in dramatic canvases in the Contarelli Chapel in San Luigi dei Francesi, Rome.

Maurice
Legend[1] claims that Maurice, who probably lived in the 3rd century AD, was the commander of the Theban Legion (Christian soldiers from Thebes in Egypt who served the Romans in Gaul). They were ordered to offer sacrifice to pagan gods, and when they refused the entire troop was massacred. Maurice was particularly venerated in the area around the canton of Valais, Switzerland, where an abbey was dedicated to him. In a painting by Malthius Grünewald he is generally shown as dark-skinned or Moorish, and wearing armour. Maurice is patron saint of northern Austria, and may be represented carrying a banner bearing an eagle, the country's emblem.

Medea
In mythology[1] the sorceress Medea was consumed with passion for the hero Jason and sailed away from Colchis with him after he had secured the Golden Fleece. They found Aeson, Jason's father, on the brink of death, but Medea's elaborate spells restored him. Pelias, who had usurped Aeson's throne, was bowed down with age and so Medea, seeking to avenge the usurpation, convinced Pelias' daughters that he too could be young again. In some accounts she told them that they could rejuvenate their father by emptying his veins, and she later pretended to fill them with youthful essence; in others she is said to have advised the daughters to cut Pelias up and boil him. His throne restored, Jason abandoned Medea to marry the

daughter of the king of Corinth. In anger Medea killed her own children, Jason's bride and his father-in-law.[2] Turner, in his *Vision of Medea*, shows Medea practising her black arts.

Medusa

In mythology[1] Medusa was one of three Gorgon sisters, renowned for her beauty, and especially her lovely hair. Neptune robbed her of her virginity in a Temple of Minerva, and to punish her for violating the sacred spot, the goddess changed Medusa's hair into a mass of fearsome snakes. One glance at her face would turn the beholder to stone, and after Perseus decapitated her he used her head to petrify his enemies. Minerva incised Medusa's image on her shield; Caravaggio re-created such a shield in paint.

Melancholia

In the Middle Ages a melancholic temperament was thought to be caused by an excess of black bile, and was associated with intellectual pursuits. Melancholia, daughter of Saturn (in Greek myth, Cronos) was of an introspective nature, and may appear in art in an attitude of gloomy contemplation. Dürer's engraving *Melancholia* shows a winged figure, heavily slumped. Scholarly objects – a sphere, a geometric block and tools – lie in disorder, while a book remains unopened in her lap and a pair of compasses unnoticed in her hand.

Meleager

In mythology[1] the Fates predicted that Meleager, son of Oeneus, king of Calydon, would live as long as a log burning on the fire lasted. His mother, Althea, therefore removed the log and carefully preserved it. When Meleager was a young man, his father neglected to make Diana (Artemis) an offering, and in her wrath she sent down a wild boar – the Calydonian boar – to ravage his lands. Meleager gathered a large band of heroes, huntsmen and hounds, and a great chase ensued. The fleet-footed huntress Atalanta joined the company and Meleager fell in love with her. She was the first to wound the boar, while Meleager drove in the fatal spear. He gave the boar's head to Atalanta as a trophy, but his mother's envious brothers tried to wrestle it from her and were killed by Meleager. Althea, remembering the prophecy, kindled a fire and flung on the log; Meleager died as it burned. Diana, placated by this tragedy, turned the women who mourned for him into birds and dispatched them into the sky. *The Hunt for the Calydonian Boar*, one of a series of eight paintings by Charles Lebrun, depicts the best-known episode of the story of Meleager.

Mercury

The athletic messenger of the gods, Mercury (in Greek myth, Hermes), was the son of Jupiter (Zeus). Because he acted as a guide and ambassador, he may be shown as a personification of diplomacy and eloquence. As a teacher he was entrusted with the education of Cupid (Eros), depicted by Correggio in *The Education of Cupid.* Mercury was the protector of travellers and led the souls of the dead down to the Underworld. He was also the god of dreams and sleep, and carried a "wand which he can use at will to cast a spell upon our eyes or wake us from the soundest sleep".[1] His wand, or caduceus, often shown with snakes entwined around it and

Medusa: *see* Perseus; Coral
[1] Ovid, *Met IV:774–803*

Melancholia: *see* Temperaments

Meleager: *see* Atalanta
[1] Ovid, *Met VIII:260–546* & Philostratus the Younger, *Imagines 15*

Mercury: *see* Herse; Io
[1] Homer, *Odyssey V:47*
[2] Ovid, *Met II:676–706*

The god Mercury, after Mercury, *a woodcut by Hans Baldung-grien (16th century).*

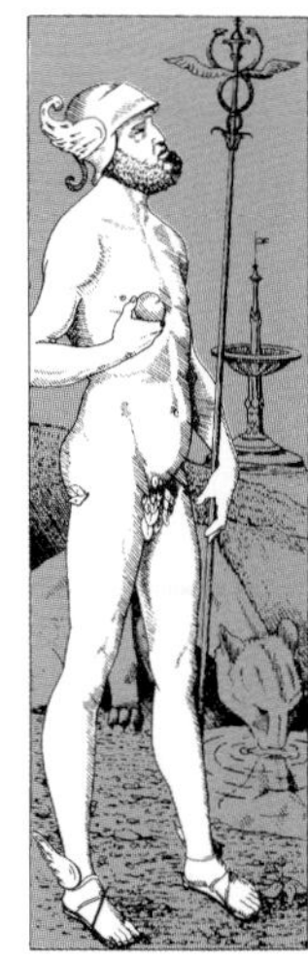

Michael, Saint (Archangel):
see
ANGELS; Last Judgment; Satan
[1] *Revelation 12:7–9*

Midas:
[1] Ovid, *Met XI:85–193*

Milky Way:
[1] Hygnus, *Poetica Astronomica II:43*

Milo of Croton:
[1] *Valerius Maximus 9:XII*

may have wings. Mercury wore winged sandals "of untarnishable gold". He may also wear a winged *petasus*, a hat with a low crown and small brim. Giambologna cast a potent image of the god in flight.

On the day he was born, Mercury made a lyre from a tortoise shell and stole Apollo's cows, walking them backward so that they could not be traced.[2] He is therefore seen as both inventive and light-fingered. When Apollo discovered the theft, he was so enchanted by the lyre that he agreed to exchange it for his herd and the caduceus. Mercury was the god of good luck, but also of commerce, wealth and thieves.

Michael, Saint (Archangel)

Michael, the heavenly messenger who was also adopted as a saint, was the prince of angels and the military leader who threw the Devil from heaven. "And there was war in heaven: Michael and his angels fought against the dragon; and the dragon fought and his angels, and prevailed not; neither was their place found any more in heaven."[1] He is depicted fighting the dragon by several artists including Dürer, or as a beautiful young man with wings (often in white or in armour, with lance and shield) standing over a dragon – for example, by Piero della Francesca. In scenes of the Last Judgment he holds scales on which he weighs the souls of the dead.

St Michael with his scales, after The Virgin and Child with an Angel, the Archangel Michael and the Archangel Raphael with Tobias *by Pietro Perugino (*c.*1490, National Gallery, London).*

Midas

The story of Midas, the legendary king of Phrygia, represents human folly and greed.[1] Midas entertained Bacchus' companion, Silenus, at a festival lasting ten days and nights. Bacchus was so grateful that he granted Midas a wish. The king asked that everything he touched be turned to gold. However, he had not anticipated being unable to eat and drink, as his food and wine were also transformed. Distraught, he begged for forgiveness for his greed. In *Midas Washing at the Source of the Pactolus* Poussin illustrates how Midas washed away folly in the River Pactolus, so that its sands became gold dust.

Now averse to riches, Midas retired to the country – but he had learned little wisdom. He worshipped Pan, who competed on his reed pipes against Apollo, the god of music. Apollo was pronounced the victor, but Midas foolishly objected; whereupon Apollo gave Midas ass's ears as a perpetual hallmark of his deafness to musical quality. Domenichino painted *The Judgment of Midas* as one of a series of rural scenes, several of which show Apollo in a vengeful mood.

Milky Way

There are various accounts of the origin of the Milky Way, which stretches in a luminous band across the night sky.[1] One is that Jupiter (Zeus) held his son Hercules (Heracles) to sleeping Juno's (Hera) breast to secure his immortality. After the infant had drunk, the flow of milk continued, some splashing upward creating constellations, some falling to earth as lilies. In *The Origin of the Milky Way* Tintoretto shows Hercules waking his unwitting wet-nurse.

Milo of Croton

A Greek athlete of the 6th century BC, Milo had remarkable strength.[1] However, he fell prey to wild animals when his hand caught in a split tree-trunk, which he was trying to prise open. Pierre Puget's sculpture *Milo of Croton* shows him screaming in agony as a lion sinks its teeth into him.

Minerva

One of the principal Olympian deities, Minerva (in Greek myth, Athene) was goddess of wisdom and war, but, unlike Mars (Ares), she fought in defence of justice. The owl of wisdom was sacred to her. She possessed a noble beauty and is usually shown in armour, carrying a lance or halberd and a shield, which may bear the image of Medusa. The daughter of Jupiter (Zeus), she often gave him counsel. She was born from his head, because Jupiter had been told in a prophecy that his first wife, Metis, would give birth to one who would surpass him, so when she became pregnant he swallowed her. But he suffered so much pain as a result that he had to beg Vulcan (Hephaestus) to split open his head – and Minerva issued forth.

Minerva competed with Neptune (Poseidon) for the region of Attica, which was promised as the prize for whichever of them gave the most useful present to its inhabitants. Neptune hit the ground with his trident and brought forth a spring or, in some accounts, a horse; Minerva created the olive tree, a symbol of peace, and the land was awarded to her. The olive tree was cultivated by Cecrops, who founded Athens, capital of Attica; and Minerva became the city's patroness, her temple being built on the Acropolis. She may be shown with an olive tree or branch, which may also decorate her dress, as in Botticelli's *Minerva and the Centaur*. Minerva was the goddess of crafts,

A detail showing the goddess Minerva, after Minerva and the Centaur *by Botticelli (*c.*1480, Uffizi, Florence).*

particularly spinning and weaving; she invented the flute, and was invoked by those in pursuit of reason, learning and the civilized arts.

Miniato, Saint

According to legend, Miniato was a 3rd-century Florentine Christian martyr. He survived ordeals with wild beasts in the ampitheatre but was eventually beheaded; he then carried his head from the bottom of a valley to the summit of a hill above Florence where the Romanesque church dedicated to him now stands. Here he can be seen as a young man crowned and holding the martyrs' palm in a 1390s painting by Agnolo Gaddi.

Minotaur

The mythological Minotaur[1] was the offspring of Pasiphaë, wife of King Minos of Crete – the result of her mating with a bull. It had the body of a man and a bull's head, and was kept

Minerva: *see*
Arachne; MUSES; Vulcan

Miniato, Saint: *see*
Martyrs

Minotaur: *see*
Ariadne; MUSES; Vulcan

[1] Philostratus the Elder, *Imagines I:16*

Model: *see*
Doctor; Geminianus, St; Jerome, St

Monica, Saint: *see*
Augustine, St
[1] St Augustine, *Confessions IX:8–13*

Moon: *see*
Diana

Moses: *see*
Aaron
[1] *Exodus 34:30*
[2] *Exodus 2:1–10*
[3] Josephus, *Antiquities II ix 7*
[4] *Exodus 2:11–21*
[5] *Exodus 3:1–17*
[6] *Exodus 4:1–4*
[7] *Exodus 7:9–10*
[8] *Exodus 7–11*
[9] *Exodus 12:23–29*
[10] *Exodus 14:5–30*
[11] *Exodus 16:4–35*
[12] *Exodus 17:6*
[13] *Exodus 17:8–12*
[14] *Exodus 20:1–17*
[15] *Exodus 31:18*
[16] *Exodus 32:1–19*
[17] *Numbers 21:5–9*
[18] *John 3:14*

in a Labyrinth where, once every nine years, seven youths and seven maidens were sacrificed to it. However, on one of these occasions the hero Theseus entered the Labyrinth with the children, killed the Minotaur and, aided by a ball of twine given to him by Minos' daughter, Ariadne, escaped with the children. The creature generally represents brutality and base animal instincts, but in the 1930s Picasso depicted a Minotaur to express the dual nature of man.

Missal
A missal, or book of the Mass, contains the services and prayers for the Roman Catholic liturgical year. It was often decorated with appropriate scenes; its frontispiece might be the Crucifixion or Christ in Majesty, sometimes surrounded by scenes from the Life and Passion of Christ.

Mithras
Mithras was the ancient Persian god of light and wisdom, and ruler of the universe. His cult spread into Europe during the 2nd century AD, and was popular among Roman soldiers, rivalling Christianity, with which it had affinities. In a relief in a temple dedicated to Mithras beneath San Clemente, Rome, Mithras is seen in his Phrygian cap plunging a dagger into the neck of a sacrificial bull.

Model
A model of a church may be held by St Jerome as one of the Four Doctors of the Church, or by other saints who founded monastic Orders. Saints may hold a model of the town or city of which they are patron; an example is St Emidius, patron of Ascoli Piceno in the Italian Marches, seen in Carlo Crivelli's *Annunciation*. A model of a building shown with its patron and architect may illustrate the enlightenment and generosity of the patron and the genius of the designer. Thus Vasari painted *Cosimo de Medici Receiving the Model for San Lorenzo from Brunelleschi*.

Monica, Saint
Monica (AD332–87) was the mother of St Augustine.[1] Converted to Christianity in Africa, she led a saintly life and tried to bring up her son in her faith. After she was widowed, she followed Augustine to Italy, where they were strongly influenced by St Ambrose of Milan, and Augustine was converted. She died at the port of Ostia, near Rome, as they were setting out for Africa. Monica appears in scenes of the life of St Augustine.

Moon
Luna (in Greek myth, Selene) was goddess of the moon and sister of the sun. She was later connected with the goddess Diana (Artemis), who is identified by a crescent moon in her hair or in the sky. The moon as a symbol of chastity was associated with the Virgin, notably in paintings of the Immaculate Conception. The sun and moon together may refer to the unity or cycle of time, to the universal, or to a marriage of dual natures. Both these heavenly bodies may be shown in the sky at the Crucifixion. The moon also signifies, simply, night.

Moses
Moses, the Old Testament prophet, led the Israelites out of captivity from Egypt, received the Ten Commandments from God, and organized the

A detail showing the baby Moses being found in the rushes, after The Finding of Moses *by Poussin (17th century, National Gallery, London).*

Jewish religion. He is invariably depicted as a vigorous elderly man, with a long flowing white beard. He is often shown with shafts of light radiating from either side of his head, for "the skin of his face shone" when he received the word of God.[1] These shafts are sometimes represented as horns, owing to an early mistranslation from Hebrew into Latin, in which "shone" was taken to mean "horned". He may also hold the tablets on which the Commandments were written, or a staff. The best-known episodes from his life are as follows:

THE FINDING OF MOSES
The populous Israelites were the slaves of the Pharaohs. Fearing their numbers, the Pharaoh resolved to kill all male Jewish children. To escape the massacre, his mother hid the infant Moses in a basket by the edge of the Nile; he was found by the Pharaoh's daughter, who adopted him.[2]

THE PHARAOH'S CROWN
In Jewish legend the Pharaoh placed a crown on Moses' head when he was a boy.[3] Moses trampled on it, and the scene came to represent the salvation of his people. This was interpreted as an omen that Moses would overthrow the king; so a trial was ordered whereby Moses had to choose between a bowl of burning coals and one of cherries. He would be exonerated if he chose the former. Moses grabbed the coals and put them into his mouth, an act which indicated his future greatness.

THE DAUGHTERS OF JETHRO
As a young man, Moses killed an Egyptian for beating a Jew and fled to the land of Midian. Here he met the seven daughters of Jethro, who were prevented from watering their flocks by shepherds. Moses drove off the shepherds and in reward was given one of the daughters as his bride.[4]

THE BURNING BUSH
As Moses watched over Jethro's flock, an angel appeared from a bush that was in flames without actually burning. From the bush God told Moses to lead his people out of Egypt into a land flowing with milk and honey.[5]

THE STAFF OF MOSES
Moses asked for a sign to prove that he was acting on God's command. God told him to cast his staff on the ground: it became a serpent but when he picked it up it became a staff again.[6] Returning to Egypt with his brother Aaron, Moses begged the Pharaoh to free their people. The ruler was unmoved either by pleas or by the sign given by the miraculous staff.[7]

THE PLAGUES OF EGYPT
Moses, with God's help, brought down ten plagues on the land of Egypt.[8] With each one, however, the

Moses and the Burning Bush, after The Burning Bush *by Nicholas Froment, (1476, St Sauveur Cathedral, Aix-en-Provence).*

Pharaoh's resolve was strengthened. Finally Moses threatened that all the first-born of the Egyptians would die unless the Israelites were released. The angel of death "passed over the houses of the children of Israel" and smote the "firstborn of Pharaoh that sat on his throne unto the firstborn of the captive in the dungeon, and all the firstborn of cattle".[9]

For seven days the Israelites ate unleavened bread according to God's command, thus initiating the celebration of the Passover. After this the Pharaoh agreed to let the Israelites leave Egypt.

A detail showing the plague of locusts, after an illustration in the Nuremberg Bible (early 16th century).

MOSES DIVIDES THE RED SEA

When the Pharaoh heard that Moses was leading his people to the Promised Land, he pursued them with an army. At the Red Sea the Lord told Moses to raise his staff, and the waters parted to allow the Israelites through. When the Egyptians tried to follow, the waters covered them.[10]

THE FALL OF MANNA

In the wilderness the Israelites became lost and were without food. God told Moses that he would "rain bread from heaven", and the following morning the ground was covered with manna, described as being like coriander seed, white and tasting like wafers made with honey. This was their food for 40 years.[11]

MOSES STRIKES THE ROCK

When the Israelites were thirsty the Lord commanded Moses to strike the rock of Horeb with his staff. Water poured forth, quenching the thirst of the people and their flocks.[12]

THE VICTORY OVER THE AMALEKITES

In the wilderness the Amalekites fought the Israelites. Moses instructed Joshua to fight while he himself watched the battle from the top of a hill. "And it came to pass, when Moses held up his hand, that Israel prevailed: and when he let down his hand, Amalek prevailed." As Moses' arms grew weary, Aaron and Hur held them up for him.[13]

THE TEN COMMANDMENTS

On Mount Sinai God instructed Moses on the Ten Commandments.[14] Moses informed his people and returned to Mount Sinai for 40 days and nights to be instructed in making an elaborate Ark to hold the covenant. Then God "gave unto Moses, when he had made an end of communing with him upon Mount Sinai, two tables of testimony, tables of stone, written with the finger of God".[15]

THE GOLDEN CALF

While Moses was on Mount Sinai, the Israelites asked Aaron to make a false god. Aaron took their jewelry and fashioned a golden calf, which the people worshipped. God instructed Moses to return from the mountain, for his people had "corrupted themselves". He went down with the two tables of testimony, and "saw the calf, and the dancing: and Moses' anger waxed hot, and he cast the tables out of his hands, and brake them beneath the mount".[16]

THE BRAZEN SERPENT

The Israelites, weary of their nomadic wandering, complained, whereupon "the Lord sent fiery serpents among the people, and they bit the people; and much people of Israel died". They begged Moses to rid them of the serpents, and "the Lord said unto Moses, Make thee a fiery serpent, and set it upon a pole; and it shall come to pass, that every one that is bitten, when he looketh upon it, shall live".[17]

Episodes from the life of Moses were depicted with other Old Testament prophets, such as Bartolo di Fredi's frescoes (Collegiata, San Gimignano). He was seen as a type of Christ, with the Brazen Serpent prefiguring the Crucifixion.[18]

Other scenes from the life of Moses were also paired with those from Christ's, such as Tintoretto's *The Fall of Manna* and *The Last Supper* flanking the High Altar of San Giorgio Maggiore, Venice. As Moses set down the law of the old covenant, so Christ dispensed the new. This was clearly indicated in frescoes by a number of artists, including Botticelli (Sistine Chapel, Vatican, Rome) and Perugino. As God's appointed vicar on earth, St Peter was often likened to Moses.

Isolated incidents from the life of Moses might be chosen for artistic reasons; in *Moses Defending the Daughters of Jethro* Rosso Fiorentino had the chance to show muscular figures wrestling; the elegance of Pharaoh's daughter finding the infant Moses appealed to both Poussin and Giambattista Tiepolo; Turner's *The Fifth Plague of Egypt* shows the dying Egyptians against a stormy landscape.

Mucius Scaevola

A legendary hero of the Roman republic, Mucius risked his life for his people.[1]

When Rome was besieged by the Etruscans, Mucius disguised himself and entered the enemy camp of Lars Porsena, intending to assassinate him. Instead he stabbed a secretary, mistaking him for the king, and was seized. To prove the fearlessness of the Romans, he thrust his right hand into a fire and held it there. Greatly impressed, Porsena made his peace with Rome. Mucius was thereafter left-handed (*scaevola*). His image, a symbol of constancy, was used in the decoration of public places, as in Ghirlandaio's *Mucius Scaevola* (Palazza Vecchio, Florence).

MUSES

See panel on following page.

MUSIC/MUSICAL INSTRUMENTS

See panel on page 157.

Myrtle

The evergreen myrtle, sacred to Venus (Aphrodite), signifies eternal love. Venus once covered herself in its leaves to hide from satyrs.[1]

In the Underworld, Aeneas saw a myrtle-wood which hides all those broken by love. Myrtle is also connected with marriage and crowns the bridal figure in Titian's *Sacred and Profane Love*.

Mucius Scaevola:

[1] Livy, *The History of Rome II xi*

Myrtle:

[1] Ovid, *Fasti IV:139–150*

[2] Virgil, *Aeneid VI:441–443*

MUSES: *see* Apollo; LIBERAL ARTS; MUSIC/MUSICAL INSTRUMENTS

[1] Ovid, *Met V:250–263*

MUSES

In mythology the Muses presided over and inspired music, poetry, dancing and the Liberal Arts. They were protected by Apollo, with whom they are often seen on high Mount Parnassus as young and beautiful virgins. Raphael's fresco *Parnassus* (Stanza della Segnatura, Vatican, Rome) shows Apollo and the muses along with poets, both ancient and modern. There were traditionally thought to be nine Muses: Clio (the muse of history), Euterpe (music), Thalia (comedy), Melpomene (tragedy), Terpsichore (dancing), Erato (lyric poetry), Polyhymnia (sacred song), Calliope (epic poetry) and Urania (astronomy). As attributes they may be shown with books, musical instruments or other related objects. They were the children of Jupiter (in Greek myth, Zeus) and Mnemosyne (Memory).

The Muses with Apollo, after The Poet's Inspiration *by Poussin (*c.*1628–29).*

The home of the Muses was the wooded Mount Helicon where they were visited by Minerva (in Greek myth, Athene), who wished to see the miraculous Hippocrene, a fountain which a blow from the winged horse Pegasus' hoof had caused to flow from the earth.[1] The Muses were also said to have guarded the springs of lofty Mount Parnassus, on which the Castalian spring was thought to be the source of poetic inspiration.

A museum (literally, a home or seat of the Muses) was originally the term applied to an institution dedicated to learning, literature and the arts; an example was the Academy at Alexandria in the 3rd century BC. A museum still suggests a place where antiquities are housed, as distinct from a gallery, also of ancient origin, where colonnades were used for the display of pictures.

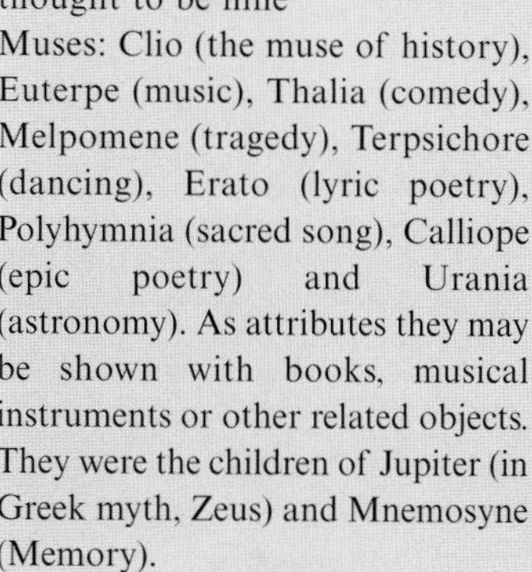

Name	**Meaning**	**Branch of the Arts**
Calliope	Beautiful voice	Epic poetry
Clio	Fame	History
Erato	Lovely	Lyric poetry
Euterpe	Joy	Music
Melpomene	Singing	Tragic drama
Polyhymnia	Many songs	Mime and sacred lyrics
Terpsichore	Joyful dance	Dance
Thalia	Good cheer/Plenty	Comic drama
Urania	Celestial	Astronomy

MUSIC/MUSICAL INSTRUMENTS

The Greek word for "music" literally means "the art of the Muses", and musical instruments are their attributes. Certain instruments have special associations through their sound and appearance: the trumpet is heraldic, proclaiming a messenger, announcing the famous or calling up the dead; the harp suggests the divine, and is often played by choirs of angels; the earthy bagpipe belonged to the lower classes and was played by shepherds; medieval pipes and the small round-backed lute were minstrels' instruments and accompanied folk dances; and tambourines and cymbals provided the accompaniment to orgiastic Bacchanalian dancing. The syrinx (reed pipes of uneven length) was sacred to Pan, and the lyre to Apollo, god of music and lyric poetry.

In allegory, the civilized lyre may be contrasted with weapons of war, and musical instruments may represent the sense of hearing.

In paintings, the inclusion of certain instruments could indi-cate modernity: as with, for example, the small portable organ, popular during the 14th century; and the viol, which was developed during the Renaissance, and appears in Giovanni Bellini's *San Zaccaria Altarpiece*.

Angels after Virgin and Child Enthroned *Cosmé Tura (*c.*1480, National Gallery, London).*

Orpheus, or a woman playing or singing, may personify music. It was an important part of family life, and in a painting may indicate domestic harmony. Music has also long been associated with love, exemplified by the 17th-century Dutch saying, "Learn on the lute, learn on the virginals to play, For strings have the power to steal the heart away." Flirtatious couples playing music together may allude to sexual pleasure, and a flute or pipe has a phallic connotation.

MUSIC: *see*
Apollo; Marsyas; MUSES; Orpheus; Pan

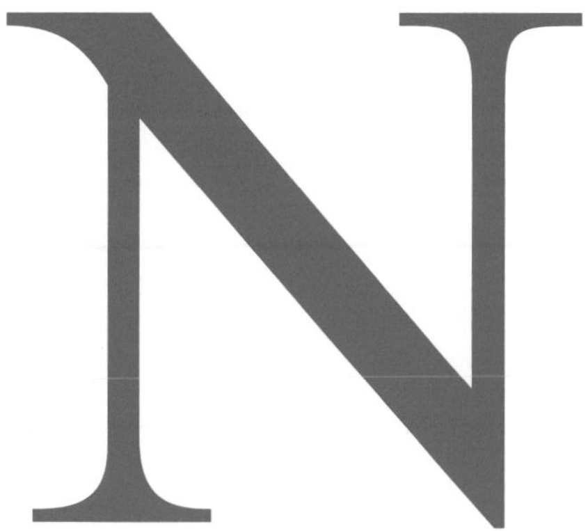

Narcissus: *see*
Echo
[1] Ovid, *Met III:339–510*

Nastagio: *see*
Cassone
[1] Boccaccio, *Decameron, 5th Day, 8th Story*

Narcissus

In mythology,[1] the youth Narcissus was so beautiful that many nymphs, including Echo, fell in love with him. Yet he scorned them all, and one cried, "May he himself fall in love with another, as we have done with him! May he too be unable to gain his loved one!" In the heat of the day Narcissus came to a sheltered spot with a clear pool of shining silvery water, and as he leaned down to drink he became enchanted by his own reflection. No thought of food or sleep could draw him from the spot, so he wasted away. Nymphs mourned his death, but when they searched for his body they found in its place the flower that bears his name.

A detail showing Narcissus, after Narcissus *by Nicolas-Bernard Lépicté (1771, Musée Antoine Lécuyer, Saint Quentin, France).*

The theme of Narcissus is one that has attracted artists since the Renaissance. He is usually shown gazing into the pool, or lying dead on the ground while Echo mourns him. Salvador Dali created a memorable image in which Narcissus' body is shown metamorphosing into the flower.

Nastagio

The poet Boccaccio (1313–75) told how the wealthy Nastagio degli Onesti fell in love with a beautiful girl of higher birth.[1] She rejected him and, brooding over the cruelty of his beloved, he wandered through the woods. There he saw a damsel running naked toward him, pursued by two fierce mastiffs and a knight on horseback, who threatened her with death. Nastagio resolved to help the girl, but then the knight told his remarkable story: his love had also been unrequited and he had taken his own life in despair. His beloved had died shortly after without repenting of her cruelty, so he cut out her cold heart with the rapier he had used on himself. Yet she rose as if unharmed, and the chase began again. Nastagio invited his own love and her family to a banquet in the woods, where they witnessed the scene and she agreed to marry him. Botticelli painted *The Story of Nastagio degli Onesti* as a series of panels: a warning to women who scorn their lovers.

Nemesis

Nemesis, the daughter of Night (Nyx), punished those insolent to the gods, and so she was the goddess of vengeance or retribution. Like Fortune, she may stand on a wheel or globe and have a scourge hanging from her girdle. In Dürer's engraving *Nemesis*, she is shown naked, holding a bridle in one hand for the undisciplined and a cup in the other with which to reward the virtuous.

Neptune

Neptune (in Greek myth, Poseidon) was the son of Saturn (Cronos) and Ops (Rhea), and shared his father's realm with his brothers Jupiter (Zeus) and Pluto (Hades). Neptune's kingdom was the sea, rivers and fountains; he was also responsible for earthquakes and, like Jupiter, he could wreak havoc with the elements.

After the Trojan War, Juno (Hera) commanded the winds to unleash a storm to deter Aeneas' fleet, but Neptune rose from the waves and made the ocean calm. He commonly appears as a slightly dishevelled, but vigorous and majestic man with cascading locks. His attribute is a trident with which he would rouse the winds and whip up tempests, and he usually rides a chariot, sometimes made from a shell, drawn by sea-horses (*hippocampi*) or dolphins. He is

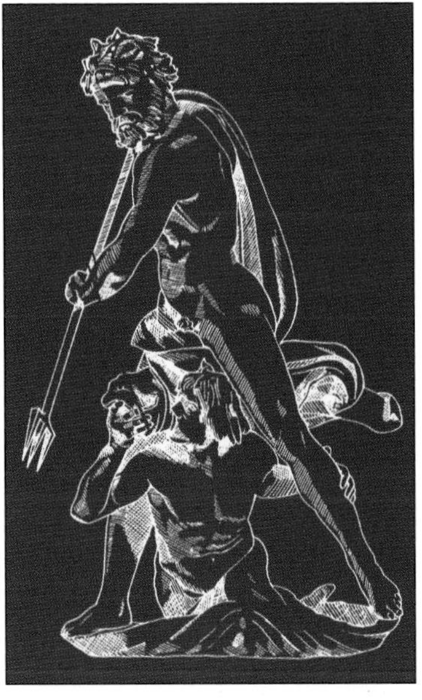

Neptune, after the sculpture Neptune and Triton *by Bernini (1622, Garden of the Villa Montalto, Rome).*

also often accompanied by mermaids and mermen (Tritons) blowing conch shells, and sea-nymphs or Nereids, or the Naiads who lived in springs, rivers and lakes.

Neptune's many loves included Amymone, Caenis and Coronis. To escape his attentions the sea-nymph Amphitrite fled to the farthest limits of the sea but was persuaded to marry him by a dolphin; their son was the merman, Triton. Neptune was also father of the Cyclops, Polyphemus. In allegory he may represent water; he is often depicted as the god of the sea, and his majestic figure is appropriate for the decoration of fountains.

Nicholas of Bari or Myra, Saint

All that is known of Nicholas is that he was Bishop of Myra in Asia Minor

Nemesis: *see*
Night

Neptune: *see*
Coronis; Elements; Jupiter; Polyphemus

Nicholas of Bari or Myra, Saint:
[1] *Golden Legend, St Nicholas*

Nicodemus: *see* Lamentation; Passion of Christ, The
[1] *John 3:1–9*
[2] *John 7:51*
[3] *John 19:39*

Night: *see* Sleep; Nemesis

St Nicholas and the three children, after The Legends of St Nicholas *by Gerard David (1484–1523, National Gallery of Scotland).*

during the 4th century. Legend[1] tells how a noble but poor man was thinking of prostituting his three virgin daughters because he was unable to provide them with a dowry; Nicholas threw three golden balls or bags of gold through the window of their house and withdrew unseen, thereby saving them from their fate.

Once, seamen threatened by a violent storm invoked Nicholas, and he appeared, and assisted them with the rigging until the storm died down. When famine spread through his bishopric, Nicholas learned that several ships were anchored in the harbour laden with grain. The saint promised the fearful sailors that if they gave the grain to his starving people, the customs men would not find their cargo short. Nicholas was also said to have saved three soldiers from decapitation; had an innocent prince released from prison; and brought to life three children hidden in a brine tub who had been murdered by their innkeeper father to feed to his guests during a plague.

The cult of Nicholas grew after the 11th century when his relics were taken from Myra to Bari in Italy. Scenes of his rescuing the three daughters and of the sailors' rescue were particularly popular, as seen in Fra Angelico's predella to the Perugia Polyptych. He is usually painted as a bishop, and his attribute is three golden balls at his feet, as shown in Raphael's *Ansidei Madonna*.

He is patron saint of sailors and of children, and also the origin of Father Christmas (Santa Claus being a derivative of St Nicholas), an identification probably derived from his patronage of children and his charitable acts of presenting gifts by night.

Nicodemus

Nicodemus was the Pharisee told by Christ that his spirit would be born again in the faith.[1] When the Pharisees were deliberating over the fate of Christ, Nicodemus asked that Christ should be heard before he was judged.[2] He was present at the Deposition, tending the dead Christ, and he brought a mixture of myrrh and aloes to embalm him at the Entombment.[3] Nicodemus usually appears in simple dress.

Night

The goddess of the night in mythology, Night (in Greek myth, Nyx) was the daughter of Chaos and mother of the day. Together Night and Day represented the passage of time and inevitable death. Night was the mother of the Fates, Discord, Death, and dreams. Her black-winged figure was feared even by Jupiter (Zeus).

Her chariot may be shown drawn by owls and bats, and she may wear a star-spangled cloak, have a crown of poppies, or carry two children (one black, one white). She may also be presented with a mask, a crescent moon or an owl: all are seen in Michelangelo's *Night*.

Night and her attributes, after The Night *by Vasari (16th century, Gallery Colonna, Rome).*

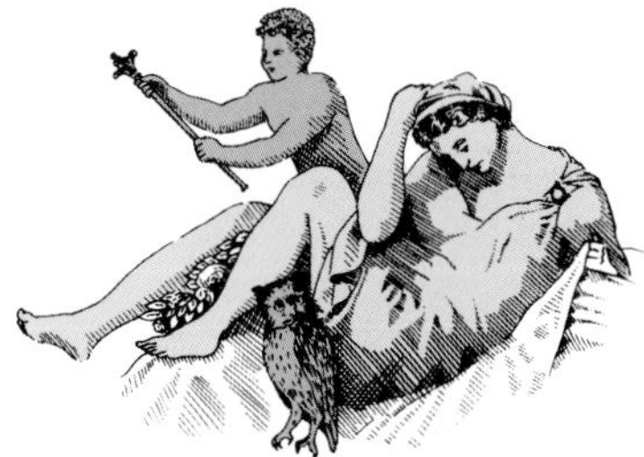

Niobe

In mythology[1] Niobe, the daughter of Tantalus, boasted that she was as beautiful as any goddess, and that her seven sons and seven daughters (the Niobids) were more beautiful than Apollo and Diana (Artemis). Their mother, Leto, along with the other gods, were outraged and; one by one, Niobe's children were killed as punishment. Richard Wilson, the 18th-century British painter, depicted Apollo and Diana shooting the Niobids from the clouds in *The Death of Niobe's Children*. Niobe's husband, Amphion, king of Thebes, drove a sword into himself to end his heartache. Niobe vainly implored the gods to save their youngest child, and Jupiter (Zeus) took pity on her, turning her into a marble statue that wept unending tears.

Noah

The Old Testament patriarch descended from Adam and Eve, Noah alone won God's favour when he saw "that the wickedness of man was great on the earth". God regretted that he had made mankind and resolved to destroy the race in a great flood. But he instructed Noah to build an ark into which he should take his wife, his three sons Shem, Ham and Japheth and their wives, and a male and female of every living creature.[1] The rains lasted for 40 days and 40 nights.[2] When the waters abated Noah sent forth a raven and a dove to find land, but it was still flooded.[3] When he sent out the dove a second time it returned with an olive leaf in its beak.[4] The ark landed on Mount Ararat, and God commanded Noah to replenish the earth and multiply.

Noah and his sons burned sacrifices, and God sent a rainbow every time the clouds gathered, as a reminder of his pact that he would no longer curse the earth.[5] Noah began to farm and planted a vineyard. On one occasion he became drunk on his wine and lay uncovered. Ham reported the nakedness to his brothers, Shem and Japheth, who took up a cloak and covered Noah, averting their eyes in respect. When he awoke and discovered Ham's behaviour, Noah cursed Ham's son, Canaan, condemning him to be for ever the servant of Shem and Japheth.[6]

When Noah entered the ark he was in his 600th year, and he has been consistently portrayed as an elderly man with a white beard. In late medieval and Renaissance art, scenes from the story of Noah appear in cycles of the Old Testament illustrated by Ghiberti (Baptistry, Florence), and by Michelangelo (Sistine Chapel, Vatican, Rome). Isolated scenes were also painted, particularly the animals entering the ark, as in Jan Bruegel the Elder's *The Entry of the Animals into Noah's Ark*. The dove returning with the olive leaf, a sign of peace and reconciliation between mankind and God, was painted with affection by John Everett Millais in *The Return of the Dove to the Ark*.

NUDE

See panel on following page.

Numa Pompilius

The legendary successor of Romulus as king of Rome, Numa Pompilius (7th century BC) was a philosopher and poet who presided over a golden age, when temples were built and religious rites established.[1] He appears

Niobe:
[1] Ovid, *Met VI:146–312*

Noah: *see* Dove; Olive
[1] *Genesis 6:5–19*
[2] *Genesis 7:17–21*
[3] *Genesis 8:6–9*
[4] *Genesis 8:10–11*
[5] *Genesis 9*
[6] *Genesis 9:20–29*

Numa Pompilius:
[1] Plutarch, *Lives, Numa Pompilius*

NUDE: *see*
Acteon; ADAM AND EVE; Noah; Pygmalion; Truth
[1] *Genesis 2:25*
[2] *Genesis 3:7*

NUDE

The nude in art, whether male or female, can be a representation of power, delight, fecundity or shame. Sculpted or painted, the nude was intended to transport the viewer into a world of the imagination. The nude occurs in both mythological and biblical narratives. Venus (Aphrodite), goddess of beauty and love, is often shown unclothed but Minerva (Athene), goddess of wisdom, only rarely so. Elsewhere a nude might signify poverty or truth.

Inherited from ancient Greece was the idea of a Golden Age when mankind was in harmony with nature and clothes were not needed. Likewise, Adam and Eve wandered in the Garden of Eden and "they were both naked, the man and his wife, and were not ashamed."[1]

The female nude may express the abundance of nature and the source of life. However "natural" the result appears, the artist has often perfected the form. Inspired by classical prototypes, the idealized male may be given strength and grace, and the female charms that accord with taste and fashion. Even if the subject warns against the dangers of love, the figure may still be profoundly sensual. From the Renaissance until the second half of the 19th century, the female nude was painted in innumerable ways to delight the male spectator, so that he might dream, like Pygmalion, that she comes alive.

To be without clothes is also to be vulnerable. When Adam and Eve were expelled from Paradise, "the eyes of them both were opened, and they knew that they were naked; and they sewed fig leaves together, and made themselves aprons."[2] They knew shame for the first time. Moreover, the Old Testament deemed that "the nakedness of thy father or the nakedness of thy mother, shalt thou not uncover", hence the embarrassment felt by Shem and Japheth when they saw Noah exposed in his drunkenness. Christ's nakedness or near-nakedness at the Flagellation and Crucifixion, or in a Pietà, presents him as defenceless and thus heightens the sense of sorrow. Most shaming of all is the nakedness of those who suffer in hell.

Nymphs: *see*
Callisto; Diana; Galatea; Hylas; Pan

in public settings, such as Perugino's frescoes *Numa Pompilius* (Collegio del Cambio, Perugia), as an example of a virtuous ruler.

Nymphs

In mythology nymphs were beautiful, earthly young women. There were nymphs of the mountains, woods, hills and dales who brought up Jupiter (in Greek myth, Zeus) and Bacchus (Dionysos); Naiads, or nymphs of the springs, rivers and lakes; and Nereids, or nymphs of the sea, such as Galatea and Thetis. They were mortal, but had long lives and prophetic gifts. Desired by satyrs, and sometimes by mortals, they were chaste and attended Diana (Artemis). Nymphs were sometimes shown with a satyr, as in Watteau's *Nymph Surprised by a Satyr*. They provided the perfect opportunity to show beautiful women bathing.

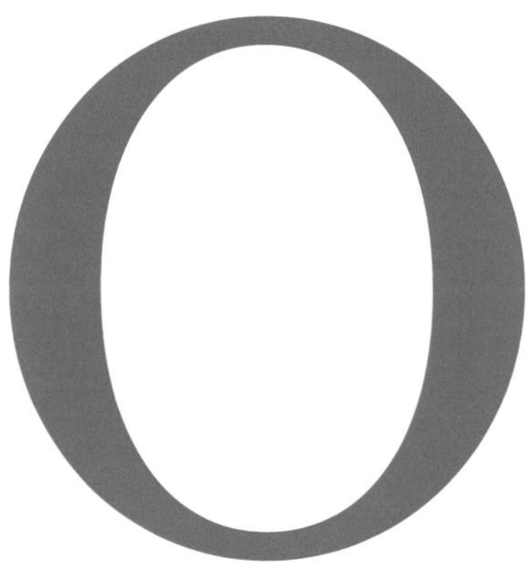

Oedipus

In mythology the Greek Oedipus[1] was descended from Venus (in Greek myth, Aphrodite) and was therefore the target of Juno's (Hera's) wrath. He was the son of Laius and Jocasta, king and queen of Thebes. An oracle had told Laius that he would be killed by his son, so when Oedipus was born he was abandoned on a hillside. However, a shepherd rescued him, and Oedipus was brought up by the shepherd and his wife. In his youth Oedipus was goaded by some friends about his parentage, so he consulted the oracle of Delphi as to who were his true mother and father; he was told never to return home, for he would kill his father and marry his mother. He therefore fled from his supposed parents. In due course he encountered Laius, who ordered him to make way for his chariot. A fight ensued in which Oedipus killed his father, whom he did not know. He journeyed on to Thebes, at that time terrorized by a Sphinx, who posed a riddle to anyone she encountered, and devoured those who could not answer. In *Oedipus and the Sphinx*, Gustave Moreau depicted the monstrous creature staring into Oedipus' eyes.

Having answered the Sphinx's riddle correctly, Oedipus was rewarded with the kingdom of Thebes and the hand of Jocasta. Thus he unwittingly married his mother, with whom he later had four children. When a plague broke out, an oracle predicted that it would not cease until the murderer of Laius was revealed. When Oedipus discovered the truth about his parentage, he put out his own eyes and banished himself to Attica, led there by his daughters, Antigone and Ismene.

Olindo and Sophronia

Jerusalem Delivered, the religious epic poem about the First Crusade, by Torquato Tasso (1544–95), tells of how the Saracen king ordered a Christian woman Sophronia to be burned at the stake. Olindo, her lover, chose to die with her. Just as the pyre was about to be lit, a pagan knight Clorinda offered to help in the war

Oedipus: *see* Sphinx

[1] Apollodorus, *The Library III v 7–9*

Olindo and Sophronia: *see* Rinaldo; Tancred

[1] Tasso, *Jerusalem Delivered II:xxvii–liii*

The archangel Gabriel holding an olive branch, after The Annunciation *by Simone Martini (1330, Uffizi, Florence).*

Olive Branch: see Minerva; Noah

Ops: *see* Cybele

Orestes: *see*
[1] Aeschylus, *Oresteia* and Euripedes, *Iphenigia*

Orion:
[1] Apollodorus, *The Library I.iv.3–5*

Orpheus and Eurydice:
[1] Ovid, *Met X:1–85*

with the Crusaders in exchange for their lives.[1] Friedrich Overbeck's *Olindo and Sophronia* shows the lovers tied to the stake.

Olive Branch

In mythology the olive was sacred to Minerva (in Greek myth, Athene), and in both the classical and Christian worlds it was a symbol of peace. After the Old Testament flood, Noah sent a dove out to see if the waters had receded. The bird returned with an olive branch to signify that it had found dry land and that God had made peace with man. The Angel Gabriel may carry an olive branch, as in Taddeo di Bartolo's *Annunciation.*

Ops

Ops (Rhea) was married to Saturn (Cronos) and gave birth to Jupiter (Zeus). The goddess of the harvest, Ops was associated with Cybele.

Orestes

In mythology[1] Orestes killed his mother Clytemnestra and her lover in revenge for their murder of his father Agamemnon. Tormented by grief and pursued by the Furies, he was eventually acquitted of matricide.

Academic painters favoured the key events in these multiple tragedies. In *The Dispute Between Orestes and Pylades* the Dutch painter Pieter Lastman (1583–1633) depicts Orestes and his friend Pylades disputing who should sacrifice himself to the gods.

Orion

In mythology[1] the giant Orion was a hunter and the subject of several tales. He once tried to rape Princess Merope of Chios, for which he was blinded by her father. Orion went to Vulcan's (in Greek myth, Hephaestus') forge and set Cedalion, one of Vulcan's assistants, on his shoulders to guide him toward the sunrise, so that its rays might restore his sight: Poussin illustrated the scene in *Landscape with Orion.* Later, Aurora fell in love with him and carried him off to Delos, where he was killed, either for challenging Diana (Artemis) to a match of quoits or for offending one of her maidens. Others state that Orion was killed by a scorpion's bite delivered by Diana because he had tried to violate her. Both the scorpion and Orion were transformed into constellations.

A detail showing Orpheus, carrying his lyre, and Eurydice led by Hymen, the god of marriage.

Orpheus and Eurydice

Orpheus[1] was the son of the Muse Calliope and the god Apollo. He played the lyre so beautifully that animals were charmed, rivers ceased flowing, and mountains and trees moved to hear his music.

Orpheus fell in love with the wood-nymph Eurydice, but at their wedding omens foretold an unhappy outcome and even Hymen, god of marriage, was gloomy. As the innocent new bride wandered in the meadows with her band of Naiads, a serpent bit her ankle and she fell lifeless to the ground. In *Landscape with Orpheus and Eurydice* Poussin painted the ill-fated wedding where a frightened Eurydice has just seen the serpent that will kill her.

The grieving Orpheus ventured into the Underworld to find Eurydice. He sang to Pluto (in Greek myth, Hades) and Proserpina (Persephone), playing his lyre, and begged them to change Eurydice's destiny. His music charmed even the tormentors of Tartarus, and the king and queen of the Underworld could not refuse his plea. They restored Eurydice to him, charging him not to look back at her until the pair had reached the upper realms. Just before they emerged into daylight, however, Orpheus looked back. At once, Eurydice slipped down into the depths, her last farewell hardly reaching his ears.

In *Orpheus Charming the Beasts* Roelandt Savery shows Orpheus playing to every type of animal and bird in the shade of trees that had moved to give him shelter from the sun.

The story of Orpheus may be used as an allegory of eloquence, as in Giambattista Tiepolo's *Modello*.

Oysters/Oyster Shells

In 17th-century Holland, oysters were considered a delicacy and an aphrodisiac. Medical authorities of the day confirmed that they "arouse appetites and the desire to eat and to make love, which pleases both lusty and delicate bodies".[1] They often appear in brothel scenes and may denote a prostitute: oyster-selling was regarded as one of the lowest forms of trade. In Jan Steen's *Easy Come, Easy Go*, an old woman shucks oysters for a man while a young girl offers him a glass of wine.

Oysters/Oyster Shells:
[1] Johan van Beverwijck, *Schat der Gesontheydt*

Palm: *see*
Joseph, Husband of the Virgin; Martyrs; Passion of Christ, The; Virgin, The
[1] *John 12:13*

Pan: *see*
Arcadia; Faunus and Fauns; Herm; Midas; Satyr
[1] Ovid, *Met I:689–712*

Pandora: *see*
ADAM AND EVE; Prometheus
[1] Hesiod, *Works and Days 60–142*

Palm

In antiquity palm leaves were used to signify victory, especially military triumph, and were bestowed upon the illustrious by personifications of Victory or Fame.

Christianity adopted the palm for martyrs who had triumphed over death. During the Flight into Egypt the fruit of the palm tree fed Joseph and the Virgin, who is shown at her death being presented with a palm. The palm is also associated with Christ's Entry into Jerusalem, when the people "took branches of palm trees, and went forth to meet Him, and cried Hosanna; 'Blessed is the King of Israel that cometh in the name of the Lord'".[1] This event is remembered in the Christian celebration of Palm Sunday.

Pan

In mythology Pan was the god of flocks, shepherds, and those who dwelled in the country. He lived in the woods and mountains of Arcadia, and was also thought to be the instigator of sudden, inexplicable fear, hence "panic". He had a human torso and arms, with the legs, hooves, tail, and two small horns of a goat. He was associated with the Roman god Faunus, chief of the satyrs. Often in the company of Bacchus (in Greek myth, Dionysos), he was a figure of lust, sometimes seen in pursuit of nymphs. In *The Triumph of Pan*, Poussin depicts him as a garlanded herm surrounded by revellers.

Pan invented the musical pipes or syrinx. The story[1] tells how he pursued Syrinx, a beautiful wood-nymph of Arcadia, who fled until she reached a river. She prayed to be transformed, and just as Pan thought he had caught her, he found he was clasping the marsh reeds. As Pan sighed in disappointment, the reeds produced a sweet sound that delighted him. He cut unequal lengths of reed, bound them together and named his pipes after the nymph.

Pandora

Vulcan (in Greek myth, Hephaestus) made Pandora[1] out of clay for Jupiter (Zeus), who wished to punish

Prometheus for stealing the gods' fire. Pandora came to life and the gods showered her with gifts: Venus (Aphrodite) gave her beauty and the art of pleasing, the Graces made her captivating, Apollo taught her to sing, Mercury (Hermes) instructed her in eloquence, and Minerva (Athene) gave her rich jewelery. Jupiter (Zeus), however, gave her a box which he told her to give to the man who married her. She was then sent to earth as a wife for Epimetheus, who, ignoring the advice of his brother Prometheus never to accept a gift from the gods, made her his wife. Epimetheus introduced Pandora into society and, overcome with curiosity, she opened the box: evils poured out and spread over the earth to afflict mankind ceaselessly. Only Hope, the consoler of sorrow, remained inside. Pandora's story became the counterpart of Eve's temptation and the Fall of Man, and in *Eva Prima Pandora* the 16th-century painter Jean Cousin shows Pandora with both an apple and an urn of troubles. Pandora was also portrayed in the 19th century; Rossetti depicted her several times as a troubled beauty holding her casket from which an evil vapour escapes.

Pantocrator

The Pantocrator (from the Greek, meaning "all-ruling") was the image of Christ as the Almighty, and originated in Byzantine iconography. According to this convention Christ usually looked straight at the viewer, his expression stern. He blesses with his right hand and may hold the Gospel in his left. The influence of this image is seen in the late 13th-century mosaics in the Baptistry, Florence, in which Christ sits in

A detail of Christ Pantocrator (spelled out in Greek around the image), after a mosaic in the Baptistry, Florence.

judgment: he draws up those who are chosen with his right hand and with his left hand he condemns the sinful.

Paolo and Francesca

In Dante's *Inferno* (the first part of his epic poem *Divina Commedia*) Francesca de Rimini tells the poet her story.[1] She was the daughter of a friend of Dante, and married the deformed Gianciotto, son of the lord of Rimini. However, she fell in love with Paolo, her husband's younger brother, and they became lovers. Gianciotto discovered them together and stabbed them to death. Their punishment was to drift for ever on the wind in the second circle of hell. This tragic theme was taken up in the 19th century. In *Paolo and Francesca* Rossetti shows Paolo kissing Francesca as they read together.

Paris

In mythology Paris, the son of King Priam of Troy, was destined at birth to be the ruin of his country. His father ordered his death, but the slave who had been entrusted with the task did not kill him. Instead, Paris was abandoned on Mount Ida, where he

Paolo and Francesca: *see*
Dante
[1] Dante, *Inferno V:88-142*

Paris: *see*
Discord; Feast of the Gods, Trojan War
[1] Hyginus, *Fabulae XCII*

A detail showing Paris confronted by the three goddesses, after The Judgment of Paris *by Rubens (*c.*1634, Prado, Madrid).*

was found and brought up by shepherds. He too became a shepherd, and the nymph Oenone fell in love with him.

In the portentous Judgment of Paris, he was charged with awarding Discord's golden apple to whichever goddess he deemed the fairest: Juno (in Greek myth, Hera), Minerva (Athene) or Venus (Aphrodite).[1] In order to judge them thoroughly, he asked them to undress. Juno told Paris to make Venus take her girdle off as it would bewitch him, and Venus encouraged Minerva to remove her helmet. Juno offered him Asia if he chose her; Minerva said she would make him a great warrior and conqueror; and Venus promised him the beautiful Helen of Sparta, together with Love, Desire, the Graces, Passion and Hymen. Venus won the apple.[2]

His choice incurred the resentment of Juno and Minerva, and his abduction of Helen, the wife of Menelaus, king of Sparta, incited the Greeks to take up arms and retrieve her. He thus instigated the Trojan War, in which he fought without enthusiasm. The war ended with the destruction of Troy.

Paris may be seen with Helen, bewitched by Venus, but the Judgment of Paris, in which he is painted as a shepherd, was a more popular subject, allowing the depiction of three beautiful female nudes. In such treatments, the disastrous outcome of his choice is usually ignored.

Passion of Christ, The

The Passion of Christ follows on directly from the Life of Christ and is described by all four Gospels, although not always in exactly the same detail and sequence. In art the scenes are depicted individually as devotional images or as entire narrative cycles.

The central episodes have given rise to the Instruments of the Passion, including the Cross, the column of the Flagellation, the Crown of Thorns, the spear or lance and the 30 pieces of silver (the sum paid to Judas for betraying Christ).

CHRIST IN JERUSALEM

The narrative usually begins with the **Entry into Jerusalem**, in which Christ, riding on a humble donkey leading a colt, was greeted by a multitude. Some spread their garments in his way, others cut down branches from olive and palm[1] trees, strewed them in his path and praised him. Some artists have also included the story of Zaccheus, who climbed a tree in order to see Christ, and later gave half his goods to the poor; this may have taken place as Christ entered Jericho.[2]

In a famous scene, **Christ Driving the Money Lenders out of the Temple**,

A detail of Christ entering Jerusalem, after a panel from Maestà *by Duccio (1308–1311, Siena Cathedral).*

Christ is depicted outraged and indignant, expelling the merchants who are trading there illegally.[3]

Christ disputed with the chief priests, and they wished to arrest him but feared the multitude, who viewed him as a prophet. He denounced the Pharisees as hypocrites[4] and foresaw that their temples would be destroyed. They gathered at the house of the high priest, Caiaphas, and plotted Christ's downfall. One of the 12 disciples, Judas Iscariot, went to them and said, "What will ye give me, and I will deliver him unto you?", and they offered him 30 pieces of silver.[5]

THE LAST SUPPER AND BETRAYAL

To celebrate the Passover, Christ gathered the disciples together. At this, the **Last Supper**, Christ announced, " 'one of you shall betray me,' and they were exceedingly sorrowful, and began every one of them to say unto Him 'Lord is it I?' " He instigated the sacrament of Holy Communion by blessing the bread and wine, which were thereafter to represent his flesh and blood, sacrificed to redeem mankind.

The Last Supper was an appropriate subject for monastic refectories; the moment usually chosen was the

A detail of Christ, after The Last Supper *by Leonardo da Vinci (*c.*1495, Santa Marie delle Grazie, Milan).*

breaking of bread and drinking of wine: the theme of the transubstantiation.[6] However, Leonardo da Vinci's *Last Supper* shows the instant of Christ's announcement of his betrayal and the various emotional reactions of the disciples. After the supper Christ poured water into a basin and began **Washing the Feet of the Disciples**, a humble act against which Peter protested.[7]

Just before his arrest Christ went with the disciples to the Garden of Gethsemane and took Peter, James

Passion of Christ, The: *see* Christ, The Life of; Descent into Hell; Joseph of Arimathea; James the Great, St; John the Evangelist, St; Judas Iscariot; Mary Magdalene; Nicodemus; Peter, St; Thomas, St; Virgin, The

[1] *John 12:13*
[2] *Luke 19:1–8*
[3] *Matthew 21:12–13*
[4] *Matthew 23:13*
[5] *Matthew 26:14–15*
[6] *Matthew 26:20–29*
[7] *John 13:4–16*
[8] *Matthew26:36–51*
[9] *Matthew 26:69–75*
[10] *Matthew 27:3–5*
[11] *Mark 14:57–65*
[12] *Matthew 27:1–2*
[13] *John 19:5*
[14] *Matthew 27:24–31*
[15] *Luke 23:33–43*
[16] *John 19:34*
[17] *Matthew 27:59–61*
[18] *Luke 24:1–7*
[19] *John 20:14–17*
[20] *Luke 24:13–21*
[21] *John 20:27*
[22] *Acts 1:9–11*
[23] *Acts 2:1–4*

and John aside, asking them to keep watch while he prayed. However, they fell asleep. Paintings of the **Agony in the Garden** often show the three sleeping disciples, while Christ has a vision of the Chalice of the Eucharist or the Instruments of the Passion; in the middle distance Judas may be seen leading an armed multitude toward Christ. In the **Betrayal of Christ**, Judas went straight up to him and, with the words "Master, Master", gave him the **Kiss of Judas**. In anger, Peter cut off the ear of a servant of the high priest.[8]

The disciples deserted Christ but Peter followed him and sat with the servants of the high priests. Then came the **Denial of Christ**, as Christ had foretold, in which Peter was asked three times if he had been with Christ and denied it three times, saying, "I do not know that man." Thereupon the cock crowed and he remembered the words of Christ's prophecy and wept bitterly.[9] Judas discarded his pieces of silver and hanged himself.[10]

The Trial of Christ

In the **Trial of Christ** Christ was brought before four judges: the high priests, Annas and Caiaphas; Herod, tetrarch of Galilee; and Pontius Pilate, Roman governor of Judea, who examined him twice. Before Caiaphas Christ avowed that he was the Son of God. At this Caiaphas rent his own garments in anger, accused him of blasphemy and condemned him to death. The **Mocking of Christ** followed, in which Pilate's servants spat on his face, buffeted him and hit him with the palms of their hands.[11]

The high priests and elders then took him to Pontius Pilate for trial by civil law.[12] **Before Pilate**, Christ said not a word that could condemn him. He also appeared **Before Herod**. Again he remained silent and was mocked before being returned to Pilate. According to a tradition of the Passover, Pilate was able to release one prisoner chosen by the people. He brought Christ to them, saying, ***Ecce Homo*** ("Behold the man"),[13] and asked them whom they would choose to release Christ or the thief Barabbas. The chief priests incited the crowd to reply, "Barabbas", and they demanded that Christ be crucified. Pilate washed his hands before them, saying "I am innocent of the blood of

A detail after The Mocking of Christ *by Giotto (dedicated in 1306, Arena Chapel, Padua).*

this just person."

Pilate ordered Christ to be whipped, which has inspired many scenes of the **Flagellation**. His soldiers then dressed him in a scarlet (or purple) robe, gave him a reed, placed a mock crown on his head and hailed him, "King of the Jews" (**Crowning with Thorns**). They spat on him and took the reed and hit him violently around the head.[14] This scene has sometimes been combined with the previous Mocking of Christ. John describes it as occurring before the Ecce Homo episode, so in some depictions of the Ecce Homo Christ is shown wearing the attributes of mock kingship, such as the Crown of Thorns.

The Crucifixion, Deposition and Entombment

The **Road to Calvary** (the *Via Dolorosa*) presents Christ carrying the Cross to the place of his **Crucifixion**, accompanied by a great crowd. As they crucified him, he said, "Father forgive them; for they know not what do." Soldiers cast lots for his garments and inscribed over his head: "Jesus of Nazareth, King of the

A detail showing the Crucifixion, after The Crucified Christ *by Raphael, (1504, National Gallery, London).*

Jews" (INRI). Two thieves were crucified with him, a penitent one on his right, an impenitent on his left. The impenitent thief mocked him along with the crowd, but was rebuked by the other, to whom Christ said, "Today thou shalt be with me in paradise."[15]

Among the holy women who watched near the Cross were his mother Mary, Mary Magdalene and Mary, the mother of James and Joseph. John, the disciple most loved by Christ, was also present. All these characters may be seen in depictions of the Crucifixion. Just before he died, a sponge soaked in wine and water was offered to Christ. Afterwards a soldier pierced his side; blood and water flowed from the wound.[16]

A detail showing Christ's descent from the Cross, after The Deposition *by Rubens (1612, Antwerp Cathedral).*

In scenes of the **Deposition** or **Descent from the Cross** Joseph of Arimathea and the Pharisee Nicodemus, are present and minister to him. They are also seen at the

Christ placed in his tomb, after The Entombment *by Dieric Bouts (*c.*1450, National Gallery London).*

Entombment, placing Christ's wrapped and anointed body in the sepulchre. After this, Mary Magdalene and another Mary sat and kept vigil by the tomb.[17]

THE RESURRECTION AND ASCENSION

The **Resurrection** of Christ was confirmed by his appearance, first to Mary Magdalene and then to his disciples. On the third day after the Crucifixion the holy women, without the Virgin, went to the tomb and found that the stone had been rolled away. On entering they discovered two angels clothed in brilliant white, who asked, "Why seek ye the living among the dead? He is not here but has risen."[18] Mary Magdalene turned around and saw Christ, but mistook him for a gardener. He revealed himself to her saying, "Touch me not." The Latin version of these words has given the scene its name – ***Noli me tangere***. Christ told her to go to the disciples and tell them that he was risen.[19]

That same day two disciples, one Cleopas, the other anonymous, went to the village of Emmaus, and Christ joined them on the journey. They did not recognize him until that evening at supper when he broke the bread and blessed it.[20] The scene is rendered as the **Supper at Emmaus**. As he had commanded, the 11 remaining disciples went to Galilee, and when they saw him they worshipped him. To Thomas, who doubted, he said, "Reach hither thy finger ... and thrust it into my side; and be not faithless, but believing."[21] Thomas reached out and touched Christ's stigmata, and only then was he convinced. This formed the basis for the popular image of **Doubting Thomas**. Christ commanded his disciples to teach all nations and baptize them.

Apart from Luke's brief mention of Christ being carried up to heaven, the following events do not appear in the Gospels but were often included in narrative cycles of the Passion. The **Ascension** occurred 40 days after the Resurrection. Christ was with his disciples outside Jerusalem when he was taken up in a cloud, and as they watched, two angels appeared to tell them that they too would be received in heaven.[22]

At **Pentecost**, the Apostles were together, when "suddenly there came a sound from heaven as of a rushing mighty wind and it filled all the house where they were sitting. ... And they were all filled with the Holy Ghost, and began to speak with other tongues."

The **Descent of the Holy Ghost** marks the end of the Passion and the beginning of the Acts of the Apostles and so the establishment of the Christian Church.

Passion Flower
The passion flower was probably named in the 16th century by missionaries to South Africa who likened its composition to the Instruments of the Passion. Its leaves represent the spear, its tendrils the scourges, its petals the disciples, without Peter and Judas, and its anthers the five wounds. The stem of the ovary was seen as the column of the Cross, or of the Flagellation, the stigmas represented the three nails, and the filaments within the flower were the Crown of Thorns. The 19th-century painter Charles Collins, in *Convent Thoughts*, shows a young nun contemplating the flower.

Patroclus
In Homer's *The Iliad* Patroclus was companion to the Greek hero Achilles, whose place he took against the Trojans. He was slain by Hector, which galvanized Achilles into joining the Greek warriors and seeking revenge on Hector. Achilles killed the warrior in single combat and then drove around the walls of Troy, dragging Hector's body.

In paintings Patroclus may be seen escorting Briseis, Achilles' concubine, to Agamemnon. Other depictions show the huge funeral pyre built for him by Achilles, as in Jacques-Louis David's *Funeral of Patroclus*.

Paul, Saint (Apostle)
Paul and Peter, the most important Apostles, brought Christianity to the Jews and the Gentiles and founded the Church. Images and scenes from their lives often appear paired in painting. Paul (died *c.*AD67) may have a high forehead and a bushy beard, and hold the sword of his martyrdom or a book, the doctrine of his missionary work.

Before his conversion Paul was known as Saul and was a strict Pharisee with Roman citizenship. He witnessed the martyrdom of St Stephen, following which he "made havoc of the church and entered every house, he dragged off men and women and committed them to prison".[1] To continue his persecutions, he travelled to Damascus. On the road he had a vision: "suddenly there shined round about him a light from heaven; and he fell to the earth and heard a voice saying unto him, 'Saul, Saul, why persecutest thou me?' "[2] When he stood up he was blind, and was led to Damascus, where Christ acknowledged him as "a chosen vessel", and after three days his sight was restored by a disciple. Saul was subsequently converted and baptized as Paul.

In 1621 Caravaggio painted a dramatic picture of his conversion for the church of Santa Maria del Popolo, Rome.

Paul had to escape from his Jewish enemies by night and was lowered over the city wall in a basket. In Jerusalem he met Peter and the disciples and began his life as a missionary. Raphael's cartoons for tapestries for the Sistine Chapel in Rome show some episodes from the Acts of Peter and Paul. For example, Raphael shows how Paul and Barnabas were preaching in Cyprus when they were called by the Roman deputy Sergius Paulus, who wished to hear the word of God. However, the sorcerer Elymas sought to prevent the encounter. Paul struck him blind and Sergius Paulus was converted.[3] In Lystra Paul and Peter cured a cripple

Patroclus: *see* Trojan War

Paul, Saint: *see* Peter, St; Martyr

[1] *Acts 8:3*
[2] *Acts 9:3–4*
[3] *Acts 13:6–12*
[4] *Acts 14:8–18*
[5] *Acts 17:16–34*
[6] *Acts 28:1–6*

Peace: *see*
Cornucopia; Dove; Olive

Peacock: *see*
Io

Pegasus: *see*
Bellerophon; MUSES; Perseus

A detail showing a peacock, after The Annunciation with St Emidius *by Carlo Crivelli (1486, National Gallery, London).*

who had never been able to walk, and when the people saw the miracle they believed that the gods had come down in the likeness of men and hailed them as Jupiter and Mercury. The priest of Jupiter brought garlands and an ox to sacrifice; Paul and Barnabas tore up their clothes and, crying out, restrained the people from making the sacrifice.[4]

In Athens Paul saw a city devoted to idolatry. He disputed daily in the market, where he encountered philosophers who took him to the tribunal in order to hear his doctrine. Paul's sermons converted some of the crowd, including Dionysius the Areopagite.[5]

In Macedonia Paul was preaching with Silas, when they were flogged and thrown into prison for exorcizing a demon from a woman. The gaoler made their feet fast in the stocks, but at midnight there was a great earthquake and their shackles unlocked and the doors burst open.

At Ephesus, Paul's preaching caused pagans to bring out their books and burn them, but in Jerusalem he was imprisoned by the Roman Governor, and after two years he appealed as a Roman citizen for trial at the emperor's court.

Paul was sailing to Rome with other prisoners when they were shipwrecked on Malta. The inhabitants kindled a fire for them against the cold and rain. As Paul gathered sticks and laid them on the fire, a viper came out of the heat and wrapped itself around his hand; Paul shook it off and suffered no harm, and the Maltese took him for a god:[6] Adam Elsheimer set the scene on a stormy night.

Paul's activities in Rome are uncertain, but he is thought to have written his epistles while in prison there. He was believed to have been beheaded at the site of the Tre Fontane in Rome at the same time as St Peter's martyrdom. He is buried on the site where the church of San Paolo Fuori le Mura now stands in Rome.

Peace

A personification of Peace may have a cornucopia, sheaves of corn or garlands of flowers, or be surrounded by the fruits of the bountiful earth which she nurtures. Children also may be nearby. She may be invoked preventatively to illustrate the benefits of peace, but she was also celebrated at the end of war.

The sculptor Adrian Jones shows her riding in triumph in a *quadriga*, a chariot drawn by four horses harnessed abreast, surmounting the Arch of Wellington at Hyde Park Corner, London (1912). An olive branch and dove are also attributes of Peace.

Peacock

This bird is the attribute of Juno (in Greek myth, Hera), whose chariot is drawn by a pair of peacocks. It was believed that the peacock's flesh never decayed, so it may also symbolize immortality.

Because of its sumptuous plumage, the peacock is associated with pride, but its decorative qualities have been much admired and utilized, especially in the Arts and Crafts and Art Nouveau movements.

Pegasus

In mythology Pegasus was the winged horse that sprang from the blood of the gorgon Medusa after Perseus

A detail after Pegasus *by Giambattista Tiepolo (18th century).*

beheaded her. It carried Perseus on his exploits, as well as Bellerophon, who rode it without the consent of the gods of Olympus.

Pelican

It was believed[1] that a pelican nourished its young with its own blood, and the bird was therefore used to represent self-sacrifice and charity. It was likened to Christ, whose blood brought salvation.

Penelope

The story of Penelope[1] is one of patient conjugal devotion. The wife of Ulysses (Odysseus), Greek hero of the Trojan War, the beautiful Penelope did not know if her husband had survived the ten years of fighting.

Believing him dead, many suitors came to press for her hand, and she conceded that she would marry as soon as she had finished weaving a shroud for Lord Laertes, her father-in-law – a large and delicate piece of work. In order to remain true to her husband she spun by day and unpicked her work by night, fooling the suitors for three years.

Penelope is seen weaving, often at a loom with handmaids and servants – for example in Giovanni Stradano's depiction of the theme in the Palazzo Vecchio, Florence.

Perseus

In mythology[1] it was prophesied that Perseus, the son of Jupiter (in Greek myth, Zeus) and Danaë, would murder his grandfather, Acrisius. Accordingly, Acrisius banished both mother and son to avoid his fate. As a young man Perseus was sent by his mother's suitor to capture the head of the gorgon Medusa, a task intended to kill him, since all who looked on her were turned to stone. Mercury (Hermes) and Minerva (Athene), however, favoured Perseus, and gave him armour and winged feet. Paris Bordone illustrates the scene in

Perseus brandishing the gorgon's head, after Phineas and his Followers Turned into Stone *by Luca Giordano (c.1680, National Gallery, London).*

Perseus Armed by Mercury and Minerva. As he approached Medusa, Perseus was guided by her reflection in his bronze shield, and was able to behead her without looking at her directly. From her blood sprang the winged horse Pegasus.

As Perseus flew home with

Pelican:
[1] *Physiologus*

Penelope: *see* Ulysses
[1] Homer, *Odyssey II:97–105*

Perseus: *see* Danaë; Medusa; Pegasus
[1] Ovid, *Met IV:604–803*
[2] Ovid, *Met V:1–249*

Peter, Saint: *see* Christ, Life of; Martyrs; Passion of Christ; Paul, St

[1] *Matthew 16:18–19*
[2] *John 21:16*
[3] *Matthew 4:18–20*
[4] *Luke 5:1–10*
[5] *Matthew 17:24–27*
[6] *Matthew 26:51–75*
[7] *Acts 5:15*
[8] *Acts 3:1–5*
[9] *Acts 4:32–37; 5:1–7*
[10] *Acts 9:36*
[11] *Acts 12:1–12*
[12] *Golden Legend, St Peter*

Medusa's head, drops of her blood scattered on the earth and became deadly serpents. On the way, Perseus spotted a beautiful girl chained to a rock and immediately fell in love with her. She was Andromeda, a princess of Ethiopia, about to be sacrificed to a sea-monster because her mother thought herself more beautiful than the Nereids, and had thereby angered Neptune (Poseidon). Perseus vanquished the monster, and a luxurious wedding banquet was prepared for the couple. At this event a riotous mob entered the palace, led by Phineus,[2] Andromeda's suitor, who had come to avenge the theft of his bride. A furious fight ensued, at the end of which Perseus held up Medusa's head and turned Phineus and his men to stone. Since the Renaissance, scenes of Perseus rescuing Andromeda have been popular, exemplified by Piero di Cosimo and Joachim Wtewael.

Another scene represented is the fight at the wedding, as in Luca Giordano's *Phineus and his Followers Turned to Stone*.

Perseus also used the gorgon's head to turn Atlas to stone, thus creating the Atlas Mountains in Morocco.

Peter, Saint (Apostle, Disciple)

Peter (died AD64), the Prince of the Apostles, held a unique position among the disciples of Christ, and in painting he stands in the favoured place on Christ's right. Peter was missionary to the Jews, as St Paul was to the Gentiles, and both were founders of the Church. Peter is *Petrus* or rock in Latin: Christ said "thou art Peter, and upon this rock I will build my church; and the gates of hell shall not prevail against it. And I will give thee the keys of the kingdom of heaven".[1] After the Resurrection Christ appeared to St Peter and instructed him to "feed my sheep".[2] His unique position was confirmed when Christ agreed to let him walk upon the water.

St Peter, after Christ's Charge to St Peter *by Raphael (1515–16, Sistine Chapel, Rome).*

Peter was considered to be the first Bishop of Rome and successive popes inherited his chair. He is represented as a vigorous elderly man with curly white hair and beard, and he often wears a golden-yellow cloak over green or blue. His most common attribute is a pair of keys.

Peter appears frequently in the Gospels. He was present at the Transfiguration and the Agony in the Garden, and he is painted in numerous scenes of the Life and Passion of Christ. He was one of the first to be called: "and Jesus, walking by the sea of Galilee, saw two brethren, Simon called Peter, and Andrew, casting a net into the sea; for they were fishers. And he said unto them, Follow me, and I will make you fishers of men. And they straightway left their nets and followed him."[3]

Reference to Peter's future

missionary work was also made during the episode known as the Miraculous Draught of Fishes. Christ asked Peter to take him on board so that he could preach to the multitude gathered on the shore. Peter informed him that, although they had toiled all night, they had caught nothing; and Christ told him to cast their nets out into the deep water once more. They caught so many fish that their nets began to break, and Christ said, "fear not; from henceforth thou shalt catch men".[4] As the cartoon by Raphael shows, Peter fell to his knees, as this was the moment when he recognized Christ as the Messiah.

As part of a cycle of the Life of St Peter, Masaccio frescoed the episode of the Tribute Money (Brancacci Chapel, Santa Maria del Carmine, Florence). At Capernaum the tax-gatherer asked Peter if Christ had paid the tribute money. Christ told Peter to cast his line into the sea: the first fish he hooked would have a coin in its mouth to pay the tax.[5]

Before the Last Supper Peter was reluctant to let Jesus wash his feet. At Christ's arrest he cut the ear off one of the servants in the crowd. He denied that he knew Jesus three times before the cock crowed, fulfilling Christ's prophecy.[6]

After the Ascension, Peter was an active missionary, preacher and performer of miracles: "they brought forth the sick into the streets and laid them on beds and couches";[7] and the very shadow of the saint passing by cured them. In Jerusalem, with St John, he healed a cripple at the gate of the Temple,[8] and they persuaded the rich to sell their land and give the proceeds to the poor. Ananias and his wife Sapphira, however, kept back part of the money, for which Peter struck them dead.[9] At Joppa he performed a miracle by raising Tabitha from the dead, a woman "full of good works and almsdeeds".[10] During the persecutions of Herod Peter was thrown into prison. Raphael's fresco in the Stanza d'Eliodoro in the Vatican, illustrates how an angel put the guards to sleep, the chains fell from Peter's hands, and he was led to freedom.[11]

Tradition claims that Peter went to Rome, where he formed the first Christian community. Legend[12] tells of how the sorcerer Simon Magus followed him, and his black arts won favour with the emperor Nero. Simon boasted that he could raise the dead and could fly from the top of a tall tower; the painter Solimena shows him tumbling to his death (San Paolo Maggiore, Naples). Nero then ordered Peter's arrest, but the Apostle converted his jailers and was set free, whereupon his followers begged him to flee. As Peter was walking out of Rome on the Via Appia Antica, Christ appeared, burdened with his cross. Peter asked *Domine, quo vadis?* ("Lord, where goest thou?"), to which Christ replied "To Rome, to be crucified again." Annibale Carracci shows the surprised saint with Christ pointing the way. Peter returned to Rome, where he was arrested and imprisoned. He was crucified head down at his request, to differentiate himself from Christ, and was buried in the catacombs directly below the present site of the dome of St Peter's.

Peter, Saint (Martyr)

Peter (1205–52) heard St Dominic preach and joined his Order, himself becoming an outstanding preacher.

Peter, Saint (Martyr): *see* Martyrs

[1] *Golden Legend, St Peter Martyr*

Phaethon: *see* Swan
[1] Ovid, *Met I:747–779; II:1–400*

Philemon and Baucis: *see* Hermes; Jupiter
[1] Ovid, *Met VIII:611–724*

Philip, Saint: *see* Martyrs
[1] *John 6:5–7*
[2] *Acts 1:13*
[3] *Golden Legend, St Philip*

He became Inquisitor General and vigorously suppressed heresy, but he made enemies as a result of this. As Giovanni Bellini shows, he was assassinated along with a friar who accompanied him on his way from Como to Milan.[1] An important saint for the Dominicans, Peter Martyr wears the black-and-white habit of the Order and often has an open wound in his head, or a knife firmly planted in his skull, as depicted by Cima da Conegliano (Brera, Milan).

Phaethon

Phaethon[1] was the son of the sun god Phoebus (identified with Apollo). The god reluctantly agreed to let Phaethon drive his chariot for one day, though only Phoebus could control the fiery steeds, illustrated by Poussin in *Apollo and the Chariot of Phaethon.*

Dawn turned the sky pink, the stars fled, and Phaethon leaped eagerly into the chariot. He drove near the constellation of Scorpio and its menacing tail frightened him so much that he dropped the reins. The horses bolted and plunged so near the earth that it caught fire, woods blazed and springs dried up. The earth cried out for help to Jupiter (in Greek myth, Zeus), who hurled a thunderbolt at Phaethon and dashed him from the chariot. Phaethon fell headlong into a river, and his charred body was buried by nymphs.

His mother Clymene and his friend Cygnus mourned him and his sisters flung themselves on his tomb. They were turned into trees and their flowing tears, hardened by the sun, became amber.

A theme of human pride and folly, the Fall of Phaethon was popular in Baroque art and was a suitable subject for ceilings, as in Sebastiano Ricci's *The Fall of Phaethon* (Palazzo Fulcis Bertoldi, Belluno).

Philemon and Baucis

In mythology[1] Jupiter (in Greek myth, Zeus) and Mercury (Hermes) disguised themselves as mortals to observe good and evil in mankind.[1] In the hills of Phrygia they looked for somewhere to rest, but were turned away from a thousand homes until they came to the tiny cottage of the elderly Philemon and his wife Baucis. This couple treated their guests with kindness, and were amazed to find that their flagon of wine refilled itself. They had a single goose, which they wanted to kill in honour of their guests, but the bird took refuge with the travellers. The gods then revealed themselves and announced that they would destroy the inhospitable land. Philemon and Baucis climbed up a steep mountain with them and watched their country drown in marshy waters. Their home, however, was turned into a temple with marble columns and a golden roof. They asked to serve as priests at the shrine of the gods and requested that, when their time came to die, they should do so together. Both wishes were granted and they were turned into trees growing side by side. Artists have focused on the hospitality of the old couple, and have shown the gods sitting at table and the goose being chased or standing nearby, as in *Philemon and Baucis* by a painter of the School of Rubens.

Philip, Saint (Apostle, Disciple)

Philip (died *c.* AD80) appears rarely in the Gospels. He doubted that Christ could feed the 5,000 with only five loaves of bread and five fishes,[1] and he may be shown holding the loaves or in close proximity to them. At the Last Supper Philip asked Christ to "show us the Father", and Christ replied "I am in the Father and the Father in me." Philip participated in the gathering of Christ's disciples after the Ascension.[2] Details of his later life are unknown, but legend[3] tells of how he preached to the pagans of Hierapolis who laid hold of him, thrust him in front of a statue of Mars, and ordered him to make a sacrifice.

Filippino Lippi illustrates the episode of Philip vanquishing a dragon as it emerged from the base of the statue of Mars and killed the priest's son and two tribunes, infecting the rest with its stench so that all were made ill. The infuriated infidels seized Philip and nailed him to a cross.

Philip of Neri, Saint

Known as the "Apostle of Rome", Philip (1515–95) was an important figure in the Counter Reformation. Aged 18 he abandoned his father's business to study philosophy and theology in Rome, where he founded a brotherhood of laymen, known as the Oratorians, to look after pilgrims and the sick. In recognition, the pope granted him the church in Rome, which he rebuilt as the Chiesa Nuova. Philip of Neri is shown as an Oratorian in black with a biretta, sometimes in the company of his friend St Carlo Borromeo. However, Piazzetta shows the saint with a vision of the Virgin and Child: he is wearing a bishop's mitre and cardinal's hat, honours that he rejected in his life (Santa Maria della Fava, Venice).

Philosophy

Philosophy was praised as the highest intellectual persuit because it investigated through reasoned argument and was concerned with the cause and nature of things. Through the application of wisdom, truth and knowledge, it gave rise to true judgment. Philosophy may be personified as a woman enthroned with a book or represented by the great philosophers of antiquity.

Phocion

The Athenian general Phocion (died *c.*318BC) led a virtuous life of self-control, modesty and patriotism.[1] He was accused of treason, however, and was forced to take a dose of the deadly poison hemlock. As a posthumous humiliation he was not allowed to be buried in Athens. Poussin depicts the scene in *A Landscape with the Body of Phocion Carried Out of Athens*; a pendant picture shows his wife gathering his ashes and taking them back to Athens for an honourable burial.

Phoenix

The phoenix was a legendary bird[1] of great beauty, thought to be unique. It is said to have its origins in the City of Heliopolis, ancient centre of sun worship, where sacrifices were made to the heron-like bird as the creative spirit of the sun.

The phoenix was said to transform in its own fire. It lived for hundreds of years in the desert, at the end of which period it built an aromatic nest and immolated itself, only to be reborn after three days in a fire ignited by the sun. It then sacrificed the nest and the ashes of its previous incarnation to the altar of the sun in Heliopolis. In

Philip of Neri, Saint: *see* Religious Dress; RELIGIOUS ORDERS

Phocion:
[1] Plutarch, *Lives, Phocion*

Phoenix:
[1] Pliny the Elder, *Natural History X:3*

Phrygian Hat: *see* Paris; Trojan War

Phryne:
[1] Quintilian, *II xv 9*

Pig:
[1] *Leviticus 11:2–7*

Pilgrims: *see* James the Great, St

Pluto: *see* Cerberus; Ceres; Hades; Proserpina

Polyphemus: *see* Galatea; Ulysses
[1] Homer, *Odyssey IX:187–474*

early Christian funerary sculpture it is a symbol of the Resurrection and the hope of victory over death.

Phrygian Hat
The hat worn by a native of Phrygia, an ancient country of Asia Minor, was conical with the top turned over at the front. It was worn by Persians and by Trojans, especially Paris.

Phryne
Phryne was the beautiful mistress and model of the famous classical sculptor Praxiteles (early 4th century BC). She was once accused of impiety, and her lawyer, seeing that her case was in doubt, unveiled her in court, and she was immediately acquitted.[1] In *Phryne Before the Judges* Jean-Léon Gérôme shows her naked before her judges, covering her eyes with shame.

Pig
According to the Old Testament, God told Moses and Aaron to "speak unto the children of Israel, saying: These are the beasts which ye shall eat among all the beasts that are on the earth." The meat of the pig was not included as it was deemed unclean.[1] Pigs were also considered greedy animals and prone to lust.

Pilgrims
A pilgrimage to a sacred place was made out of religious devotion or as a penance. In the early 13th century the Inquisition imposed pilgrimages as a punishment upon penitent heretics, who were expected to return with evidence that they had reached their destination. In the Middle Ages the principal places of pilgrimage were the Holy Land, Rome and Santiago de Compostela. Pilgrims would bring back a Cross and palm from the Holy Land, and a cockle shell from the shrine of St James at Santiago. Typically, a cockle shell in the hat denotes a pilgrim, who would also wear a simple cloak and carry a staff.

Pluto
Pluto (in Greek myth, Hades), the son of Saturn (Cronos) and Ops (Rhea), was ruler of the Underworld, a realm allotted to him by his brother Jupiter (Zeus) after the latter's usurpation of their father, as the chief of gods. Unable to find a bride to share his gloomy domain, Pluto assaulted Proserpina (Persephone) and dragged her down to be his queen. In *The Rape of Proserpina* Bernini portrayed him as a resolute, vigorous man with his attribute Cerberus, the three-headed dog that guarded the entrance to the Underworld.

Polyphemus
In mythology the savage Polyphemus, son of Neptune (in Greek myth, Poseidon), was chief of the Cyclopes, a race of one-eyed giants who were assistants of Vulcan (Hephaestus). Wandering homeward from the sack of Troy, Ulysses (Odysseus)[1] came to an island, probably Sicily, where Polyphemus looked after his flocks. Taking 12 men and some potent wine, Ulysses entered the monster's cave and awaited his return. Polyphemus drove his flock into the cave and sealed the entrance. He discovered the strangers and, tearing two of them limb from limb, feasted on them; in the morning he ate two more. That evening Ulysses persuaded the Cyclops to drink the wine, until the giant fell down senseless. Ulysses

drove a burning stake into the giant's eye and escaped next morning with his remaining men clinging to the bellies of the sheep: the blinded Polyphemus stroked the back of each sheep as it passed him on its way to pasture. In revenge Neptune made Ulysses' journey home lengthy and hazardous. Turner's *Ulysses Deriding Polyphemus* shows Ulysses' boat pulling away while phosphorescent Nereids guide his ship; the bulk of Polyphemus forms part of the mountain seen through the clouds.

Polyxena

Polyxena was the beautiful daughter of King Priam of Troy. She and the Greek hero Achilles fell in love, but her brother Hector refused to let her marry an enemy of the Trojans. Achilles killed Hector during battle and was himself killed by Paris to avenge Hector's death. After the defeat of Troy the ghost of Achilles requested that Polyxena be sacrificed to honour his tomb. In *The Sacrifice of Polyxena* Giovanni Battista Pittoni shows her being led with dignity to the tomb where she asks Neoptolemus, Achilles' son, to kill her, preferring death to enslavement by the Greeks.[1]

Pomegranate

A pomegranate is the attribute of Proserpina (in Greek myth, Persephone), who was abducted by Pluto (Hades), king of the Underworld. Ceres (Demeter), Proserpina's mother, was told by Jupiter (Zeus) that her daughter could return home only if she had eaten nothing in the Underworld. Without knowing the terms of her freedom, Proserpina had eaten some pomegranate seeds. As a compromise she was released back to the upper world for half the year. Dante Gabriel Rossetti's *Proserpina* shows her contemplating the restrictions of her life.

The myth represented the bleakness of autumn and winter and the regeneration of spring and summer, symbolized by the pomegranate.

Christianity adopted the pomegranate as a symbol of the Resurrection and sometimes of the Church. The Christ Child is sometimes seen holding a pomegranate: for example, in *Madonna della Melagrana* by Botticelli.

Pomona and Vertumnus

In mythology[1] Pomona was a wood nymph who was devoted to the cultivation of fruit trees, from which she derived her name (*poma* meaning "fruit" in Latin).

She carried a curved knife for pruning, and watered the plants from trickling streams. To keep satyrs out she fenced herself inside her orchards, but Vertumnus (a satyr, though he may not be depicted as such) fell in love with her and adopted various disguises to approach her: as a rough harvester, a vineyard worker, a soldier and a fisherman.

Dressed as an old woman, he entered her garden and lavishly praised Pomona's fruit trees. Disguised, he tried to persuade her to court Vertumnus, likening marriage to a tree that supports a vine, but to no avail. Finally, he threw off his disguise and the nymph, entranced by his beauty, was smitten with a passion equal to his own.

This bucolic subject was chosen for the decoration of villas: for example, the Villa Medici, which was adorned

Polyxena: *see* Trojan War
[1] Ovid, *Met XIII:439–480*

Pomegranate: *see* Proserpina

Pomona and Vertumnus: see Satyr
[1] Ovid, *MetXIV:623–771*

A detail showing the Christ Child holding a pomegranate, after Madonna della Melegrana *by Botticelli (1480s, Uffizi, Florence).*

Priapus: *see*
Bacchus; Pan
[1] Ovid, *Fasti I:393–441*
[2] Ovid, *Met IX:346–348*

Prometheus: *see*
Pandora
[1] Hesiod, *Works and Days 48–104* and *Met I:76–89*
[2] Apollodorus, *The Llibrary I vii 1*
[3] Apollonius, *Argonautica II:1242–1261*

Proserpina: *see*
Ceres; Hades; Pluto
[1] Ovid, *Met V 346–571*

by Pontormo; while other artists chose the scene of the disguised Vertumnus wooing Pomona, such as Domenico Fetti in his *Vertumnus and Pomona*.

Priapus

In mythology Priapus, the son of Venus (in Greek myth, Aphrodite) and Bacchus (Dionysos), had enormous genitals, and his mother banished him to the mountains because of his deformity. He was the god of licentiousness and fertility, the latter especially in respect of orchards, vines and gardens. He attended a feast of Bacchus where he lost his heart to the nymph Lotis, but she scorned him.[1] When night came Lotis fell asleep on the grass and Priapus was about to ravish her when the ass belonging to Silenus' companion (the son of Pan) brayed raucously and Lotis awoke. In terror she pushed Priapus away and fled. The gods took pity on her and transformed her into the lotus tree to protect her from the lustful Priapus.[2] Giovanni Bellini shows this scene in *Feast of the Gods*.

Prometheus

The Titan Prometheus was a master of cunning. He fashioned man from the newly-made earth in the image of the gods,[1] as depicted by Piero di Cosimo in two paintings of the story of Prometheus. As punishment Jupiter (in Greek myth, Zeus) deprived humankind of fire. With the help of the goddess Minerva (Athene), Prometheus, on humankind's behalf, climbed to the heavens and retrieved a spark from the chariot of the sun. In retribution for this act Jupiter spread evils over the world, released via Pandora's box, and set Prometheus on Mount Caucasus, chained to a rock. Each day an eagle came and devoured his liver, and each night the organ regenerated until, after many years, Hercules set him free.[2] As Jason and the Argonauts sailed through the steep crags of the Caucasian mountains they saw the eagle and heard the anguished cries of Prometheus as his liver was torn out.[3]

The most popular theme in art from the story of Prometheus was his torture, especially in the 17th century. Rubens, for example, shows his muscular body racked with pain.

The story has various resonances: the courage needed to disobey the gods, the "fire" of intelligence distinguishing man from the beasts and the way in which Prometheus ended the Golden Age, bringing wisdom to mankind.

A detail showing Prometheus, after Prometheus Carrying Fire *by Cossier (mid-17th century, Prado, Madrid).*

Proserpina

Known as Persephone to the Greeks, Proserpina[1] was the daughter of Ceres (Demeter), goddess of the corn, and Jupiter (Zeus). She was gathering flowers when "at one and the same time, Pluto [Hades] saw her, and loved her and bore her off – so swift is love". She cried out to her mother while struggling to break free, but her captor urged his chariot on. A nymph rose from the waters and tried to block his path but Pluto hurled his sceptre into the depths of the pool. The ground opened up to receive his chariot as it hurtled down to the gates into the Underworld, guarded by Cerberus. Bernini's statue in the Borghese Gallery, Rome, captures the horror of the abduction.

Unable to find her daughter, Ceres grew angry and decided that she would stop the crops from growing unless Proserpina returned. Jupiter took pity on Ceres, granting her request only if Proserpina had eaten nothing in the Underworld. However, Pluto's new queen had tasted a few pomegranate seeds. Given the triviality of this, Jupiter allowed her to return to earth and live with her mother for six months of the year. During the other half of the year Proserpina lamented her fate as queen of the Underworld.

Psyche

In an ancient Roman tale,[1] Psyche's beauty rivalled that of Venus (in Greek myth, Aphrodite), and the angry goddess commanded Cupid (Eros) to make her fall in love with an idiot.[1] However, Cupid himself fell in love with Psyche and took her to an enchanted castle. He forbade her to look at him and came to her only at night, vanishing at daybreak. Psyche's jealous sisters tricked her into looking at her sleeping lover by the light of a lamp. When she saw his beauty she too fell in love, but a drop of scalding oil woke the god, and he angrily soared away. A distraught Psyche roamed the earth looking for Cupid until she found the house of Venus. Here she became Venus' slave and her mistress set her a series of almost impossible tasks: to separate a pile of mixed grain, which she achieved with the help of ants; to procure golden wool from dangerous sheep, in which a reed from the sacred waters instructed her; to fetch water from a sacred stream guarded by dragons, in which Jupiter's (Zeus') eagle came to her aid; and to collect a some of Proserpina's beauty from the Underworld, in which a tower guided her safely to Hades. At last Cupid begged Jupiter to take pity on Psyche; a council of the gods was held, and Psyche was given a cup of nectar to make her immortal. The great wedding feast of Cupid and Psyche was arranged, and she later bore him a daughter called Pleasure.

The story of the beautiful couple was a popular and happy romantic tale. Its numerous episodes and final wedding scene have been used to cover large areas or fill the many vaults of a ceiling, as in Raphael's frescoes in the Loggia (Villa Farnesina, Rome). Episodes from the story were also painted as a series, such as the 12 canvases of Luca Giordano's *Cupid and Psyche*. Alternatively, artists painted isolated scenes, such as Fragonard's *Psyche Showing her Sisters her Gifts from Cupid*, and François Gérard's *Psyche Receiving her First Kiss*.

Putto

A *putto* (plural *putti*) is a very young, winged boy, also known as an *amoretto* or "little Cupid". *Putti* may be little angels or cherubs in religious paintings, or add a humorous note to secular paintings about love. They often accompany Venus or may worship her statue during the Feast of Venus. In Titian's *The Worship of Venus*, countless *putti* gather apples, sacred to the goddess, from the floor of the orchard or fly up to pick them from the trees and tumble about playing ball.[1]

Pygmalion

In mythology the race of Propoetides denied the divinity of Venus and in her anger she turned their women into prostitutes.[1] When Pygmalion saw

Psyche: *see* Cupid
[1] Apuleius, *The Golden Ass, VII; VIII; IX*

Putto: *see* ANGELS
[1] Philostratus the Elder, *Imagines I:6*

Pygmalion:
[1] Ovid, *Met X:243–297*

Pyramus and Thisbe:
[1] Ovid, *Met IV:55–166*

Pythagoras: *see* LIBERAL ARTS

their wicked lives he vowed to remain celibate. He carved a snowy ivory statue, more beautiful than any living woman, and fell in love with his own creation. He would stroke and embrace it, and wooed it as if it were alive. At the Festival of Venus, he prayed to the goddess to bring his statue to life, and she consented, and was present at their marriage. The subject was of interest to 18th- and 19th-century painters: François Boucher painted *Pygmalion*; in a painting of the same title Jean-Léon Gérôme shows Pygmalion embracing his statue; and Edward Burne-Jones painted the series *Story of Pygmalion*.

Pyramus and Thisbe

In mythology Pyramus and Thisbe, who had grown up next door to each other, fell in love.[1] Their parents forbade their marriage, however, and the lovers communicated through a slender chink in the wall between their houses, cursing the wall for preventing their embrace. They determined to escape at night and planned to meet outside the city, near a mulberry tree by a tomb. Thisbe slipped out first, but, near the appointed tree, was frightened by a bloodied lion arriving from a recent kill.

As she fled to a cave, her veil slipped from her shoulders and the lion tore it to shreds. Pyramus came upon the blood-stained garment and, thinking his beloved dead, plunged a sword into his side. Thisbe found him dying and took her own life. Their blood turned the fruit of the mulberry tree red for evermore. In *Landscape with Pyramus and Thisbe* Poussin shows Thisbe rushing across to the fatally wounded Pyramus, against a stormy landscape.

Pythagoras

The celebrated Greek philosopher Pythagoras (*c.*582–507BC) held that all relationships could be expressed in numbers and discovered that there was a numerical relationship between the length of a string and the sound it made when plucked.

He may appear as a personification of arithmetic in representations of the Liberal Arts.

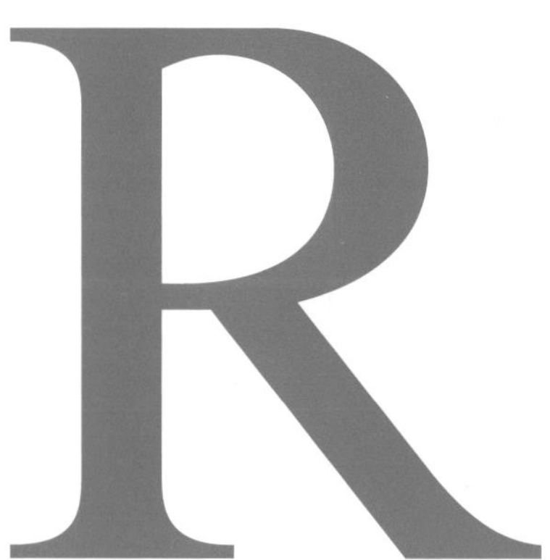

Rabbit
A rabbit or hare is sometimes used as a symbol of lust because of its renowned fertility. For example, a hare appears at the feet of Pisanello's personification, *Lust*.

Rainbow
In mythology the goddess Iris is associated with a rainbow, on which she brought messages from the gods to mortals. In the Old Testament, a rainbow was sent by God as a symbol of reconciliation with mankind after the Flood.[1] It is also depicted surrounding Christ's throne in the Last Judgment after the vision in Revelation.[2]

Raphael, Saint (Archangel)
Like the other archangels, Raphael is often shown as a winged youth; his name means "God heals". He acts as a guardian angel and is traditionally a protector of the young and of travellers. He acted as a guide for Tobias, in whose company he is usually seen. Tobias may hold a fish and Raphael a jar containing the fish gall with which he restored Tobias' father's sight. He is shown with these attributes in Francesco Botticini's *The Three Archangels and Tobias*.

A detail of Raphael, after Botticelli's Archangel Raphael and Tobias *(15th century, Galleria Reale, Turin).*

Rebecca
In the Old Testament[1] Abraham sent his servant Eliezer to find a wife for his son Isaac among Abraham's own

Rainbow: *see* Iris; Noah
[1] *Genesis 9:13*
[2] *Revelation 4:3*

Raphael, Saint: *see* ANGELS; Tobias

Rebecca:
[1] *Genesis 24*

Religious Ceremonial Objects: *see*
Aaron; Blood; Christ, The Life of; John the Evangelist, St; Laurence, St
[1] *Mark 14:23–25*

Religious Dress: *see*
Jerome, St; Religious Ceremonial Objects

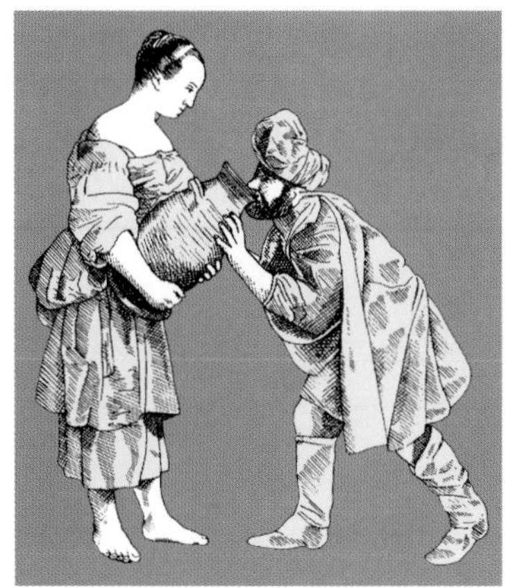

A detail of Rebecca, after Eliezer and Rebecca *by Salomon de Bray (*c.*1640, Musée de la Chartreuse, Douai).*

kin. Eliezer reached a well at dusk, when women of the city came to fill their pitchers, and he realized that he would find the girl by asking for water. Rebecca willingly drew water for him and for his camels, and Eliezer rewarded her with jewelry. Resting that night at her father's house, Eliezer announced that Rebecca had been divinely chosen to be Isaac's wife. The meeting at the well was often painted, especially in the 17th and 18th centuries. Rebecca is shown offering water or being presented with jewels by Eliezer. Giambattista Tiepolo's *Rebecca* is regal, but in many other paintings she can have an air of coyness or even flirtatiousness.

Religious Ceremonial Objects

Many religious objects have gathered significance from Old and New Testament teaching, and are related to particular sacraments, incidents or people. A **censer**, or thurible, is the vessel in which incense burns, and may be the attribute of Aaron or of deacon saints such as Laurence. A **chalice** is the sacramental cup of the Eucharist. At the Last Supper, Christ "took the cup, and when he had given thanks, he gave it to them; and they all drank of it. And he said unto them, This is my blood of the new testament, which is shed for many. ... I will drink no more of the fruit of the vine, until that day that I drink it new in the kingdom of God."[1] The cup of salvation is, therefore, an important feature in painting illustrating the service of the Eucharist, and is shown with various saints or priests officiating. It may be presented to Christ by an angel during the Agony in the Garden. A chalice with snakes is the attribute of St John the Evangelist. A **corporal** is the cloth on which the chalice is placed during the Eucharist before consecration.

A **ciborium** is a cup with an arched cover which is reserved for the Host. A ciborium may also be a canopy covering an altar or shrine. A **pyx** is a small portable receptacle for the Host. The Host is preserved in a **tabernacle**. A **monstrance**, an open or transparent receptacle, holds the consecrated Host for display at the service of benediction. It is also carried in processions, especially at the Corpus Christi – a celebration of the Sacrament of the Eucharist, founded in 1264 by Pope Urban IV. Similar containers termed **reliquaries**, usually highly ornate, hold holy relics and were used to perform miracles. They are seen carried in procession, as in the *Stories of the Relic of the True Cross* by Bellini and artists of his studio.

Religious Dress

The dress of ministers of the Church – bishops, priests and deacons –

denotes their rank and the office they are performing.

When celebrating Mass, they wear a **chasuble**, a highly decorated outer garment; a **maniple**, a band of silk worn on the arm; and a **stole**, a narrow embroidered band worn around the neck and crossed over the chest. A **cope** (a large semi-circular cape with a deep collar) is worn in processions and on important occasions. Otherwise, a **cassock** and **biretta** (a square, ridged hat) are worn; these are usually purple for bishops and black for priests and deacons.

Some elements of the liturgical dress may be common to all ministers. For example, a bishop's mitre is also worn by the pope as bishop of Rome.

In paintings, ministers of the church are usually depicted in the highest office they attained in their lives. Early saints, however, such as St Jerome, were given their office posthumously.

The church's hierarchy of ministers is recognizable from the following attire: the Pope has a **tiara**, a conical hat with three crowns, or wears a white cassock with a short red cloak; Cardinals wear a scarlet cassock, and have a scarlet broad-brimmed hat with a low crown; Bishops wear a chasuble or cope, and a **mitre** (a tall, decorated head-dress with a cleft) and carry a **crozier**, the original staff of the Apostles, which became highly elaborate. Deacons may be seen carrying a **censer**. The regular clergy belong to a religious Order, and therefore they are seen wearing the habit of their Order.

RELIGIOUS ORDERS

See panel on following page.

Rémi (Remigius), Saint

Son of a count of Gaul, Rémi (AD*c.*438–*c.*533) was appointed Bishop of Rheims at the age of 22. According to legend[1] Clovis I, king of the Franks, vowed to follow his wife's faith if he became glorious in battle. This ambition fulfilled, he was baptized by Rémi but, when he arrived at the font, the sacred oil was found missing; a dove flew down with a phial in its beak and from this the king was anointed. The Master of St Giles shows Rémi as a bishop baptizing the king, and also his conversion of many heretics.

Rinaldo

Rinaldo was a Christian hero who features in the epic poem *Jerusalem Delivered* by Torquato Tasso (1544–95), which describes the siege and capture of Jerusalem from the Saracens during the First Crusade. Rinaldo was lulled to sleep by the Saracen sorceress Armida, who planned to kill him but was suddenly overcome by his beauty.[1] In *Rinaldo and Armida*, Poussin shows Cupid (Eros) holding back the hand in which she clutches a dagger; and in another version he depicts her carrying Rinaldo away to her enchanted castle.

The companions of Rinaldo, Carlo and Ubaldo, set out to rescue the knight, fighting a dragon and savage beasts on their way. Nymphs bathing naked tried to lure them into laying down their arms, but they passed on unmoved. They found Rinaldo in Armida's thrall, gazing into her eyes as she held up a mirror so that each could see the passion of their love. In his *Rinaldo and Armida* Giambattista Tiepolo shows this moment, and the subject may be used to illustrate men's

Rémi (Remigius), Saint:
[1] *Golden Legend, St Remy*

Rinaldo: *see*
Olindo and Sophronia;
Tancred
[1] Tasso, *Jerusalem Delivered XIV:lxvi–lxx*
[2] Tasso, *Jerusalem Delivered XVI:xx–xxxiv*

RELIGIOUS ORDERS: *see* COLOURS: Religious Dress; individual names of saints

RELIGIOUS ORDERS

Monasticism was in existence before the legalization of Christianity (AD313). Hermits formed communities dedicated to prayer and the Christian doctrine, but St Anthony is usually considered to have been the founder of monasticism in the 3rd century. The different Orders were distinguished by the habit they were seen wearing. An abbot or abbess is shown with the pastoral staff, which signifies office, but otherwise wears the dress of his or her Order. The following is a brief description of some of the most frequently painted Orders and their identifying attributes:

The **Benedictines** were founded by St Benedict *c.*AD529 at Monte Cassino. It is the oldest Order in Europe, and the abbey, founded in 910 at Cluny, became a major religious centre in the Middle Ages. The rule stressed communal living, physical labour and learning. Their habit is black.

There were also several reformations of the Benedictine Order, resulting in: the **Camaldolese**, founded by St Romuald in the early 11th century, who wear white; the **Vallombrosians**, founded by St John Gualbert *c.*1038, who wear light grey; the **Carthusians**, founded by St Bruno *c.*1090, who wear white; and the **Cistercians**, founded by St Bernard of Clairvaux *c.*1115, who wear white, too. The **Olivetians** and **Oratorians** were also reformed Benedictines, and paintings for these Orders may show their founder wearing white.

Augustinians were founded *c.*1060 and were named after St Augustine, whose example they followed. He had lived in a community and looked after the material needs of the church and of the poor. Their habit is black.

The Order of **Franciscans** was founded in 1210 by St Francis of Assisi. These friars were called *frati* (brothers) instead of *padri* (fathers) to emphasize their humility, and St Francis added the term *minori* to members of his community. They were noted as missionaries and preachers and took vows of poverty, chastity and obedience. They renounced all forms of ownership and were mendicants, living solely on alms. Their hooded habit was first grey, hence the "grey friars", but two centuries later it changed to brown and was bound at the waist with a knotted cord. They are shown barefoot or wearing only simple sandals. With St Clare, St Francis also established the **Poor Clares** in 1212, the first community for poor women.

Dominicans were founded in 1216 by St Dominic. Like the Franciscans they took vows, particularly of poverty, and were mendicants. They were preachers but were also known for placing emphasis on study and teaching. Their habit is a white gown with a black hooded cloak.

Jesuits were founded by St Ignatius Loyola and approved by the Papacy in 1540 as the Society of Jesus. They were active missionaries and believed in education, charity and moderation. Their habit is black and has a high collar.

enslavement by women. When Armida departed, Ubaldo stepped forward and showed Rinaldo his true image in his shield, at which Rinaldo threw off his crown of flowers.[2] Charles van Loo painted episodes from the poem (Palazzo Reale, Turin), including the warrior listening to Armida's pleas as he returned to the Crusade with Carlo and Ubaldo.

Roch (Rocco), Saint

Born in Montpellier, France, Roch (14th century) gave up his worldly goods to begin a pilgrimage to Rome. During a series of plagues, which culminated in the Black Death, he devoted himself to nursing the sick in northern Italy; after many years' devotion he caught the plague himself, and was fed by a dog. The disease attacked him so virulently that no one recognized him and he was thrown as an imposter into prison, where he died. Like St Sebastian (with whom he may be depicted), he was invoked against illnesses, especially in northeastern Italy. Tintoretto painted scenes from his life in the Scuola di San Rocco, the institution dedicated to him in Venice. Lorenzo Lotto's image of Roch in his *Saints Christopher, Roch and Sebastian* shows him typically dressed as a pilgrim with staff, lifting up his tunic to reveal a sore on his inner thigh. He may also be accompanied by a dog.

Romuald, Saint

Born in Ravenna, Romuald (*c.*AD950–1027) was horrified when his father murdered a relative during a dispute over property, and sought refuge in solitude. He became a Benedictine, but seeing the necessity for reform he established an independent Order known as the Camaldolese, named after his hermitage near Arezzo, which was devoted to silence. Andrea Sacchi shows Romuald as an old man with a crutch, with members of his Order in their white habits, as he has his vision of men in white climbing up a ladder that stretches from earth to heaven.

Romulus and Remus

According to legend[1] Rhea Silvia was a descendant of Aeneas, the Trojan hero destined to be the forefather of the Romans. The mother of the twins Romulus and Remus, she was a Vestal Virgin, who had been raped by Mars. For this she was thrown into prison and her children were cast into the River Tiber, but the twins survived as a result of being suckled by a she-wolf. Rome was founded in 753BC when Romulus traced out the city walls on the Palatine with a sacred plough, killed his brother and gave his name to the new city. The she-wolf was a symbol of Rome, an Etruscan bronze of this subject (late 6th or early 5th century BC) originally stood on the Capitol; Romulus and Remus were added to the statue by Antonio Pollaiuolo in the late 15th century.

Rosary

A rosary is a string of beads, divided into five sections, and each one having one large bead and ten small. It and is used for keeping count during meditations and prayers on the life of Christ and the Virgin.

Known as the Mysteries, the prayers are divided into three groups of five: Joyful, Sorrowful and Glorious. A rosary may be included in paintings of the Virgin and Child, such as Bergognone's *Virgin and Child*; or of

Roch (Rocco), Saint: *see* Sebastian, St

Romuald, Saint: *see* RELIGIOUS ORDERS

Romulus and Remus: *see* Sabine Women; Vesta and Vestal Virgins

[1] Livy I, *iv* and Plutarch, *Lives, Romulus*

Rose: *see* Flowers; Venus; Virgin, The

St Dominic, who was said to have instituted its use as an emblem of devotion.

Rose

The rose is the flower of Venus (Aphrodite): in mythology it was believed that the flower first bloomed when Venus was born from the sea. The flower also heralds spring, and both themes have been immortalized by Botticelli in the *Birth of Venus Primavera*. In chivalrous imagery, rose gardens may surround a maiden, its thorns protecting her chastity. Numerous portraits of women include roses to enhance their beauty, and in Dutch still lifes, or *vanitas* paintings, roses may indicate that beauty and life are both ephemeral.

In medieval Christianity the petals of the flower were taken to represent the five wounds of Christ; a red rose growing among thorns signified the early martyrs and their persecutors; and a white rose reflected the spotless purity of the Virgin. In the Garden of Eden the rose grew without thorns, and its fragrance and beauty were a reminder of the glory of Paradise. Saints and angels often hold roses as an indication of the heavenly bliss they have entered.

A golden rose was sent by the Pope to sovereigns whom the Church esteemed, and since the Middle Ages roses have played an important part in heraldry. The wars which racked England during the 14th century gained the name the Wars of the Roses from the white rose of the House of York and the red rose of the House of Lancaster. With peace restored, the flower was adopted by the Tudor dynasty and became a royal device.

A detail showing Ruth, after Summer *or* The Meeting Between Ruth and Boaz *by Poussin (1660–64, Louvre, Paris).*

Ruth

In the Old Testament,[1] Ruth was from the land of Moab, but married into a Jewish family who had settled there. When her husband and father-in-law died, she left her country to accompany Naomi, her mother-in-law, to Bethlehem. Naomi begged her not to stay but Ruth refused to abandon her. They arrived at the beginning of the harvest and Ruth asked the Israelite Boaz if she might glean in his fields. He granted her permission, telling his reapers to leave her extra corn from their sheaves. Eventually they married, and from their union evolved the line of David and, therefore, of Christ.

In *Summer* or *The Meeting Between Ruth and Boaz*, Poussin chose this subject to illustrate the season of summer.

Sabine Women
According to legend[1] Romulus founded Rome in 753BC. Since there were few women in the settlement, he was concerned about the future growth and greatness of Rome, so he invited the neighbouring Sabines to a festival and, at a given signal, the Romans raped the Sabine women. They were careful to choose unmarried women, for the intention was to unite with their neighbours "by the greatest and surest bonds"; only one married woman was mistakenly chosen. The Rape of the Sabine Women was treated by numerous sculptors and painters, such as Giambologna (Loggia dei Lanzi, Florence) and Pietro da Cortona.

Romulus refused to let the women return, so their dishonoured fathers and brothers marched against Rome. During the battle, the women came running out "with miserable cries and lamentations, like creatures possessed, in the midst of the army and among the dead bodies, to come at their husbands and their fathers, some with their young babes in their arms, others with their hair loose about their ears, but all calling, now upon the Sabines, now upon the Romans, in the most tender and endearing words." Jacques-Louis David drew upon this dramatic account in *The Intervention of the Sabine Women*. Both armies melted with compassion and the women ended the fight by pleading with both sides to unite.

Sabine Women: *see* Lamentation; Romulus and Remus

[1] Plutarch, *Lives, Romulus*

Sacra Conversazione
The *sacra conversazione*, or "holy conversation", is a type of devotional altarpiece that was developed *c.*1440, in which various saints flank the Madonna and Child, with the Madonna often shown enthroned, in the same pictorial space, rather than in separate panels. An example is Domenico Veneziano's *St Lucy Altarpiece* or *Madonna and Child with Saints*.

Sacraments
The seven sacraments of the Catholic church are Baptism, Confirmation,

Sail: *see* TRIUMPHS

Saints: *see* individual names

Salome: *see* John the Baptist, St

[1] *Matthew 14:1–11*

the Eucharist, Penance, Ordination, Matrimony and Extreme Unction. They were painted only occasionally in the Renaissance, Rogier van der Weyden's *Seven Sacraments Triptych* being a rare example. Later Poussin executed two large series of seven separate paintings, both series entitled *The Seven Sacraments*. Five of the subjects were taken from the lives of Christ and the Virgin: *Baptism* is represented by John the Baptist and Christ; *Penance* by Mary Magdalene washing Christ's feet; *Ordination* by Christ giving the keys of heaven to St Peter; *Matrimony* by the marriage of the Virgin and Joseph; and the *Eucharist* by the Last Supper. *Extreme Unction* is a man receiving the Sacrament as he lies dying surrounded by mourners. *Confirmation* is set in the catacombs, and evokes the atmosphere of the early Christian age.

Sail

A full sail or billowing drapery may illustrate the winds. In mythological painting a sail may suggest prosperity and success, as in works depicting triumphs. Because the winds are not constant, a sail may also be the attribute of Fortune, to represent her inconstancy.

Saints

Saint was the title given to the Apostles, the Evangelists, and the numerous martyrs who died during the Roman persecutions. Pope Alexander III (1159–81) gave the Papacy the exclusive right to canonize others, such as popes and monarchs.

Saints are shown with haloes, and their attributes usually relate closely to their lives. They can appear in paintings together regardless of the period in which they lived. In visions of Paradise, such as that by Nardo di Cione (Strozzi Chapel, Santa Maria Novella, Florence), saints, accompanied by angels, surround the throne of Christ, according to their hierarchy. Like a jury, they may also flank Christ at the Last Judgment.

The reasons for the choice of a particular saint in art are manifold. The saint could be the patron of the city or the titular saint of the church or chapel for which the work was commissioned. Paintings for a monastic Order often include its founder. The saint may be the namesake of the patron or the protector of the patron's family. The image of a saint may also be commissioned for the significance of particular episodes in his or her life; for example, St Sebastian recovered from his wounds and was therefore invoked against the plague.

Salamander

In antiquity the salamander was a mythical, lizard-like reptile thought to live in, and be impervious to, fire. It nourished the good and destroyed the bad, and was adopted as an emblem of Francis I of France. It was usually shown surrounded by flames.

Salome

In the New Testament,[1] Salome danced at a banquet to celebrate the birthday of Herod, her stepfather. Her dance pleased him so much that he promised to give her whatever she requested as a reward. John the Baptist had preached against Herod's marriage to Salome's mother, Herodias, and Herodias instructed her daughter to demand John's head.

Salome shown dancing before Herod, after The Dance of Salome *by Filippino Lippi (1452–66, Prato Cathedral, Florence).*

In cycles of the life of John the Baptist the decorative episode of the dance of Salome often occupied a prominent position, as in Filippino Lippi's frescoes (Prato Cathedral, Florence). Salome's story of intrigue and murder also inspired many other artists, notably Aubrey Beardsley, who made illustrations to the play *Salome* by Oscar Wilde (1856–1900).

Salvator Mundi

Salvator Mundi, or Saviour of the World, was the name applied to a type of devotional image showing Christ holding a globe, as in a painting of *c.*1510 by Carpaccio. Christ may be making the sign of benediction, pointing above to the divine, wearing a Crown of Thorns, or any combination of these.

Samson

An Old Testament Judge, Samson had great physical strength, and is shown as muscular with long hair. His attribute is often a broken pillar.

The Israelites had been ruled by the Philistines for 40 years when an angel announced to Manoah and his barren wife that they would conceive a son, to be named Samson, who would liberate their people. He warned that Samson's hair must never be cut. Manoah made an offering to the Lord, and as he lit the altar fire the angel ascended to heaven in the flames.[1] Like the mythological Hercules, the young Samson slew a lion with his bare hands.[2] He was captured by the Philistines, but he broke the ropes binding him and killed 1,000 men with the jawbone of a donkey. This weapon also provided him with a stream of water to quench his thirst.[3]

Samson fell in love with Delilah who, bribed by the Philistine kings, sought to discover the secret of his strength. At last he revealed the truth, and Delilah, having lulled him to sleep in her lap, called upon the Philistines to shave his head. This done, they bound him, put out his eyes, set him in bronze chains and put him to work at a prison mill. There, however, his hair began to grow again. When brought out to entertain an audience of Philistines, including their five kings, he was placed between pillars supporting the building. Samson asked God to restore his strength, and he brought down the pillars and whole building, killing himself, as well as more Philistines than he had ever killed during his life.[4]

A detail after Rubens' Samson and Delilah *(*c.*1609, National Gallery, London).*

The most commonly painted episode of his life is the sleeping Samson betrayed by Delilah to the Philistines, as in Rubens' *Samson and Delilah*. The subject illustrates how even the strong can be rendered powerless by a woman. Other episodes were also favoured, such as the annunciation of Samson's birth, or the angel ascending in the flames of Manoah's sacrifice. Rembrandt

Samson: *see* Cassone; Hercules

[1] *Judges 13:1–20*
[2] *Judges 14:5–6*
[3] *Judges 15:13–19*
[4] *Judges 16:1–30*

Sappho:
[1] Ovid, *Heroids XV*

Sardanapalus:
[1] Diodorus of Sicily, *II.27*

Satan: *see*
ANGELS; Descent in Hell; Passion of Christ, The
[1] *Isaiah 14:12*
[2] *Matthew 12:24*
[3] *Revelation 12:9*

Saturn: *see*
TIME
[1] Ovid, *Fasti IV:197–206*

depicted the gory scene of *The Blinding of Samson.*

Sappho
Sappho (7th century BC), lived on the island of Lesbos and was famous for her poetry, her beauty and the violence of her passions.[1] She fell in love with Phaon, who refused her, whereupon she threw herself into the sea. The Lesbians honoured her as a goddess after her death. Sappho and Phaon are shown together in Jacques-Louis David's *Sappho and Phaon*, and Gustave Moreau painted *Sappho Leaping into the Sea.*

Sardanapalus
The king of Assyria in the 7th century BC, Sardanapalus was besieged in his capital and ordered his wives, his favourite concubine Myrrha, his servants and his treasures to be burned on a funeral pyre with him.[1] Delacroix's extravagant *Death of Sardanapalus* was based on Byron's play *Sardanapalus* (1821).

Satan
In the Christian faith, Satan was a rebel angel who rose up in pride against God, and fell from heaven, vanquished by St Michael and his armies. Thereafter his sole aim was to foster evil. As an angel, his name had been Lucifer.[1] He was also associated with the false god Beelzebub, called by the Gospels "the prince of the devils".[2] In images of the Last Judgment Satan is represented as the Lord of Hell, an incarnation of evil, who feeds on sinners and is surrounded by demons and the condemned, as in Taddeo di Bartolo's fresco (Collegiata, San Gimignano).

The Book of Revelation describes how "the great dragon was cast out, that old serpent called the Devil, and Satan, which deceiveth the whole world; he was cast out into the earth, and his angels were cast out with him."[3] Thus the Devil may take on the guise of a dragon, in the fights with Saints Michael and George; or a serpent, in the Temptation of Eve. After the Crucifixion, Christ descended into Limbo and vanquished the Devil.

A detail showing Satan, after The Temptation of Christ *by Botticelli (1482, Vatican, Rome).*

Satan may also be represented as a hybrid with horns, pointed ears, a tail, claws, cloven hoofs, the wings of a bat and the face of an animal.

Saturn
In mythology Saturn (in Greek myth, Kronos) was the son of the Earth (Gaea) and Uranus, the ruler of heaven. Uranus banished his children the Cyclopes, Hekatoncheires and Titans to Tartarus in the Underworld, an act for which Saturn took revenge by castrating his father with a scythe.

However, Venus (Aphrodite) was

born from Uranus' sperm as it spread over the waters. Vasari chose this subject for the ceiling of the room known as the *Four Elements* (Palazzo Vecchio, Florence).

Saturn inherited his father's kingdom, but an oracle warned that he would be ousted by his son. He therefore ate his offspring as fast as they were born, a monstrous act depicted by Goya in *Saturn Devouring his Children*. Saturn's wife, Ops (Rhea), could no longer bear to see her children perish, so when Jupiter (Zeus) was born she gave Saturn a stone in place of the baby.[1] Later, Saturn was overthrown by Jupiter and fled to Italy were he taught agriculture and the Liberal Arts. His benevolent and tranquil rule was linked to the Golden Age.

Saturn is the god of agriculture and is represented as an old man with a scythe. He may also personify Time, although this allusion came about from a confusion between the Greek name for the god, Kronos, with *cronos*, the Greek word for time.

Satyr

Satyrs were men with goat's horns, legs and hooves. They inhabited the countryside as the carousing attendants of Bacchus (in Greek myth, Dionysos), and became associated with lust. However, a satyr appears with peasants in Jacob Jordaens' *Satyr and the Peasant*, pointing out the incongruity of blowing on soup to make it cool and on hands to warm them.

Saul

In the Old Testament Saul[1] was chosen by God and anointed by Samuel as the first king of the 12 tribes of Israel. He waged war on the Philistines and Amalekites, but God rejected him for his leniency to his enemies. Saul found comfort with David, the court musician, who played the harp so beautifully that Saul made him his armour-bearer.[2] Rembrandt's *David Harping Before Saul* shows sympathy with the melancholic king. On the eve of battle with the Philistines, Saul consulted the Witch of Endor, from whom he learned that his army would be defeated and his three sons killed. When this happened, he fell on his own sword, as shown in Bruegel's panoramic *The Suicide of Saul*.

Scales

Scales are the attribute of Justice who weighs right against wrong, and of St Michael, said to weigh souls at the Last Judgment. They also denote the zodiacal sign of Libra. They may be seen with relevant trades, for example in Quentin Metsys' *The Moneylender and his Wife*.

Sceptre

A sceptre is a staff held by someone in authority, especially a monarch or an emperor. The tip may have an appropriate emblem or attribute.

Scholastica, Saint

Little is known of Scholastica[1] (AD*c*.480–*c*.543) except that she was St Benedict's sister. She probably founded a Benedictine nunnery near Monte Cassino and became the chief female saint of that Order. At her last meeting with her brother she asked him to delay his departure from the nunnery; when he refused, her prayers brought on a thunderstorm which prevented him from leaving. They

Satyr: *see*
Faunus and Fauns; Pan

Saul: *see*
David; Witch of Endor
[1] *I Samuel 10:1*
[2] *I Samuel 16:16–23*

Scales: *see*
Michael, St; Zodiac

Sceptre: *see*
Religious Ceremonial Objects

Scholastica, Saint: *see*
Benedict, St; Dove; Lily
[1] *Golden Legend, St Benedict*

Scipio: *see* CONTINENTS; Cybele
[1] Livy, *History of Rome XXVI:i*

Sebastian, Saint: *see* Arrow
[1] *Golden Legend, St Sebastian*

spent the whole night in holy conversation and mutual edification. Three days later she died, and Benedict saw her soul rising to heaven in the form of a dove. Scholastica may appear in pictures beside her brother. She generally wears the black of the Benedictine Order, and she may hold a lily and be accompanied by the dove of the legend.

Scio

In 1822, during the Greek wars of independence, patriots on the island of Scio (or Chios) attacked the Turkish garrison. The Turks retaliated by massacring innocent men, women and children. This inspired great sympathy in the West and the subject was notably painted by Delacroix in *The Massacre of Scio: Greek Families Awaiting Death or Slavery*.

Scipio

The Roman family of Scipio was awarded great honours during the years of the Republic. General Cornelius Scipio Africanus (235–183BC) was so named after his victories over Hannibal and the destruction of Carthage (in Africa), which ended the Punic Wars. He was the subject of the historical poem *Africa* by Petrarch (1304–74). Scenes of his triumph may allude to contemporary victories, and may be used for public decorations to accompany a dignitary's ceremonial entry into a city. The virtuous Scipio also had a bust of the mother goddess Cybele brought to Rome, as it had been prophesied that the presence of this bust was necessary for the defeat of Hannibal. The theme was shown in Mantegna's *Introduction of the Cult of Cybele into Rome*.

The Continence of Scipio was a popular theme in art.[1] After a victory at New Carthage, Scipio captured a beautiful young girl who was betrothed to the young Allucius. Hearing of this, Scipio restored the girl to her betrothed and requested only that Allucius be a friend to Rome; he gave the girl's ransom to the couple as a wedding gift. The theme was painted to signify self-control, as well as the generosity of a noble and virtuous general toward the innocent. Artists such as Sebastiano Ricci in *The Continence of Scipio* chose to set the scene before Scipio's magnanimous act to enhance the suspense.

SEASONS

See panel on following page.

Sebastian, Saint

Sebastian (3rd century AD) was an early martyr, venerated from the 4th century onward. In legend,[1] he was a Christian officer in the Roman Praetorian Guard who persuaded two fellow officers to die rather than renounce Christ. When his faith was discovered, the emperor ordered that he be executed. He was shot with so many arrows that "he looked like a porcupine", and the soldiers left him for dead. He miraculously survived and was nursed by a Christian woman Irene. Georges de la Tour shows her tending the saint. A few days later, when Sebastian stood on the steps of the imperial palace to rebuke the emperor, he was recognized and stoned to death. As Carracci illustrates, his body was tipped into the Cloaca Maxima, the main Roman drain. Sebastian revealed the location of his body to a Christian woman in her dream; it was retrieved and buried

St Sebastian, after Bellini's panel from the polyptych of St Vincent Farrer (1464–68, SS Giovanni e Paolo, Venice).

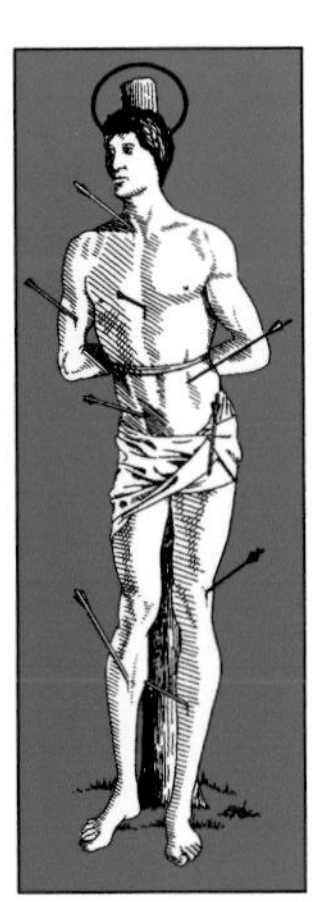

SEASONS

The four seasons of the year are often represented in art by the agricultural activities and the weather with which they are associated. Giuseppe Archimboldi ingeniously transformed the agricultural produce of the seasons into faces.

Poussin inventively included scenes from the Old Testament in his series of the four seasons: Adam and Eve in Paradise are spring; the meeting of Ruth and Boaz is summer; spies returning from the Promised Land are autumn; and the Flood is winter. Bruegel painted six panels each to illustrate a two month period; for example, *Hunters in the Snow* is thought to represent January and February.

In the tradition of Italian art, the seasons may also be represented by the gods of antiquity. Spring is the time to plant, so may be personified as a young girl with flowers, a spade or hoe, or as Flora, goddess of flowers. Summer is the time to harvest, so may be a girl with sheaves of corn, fruit or a sickle, or Ceres (in Greek myth, Demeter), goddess of the harvest. Autumn, the time for pressing wine, may be a figure with grapes or a vine, or Bacchus (Dionysos), god of wine. Winter is often an old man warming himself by a brazier in a snowy landscape, or Vulcan (Hephaestus), god of the forge.

Since antiquity the seasons have been likened to the four ages of mankind: "For in early spring it is tender and full of fresh life, just like a little child ... all things are in bloom and the fertile fields run riot with their bright-coloured flowers; but as yet there is no strength in the green foliage. After spring has passed, the year, grown more sturdy, passes into summer and becomes like a strong young man ... Then autumn comes, with its first flush of youth gone, but ripe and mellow ... And then comes aged winter, with faltering step and shivering, its locks all gone or hoary."[1] The theme of the seasons as the ages of man was illustrated by David Teniers in *Spring, Summer, Autumn, Winter*.

SEASONS: *see* Bacchus; Ceres; Flora; FLOWERS; Vulcan

A detail of a man threshing, after Bruegel's The Corn Harvest (August and September) *(1565, Metropolitan Museum of Art, New York).*

on the Via Appia Antica, Rome, near the basilica now dedicated to him.

Sebastian was invoked against disease because he survived his wounds, and the image of him pierced with arrows is shown far more often than his martyrdom. He was particularly popular with painters of the Italian Renaissance, who frequently portrayed him as a handsome naked youth, riddled with arrows, looking heavenwards for inspiration. Mantegna's painting is a typical example.

Semele

Semele, the daughter of Cadmus, king of Thebes, was loved by Jupiter (in Greek myth, Zeus).[1] Juno (Hera), Jupiter's wife, furious to find Semele with child, persuaded her to ask the god to appear in his full glory, as he did to Juno herself. Semele's mortal frame could not endure the god's embrace, and his lightning turned her to ashes. Her child Bacchus (Dionysos) was snatched from her womb before she died, and was sewn

Semele: *see* Bacchus; Juno

[1] Ovid, *Met III:253–315* and Philostratus the Elder, *I:14*

Semiramis:
[1] Valerius Maximus, *9:III*

Seneca:
[1] Tacitus, *Annals XV:60–64*

Sennacherib:
[1] *Isaiah 37:36*

Sheba, Queen of: *see* True Cross
[1] *I Kings 10:1–12*
[2] *Golden Legend, The Finding of the Holy Cross*

into Jupiter's thigh until his birth. In *Jupiter and Semele* Gustave Moreau painted a youthful Jupiter on his throne, with a nude Semele in his lap, gazing at his brilliance.

Semiramis

In Babylonian legend, the beautiful Semiramis was the wife of Menones, who hanged himself when Ninus, founder of Nineveh, demanded her from him. Through Ninus she acquired the crown of Nineveh. She then had Ninus put to death, and henceforth displayed a warlike disposition. Once, on hearing news of a revolt in Babylon, she took up arms immediately, though her hair was undone and she was only half dressed.[1] As empress of Assyria she travelled throughout her kingdom building monuments. She was eventually killed by her son. Rossini (1792–1868) made her the subject of an opera, which inspired Degas' *Semiramis Constructing a Town*.

Seneca

The Stoic philosopher Seneca (4BC–AD65) was tutor to Emperor Nero. When Nero accused him of conspiracy, he was ordered to take his own life.[1] Seneca's wife wanted to die with him but was prevented from doing so.

Jacques-Louis David's *Death of Seneca* depicts how, with calm dignity, he opened his veins. His animated last words were recorded by friends. To hasten death he drank poison as well, but to no effect, so he asked to be placed in a hot bath to make his blood flow more freely.

SENSES

See panel, right.

SENSES

The depiction of the five senses – hearing, sight, smell, touch and taste – was particularly popular in the 17th century: an example of which is Gonzales Coques' series of *c.*1650. They are often represented by relevant objects, such as musical instruments for hearing, and pipe smoke or flowers for smell.

In Coques' *Touch* a man is seen letting blood drain from his arm. The senses may also be suggested in paintings such as Willem Buytewech's *Merry Company*, or in still lifes, to act as a reminder of the vanities of the material world.

Sennacherib

In the Old Testament, King Sennacherib and his Assyrian warriors had conquered all the cities of Judah and were about to attack Jerusalem. One night, however, an angel of the Lord entered the Assyrian camp and smote dead 185,000 soldiers as they slept.[1] Rubens' *The Defeat of Sennacherib*, shows the king and his army not asleep but on horseback, plunged into chaos as a host of angels swoops down in a blaze of heavenly light.

Sheba, Queen of

In the Old Testament the Queen of Sheba came to Jerusalem to see if the rumours she had heard about King Solomon's wealth were true. Like the Magi worshipping the Christ Child, she brought a magnificent array of spices, gold and precious stones as gifts.[1] He in return gave her "all she desired". Their meeting was depicted

Venus standing in a scallop shell. A detail after The Birth of Venus *by Sandro Botticelli (1484–86, Uffizi, Florence).*

by Ghiberti (Baptistry, Florence).

In legend,[2] on her way to visit Solomon, the queen recognized and worshipped the wood of the True Cross.

Shell

In mythology a scallop shell was the attribute of Venus (in Greek myth, Aphrodite), who was born from the sea. Shells were also the chariots of Neptune (Poseidon) and Galatea. Conch shells may be used as trumpets by Tritons (mermen) and other figures, such as the impudent satyr in Botticelli's *Mars and Venus*. In Dutch 17th-century still lifes, such as that of Abraham van Beyeren, exotic shells allude to the newly discovered territories, and display the artist's skill.

Ship

In Christian art a ship might represent a safe haven for the faithful, symbolized by Noah's ark, or the "Navicella" in which the disciples were sailing on the Sea of Galilee, in the incident of Christ Walking on the Waters.[1] The "nave" of a church derives from the Latin *navis*, ship.

Ship of Fools

In *Das Narrenschiff* (1494) by the German satirist Sebastian Brant (1458–1521), a variety of fools are shipped off to the land of fools, without pilot or direction. This satire on human vice and folly inspired allegorical illustrations, such as Bosch's *Ship of Fools*.

Sibyl

In antiquity sibyls were women inspired by the gods, and had the gift of prophecy. There were believed to be ten in all, in Persia, Libya, Delphi, Cumae in Italy, Erythrae, Samos, Cumaea in Aeolia, Marpessa on the Hellespont, Ancyra and Tiburtis. The most famous were the Delphic and the Cumaean oracles of Apollo. In Roman tradition, their prophecies were written down, and these "Sibylline Verses" were carefully preserved, even surviving a fire. Probably written by Christians in the 2nd century, some of the verses tell of Christ's Passion.

The emperor Augustus was said to have been told of the Advent of Christ by the Tiburtine Sibyl, at the place where the Church of the Araceoli (Altar of Light) now stands next to the Capitol in Rome. In *Augustus and the Tiburtine Sibyl* Antoine Caron shows the emperor kneeling to the Sibyl while she points to a vision of the Virgin and Child. Analogous with the Old Testament prophets, sibyls were portrayed as matronly figures, and commonly have inscriptions to identify them. They fill spaces in polyptychs, such as Jan van

Shell: *see*
James the Great, St; Neptune; Venus

Ship:
[1] *Matthew 14:24–27*

Sibyl: *see*
Apollo

Silenus: *see*
Bacchus; Midas; Satyr

Simon, Saint: *see*
Martyrs
[1] *Golden Legend, SS Simon and Jude*

Sirens: *see*
Jason and the Argonauts; Ulysses
[1] Homer, *Odyssey XII*

Sisera:
[1] *Judges 4:21*

Sisyphus: *see*
Ixion; Tantalus; Tityus
[1] Homer, *Odyssey XI:593–600*

Eyck's *Ghent Altarpiece*, and in chapels, as in Raphael's *Sibyls* (Chigi Chapel, Santa Maria della Pace, Rome). Their images decorate the floor of Siena Cathedral, and Michelangelo placed them, with the Old Testament prophets, around scenes from the Book of Genesis (Sistine Chapel, Vatican, Rome).

Silenus
In mythology Silenus was the companion of Bacchus (in Greek myth, Dionysos) in revelry. Sometimes described as the son of Pan or Mercury (Hermes), he is depicted as a fat, merry, old man riding an ass, in varying degrees of drunkenness. Rubens' *Drunken Silenus Supported by Satyrs* shows him inebriated to the point of helplessness.

Simon, Saint (Apostle, Disciple)
Little is known of Christ's disciple Simon (1st century AD), who was called the Zealot or the Canaanite. According to legend,[1] he preached with St Jude, in Egypt and in Persia, where they performed miracles, baptized the converted, and were martyred. Some say that Simon was crucified, others that he was sawn in two; he may therefore be shown with either a cross or a saw.

Sirens
In mythology Sirens were half-woman, half-bird, and their beautiful singing drew sailors to their destruction on the rocks. They lived among the skeletons of men whom they had bewitched. Both Jason and Ulysses had to sail near them on their homeward journeys. Ulysses escaped by plugging his crew's ears with wax and having himself bound to the mast until they had safely passed.[1] This subject interested Victorian painters, such as J. W. Waterhouse, who depicted *Ulysses and the Sirens*. Although the Sirens were usually thought to be monsters, Gustave Moreau, in *The Sirens*, presents them as three beautiful maidens with crowns.

Sisera
In the Old Testament, Sisera was the captain of the armies of Jabin, king of Canaan, who ruled over the Israelites. Jael, who belonged to tribe at peace with Jabin, invited Sisera into her tent, gave him a drink and let him rest. Then she "took a nail of the tent, and took a hammer in her hand, and went softly unto him, and smote the nail into his temples, and fastened it into the ground."[1] Like Judith, Jael was seen as a heroine and liberator of the Israelites.

Sisyphus
In myth the devious king of Corinth, Sisyphus, was condemned to Tartarus, in Hades, with Tantalus, Ixion and Tityus. His eternal torment was to push a huge boulder up a hill; every time he was about to send it toppling over the crest, it would roll back, to the bottom.[1] In *Sisyphus*, one of four large paintings of the condemned men, Titian shows him struggling with the rock on his shoulder; the only other to survive shows Tityus.

Skull
A skull is a reminder of death, a *memento mori*. It was used as an aid to meditation by monks, especially Franciscans and Jesuits, and by saints, especially the hermit St Jerome and the penitent Mary Magdalene. Skulls

were often included in Dutch still lifes, such as Harmen Steenwyck's *Allegory of the Vanities of Human Life*. In an allegory of the Ages of Man, a skull may be held by an old man; or it may represent the passing of time, as in Frans Hals' *Young Man Holding a Skull.*

Paintings of the Crucifixion may have a skull at the foot of the Cross. The site of the Crucifixion was named Golgotha, or place of the skull, probably because bodies were left here to be pecked by the birds. Legend also claimed that Christ was crucified on the spot where Adam had been

A detail of a skull, after Allegory of the Vanities of Human Life *by Harmen Steenwyck (1612, National Gallery London).*

buried. In scenes of the Crucifixion, Adam's skull was shown as uncovered to indicate that Christ's sacrifice was for the redemption of mankind.

Sleep

In mythology Sleep dwelled in a silent cave, where poppies bloomed in abundance; from here he dispatched his son, Morpheus, to deliver dreams through the night.[1] Dreams may be depicted as visions of delight or horror, the latter vividly portrayed in Henry Fuseli's *Nightmare*. Goya transformed irrational ideas into owls, bats and a cat in *The Dream of Reason Produces Monsters*. Death was the brother of Sleep, and both were the children of Night. They may be personified as one dark- and one light-skinned *putto*, and are seen curled up asleep at their mother's feet in Poussin's *Diana and Endymion.*

In 17th-century Dutch paintings a man asleep in the company of a young woman might have a lewd significance. Gerard ter Borch's *Women Drinking Wine with a Sleeping Soldier* (the man has been overcome by wine and tobacco) would have been considered a warning against sin. Jacob Duck's buxom *Sleeping Woman* is overtly erotic.

Sloth

One of the seven Vices, Sloth may be represented by a scene of physical or mental idleness, the latter leading to melancholy. Popular as a theme in 17th-century Dutch art, is idleness suggested by a woman dozing or day-dreaming. Nicholaes Maes' *Interior with Sleeping Maid and Her Mistress* shows a mistress soliciting our exasperation with a sleeping maid whose chores are not finished. In many paintings there are suggestions that slothful sleep has been brought on by lust. The ass and pig were used as symbols of laziness.

Snake/Serpent/Asp

From ancient times it was believed that the snake had great tenacity for life and possessed medicinal powers. A serpent coiled around a staff, the caduceus, is the attribute of Aesculapius (in Greek myth, Asklepios), god of medicine. Given to Mercury (Hermes) by Apollo, the caduceus remains an emblem of the medical profession to this day. A

Skull: *see* STILL LIFE

Sleep: *see* Sloth

[1] Ovid, *Met XI:592–615*

Sloth: *see* VICES

Snake/Serpent/Asp: *see* ADAM AND EVE; Aesculapius; Caduceus; Cleopatra; John the Evangelist, St; Medusa; Moses

[1] *Matthew 10:16*
[2] *Genesis 3:1–14*
[3] Virgil, *Eclogues III:92–93*

A detail showing Cleopatra with the asp about her neck, after Cleopatra *by Piero di Cosimo (c.1485–90, Musée Condé, Chantilly).*

Sol: *see* Apollo

Solomon: *see* Sheba, Queen of; True Cross
[1] *I Kings 3:16–28*
[2] *I Kings 11:1–14*

brazen serpent was used by Moses to cure Israelites of snake bites.

In the classical world the snake was also thought to be wise, an idea continued in the Gospels: "Be ye therefore wise as serpents, and harmless as doves."[1] However, in the Old Testament, the serpent had been synonymous with evil, and its wisdom was the cunning of the Devil: "the serpent was more subtil than any beast of the field".[2] In representations of the Temptation the snake is often given the head of a woman, because Eve, tempted by the snake, in turn gave the fruit to Adam, and woman is thus a temptress. In paintings of the Immaculate Conception, the Virgin may stand on a snake to show triumph over evil. The snake has been a phallic symbol from earliest times. The Devil and his demons are often shown with snake-like sexual organs.

A snake may also be poisonous, and the attribute of St John the Evangelist is a chalice full of snakes, based on the legend that he drank poison without suffering any harm. The idea of "a snake lurking in the grass"[3] suggests hidden danger even in the midst of peaceful nature, or at the ill-starred wedding of Orpheus and Eurydice.

An asp was the traditional emblem of Egypt, conspicuous on the royal diadem. No one bitten by an asp survived, and it was, therefore, an appropriate symbol of the invincibility of Egyptian rule. Cleopatra committed suicide with an asp's bite.

Socrates

The celebrated Greek philosopher Socrates (469–399BC), who taught by a sequence of questions and answers, believed that wisdom lay in the recognition of one's ignorance. The Greek Assembly charged him with corrupting youth, and he committed suicide in captivity. Jacques-Louis David's *Death of Socrates* shows him surrounded by grieving students, as he calmly drinks a cup of hemlock.

Sol

Sol (in Greek myth, Helios) was the sun god, particularly venerated in Persia. His chariot was drawn by snow-white horses and brought light to the day; in the evening it descended into the ocean.

In late classical poetry Apollo assumed Sol's role; the former is more often represented in art.

Solomon

In the Old Testament, Solomon was the son of David and Bathsheba, and king of Israel. He was renowned for his wisdom, a gift from God, which was exemplified in the Judgment of Solomon,[1] when two harlots who had given birth claimed to be the mother of the one surviving child. In *The Judgment of Solomon* Poussin shows how, to end their dispute, the king ordered the baby to be cut in two. He at once recognized the true mother as the one who abandoned her claim.

Solomon had a long and prosperous reign, preferring to amass wealth than wage war. He built a palace and the Temple of Jerusalem, which was covered with gold and sumptuous ornaments. Its spiral columns, in the Solomonic style, were brought to Rome and provided a source for Raphael's *Healing of the Lame Man at the Beautiful Gate*, and the inspiration for Bernini's canopy over the high altar of St Peter's, Rome.

Solomon had 700 wives and 300

concubines.[2] Many of these were foreign and worshipped pagan gods, whose cults Solomon also followed. Luca Giordano's *Altar of Solomon* shows the king at an altar worshipping a statue, surrounded by women.

Sophonisba

The story of Sophonisba is an example of ancient virtue.[1] A Carthaginian beauty and daughter of General Hasdrubal, during the Second Punic War she fell captive to the Romans. Masinissa, her husband, suggested that she drink poison, choosing death rather than the dishonour of capture.

The subject was popular in the 18th century, and Giambattista Tiepolo's *Sophonisba Receives the Poison* shows her receiving a cup with composed dignity.

Soul

In Christian art the soul of the dead was usually depicted as an infant, carried to heaven by an angel, as in El Greco's *The Burial of the Count of Orgaz*, or in the case of sinners, taken to hell by demons.

A detail showing a soul being transported to heaven, after El Greco's The Burial of the Count of Orgaz *(1586–88, Toledo, Spain).*

Sphinx

In classical antiquity the Greeks adopted the Egyptian sphinx as an emblem of wisdom, adding the head and breasts of a young girl to its lion's body. Juno (in Greek myth, Hera) had sent just such a creature to terrorize the neighbourhood of Thebes by asking passers-by a riddle and devouring any who could not answer. The question was, "Which animal walks on four feet in the morning, on two at noon and on three in the evening?" Oedipus gave the right answer: a man, who crawls as a baby, stands upright in manhood and walks with a stick in old age.[1] Ingres' *Oedipus and the Sphinx* shows Oedipus calmly confronting the ceature.

The sphinx may also indicate the African continent or the River Nile. From the Renaissance it has been used (along with the griffin, which has an eagle's head and wings and a lion's body) to embellish furniture.

Spinario

This antique bronze statue (Musei Capitolini, Rome) of a boy pulling a thorn from his foot was often cited and copied from the Renaissance on. It was said to represent the diligence of a messenger who plucked out the thorn only after giving his message.

SPQR

SPQR, the monogram of *Senatus Populusque Romanus* ("The Senate and People of Rome"), was inscribed on the standards of ancient Rome and is seen in re-creations of the era, such as Mantegna's *Triumphs of Caesar.*

Stag

The stag or hart was hunted by Diana (in Greek myth, Artemis).[1] She also

Sophonisba:
[1] Livy, *The History of Rome XXX:xv*

Sphinx: *see* CONTINENTS; Oedipus; Spinario
[1] Apollodorus, *The Library III v 8*

Stag: *see* Actaeon; Aeneas; Diana; Eustace, St; Giles, St; Hubert, St; Julian, St
[1] Virgil, *Aeneid VII:480–500*
[2] *Psalms 42:1*

Stations of the Cross: *see* Passion of Christ, The; Veronica, St

Stephen, Saint: *see* Laurence, St; Martyr
[1] *Acts 6:8*
[2] *Acts 7:58*
[3] *Golden Legend, The Finding of Stephen*

Stigmata: *see* Catherine of Siena, St; Francis of Assisi, St

Susannah and the Elders:
[1] *Apocrypha, The Story of Susannah*

A detail showing a white hart, after a panel from the Wilton Diptych *(c.1395, National Gallery, London).*

changed Actaeon into a stag for intruding on her as she bathed.

In Christian art stags may drink at the spring of life-giving waters,[2] as seen in early Christian mosaics (Galla Placidia, Ravenna). A stag is the attribute of Saints Eustace, Giles, Hubert and Julian. In secular art, Edwin Landseer's aggressive *Monarch of the Glen* echoes the proud, self-satisfied character of the Victorian ruling class. Stags were also frequently used by royalty and by the aristocracy as a heraldic device; a white hart was adopted as Richard II of England's emblem, and is seen on the badges of the angels in the *Wilton Diptych*.

Stations of the Cross

The Stations of the Cross record significant moments of the Passion of Christ on the road to Calvary (*Via Dolorosa*). In the Middle Ages, images appropriate to these moments were ranged at intervals in a church for devotional purposes. Later, scenes from the Crucifixion were added, so that the whole series comprised: Christ condemned to death; Christ carrying the Cross; his three falls; his encounter with the Virgin; Simon the Cyrenian helping him to carry the Cross; Veronica's veil; Christ speaking to the daughters of Jerusalem; Christ stripped of his garments; Christ nailed to the Cross; the release of his spirit; the Deposition; and lastly the Entombment.

Stephen, Saint

Stephen (died *c.*AD35) was venerated as the first Christian deacon and martyr. As the number of Christ's disciples grew, Stephen was appointed deacon with six others to minister to the Greek-speaking widows in Jerusalem. He disputed with the blasphemous and worked "great wonders and miracles among the people".[1] Brought before the Jewish council, he argued that the coming of Christ had been foretold by the prophets and that the Crucifixion was an act of murder. The elders "cast him out of the city and stoned him".[2]

In legend,[3] some 300 years after Stephen's death, Lucian, a priest in Jerusalem, was told in a dream where to find the saint's grave. His relics found their way to Rome, where they were placed in the tomb of St Laurence in the church dedicated to him outside the city walls. Apparently, when the tomb was opened, Laurence moved to make room for Stephen.

In Italian and French art of the Renaissance, Stephen is generally seen as a young deacon with his attribute of a stone, the instrument of his martyrdom. Scenes from his life were painted by Carpaccio, originally for the Scuola di San Stefano in Venice. In Fra Angelico's narrative cycle in the Nicholas V chapel (Vatican, Rome) he is paired with St Laurence.

Stigmata

These five marks, from the wounds Christ received at the Crucifixion in the hands, feet and side, were said to have transferred themselves to Saints Francis of Assisi and Catherine of Siena, because of their exceptional devotion.

STILL LIFE

See panel on following page.

Susannah and the Elders

In an apocryphal Old Testament story Susannah was married to the wealthy

STILL LIFE

The painting of still lifes, or inanimate objects, emerged as a subject in its own right during the 17th century. Such an idea, however, had existed since classical antiquity, when the celebrated Zeuxis was reputed to have painted a bunch of grapes so naturalistically that birds tried to eat them. Still lifes were particularly popular in Holland, which had a tradition of delight in the everyday world. In such paintings the choice of objects may be significant; however, carefully arranged with controlled lighting, these works were above all a display of the artist's virtuosity. Both humble and extravagant objects were included, the latter often carrying implications of wealth or aspiration. Luxuries such as silver, mother-of-pearl ojects or fashionable Chinese porcelain imported by the Dutch East India Company made the painting a luxury in itself.

The type of still life known as *Vanitas*, referring not to self-importance but to the emptiness of worldly possessions, contained objects to indicate the transience of life, as in the admonition: "Vanity of vanities, saith the Preacher, vanity of vanities; all is vanity. What profit hath a man of all his labour which he taketh under the sun? One generation passeth away and another generation cometh."[1] Such items may be a skull; a lamp or candle, which is easily extinguished; a smouldering pipe; or a watch or clock to indicate time running out.

Flower and fruit paintings, such as Jan van Os' *Fruit and Flowers in a Terracotta Vase*, may show an impossible arrangement, including specimens from different parts of the world or ones that bloom in different seasons. At first glance they may evoke the bountiful earth, but a fly, snail, lizard or mouse may have begun to destroy the fruit and indicate that everything perishes with time.

Still life painting was considered an inferior subject by academic artists, and useful only for studies. By the end of the 19th century, however, Cézanne had become a master of still life, working and reworking from familiar objects in his studio. Subsequently, Cézanne's work inspired Picasso and Braque in the development of Cubism. Van Gogh's objects often have a highly personal significance, while the Surrealist painters played with visual puns: Magritte transformed boots into feet in *The Red Model,* and Dalí's *Animated Still Life* reverses the idea of *nature morte*, (literally "dead nature"), the French for still life.

STILL LIFE: *see* FLOWERS; Shell; TIME

[1] *Ecclesiastes 1:2–4*

and honourable Joachim, in whose house two judges spent much time. They lusted after Susannah, and together they conspired to watch her bathing in her beautiful garden.[1] She commanded her maids to fetch her oils, and once she was alone, the two judges appeared and told her to lie with them or they would accuse her of adultery. She replied that she would prefer to be falsely accused than to sin in the eyes of the Lord. At her

Swan: *see*
Apollo; Leda; MUSES; Phaethon; Venus
[1] Ovid, *Met II:367–380*

Sylvester, Saint: *see*
Bull; Constantine, St; Dragon
[1] *Golden Legend, St Sylvester*

A detail after Susannah and the Elders *by Tintoretto (1557, Kunsthistorisches Museum, Vienna).*

ensuing trial she was condemned to death. As she was led away, the Lord sent a youth, Daniel, who brought the truth to light, the elders were sentenced and Susannah was set free. From the Renaissance on, artists chose to show Susannah bathing, an opportunity to paint a beautiful female nude. One example is Tintoretto's *Susannah and the Elders.*

Swan

Jupiter (in Greek myth, Zeus) transformed himself into a swan in order to lie with Leda, a queen of Sparta.

Cygnus was a youth who was transformed into a swan.[1] He was a close friend of Phaethon, the son of Helios, who died when he drove his father's chariot too close to the earth. As Cygnus mourned the death of Phaethon, his voice became thin and shrill; mistrusting the skies and hating fire, he chose to inhabit rivers, where he was changed into the swan.

The fabled "swan song" was thought to be sung just before the bird died.

A swan is associated with the Muses and with Apollo; one Greek legend claims that the soul of Apollo, and therefore of all good poets, turned into a swan. These beautiful birds may be shown drawing Venus' chariot. Jan Asselijn's *The Threatened Swan* was retitled *Netherlands Defending her Nest Against the Enemies of the State* when the artist acquired the Grand Pensionary of the Dutch Republic as his new patron.

Sylvester, Saint

Sylvester (died AD335) was one of the earliest popes, elected in 313, the same year that Christianity had been legalized. Little is known about him, but legend[1] tells that he was highly eloquent. He disputed with 12 learned Jewish doctors about Christianity and finally, as proof, restored a bull to life. He also closed the throat of a dragon whose breath had killed two wise men in the Forum.

When the emperor Constantine caught leprosy and ordered the slaughter of 3,000 children so that he could be cured by bathing in their blood, Saints Peter and Paul appeared to him in a dream and told him to summon Sylvester instead. Sylvester baptized the emperor, immersing him in a pool from which he emerged restored to health, and the children were returned to their mothers unharmed.

In 1248, in the Chapel of San Sylvestro (Quattro Coronati, Rome), scenes of Sylvester and Constantine were frescoed as an assertion of papal primacy. Scenes from the life of Pope Sylvester by Maso di Banco can be seen in the Bardi di Vernio Chapel, Santa Croce, Florence. Sylvester is usually dressed as a pope; his attributes may be a chained dragon or a bull.

Tancred

The hero of the popular epic poem *Jerusalem Delivered* by Torquato Tasso (1544–95), Tancred, like Rinaldo, was a romantic subject in painting. He fell in love with the pagan Clorinda, who fought for the Saracens, but fatally wounded her in battle, not recognizing her in armour. As she lay dying she asked Tancred to wash away her sins with water. He ran to fill his helmet from a nearby stream so that she could die in peace.[1]

Erminia, a Saracen princess who also secretly loved Tancred, escaped the besieged city of Jerusalem wearing armour and fell asleep in the woods. Domenichino's *Erminia with the Shepherds* shows how she awoke to the sound of a shepherd and his young sons singing. While they explained the delights of country life, she briefly considered abandoning war for a life of rural peace.[2]

Tancred accepted a challenge to fight the Saracen giant Argantes, but although he killed his opponent he was himself heavily wounded. Filled with fear for her lover, Erminia ran to his side with his squire Vafrino. At first they believed him dead, as Guercino's *Tancred and Erminia* shows. Seeing his lips give a sigh, however, Erminia cut off her amber hair to stop the flow of his blood, and they carried him back alive to the Crusaders' camp.[3]

Tantalus

In mythology[1] Tantalus, king of Lydia, was condemned to Tartarus in the Underworld, having been variously accused of feeding his son to the gods, or stealing their nectar or giving away their secrets. His eternal punishment was to stand in a pool "tantalized" by its refreshing waters, which nearly reached his chin; whenever he stooped to drink, the water receded. Trees dangled fruits over his head, but the wind always blew them just out of his reach.

Alternatively, Tantalus is described as being eternally prevented by the Furies from enjoying a sumptuous banquet. He was a warning to the subjects of a monarch who ruled by divine right, and was painted as a

Tancred: *see* Rinaldo; Olindo and Sophronia

[1] Tasso, *Jerusalem Delivered XII:lxiv–lxviii*

[2] Tasso, *Jerusalem Delivered VII:vi–xv*

[3] Tasso, *Jerusalem Delivered XIX:ciii–cxii*

Tantalus:

[1] Homer, *Odyssey XI:582–593*

Telemachus: *see* Penelope; Trojan War; Ulysses

Temperaments: *see* Melancholia

Teresa, Saint:
[1] *Teresa of Avila 29*

Tereus:
[1] Ovid, *Met VI:401–674*

companion to the others who suffered in hell: Ixion, Sisyphus and Tityus. Most notably, there are copies of lost paintings by Titian and Ribera.

Telemachus

In Homer's *The Odyssey* Telemachus, the son of Ulysses (Odysseus), went in search of his father, who had not returned from the Trojan War. The French writer Fénelon (1651–1715) retold the story in a romance, *Télémaque*, in which the hero was protected by Minerva (in Greek myth, Athene), disguised as his old guardian, Mentor. In *Telemachus and Mentor*, Giambattista Tiepolo shows the two striding out together. Telemachus was detained, as his father had been, by the goddess Calypso. However, he fell in love with one of her nymphs, and her companions burned his boat to further prolong his stay on their island. He finally escaped when Mentor threw him into the sea and he was rescued by a passing boat.

Temperaments

In the Middle Ages it was taught that the body contained four fluids or humours, which related to the temperaments (the Latin *temperare* means to measure). To sustain well-being the humours had to be held in a natural balance, and the dominant humour would determine a person's character. An excess of blood made a person sanguine; phlegm, phlegmatic; yellow bile, choleric; and black bile, melancholic. The balance could be thrown by planetary movements as well as diet, leading to illness and emotional upset.

Melancholia is probably the temperament most often seen in art, as in Dürer's engraving of 1514.

Teresa, Saint

Teresa of Avila (1515–82) entered a Carmelite convent in her native town aged about 20, and in 1562 founded the first of many convents of reformed or "discalced" (barefoot) Carmelites. Teresa frequently had mystical visions, which she recorded. In one heavenly rapture she described how an angel appeared: "In his hands I saw a great golden spear, and at the iron tip there appeared to be a point of fire. This he plunged into my heart several times ... and left me utterly consumed by the great love of God. The pain was so severe that it made

St Teresa, after Bernini's Ecstasy of St Teresa *(1645–52, Cornaro Chapel, Santa Maria della Vittoria, Rome).*

me utter several moans."[1] This divine experience was famously sculpted by Bernini (Cornaro Chapel, Santa Maria della Vittoria, Rome).

Tereus

In mythology[1] Tereus, the son of Mars (Ares), was a king of Thrace. He married Procne, but their wedding feast was attended by the Furies, whose presence doomed the marriage and caused Tereus to rape his beautiful sister-in-law, Philomela. To prevent her from recounting his crime he cut out her tongue. Inventively, she wove a tapestry which told of her misfortune, and when Procne saw it she plotted revenge on her husband. She killed their son, tore his limbs apart and cooked them for his father to eat. Tereus ate what he was served, then asked for his son to be brought in. In reply, Philomela thrust the child's bleeding head before him. Rubens depicts Tereus recoiling in horror, in *The Banquet of Tereus*.

Theagenes and Chariclea
The ancient romance *Theagenes and Chariclea* by Heliodorus of Syria was published in Basel in 1534. Chariclea, princess of Ethiopia, was born white owing to the effect of a marble statue of Andromeda on her mother while pregnant. Fearful of being accused of adultery, the mother had Chariclea brought up elsewhere. As a youth, Chariclea awarded Theagenes the palm of victory after an athletic race, and they immediately fell in love; the incident is shown in Abraham Bloemaert's *Theagenes and Chariclea*. After several adventures Chariclea returned to Ethiopia, where she was accepted as the king's daughter.

Thecla, Saint
Thecla (1st century AD) was said to have been converted to Christianity by St Paul;[1] breaking off her engagement to a young man, she became a bride of Christ. Persecuted for her faith, she survived torture by fire and exposure to wild beasts in the amphitheatre, eventually becoming a hermit. In her old age a chasm opened up to save her from further persecutions. She is honoured as the first female martyr by the Greek Church, although she is of doubtful historical authenticity. Churches were dedicated to her in Italy, such as the Cathedral of Este, where a painting by Giambattista Tieoplo shows her interceding on behalf of the town for release from the plague.

Theodore, Saint
Legend cites Theodore (4th century AD) as a Roman soldier who, converted to Christianity, set fire to a pagan temple, for which he was cruelly tortured with iron hooks and burned to death. Like St George, Theodore was also thought to have slain a dragon, and his attribute is a crocodile. Dressed as a knight, he stands over a dragon as the first patron saint of Venice in a sculpture in the Piazzetta of San Marco.

Theseus
The legendary hero Theseus[1] appears in art as a muscular figure, sometimes with a club, not unlike Hercules (in Greek myth, Heracles). He was mistakenly believed to be the son of Neptune (Poseidon), but his true father, Aegeus, king of Athens, had hidden a sword and sandals under a heavy rock in order to test the strength of his son and to prove his identity. Led by his mother, Theseus lifted the rock and discovered the objects, as Poussin shows in *Theseus Finding his Father's Arms*. He set out for Athens, overcoming robbers and wild beasts on the way. In the city he found the sorceress Medea living with Aegeus, and she attempted to destroy him before his identity became known. At a banquet, thinking

Thecla, Saint: *see*
Paul, St; Martyrs

Theodore, Saint: *see*
George, St; Martyrs
[1] *Apocrypha, Acts of St Paul*

Theseus: *see*
Amazons; Ariadne; Centaur; Hippolytus; Ixion; Medea; Minotaur
[1] Plutarch, *Lives*, Theseus
[2] Apollodorus, *II v 12*

Thetis: *see*
Achilles; Discord; Feast of the Gods; Paris; Trojan War
[1] Ovid, *Met XI:221–265*
[2] Homer, *Iliad I:495–512*
[3] Homer, *Iliad XVIII:428–617*

Thomas, Saint:
[1] *John 20:25–29*
[2] *Golden Legend, The Assumption of the Virgin*

Theseus to be an imposter who plotted to kill him, Aegeas was about to give Theseus a cup of poison when he recognized his sword.

In the most celebrated of his adventures, Theseus killed the Minotaur, which lived in a Labyrinth on the island of Crete. He sailed away with the Cretan king's daughter, Ariadne, but later abandoned her on the island of Naxos. Reaching home, he forgot to hoist the white sails of victory in order to notify his father of his safe return. As a result, Aegeus threw himself into the sea in grief, hence the Aegean Sea.

Theseus succeeded to the throne of Athens, and was a liberal and popular monarch. However, in love he was consistently unsuccessful; he married Phaedra, sister of Ariadne, but she fell in love with Hippolytus, Theseus' son by the Amazon, Antiope. When the beautiful youth rejected her, she told Theseus that he had tried to seduce her, a scene depicted by Pierre-Narcisse Guérin in *Phaedra and Hippolytus*. Theseus then sought Neptune's help in punishing the boy, and Hippolytus was dragged to death by his horses.

Among his other adventures, Theseus joined Hercules in his battle with the Amazons, and fought off the Centaurs who invaded the wedding of his friend Pirithous, king of the Lapiths. Theseus and Pirithous also descended into the Underworld to carry away Proserpina (Persephone), but were stopped by Pluto (Hades). In punishment Pirithous was placed on his father Ixion's wheel, and Theseus was tied to a huge stone until he was rescued by Hercules.[2] On his return to Athens, Theseus discovered his throne had been usurped by a certain Menestheus, and he fled to the island of Scyros. Here he was said to have been pushed down a steep precipice to his death by the king of the island, who feared possible usurpation from such a powerful hero.

Thetis

In mythology it was prophesied that Thetis, the most beautiful of the Nereids, would bear a child who would surpass his father. This deterred the supreme god Jupiter (in Greek myth, Zeus) from pursuing her, and so he ordered Peleus, a mortal, to become her lover instead. Thetis tried to avoid the union by changing shape into a bird, a tree and a tiger, but the mortal held her by force.[1] At their wedding, the Feast of the Gods, Discord threw down a golden apple, as prize for the most beautiful of the three important goddesses present: Venus (Aphrodite), Minerva (Athene) and Juno (Hera). This act resulted in the Judgment of Paris, which ultimately led to the Trojan War. Achilles, hero of that war, was the son of Thetis and Peleus. Homer's *The Iliad* relates, how, when the hero was insulted by Agamemnon, Thetis rose from the depths of the sea to Mount Olympus and begged Jupiter to avenge him.[2] Ingres illustrated this scene in *Jupiter and Thetis*. Thetis also asked Vulcan (Hephaestus) to make Achilles a magnificent suit of armour.[3]

Thomas, Saint (Apostle, Disciple)

Thomas, or "Didymus" the twin (1st century AD), is known for doubting the Resurrection: he declared that unless "I shall see in his hands the prints of the nails, and put my finger into the print of the nails, and thrust my hand into his side, I will not

A detail showing St Thomas, after The Incredulity of St Thomas *by Giambattista Cima da Conegliano (1517–18, National Gallery, London).*

believe." Christ instructed him to do so, saying, "Be not faithless but believing."[1] The "Doubting Thomas" theme appears in many cycles of stories following the Resurrection, including Duccio's *Maestà*, as well as in isolated episodes such as Caravaggio's vivid representation in *The Incredulity of St Thomas*, in which Christ draws Thomas' finger to the wound in his chest.

According to legend[2] Thomas also doubted the Assumption of the Virgin, but "suddenly the girdle that had encircled her body fell intact into his hands", and he believed. The supposed girdle was preserved and in 1141 brought to the Cathedral of Prato in Tuscany, where relevant scenes were frescoed by Agnolo Gaddi in the 1390s, and Donatello and Michelozzo carved a pulpit to display the relic.

TIME

Time has been represented in art in two distinct ways. Commonly it is personified as a winged old man with an hour-glass or scythe. He may convey a message, as in Pompeo Batoni's *Time*, who sits pointing to a young girl while an old woman loses her beauty. This representation of Time is finite. His daughter is Truth. The transience of time may be represented by things that wither or disappear, such as flowers, smoke or bubbles, or by objects that are reminiscent of death, such as a skull.

Time may also be shown as cyclical, denoted by the recurring months and seasons, represented by agricultural pursuits. This agricultural association gives Time his attribute of the scythe. Times of the year may also be suggested by the signs of the zodiac. Michelangelo interpreted Time as the figures of *Dawn*, *Dusk*, *Night* and *Day*, identified by their forms or movement – except that Night is given attributes of an owl, a mask, a star and a crescent moon.

TIME: *see* FLOWERS; Night; Saturn; SEASONS; Skull; Truth

Thomas Aquinas, Saint

One of the great Doctors of the medieval Church, Thomas (1225–74) was educated at the University of Naples, where he joined the Dominican Order *c.* 1244. His noble family was outraged that he chose to be a mendicant friar and had him imprisoned for a year, but this only reinforced his resolve. Released, he studied at Paris and Cologne, then devoted the rest of his life to teaching in Paris and several cities in Italy, and also to writing his *Summa Theologica* (1266–73), which became the basis of much of the Catholic doctrine.

Thomas Aquinas, Saint: *see* RELIGIOUS ORDERS

Thyrsus: *see*
Bacchus; Ivy

Tityus: *see*
Ixion; Sisyphus; Tantalus
[1] Virgil, *Aeneid VI:595–600*

Tobias: *see*
Raphael (Archangel), St
[1] *Apocrypha, Tobit 2:9–10*
[2] *Apocrypha, Tobit 4:1–2*
[3] *Apocrypha, Tobit 6:2–5*
[4] *Apocrypha, Tobit 11:11–13*
[5] *Apocrypha, Tobit 5:21*

He is depicted in the Dominican habit, and his importance as a theologian is represented in the chapter house known as the Spanish Chapel in the Dominican church of Santa Maria Novella in Florence, painted by Andrea de Firenze in the mid-14th century. He may be seen at his books and have a star on his chest, or hold a lily. Velázquez shows him supported by angels in front of a fire, a reference to the episode in which he used a burning log to chase off a woman who had come to tempt him.

Thyrsus
This rod, intertwined with vine leaves and ivy, is the attribute of Bacchus (Dionysos) and his followers. It may be tipped with a pine cone.

TIME
See panel on previous page.

Tityus
In mythology Tityus was condemned to Tartarus in the Underworld, as were Ixion, Sisyphus and Tantalus. He was the giant son of majestic Earth, and his body stretched over nine acres. His offence was to have assaulted Latona, mother of Apollo and Diana (in Greek myth, Artemis). In the Underworld a pair of vultures continually plucked out his liver, while his hands were powerless to drive them off.[1] Images of his torture, such as Michelangelo's drawing of *Tityus*, may be confused with Prometheus who suffered a similar fate.

Tobias
In the Old Testament Apocrypha Tobit, father of Tobias, lived in the Assyrian capital of Nineveh and defied the law in helping his fellow Jews in exile. For this all his goods were taken away. When Tobit gave a Jew a proper burial one night, he slept in his courtyard and was blinded by sparrow droppings.[1] Fearing imminent death, Tobit remembered money he had deposited with a man in Media and sent Tobias to reclaim them.[2] The Archangel Raphael appeared in disguise to guide him to it, and Tobias' dog accompanied them. One evening they came to the River Tigris, and when Tobias "went down to wash himself, a fish leaped out of the river, and would have devoured him." Raphael told him to catch the fish and

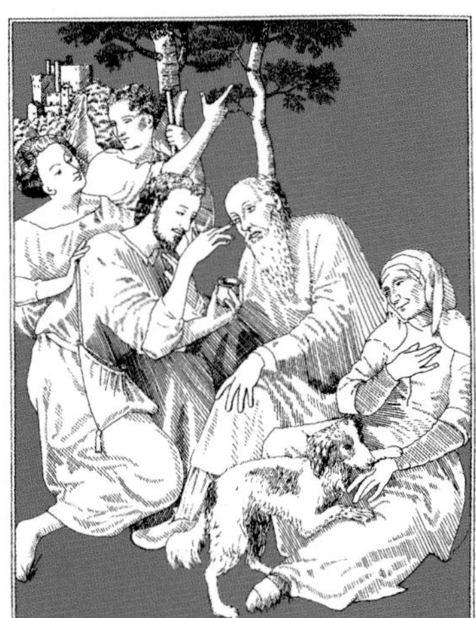

Tobias and Tobit, after The Healing of Tobit *by Jan Metsys (*c.*1550, Musée de la Chartreuse, Douai, France).*

to conserve the heart, liver and gall while they ate the rest of it.[3] They arrived at the house of Tobias' cousin Raguel, where it was arranged that Tobias would marry Raguel's daughter, Sarah. The heart and liver of the fish were burned and their scent banished the demon which had caused the death of Sarah's seven previous husbands. Raphael was sent to collect the money, the wedding was celebrated, and they returned to Nineveh to cure Tobit's blindness with the gall of the fish.[4]

The young Tobias with his divine protector was a popular subject in 15th-century Florence, where the Compagnia di Raffaello had been formed. In paintings, therefore, the principal figure is often the archangel, as in *Tobias and the Angel* by a follower of Verrocchio. The painting includes elements from the narrative which may be considered attributes: Raphael, with a dog and pot containing the fish's gall, leads Tobias holding a fish. The happy outcome of the story must have appealed to travellers: Tobit had announced as Tobias set off that "the good angel will keep him company, and his journey shall be prosperous and he shall return safe".[5] Later artists also illustrated scenes from the story; for example, Rembrandt painted *The Angel Leaving Tobias.*

Trajan

According to legend[1] the Roman emperor Trajan was on his way to war when he was stopped by a widow demanding justice for the death of her son. Moved with compassion, Trajan postponed his affairs and saw to it that the innocent boy was avenged.

On another occasion, his own son was recklessly galloping through the city and ran down the son of a widow. When Trajan of heard this, he handed over his son to the widow to replace her loss. Many years after the emperor's death, St Gregory the Great, walking through the Forum of Trajan, was reminded of Trajan's kindness, and God's voice told him

A detail after Tree of Jesse, *a book illumination (*c.*1145, Lambeth Bible, Canterbury).*

that the emperor's soul was pardoned. The subject of Trajan and the widow was painted as an example of justice.

Tree of Jesse

In the Old Testament Isaiah prophesied that "there shall come forth a rod out of the stem of Jesse and a branch shall grow out of his roots: And the spirit of the Lord shall rest upon him."[1] In the Middle Ages, therefore, the ancestry of Christ, stretching back to Jesse, father of David, was shown as a genealogical tree, the names of his forbears appearing on the numerous branches. Luke[2] traces Christ's ancestry right back to Adam. Jacobus de Voragine (1230–98), author of the *Golden Legend*, claims that both the Virgin and Christ were descended from the house of David.[3] The maternal line of Christ's ancestry is shown in paintings

Trajan:
[1] *Golden Legend, St Gregory*

Tree of Jesse: *see*
Anna, St
[1] *Isaiah 11:1–2*
[2] *Luke 3:23–28*
[3] *Golden Legend, The Life of the Blessed Virgin*

TRIUMPHS: *see*
Caesar; Galatea

TRIUMPHS

In classical Rome a triumphal march was held for the victorious general and his legions after a successful military campaign. Their booty would be paraded along the Via Sacra, followed by the captives of the campaign, who would soon be executed or else become slaves.

During the Renaissance the idea of the triumphal march was revived both in practice and as a subject to be depicted in art. The triumphs of contemporary and classical figures, personifications of the virtues and mythological figures were all represented.

After The Triumph of Galatea *by Raphael, (*c.*1514, Villa Farnesina, Rome).*

Trionfi by Petrarch (1304–74) also became the inspiration for Italian artists. In the first of these six poems, the poet has a vision of Love on a chariot of fire, which is pulled by four white horses and which holds lovers captive.

In each successive poem, the protagonist is seen to conquer his or her predecessor, so that in the second, Chastity overcomes Love after a battle between reason and passion. There follows the Triumph of Death, of Fame, of Time and of Eternity, but the most popular triumphs in art were those of Love and of Chastity.

of St Anne and the Holy Kinship.

Taddeo Gaddi's *The Tree of the Cross* shows branches growing from the Crucifixion, decorated with medallions of the four evangelists and 12 prophets.

TRIUMPHS

See panel, above.

Trojan War

The Iliad by Homer (8th century BC) describes how the Greeks (or Acheans) laid siege to the city of Troy in a war that lasted nine years. The principal Greek heroes were King Agamemnon, his brother Menelaus, Achilles, Ulysses (in Greek myth, Odysseus), Patroclus and Diomedes; the Trojan heroes were Hector and Aeneas, the son of Venus. The battle arose because Paris, a prince of Troy, had abducted Helen, wife of Menelaus, after a competition in which Paris had to choose the most beautiful of the three goddesses, Minerva (Athene), Venus and Juno (Hera). He chose Venus, who granted Helen as his prize. The gods took an active part in the war: Juno, Minerva and Neptune (Poseidon) supported the Greeks; Apollo, Venus and Mars (Ares), the Trojans. Jupiter (Zeus) both incited and checked each side,

Trojan War: *see*
Achilles; Ajax; Cassandra; Feast of the Gods; Helen; Iphigenia; Laocoön; Paris; Patroclus; Polyxena; Thetis; Ulysses

[1] Homer, *Iliad I:172–187*
[2] Homer, *Iliad I:190–199*
[3] Homer, *Iliad I:343–356*
[4] Homer, *Iliad I:495–512*
[5] Homer, *Iliad V:311–362*
[6] Homer, *Iliad VI:394–592*
[7] Homer, *Iliad XXII:395–515*
[8] Homer, *Iliad XXIV:469–804*
[9] Virgil, *Aeneid II*

sending down thunderbolts and lightning, and intervening in the destinies of those involved.

At the outset Achilles was insulted when Agamemnon appropriated his mistress, Briseis, and he withdrew from battle.[1] His mother, Thetis, begged Jupiter to avenge him and take action against Agamemnon. The Greeks suffered a series of defeats, and Hector, King Priam's favourite son, breached their defences and set fire to their encampment and one of their ships. Still sulking, Achilles agreed to let his closest friend, Patroclus, lead his force to the Greeks' aid, but Patroclus fought too long and was killed by Hector. Achilles, in magnificent armour fashioned by Vulcan (Hephaestus), returned to the war and avenged the death of Patroclus by slaying Hector.

Subjects drawn from *The Iliad* were particularly popular in the 18th and early 19th centuries; an example is Giambattista Tiepolo's *Room of The Iliad*. The scenes most often chosen were: The Wrath of Achilles, in which Achilles was about to draw his sword against Agamemnon, when Minerva held him back by his golden locks;[2] Briseis being taken away from Achilles or led to Agamemnon by Patroclus;[3] Thetis asking Jupiter to avenge Achilles;[4] Venus wounded by Diomedes as she tries to save her son, Aeneas;[5] Hector reproaching Paris for failing to take part in the war; Hector making a tender farewell to his wife, Andromache, and their baby son;[6] Achilles dragging the body of Hector, tied by the ankles to his chariot, around the walls of Troy;[7] King Priam, protected by Mercury (Hermes), in Achilles' camp, kneeling and kissing Achilles' hand, pleading for the body of Hector;[8] and Andromache and her son grieving over Hector's corpse, which had been saved by Apollo from decay and damage.

The Wooden Horse of Troy, the most famous and decisive incident of the war, is related in both Homer's *The Odyssey* and Virgil's *The Aeneid*, although the account in Virgil is fuller.[9] In order to penetrate the city of Troy, the Greeks built a hollow wooden horse which they pretended was an offering to the gods to ensure their safe homeward voyage. In *The Building of the Trojan Horse* Domenico Tiepolo shows them constructing it. Their best men were installed inside it, and the others hid from sight. The Trojans flung open their gates and rejoiced at the disappearance of their enemy. They ignored Cassandra's and Laocoön's prophetic warnings, and were tricked by Sinon, a Greek captive, into believing that the horse was dedicated to Minerva and should be brought to her temple. The horse was dragged in and, that night, Sinon released the Greeks. They cut down the sentries, let in their army and set Troy ablaze.

True Cross

According to legend,[1] when Adam grew old, his son, Seth, went to the gates of Paradise and begged for some healing ointment. The Archangel Michael appeared and gave him a branch, supposedly from the Tree of Knowledge. Seth returned to find his father dead and planted the branch over his grave. It grew into a tree which was cut down to build a house for King Solomon, but the trunk could not be accommodated, and so was laid across a stream to serve as a

True Cross: *see* Constantine, St; Helena, St; Queen of Sheba; Solomon

[1] *Golden Legend, The Finding of the Holy Cross*

[2] *Golden Legend, The Exaltation of the Holy Cross*

Truth: *see* TIME

Tuccia: *see* Sophonisba; Vesta and Vestal Virgins

[1] Pliny the Elder, *Natural History*, XXVIII:12

bridge. On her visit to Solomon, the Queen of Sheba, who had had a vision that the Saviour would one day hang upon this trunk, approached the "bridge" and knelt to worship it. She told Solomon that a man would come to destroy the kingdom of the Jews, and Solomon ordered the wood to be buried deep in the earth. When the time of Christ's Passion drew near, the wood floated to the surface of a pool and was used to make his Cross.

The story leaps several hundred years to the 4th century, when the emperor Constantine was converted to Christianity and baptized. His mother, Helena, went to Jerusalem to seek a relic of the True Cross, but Jewish scholars refused to tell her where to find it. One Jew was thrown down a dry well and, after six days without food, he capitulated and led Helena to the site of the Cross on Golgotha. Three crosses, however, were found, and since they could not distinguish Christ's from those of the two thieves, Helena and her companion placed them upright in the city and waited for the Lord to give a sign. A young man was restored to life when the True Cross was held over him, and Helena returned home with part of the supposed relic, now preserved in St Peter's, Rome.

Some two centuries later,[2] Chosroes, king of Persia, conquered Jerusalem and captured another part of the True Cross. He sat on a throne as the Father, put the wood in place of the Son, a cock in place of the Holy Ghost, and decreed that all should call him God. In the name of the Cross the emperor Heraclius defeated him and ordered the Persians to embrace the Christian faith. On his victorious return to Jerusalem, Heraclius was told by an angel to humble himself. In *The Emperor Heraclius Carries the Cross to Jerusalem* Michele Lambertini shows how he entered the city barefoot, carrying the Cross.

The story of the True Cross links the Fall of Man to the Redemption. It was painted in the late Middle Ages and early Renaissance, especially in churches that possessed a relic of the Cross, such as Santa Croce, Florence. Here Agnolo Gaddi painted frescoes of the narrative in the Chancel.

The story provided artists with a cast of celebrities, a variety of settings and a token piece of anti-semitism. Episodes were not necessarily painted in sequence. Piero della Francesca, in his *Legend of the True Cross*, put the battle scenes of Heraclius against the Persians opposite each other in the lowest tier of the cycle to create a balanced decorative scheme.

Truth

The female personification of Truth may stand naked, with the attribute of the sun's rays or the sun itself, or a book in which truth is written. She is the daughter of Time, revealer of all. She may be standing on a globe to signify that she is superior to worldly concerns; Bernini used this idea in his sculpture of *Truth*.

Tuccia

An example of abstinence, the Vestal Virgin Tuccia was, in legend,[1] accused of breaking the laws of chastity. To prove her innocence, she carried water in a sieve from the Tiber to the Temple. In *Tuccia* a follower of Mantegna paired her with Sophonisba, another example of virtuous womanhood.

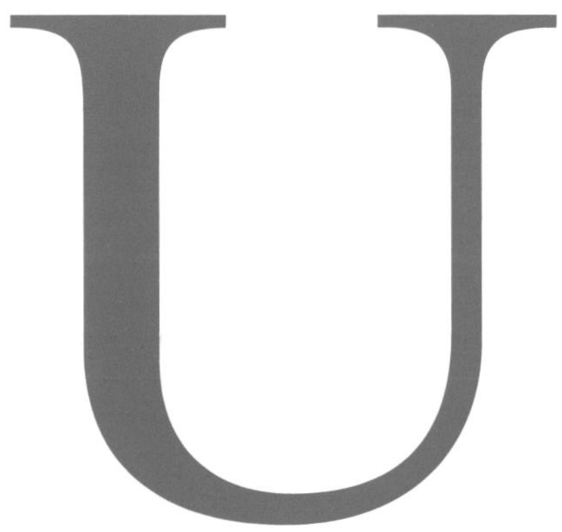

Ugolino

In the *Divina Commedia* by Dante (1265–1321), Count Ugolino, a political leader, was imprisoned with his two sons and grandsons in a tower, and the key was thrown away. The count declared he was ready to make his confession, yet was allowed neither priest nor friar. As they starved, his sons cried, "Father, we should grieve far less, if thou wouldst eat of us."[1] They all died of hunger. In *Ugolino*, Rodin shows an emaciated Ugolino kneeling over his barely living grandsons.

Ugolino: *see*
Dante
[1] Dante, *Inferno XXXI II:13–82*

Ulysses

The Greek hero Ulysses (Odysseus to the Greeks themselves) was the son of Laertes, king of Ithaca. He sought Helen as his bride but relinquished his suit to Menelaus, who was king of Sparta and later fought to retrieve Helen from Paris in the Trojan War. Instead Ulysses married Penelope. Bound by oath to protect Helen, he at first feigned madness when she was carried off to Troy. He ploughed the earth with salt, but abandoned his pretence when his infant son was placed in his path.[1] Ulysses then played a prominent part in the Trojan War, as recounted in Homer's *The Iliad*. After the death of Achilles, the Greek hero, Ajax and Ulysses fought for his armour and Ulysses emerged the victor.

In Homer's epic poem *The Odyssey*, Ulysses (Odysseus in the poem) is the central figure. After the sack of Troy, Ulysses' return to Ithaca was impeded by the gods. During his homeward wanderings, he blinded the Cyclops Polyphemus,[2] the son of Neptune, whose wrath he incurred; and he encountered the sorceress Circe[3] whose magic Mercury (Hermes) helped him to withstand.

He journeyed to the land of the dead to learn his fate, and there met his fallen comrades, including Agamemnon, who had been killed by his wife Clytemnestra and her lover.[4] Ulysses then sailed past the seductive Sirens and landed safely, whereupon his hungry crew ignored his command and killed the cattle of Helios, the sun god; in punishment, Jupiter (Zeus)

Ulysses: *see*
Circe; Helen; Homer; Penelope; Polyphemus; Sirens; Telemachus
[1] Hygenus, *Fabulae XCV*
[2] Homer, *Odyssey IX*
[3] Homer, *Odyssey X*
[4] Homer, *Odyssey XI*
[5] Homer, *Odyssey VI*
[6] Homer, *Odyssey XXI; XXII*

A detail showing Ulysses, after Ulysses and the Witch Circe *after a fresco by Pellegrino Tibaldi (mid 16th century, Palazzo Poggio, Bologna).*

St Ursula, after a woodcut from James Voraigne's Golden Legend *(1483 edition).*

destroyed both Ulysses' men and his ship with a thunderbolt. For seven years Ulysses was detained by the beautiful sea-nymph Calypso, then, after leaving her, he survived a storm with the help of the sea-goddess Ino. He landed in Alcinous and was discovered by Princess Nausicaa near a river, as in Rubens' *Landscape with Ulysses and Nausicaa*. She made him welcome in the royal house of the Phaeacians.[5] Ulysses finally returned to Ithaca laden with gifts.

Minerva protected Ulysses throughout his trials and told him of the disaster that had befallen his home in his absence: his faithful wife Penelope was being plagued by numerous disreputable suitors, who courted her as though Ulysses were dead. On his return to Ithaca he disguised himself as a beggar but was found by his son, Telemachus, and together they hatched a plot. Ulysses joined an archery contest in which Penelope was the prize, and, armed with his great bow, he and Telemachus slew all the suitors. Ulysses was thus reunited with Penelope and his father, Laertes.[6]

Ulysses is mostly shown as a heroic, muscular figure. Frescoes of scenes from *The Odyssey* may be included as part of a decorative scheme, such as those of Pintoricchio originally taken from the Palazzo Petrucci in Siena. Alternatively, his exploits may occupy a whole narrative cycle, as in the frescoes of Pellegrino Tibaldi.

Umbrella

An umbrella or parasol was used not only as shelter from the weather, but as a sign of protection or sovereignty. For example, the Holy Roman Emperor might hold one over the pope as an indication of their alliance.

Unicorn

The legendary unicorn was a beautiful white pony with a goat's beard and a single horn in the centre of its head. With this horn it purified waters poisoned by a serpent so that animals could drink. The unicorn was strong and extremely swift, but it could be caught by a virgin, whose purity it sensed and in whose lap it would rest. Tapestries now hanging in the Cloisters, Metropolitan Museum, New York, show it being hunted and captured, while those at the Cluny Museum, Paris, may be an allegory of the five senses. Both series have many chivalric references, as the unicorn was also associated with courtly love: it is likened to a man who becomes the helpless servant of the noble lady he loves.

The unicorn was absorbed into Christian symbolism and, although there are variations, most medieval bestiaries see the unicorn as Christ, and the maiden as the Virgin Mary. The creature is invincible as Christ of the Resurrection, the poisonous snake becomes Satan, and the animals drinking the purified waters are sinners seeking salvation. The unicorn is the attribute of St Justinia for her purity and of St Boniface for the solitude of his monastic life. It unicorn appears on many aristocratic and royal coats of arms.

Ursula, Saint

The history of Ursula is uncertain and her dates are unknown, but she was venerated by the early 5th century and appears in several Italian and German paintings. Legend cites her as the Christian daughter of the king of Brittany, whose hand was sought by Conon, the pagan son of the king of

Anglia. She agreed to the match on condition that he was baptized, that she should be provided with ten virgin companions, that the eleven of them should each have a retinue of 1,000 virgins, and that all should make a pilgrimage to Rome. Ambassadors were despatched, conditions were agreed, ships were rigged, and a great crowd watched them all embark. They travelled via Cologne where an angel appeared to Ursula in a dream and told her of her forthcoming martyrdom along with that of her virgins. At Basel they left their ships and continued to Rome on foot where the pope welcomed and blessed them. He decided to return with them, accompanied by cardinals and priests, as he too had been told that he would receive the martyr's palm. On their journey home they were besieged by the Huns who, like wolves ravaging a flock of sheep, slew them all. Their leader tried to pursuade Ursula to become his wife but she refused, and he shot her with an arrow.

Ursula is usually depicted as a young girl. She may be holding the martyr's palm, an arrow, a pilgrim's staff, or a white flag with the red cross of victory. She may also appear with a ship or, reflecting her royal birth, a crown or cloak lined with ermine, with which she may be protecting her numerous virgins.

Scenes from the life of St Ursula were painted in the late Middle Ages and Renaissance, particularly in Venice and the Veneto. The most famous example of such a narrative cycle was painted by Carpaccio *c.*1495; he set episodes such as the call of the ambassadors and the departure of the pilgrims against contemporary Venetian Renaissance settings. In 1641 Claude Lorrain chose to paint the single scene of *Ursula's Embarkation*, probably because it provided him with a sea-port setting at dawn.

Uzziah

Uzziah, king of Judah, conquered the Philistines but his victories made him proud and he presumed to take the priest's place in the Temple – in punishment he was smitten with leprosy. Rembrandt painted him as a resigned figure.

Unicorn: *see* Boniface, St; Justinia, St
[1] *Physiologus*

Ursula, Saint: *see* Martyrs
[1] *Golden Legend, The Eleven Thousand Virgins*

Uzziah
[1] *II Chronicles 26*

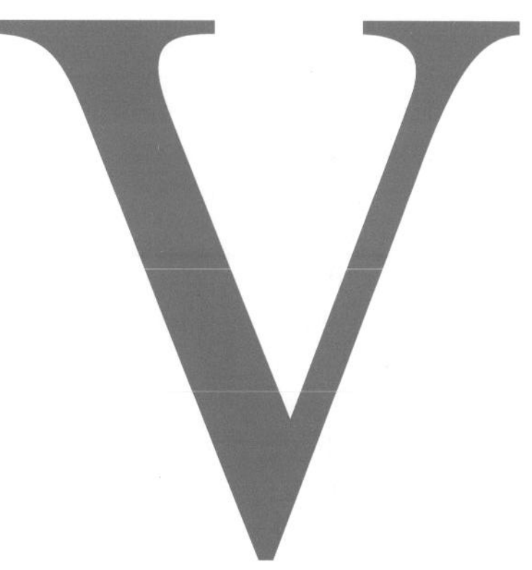

Venus: *see*
Adonis; Aeneas; Cupid; Feast of the Gods; Graces, Three; Mars; Saturn; Vulcan

Veronica, St:
[1] *Apocrypha, Gospel of Nicodemus*

St Veronica, after a panel of the Adoration of the Magi *tryptich by Hans Memling (1479, Saint Jan's Hospital, Brussels).*

Venus

One of the most celebrated deities, Venus (in Greek myth, Aphrodite) was the goddess of beauty and love. She was frequently represented in art to show the ideal of contemporary beauty. Painters of the female nude have traditionally depicted her reclining provocatively, ever since Giorgione's *Sleeping Venus*. She may also be seen at her toilet, or in scenes relating to her mythological life or as part of an allegory, but many paintings of nude women have been given the title of Venus simply as a way to remove the image from the everyday world.

Her attributes include roses and myrtle, which were sacred to her; swans and doves, which may fly near her or pull her chariot; or Discord's golden apple, awarded to her by Paris. Her special attribute, however, was her son Cupid (Eros). The Graces were her attendants and she is associated with the pleasures of life.

Venus was believed to have been born of the sea from the semen of Uranus, after he was castrated by his son, Saturn. Botticelli's *Birth of Venus* shows her being blown by the winds on her scallop shell to the island of Cyprus. She was also said to have landed at Cythera, by which name she is alternatively known, but she was soon taken to the realm of the gods.

Venus was married to Vulcan (Hephaestus), the deformed god of the forge, but she had many lovers, including Mars (Ares), Mercury (Hermes), Bacchus (Dionysos) and Neptune (Poseidon). She also became enamoured of the mortals Adonis and Anchises with whom she conceived Aeneas. Her other children included Hermaphroditus and Priapus. The ease with which Venus captivated men was increased by her magical girdle, or *cestus*, which Vulcan made for her.

Veronica, Saint

In the Apocryphal Gospels[1] Veronica is named as the woman with the issue of blood who was cured by touching the hem of Christ's robe. She was also known to possess a portrait of Christ, which legend relates she obtained when she dabbed the sweat off his face with a piece of linen as he carried the Cross to Calvary; his image miraculously remained on the cloth. This so-called veil of Veronica, found its way to Rome and became an important relic of St Peter's cathedral. Veronica's name could be derived from *vera icon*, meaning "true icon". The saint may be seen holding up the veil, as in El Greco's painting of her; or she may be amid the ugly crowd pressing around Christ before his Crucifixion, standing out because of her elegance, as depicted by Bosch.

Vesta and Vestal Virgins
Vesta (in Greek myth, Hestia) was the goddess of the hearth and home. A fire burned constantly in her circular temple, guarded by the Vestal Virgins whose ancient and honoured office survived for 1,000 years.

Entrusted to a high priest, the Vestals were selected at the age of about six. In the first ten years they learned their sacred duties; in the next ten years they performed them; and in their final ten years, they taught the novices. After this they were free to marry.

Their most important task was to ensure that the sacred fire never died, and if they failed in this they were whipped by the high priest. Additionally, if they broke their vow of chastity they were walled up alive.

The Vestals wore a white tunic with purple borders, and a purple mantle which reached the ground. Celebrated Vestals were Rhea Silvia (who was the mother of Romulus and Remus), Tuccia and Claudia.

VICES
See panel, right.

VICES
The Seven Vices or Deadly Sins are Pride, Anger, Envy, Lust, Gluttony, Sloth and Avarice. Those guilty of such sins would be condemned to Hell at the Last Judgment. Fra Angelico's *Last Judgment* shows transgressors being forced by demons to suffer violent experiences related to their crimes. The Vices were personified with varying attributes: Avarice usually holds a purse, and Dante placed specific usurers in the seventh ring of his imagined hell, in the *Inferno*; Sloth may be a woman hanging herself, because the sin suggests lack of faith; Anger may be a female figure renting her clothes. Of the seven, the Church held Lust and Avarice to be the most sinful of all.

Many other kinds of wrongdoing were also condemned: Idolatry, Infidelity, Inconstancy, Folly, Injustice, Cowardice, Vanity and Ignorance, for example. Andrea Mantegna's *Minerva Expelling the Vices from the Garden of Virtue* includes a figure of Avarice leading the group of banished Vices. Accompanied by Ingratitude, she carries an obese crowned figure of Ignorance. Following them are a lusty satyr and a centaur on whose back stands a shameless nude; a monkey named "Immortal Hatred" comprising Jealousy and Suspicion; and an armless figure of Idleness led by Sloth.

In paintings many of these figures have labels to identify them.

Vesta and Vestal Virgins: *see* Claudia; Romulus and Remus; Tuccia

VICES: *see* Dante; Luxury; Sloth; VIRTUES

Victory: *see*
Fame; Laurel; Palm

Vincent of Saragossa, Saint: *see*
Laurence, St; Martyrs
[1] *Golden Legend, St Vincent*

Vine: *see*
Bacchus; VICES

Virgil: *see*
Aeneas; Dante

Virgin: *see*
Anna, St; Christ, The Life of; Holy Family; Joachim and Anna; Joseph, Husband of the Virgin; Passion of Christ; Thomas, St; Tree of Jesse
[1] *Apocryphal Gospel of Pseudo Matthew* and *Golden Legend, The Birth of the Virgin*
[2] *Luke 1:31–35*
[3] *Isaiah 7:14*
[4] *Luke 1:28*
[5] *Luke 1:41*
[6] *Golden Legend, The Assumption of the Virgin*
[7] *Apocyphal Gospel of the Nativity of Mary IX*
[8] *Revelation 12:1*
[9] *Luke 2:34–35*

Victory

Personified as a winged female, Victory is usually seen flying down with a palm branch in one hand and a crown of laurel in the other to place on the head of those triumphant in war, athletics or poetry. She appears in Ingres' *Apotheosis of Homer*. The figure of Fame may accompany her.

Vincent Ferrer, Saint

Born in Valencia, Vincent (*c.*1350–1419) joined the Dominicans in 1367, served as a missionary among the Moslems, and supported the return of the Papacy to Rome from Avignon in 1417. His apocalyptic preaching drew crowds, and he had a following of penitents. The polyptych by Giovanni Bellini dedicated to him in SS Giovanni e Paolo in Venice shows him in the Dominican habit. The predella depicts scenes of his life: he saved a woman from drowning, rescued those buried under a ruined building, revived the dead, and liberated innocent prisoners.

Vincent of Saragossa, Saint

According to legend[1] Vincent (3rd century AD) was a deacon of Saragossa, Spain, and suffered a series of horrible tortures, including being racked, beaten and burned, but refused to deny his faith. It was agreed to keep him alive only so that his torturers could resume their torments, but he died before they could do so. His body was left in an open field and a crow drove off the wild beasts that came to devour it. It was then thrown into the sea, weighed down by a millstone, but the corpse returned to the shore faster than the sailors who had tossed it overboard. Vincent commonly appears as a young deacon, and may have the instruments of his torture, including the gridiron (also carried by St Laurence), a millstone or the crow. He is the patron saint of Lisbon.

Vine

In mythology, the vine and grapes were the attribute of Bacchus (in Greek myth, Dionysos), god of wine, and his companion, Silenus. They are also the attribute of Autumn. In Christian art grapes symbolize the Eucharist, in which wine is believed to turn into the blood of Christ. In Botticelli's *Madonna of the Eucharist* grapes appear with sheaves of corn (the body of Christ). However, some held that women and sweet wine were a danger; in 17th-century Dutch paintings figures drinking wine in the company of women are shown as susceptible to the vices of Lust and Sloth.

Virgil

The Roman poet Virgil (70–19BC) is famous for the epic *The Aeneid* which recounts the wanderings of Aeneas from the fall of Troy to his arrival in Italy, where he was destined to become the ancestor of the Romans. In *Virgil Reading the Aeneid to Augustus and Octavia* Jean-Joseph Taillasson shows the poet reading a passage of *The Aeneid* to the emperor and his sister. Virgil also wrote pastoral poems and was considered the prince of Latin poets. Out of admiration for him, Dante made Virgil his guide to the Gates of Paradise in the *Divina Commedia.*

Virgin, The

Images of the Virgin Mary or Madonna, the mother of Christ, are

*The Annunciation, after Domenico Veneziano (*c.*1445, Fitzwilliam Museum, Cambridge).*

countless and richly varied. In certain respects the Christ Child may be seen as her attribute. She was the subject of large fresco cycles and altarpieces, as well as small private devotional works. Her popularity is partly explained by her role as intercessor; partly by society's need to venerate a female, and even more, a maternal figure; and partly by the doctrine of the Christian Church, which emphasized her virginity as a foil to the sin of lust.

Early Life of the Virgin

According to legend[1] Mary was born to Joachim and Anna, as a result of the Immaculate Conception, for her mother conceived her by divine intervention, not by conjugal intercourse. From the age of three she behaved like an adult, dedicating herself to prayer and weaving. She was taken to the temple to be brought up by priests and walked up the flight of stairs to the altar unaided. She made a vow to God that she would remain a virgin, and when she was about 12 years old the perplexed priests held a council to decide how to find her a suitable spouse. Under instruction from an angel, Joseph and other suitors came to lay rods on an altar; the suitor whose rod flowered would become her spouse. In painting the rejected suitors may be seen angrily breaking their rods over their knees. Miraculously, Joseph's rod flowered and brought down the Holy Ghost in the form of a dove. Joseph and Mary celebrated their betrothal, and Mary returned to her parents.

Scenes from the early life of the Virgin, which may follow the lives of Joachim and Anna, were illustrated in cycles of mosaics, panels and frescoes, most notably by Giotto (Arena Chapel, Padua). Isolated scenes were also chosen, such as the *Presentation of the Virgin in the Temple* by Titian, or the *Sposalizio* (or *Marriage of the Virgin to Joseph*) by Raphael.

Annunciation and Visitation

The Gospels[2] relate the story of the Angel Gabriel's **Annunciation**, the moment in which the Incarnation of Christ was made known to Mary.

This is one of the most frequently depicted scenes in Christian art. Often with the lily of purity nearby, she is usually seated or kneeling in meditation, or reading a holy book, sometimes thought to be the Old Testament prophecy, "Behold, a virgin shall conceive, and bear a son."[3] The Virgin may recoil in humility from the angel's words, "Hail thou that art favoured, the Lord is with Thee."[4] God's hand may be seen dispatching rays of light and the dove of the Holy Ghost.

Immediately after the Annunciation, Mary paid a visit to her cousin Elizabeth who had miraculously conceived St John the Baptist. At the **Visitation** they embraced, and "when Elizabeth heard the salutation of Mary, the babe leaped in her womb; and Elizabeth was filled with the Holy Ghost".[5]

The Virgin and the Life of Christ

The many scnes in this part of the Virgin's life may be depicted as devotional images or in cycles of her own or of Christ's life: the **Nativity**, **Adoration of the Shepherds**, **Adoration of the Magi**, **Christ's Circumcision**, **Purification**, **Presentation in the Temple**, **Flight into Egypt**, **Massacre of the Innocents** and **Dispute with the Doctors**. Afterwards the Virgin is mentioned little in the Gospels: she does appear, however, at the **Wedding Feast of Cana** and the **Crucifixion**. After **Christ's Ascension**, Mary was present in the upper room at Jerusalem when the disciples gathered to pray at Pentecost, and the Holy Ghost descended.

Dormition and Assumption

The stories of the **Dormition** and **Assumption** of the Virgin derive from many apocryphal legends.[6] After the Resurrection of Christ the Virgin was said to have prayed daily by Christ's tomb for death and reunion with her son. The Holy Ghost told the Apostles to place the Virgin's body in the innermost of three caves near the Mount of Olives. On the way to the tomb a Jew tried to shake Mary off her litter but an angel severed his hands and they remained stuck to the bed. The Virgin heard his prayers, restored his hands, and he was converted. At the tomb, angels appeared with Moses, Elijah, Enoch and Christ, and Mary's body and soul were carried to Paradise.

A detail after Annibale Carracci's Assumption of the Virgin *(1600–1601, San Maria del Popolo, Rome).*

At the Assumption of the Virgin, the more popular subject of the two and gloriously depicted by Titian, the Virgin rose to become the **Queen of Heaven**. This image of her in glory derives from Byzantine prototypes, where she is seen enthroned as a monumental figure. The Italian *Maestà*, or Virgin and Child in majesty, might include saints and angels shown smaller than the Virgin to reflect the hierarchy of importance.

The subject of the **Coronation of the Virgin**, in which she is usually crowned by Christ, appeared in late medieval art. After her Assumption, the Virgin continued to perform miracles. Many of these episodes were illustrated; Duccio's side-panels to the *Maestà*, for example, include the scene when an angel came to her with a palm, the leaves of which gleamed like the morning star, and announced her death.

Lesser Episodes

Other, more obscure, episodes from the Virgin's life are infrequently depicted. One story tells how Joseph brought two midwives to Mary, only to find Christ already born. One of the midwives, Salome, doubted the miracle of the virgin birth and asked to examine her. When she touched Mary, her blasphemous hand withered up. She repented, and an angel told her to touch the infant Christ and thus restore her hand. Salome holds her hand over Christ in the Master of Flémalle's *Nativity*; and the Virgin may have female attendants, who refer to the midwives, in pictures of the Adoration of the Magi.

Another story relates how, during the Flight into Egypt, Christ tamed the beasts of the desert; and, when the Virgin was hungry and thirsty, commanded the branches of a tall palm tree to bend down so that she could eat, while a stream sprang from its roots to quench her thirst. This is shown in Correggio's *Madonna della Scodella*.

Later medieval legend tells of an emotional scene when Christ took leave of his mother. He told her of his sufferings to come, and said farewell to her before entering Jerusalem for the last time. This subject was popular in the North, particularly in Germany; in Altdorfer's *Christ Taking Leave of his Mother*, St John the Evangelist stands nearby and the Virgin faints at the moment of parting from her son.

Images of the Virgin

The Virgin as the mother of God is a central doctrine of the Church and images of the Virgin frequently stress her motherhood. This was apparent in the Tree of Jesse, which emphasized Christ's descent from the father of David, via the Virgin rather than Joseph. A most maternal image was the **Virgin Suckling the Christ Child**, depicted until the Council of Trent (1545–63) registered its disapproval of the Virgin's nudity. The Franciscans emphasized human tenderness, and during the Renaissance many artists portrayed the Virgin in domestic settings or a naturalistic landscape, perhaps even wearing fashionable contemporary clothes.

The virginity of the mother of Christ was also a core doctrine of the Church. She both conceived without carnal knowledge, and was herself conceived in the same way. The Immaculate Conception of her mother, St Anna, may be illustrated by an image of the Virgin sitting on her mother's lap. At the Annunciation, the angel said, "Fear not, Mary, as though I meant something contrary to thy chastity by this salutation ... as a virgin thou shalt conceive, as a virgin thou shalt bring forth, as a virgin thou shalt nourish."[7] Thus, Mary was endowed with perpetual virginity, and may be shown

Virginia:
[1] Livy, *The History of Rome III:xliv–xlviii*

VIRTUES: *see*
Charity; Hercules; Judith; VICES
[1] *Matthew 10:16*

Virtues and Vices, Battle of: *see*
VICES; VIRTUES
[1] *Ephesians 6:11*
[2] Prudentius, *Psychomachia*

protected in a symbolic walled garden, the *Hortus Conclusus*, presented as an example for saints and martyrs. She may be seen standing on a serpent or dragon, whereby she vanquishes sin.

In the early 17th century Pope Paul V proclaimed a new type of *Immacolata* derived from the Book of Revelation: "And there appeared a great wonder in heaven; a woman clothed with the sun, and the moon under her feet, and upon her head a crown of 12 stars."[8] This became a highly popular devotional image, especially with the Jesuits.

The dead Christ in the lap of the Virgin, after the Pietà *by Michelangelo (1499, St Peter's, Rome).*

The Virgin was believed to have important powers of intercession, which partly accounts for the popularity of her image and for the number of churches dedicated to her. She may be present with St John the Baptist in the Last Judgment, and in private commissions the donors may be shown being presented to her by saints. She was also painted in thanksgiving for deliverance from the plague or after a military victory. The Virgin was also a protector, and is seen as the **Virgin of Mercy** opening her cloak, under which the chosen or faithful can shelter. This image was often painted for lay confraternities of *misericordia*, or compassion, which gave aid to the sick.

The ***Mater Dolorosa***, or **Virgin Mourning**, shows her weeping alone or over the dead body of Christ. The **Seven Sorrows of the Virgin** were: the prophecy of Simeon that "This child is set for the fall and rising again of many in Israel and for a sign that is spoken against and a sword will pierce through your own soul also";[9] the Flight into Egypt; the Loss of the Holy Child in the Temple; the Meeting on the Road to Calvary; the Crucifixion; the Deposition; and the Entombment.

The ***Pietà*** developed out of the Lamentation over Christ's body, and is prefigured in images of the Virgin and Child, where the Christ Child lies in his mother's lap, seemingly dead.

Virginia

According to legend[1] Virginia, the daughter of a centurion, was desired by one of the ten principal magistrates of Rome, Appius Flaudius, who made her a slave so that he could possess her. Her father plunged a knife into her breast to save her honour, as depicted by Guillon Lethière in *Death of Virginia*. In the consequent uprising the magistrates were overthrown.

VIRTUES

See panel on following page.

Virtues and Vices, Battle of

In his preaching Paul the Apostle advised: "Put on the whole armour of

VIRTUES

The three Theological Virtues are Faith (*Fides*), Hope (*Spes*) and Charity (*Caritas*). They were personified as women: **Faith** may be resolute and majestic, with a book, a lighted candle, and a heart, cross or chalice: **Hope** may be a winged figure reaching up to a crown, looking beyond to the future in expectation; **Charity** may hold a cornucopia or bowl of fruit, emphasizing the bounty which she distributes and her kindness.

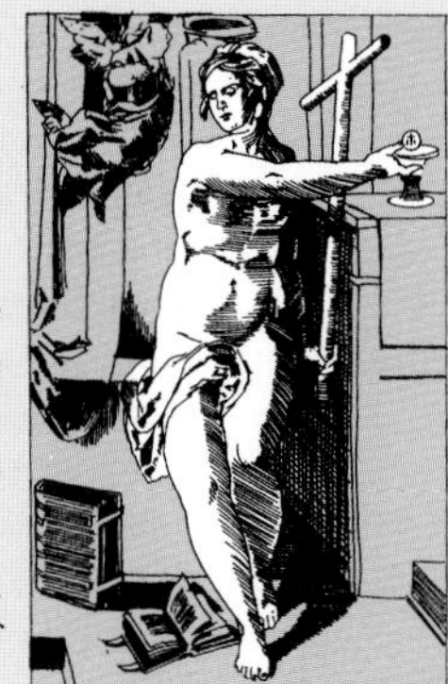

A detail showing Faith, after an engraving by Lucas van Leyden (early 16th century).

The four Cardinal Virtues, so called because they are the "hinges" on which the Theological Virtues hang, are known as Justice (*Iustitia*), Prudence (*Prudentia*), Temperance (*Temperantia*) and Fortitude (*Fortitudo*). These may likewise be female personifications.

An image of Justice, after an engraving by Lucas van Leyden (early 16th century).

Justice may hold the sword of power and scales of balance (in the later 16th century, she was shown blindfold to symbolize her impartiality and incorruptibility) or she may be seen giving alms to the righteous and punishing the wicked.

Prudence may hold a book of wisdom, or a serpent;[1] she may be shown with more than one head to signify that she learns from the past and also has foresight, or she may hold up a mirror to reflect truth.

Fortitude is a figure of strength and may be shown with a column (in reference to the biblical Samson, who while a prisoner brought down the columns of the building in which he was ordered to entertain a Philistine audience, killing himself as well as a multitude of Philistines), a shield or a lion; she may also be represented by Judith (a courageous widow of the Apocryphal Old Testament) or Hercules (in Greek myth, Heracles), who was renowned for his great strength.

Temperance is a figure of moderation, and can be seen with an unsheathed sword, or a pitcher with which to dilute her wine, or a bridle with which to enforce restraint.

The Virtues often have inscriptions for indentification.

There were also minor virtues, such as Hospitality, Humility and Innocence.

Vulcan: *see*
Aeneas; Cythera; Mars; Jupiter; Venus

[1] Homer, *Iliad XVIII:428–617*

[2] Ovid, *Met IV:170–90* and Homer, *Odyssey VIII:265–346*

God, that ye may be able to stand against the wiles of the devil."[1] The battle between the Virtues and Vices may be illustrated by personifications of the opposites, sometimes set against one another in niches:[2] Faith against Idolatry; Hope against Despair; Humility against Pride; Charity against Avarice or Envy; Justice against Injustice; Chastity against Lust; Patience against Anger; Temperance against Gluttony or Anger; Fortitude against Inconstancy; and Prudence against Folly. Such pairs are found beneath Giotto's narrative frescoes. From the Renaissance onward, the gods and goddesses of antiquity may take on the role of the Virtues and Vices: Minerva (in Greek myth, Athene), Apollo, Diana (Artemis) and Mercury (Hermes) fight for the Virtues; Venus (Aphrodite) and Cupid (Eros) for the Vices. An example is Perugino's *Battle Between Love and Chastity*. The Virtues are often armed and are usually the victors.

Vulcan

The god of the forge who presided over fire, Vulcan (in Greek myth, Hephaestus) was the patron of metalworkers. The son of Juno (Hera) and Jupiter (Zeus) for whom he made thunderbolts, he was thrown off Mount Olympus when he attempted to free his mother who had been chained up in punishment by Jupiter. Vulcan landed on the island of Lemnos, where the inhabitants caught him, but he broke his leg in the fall and became lame. He built a palace for himself and set up forges, said to be the earth's volcanoes; the Cyclopes were his attendants.

Vulcan made ingenious works of art in metal for the gods, and for mortals at the request of the gods; these included magnificently decorated shields for both Achilles and Aeneas.[1] Boucher illustrated this in *Venus at Vulcan's Forge Asking for Arms for her Son, Aeneas*. Vulcan also made for Jupiter a complete set of armour, for which he was promised whatever he wanted as a reward. Vulcan asked for the chaste Minerva (Athene), and Jupiter warned her of impending trouble. Vulcan, unable to ravish her, spilled his seed on the earth, from which Erichthonius was born. Instead Vulcan married Venus (Aphrodite), who was constantly unfaithful. One humorous story describes how Vulcan fashioned an invisible net to trap Venus with Mars (Ares). They were caught in an embrace, and Vulcan exposed them to the gods who, to his discomfort, were greatly amused. Mercury (Hermes) antagonized Vulcan by saying how much he would like to take Mars' place.[2]

In paintings, Vulcan's deformity is usually apparent; he often appears half-naked and dishevelled at his forge, holding a hammer about to strike an anvil, or with a thunderbolt held in pincers; or he may be blowing the flames, his face black with smoke.

Appropriately, he appears above fireplaces, as in Peruzzi's *Vulcan at his Forge* (Villa Farnesina, Rome).

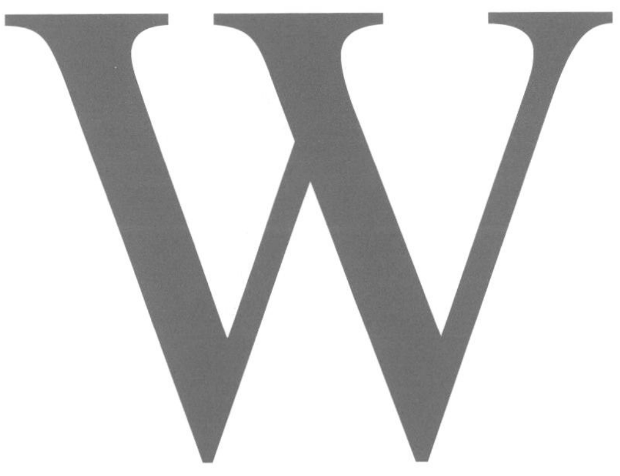

War

Classical literature recounts numerous epic tales of war, many of which tell of glorious causes and noble heroes.

From the Renaissance onward, artists have depicted the justice, generosity, magnanimity or restraint of their leaders. The wars selected may be the outcome of wounded pride or personal affront; the most famous example is the Trojan War, although not all depictions have been from classical sources. A war may also be conducted in the cause of freedom, as illustrated by Delacroix's *Liberty Leading the People*, or of missionary zeal as in the various depictions of the Crusades.

Equestrian monuments of victorious generals are found in many European cities; these commemorate the subject's successes and bolster their fame as national heroes. Uccello's tapestry-like painting *Rout of San Romano*, which resembles a jousting tournament, gives war a decorative quality. Images of war have often been commissioned for public halls as political propaganda to incite or sustain national pride.

Alternatively, artists have illustrated the futility and horror of war, and its ruinous outcome. Dürer's engraving of *Knight, Death and the Devil* of 1513 shows a warrior who rides forth oblivious to his grim companions.

As an argument for avoiding conflict in Europe, Rubens presented his *Allegory of Peace and War*, which illustrates the benefits of peace, to Charles I of England. Rubens also painted *Consequences of War*, which shows how War, led by Disaster, tramples over the civilized arts. Goya's 65 etchings entitled *Disasters of War* are brutally savage images depicting the cruelty of man. The same painter's *Colossus* likens an invading army to a giant trampling over the earth.

When, in 1937, the Basque town of Guernica was destroyed by German bombers acting on behalf of General Franco, Picasso responded with a huge painting of terrified figures, which resembles a Massacre of the Innocents.

War: *see*
Equestrian Monument; Giants; Judgment of Paris; Mars; Trojan War

A detail showing what Rubens himself called "unhappy Europe", after his painting Horrors of War *(1638, Palazzo Pitti, Florence).*

Winds: *see*
Aeolus; Flora
[1] Virgil, *Aeneid I:50–65*
[2] Ovid, *Met VI:675–721*

Witch of Endor: *see*
Saul
[1] *I Samuel 28*

Winds

In mythology there were four winds, all blowing from different directions in times of strife. Their king, Aeolus, kept them in a dark cavern and tempered their fury.[1] The East wind came from Arabia and Persia, where the morning sun rose; the balmy West wind, Zephyr, blew from shores warmed by the setting sun; the South wind brought rain and clouds; the North wind, old, bearded Boreas, whipped up storms of snow and hail.

Boreas fell in love with Oreithyia, daughter of Erechtheus of Athens, and for a long time wooed her in vain. At first he tried to win her with persuasion, but then he returned to his violent ways, shook out his wings and swept her to his home, where she became the icy despot's wife.[2]

The winds may be depicted as winged heads, with their cheeks puffed out from blowing, or as winged personifications. The cold winds may be shown as old men with shaggy beards and hoary locks, the warm winds as youths, although the South wind can appear as an old man.

A detail illustrating a wind, after Botticelli's The Birth of Venus *(1484–6, Uffizi, Florence).*

Witch of Endor

In the Old Testament,[1] Saul, king of the Israelites, expelled "those that had familiar spirits" (witches) from the land. Later he feared defeat by the Philistines and wished to consult a witch. His servants recommended the Witch of Endor and, in disguise, he went to her at night. By the witch's magic Samuel, his predecessor, manifested himself and confirmed that, having offended the Lord, Saul would be defeated. Salvator Rosa illustrated the scene in *The Spirit of Samuel Called up Before Saul by the Witch of Endor*.

Zaleucus, Judgment of
Zaleucus (6th century BC) was the magistrate of a Greek settlement in Italy. He was once required to pass judgment on his own son, who had been accused of adultery. The punishment laid down was for the transgressor to lose both his eyes. His son was found guilty of the crime, but the people were compassionate and intervened. Rather than defy the law, however, Zaleucus had one of his own eyes taken out, as well as one of his son's.[1] He is portrayed in art as an example of justice.

Zano, Saint
Zano (died *c.*AD372) was bishop of Verona. Little is known of his life except that he was a wise and zealous preacher. He may have a fish hanging from his crozier, possibly because it was early symbol of Christianity – although a local tradition claims that he was merely fond of fishing.

Zenobius, Saint
Zenobius (died *c.*AD390) was bishop of his native Florence. He is depicted in the city's art in a bishop's habit, with the fleur-de-lys, the emblem of Florence, decorating his cope, as in Domenico Veneziano's *St Lucy Altarpiece*.

The panel from the predella now in the Fitzwilliam Museum, Cambridge, England, successfully, shows the miracle of how he prayed for a dead child to be restored to life.

Zeuxis
One of the most celebrated painters of ancient Greece, Zeuxis (5th century BC) offered to paint a picture of Helen of Troy for the people of Crotona. They brought their most beautiful maidens to him to act as his models, from whom he selected five. In order to portray an ideal figure, he copied the finest physical features from each woman; this approach was taken up by Raphael in the Renaissance. In *Zeuxis Choosing his Models*, François-André Vincent shows the artist studying the models.

ZODIAC
See panel on following page.

Zaleucus:
[1] Valarius Maximus *6: V*

ZODIAC: *see* Bull; Goat; SEASONS; and individual names of gods

ZODIAC

Astrology was particularly popular from the 14th to 16th centuries. Professors were appointed at universities and astrologers were consulted by statesmen, popes and princes. The Earth was believed to be a fixed element surrounded by an unstable atmosphere composed of spheres of increasing size, which contained the planets Mercury, Venus, the Sun, Mars, Jupiter and Saturn. These moved at different speeds and were controlled by angels. Beyond the farthest sphere was a static region which housed the stars. The 12 bands of the zodiac fitted into the planetary spheres.

Astrology was endorsed by Christianity because it was thought to be directed by God. The aspect of the heavenly bodies, such as the position of a planet in a sign of the zodiac, was held to be mirrored in a person's physical and mental well-being. Horoscopes were drawn up at birth, and a chart of the heavenly spheres not only mapped out an individual's fate but also created a highly decorative scheme: the banker Agostino Chigi had a ceiling painted with his own astrological chart by Peruzzi (Loggia of Galatea, Villa Farnesina, Rome).

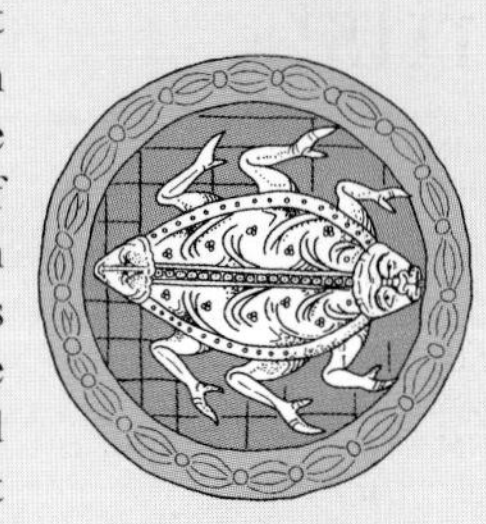

The zodiac sign of Cancer (the crab), taken from a medieval book illustration.

The signs of the zodiac were also used to illustrate the 12 months of the year, along with the corresponding agricultural labours. Each sign has a particular personification or attribute and a mythological god, goddess or other classical personificaiton.

Zodiac Sign	Symbol	God/Goddess
Aquarius	Water-bearer	Janus
Pisces	Fishes	Venus and Cupid
Aries	Ram	Mars
Taurus	Bull	Jupiter as a bull
Gemini	Twins	Castor and Pollux
Cancer	Crab	Phaethon
Leo	Lion	Hercules
Virgo	Virgin	Ceres with corn
Libra	Scales	Ceres with fruit
Scorpio	Scorpion	Bacchus
Sagittarius	Archer	Centaur
Capricorn	Goat	Amalthea

Acknowledgments

I should like to thank all those at Duncan Baird who were involved in the production of this book, Judy Dean above all. My thanks go also to the editors Alice Peebles and Caroline Bugler; to Clare McDonnell, Polly Hudson, A & J C-G, and Nicholas Ross; and to Susie Swoboda who introduced me to this fascinating subject and has never ceased to inspire.

Index of Artists

The following abbreviations are used in the Index of Artists.

Acc: Accademia, Venice
ACP: Arena Chapel, Padua
AM: Altepinoteck Museum, Munich
AMO: Ashmolean Museum, Oxford
Bavo: Cathedral of St Bavo, Ghent
BCAG: Birmingham City Art Gallery
BF: Baptistry, Florence
BGR: Borghese Gallery, Rome
BML: British Museum, London
BN: Bibliothèque National, Paris
Brera: Brera, Milan
CdC: Collegio del Cambio, Perugia
CMN: Chrysler Museum, Norfolk, Virginia
CIL: Courtauld Institute, London
DPG: Dulwich Picture Gallery
DPU: Ducal Palace, Urbino
EBA: École des Beaux Arts, Paris
EJF: Edward James Foundation
Fl: Florence
FMC: Fitzwilliam Museum, Cambridge
GCN: Galleria Campodimonte, Naples
GD: Gemaldegalerie, Dresden
HCL: Hampton Court Palace, London
HSP: Hermitage, St Petersburg
JPG: John Paul Getty Museum, Malibu
KH: Kunsthalle, Hamburg
KMV: Kunsthistorisches Museum, Vienna
KPL: Kensington Palace, London
LP: Louvre, Paris
MBA: Musée des Beaux Arts, Brussels
Md'O: Musée d'Orsée, Paris
MH: Mauristhuis, The Hague
MMP: Moreau Museum, Paris
MNY: Metropolitan Museum of Art, New York
MSM: Museum of St Mark, Florence
NGI: National Gallery of Ireland, Dublin
NGL: National Gallery, London
NGS: National Gallery of Scotland, Edinburgh
NGU: National Gallery, Umbria
NGW: National Gallery, Washington, D.C.
NMN: National Museum, Naples
OF: Orsanmichele, Florence
pc: private collection
PM: Prado, Madrid
PMA: Philadelphia Museum of Art
PP: Panthéon, Paris
PPF: Pitti Palace, Florence
PS: Pinacoteca, Siena
PVF: Palazzo Vecchio, Florence
RAL: Royal Academy of Art, London
RAm: Rijksmuseum, Amsterdam
RCW: Royal Collection, Windsor
RGB: Royal Gallery, Brussels
RGT: Reale Gallery, Turin
RMP: Rodin Museum Paris
SAF: San Annunziata, Florence
SCF: Santa Croce, Florence
SCR: Sistine Chapel, Vatican, Rome
SFA: San Francesco, Arezzo
SGV: Scuolo di San Giorgio, Venice
SKD: Stadelesches Kunstinstitut, Dresden
SKF: Stadelsches Kunstinstitut, Frankfurt
SLF: San Lorenzo, Florence
SMB: Staatliche Museum, Berlin
SMN: Santa Maria Novella, Florence
SMP: Santa Maria del Popolo, Rome
SSR: Scuola di San Rocco, Venice
SSV: Scuola di San Stefano
SzMB: Szepmuveszeth Museum, Budapest
TGL: Tate Gallery, London
UF: Uffizi, Florence
V&A: Victoria and Albert Museum, London
VF: Villa Farnesina, Rome
VR: Vatican, Rome
WCL: Wallace Collection, London

Only artists and works of art which are cited in the dictionary are listed. In most cases the date of the work and its location are given. Page numbers in italics refer to illustrations.

Index of Artists

Index of Artists

Index of Artists

Index of Supplementary Words

Entries in this index suffixed with "f" refer to feature panels in the dictionary; all cross-references refer to index entries except those prefixed with an asterisk (*), which refer to entries in the main dictionary; numerals in brackets after page numbers indicate the number of times the index entry appears on that page.

Index of Supplementary Words

Continued from front flap

• In Renaissance painting, charity is often personified as a loving mother with two or more children, one of whom she may be nursing, as in Cranach's *Charity*.

• Fraud, as in Bronzino's *Allegory of Love*, is depicted as a sweet young girl offering a honeycomb with one hand, while holding her stinging tail in the other: she is half-reptile, with the feet of a lion.

Approximately 160 line drawings, many of them two-color, show key aspects and details of works of art to highlight recurring visual themes.

Detailed and complete, *The Dictionary of Symbols in Western Art* is the ideal reference for students of art history, mythology, and religion, as well as the interested general reader.

Sarah Carr-Gomm studied art history at the University of East Anglia and took a master's degree in the Renaissance at Birkbeck College, London. Her previous books on art history include volumes on Manet and Seurat and an artistic guide to Rome. She currently teaches art history in both England and Italy.